A Modern History of Syria

INCLUDING LEBANON AND PALESTINE

Books by the same author

ARAB EDUCATION IN MANDATORY PALESTINE, 1918–48

BRITISH INTERESTS IN PALESTINE, 1800–1901

AMERICAN INTERESTS IN SYRIA, 1800–1901

A Modern History of Syria

including Lebanon and Palestine

A. L. TIBAWI

Macmillan
St. Martin's Press

First published 1969 by
MACMILLAN AND CO LTD
Little Essex Street London WC2
and also at Bombay Calcutta and Madras
Macmillan South Africa (Publishers) Pty Ltd Johannesburg
The Macmillan Company of Australia Pty Ltd Melbourne
The Macmillan Company of Canada Ltd Toronto
St Martin's Press Inc New York
Gill and Macmillan Ltd Dublin

Library of Congress catalog card no. 73-93539

Printed in Great Britain by
R. & R. CLARK LTD
Edinburgh

To Raya

Commemorating the 31st of December 1965

Contents

Acknowledgements

By an unwritten convention authors seldom venture to thank their publishers. I wish to depart from this custom by recording here sincere appreciation of my publishers and their staff concerned with the production of this book. Two deserve special mention: Mr Michael Shaw for the scholarly care he bestowed on the manuscript and the meticulous attention to details in easing its passage to the press; and Miss Angela Weight for her diligent, intelligent and successful search for illustrations.

Two of my friends in Syria were particularly helpful in answering questions and supplying, moreover, several useful illustrations: Professor N. Hatoum, University of Damascus and Mr M. Akhal, British Embassy in Beirut. It is a pleasant duty to extend to both my deep gratitude.

Last but not least is my daughter Raya, who amidst her own studies at Girton and Somerville seconded and sometimes succeeded her mother as my most vigilant literary critic. To them both I am most grateful.

List of Plates

BETWEEN PAGES 176 AND 177

A modern yarn and cloth mill near Damascus
Al-Arabi Magazine, *Kuwait*

A group of folklore singers
Al-Arabi Magazine, *Kuwait*

A contemporary village scene in the Ghūṭah
Al-Arabi Magazine, *Kuwait*

List of Maps

Transliteration

THE received English spelling of such Arabic names and words as Mecca and muezzin has been adopted. Otherwise the system of transliteration familiar to British orientalists has been followed except where it does not conform to the correct Arabic pronunciation, notably after the definitive article *al.* Even so consistency is well nigh impossible. But with very few exceptions, notably 'Faisal', all Arabic names and words receive diacritical and orthographical signs in transcription.

Introduction

GEOGRAPHICAL Syria including Lebanon and Palestine east and west of the river Jordan is the subject of this history, from the closing decades of the eighteenth century to the imposition of political divisions after the First World War. From 1921 Lebanon and both parts of Palestine are excluded, and the history continues as that of the Republic of Syria, first as a French mandated territory and then as an independent sovereign state down to the summer of 1967.

The book is in two parts: the first half is devoted to the Ottoman period, and the second to the making of modern Syria beginning with the wartime negotiations with Britain and the division of the country into British and French spheres, then leading to the operation of the French mandate and finally the affairs of the Republic of Syria since independence.

Reckoned in years, the first period is longer than the second, but the latter was so much more crowded with revolutionary events, political, economic, social and cultural, that the present allocation of space in this book is deemed fully justified. In particular I make no apology for the longer chapters at the beginning of Part Two, for they serve to show how the destiny of modern Syria was shaped, and contain moreover entirely new material culled from British Foreign Office papers only recently opened for inspection by scholars. Furthermore, these chapters offer fresh interpretations of a number of vital events which influenced and continue to influence the politics of the Arab Middle East since 1914.

I have sought to produce a history in which the people figure as prominently as their rulers. For this purpose I have taken care to study political history in conjunction with social, economic and cultural development. It will be seen that this was done consistently throughout the book without any gaps, so that the twelve chapters form a continuous narrative, with the substance and the conclusion of each chapter closely linked, in the historical and literary sense, with the beginning and substance of the next.

The treatment was, of course, governed by the nature and quantity of the available material as well as by the author's view of the comparative significance of the events under study. I have, for example, given more prominence to education and literary developments than to the ephemeral squabbles of Ottoman pashas or Syrian Arab ministers. But nothing of great significance and covered by the sources was omitted from the history of the Ottoman period. I have, however, accumulated much more relevant material on the post-war period than could be conveniently accommodated in this book. A great deal of it will be used in a forthcoming volume on Anglo-Arab relations concerning both parts of Palestine.

More recent and contemporary history is admittedly less documented, but I have personally witnessed some of its vicissitudes, and relied partly on personal acquaintance with a number of leaders and partly on my own collection of official communiques and press cuttings.

For the first half of the book I have used material derived from manuscript sources preserved in public or semi-public archives and listed in the Bibliography. I have also used native chroniclers and modern works in Arabic and other languages, collating and sifting the evidence before writing each chapter. It was evident that native chroniclers as well as modern writers tend to concentrate on politics and war and to neglect the other sides of history. To produce a balanced picture I had recourse to diplomatic and consular archives, chiefly British and partly French, and to American and British missionary records. One of the fruits of this endeavour was a new interpretation of the literary revival in Syria and the earliest Arab national stirrings.

I would call particular attention to other new material derived from over two hundred volumes in the British archives. On its basis, Anglo-Arab negotiations concerning Syria during and after the First World War are shown in a fresh light, and there are important revelations on, among others, A. J. Balfour, Herbert Samuel, Mark Sykes, T. E. Lawrence and Ronald Storrs. On the Arab side the Sharif Ḥusain and his son Faisal emerge in a new light.

For the period of the mandate I relied on the minutes of the Permanent Mandate Commission as a corrective to the French annual reports to the Council of the League of Nations. On more recent history since independence, official statements and statistics have been balanced with Arabic and foreign press reports as well as personal knowledge and observation. For the history of the last four years, a chronological quarterly and an annual record of documents, both issued by the American University of Beirut, have been used together with Arabic and foreign press reports.

I have considered and, with one or two important exceptions, disregarded the evidence of memoirs and similar accounts. I have done so not only because of the inevitable apologetic purpose of such publications, but also because of the discovery that what an author writes retrospectively in old age is sometimes at material variance with what he himself had written at the time of the events in official reports.

The study of authoritative sources simultaneously with reading published works proved a most illuminating exercise. For one thing, it exposed the dangers of generalising from scanty evidence or summing up decades of history in a paragraph or even a sentence. For another, it confirmed that among the worst enemies of historical accuracy is the uncritical quotation by authors from their predecessors, and the perpetuation thereby of unwarranted assumptions and factual mistakes.

I have left such discoveries as I made to speak for themselves; I made no attempt to compare my work with other accounts or to contradict other authors. Hence relatively few modern works are specifically mentioned in the Notes and Bibliography. But where correction of factual errors was deemed absolutely necessary it was introduced with such phrases as 'contrary to current accounts' or 'not as we have so often been led to believe'. It was not my purpose to contradict predecessors by more specific means.

Yet I would give only one example of vague and unwarranted generalisation, and factual error that divorces events from the actual date of their occurrence. Summing up the Ottoman administration in Syria at the beginning of the nineteenth century, one author asserts, without factual support, that 'Lebanon was an oasis of order amid the chaos'. The same author also writes: 'In 1839, under the influence of the British Ambassador, Stratford de Redcliffe, the Sultan Abdul-Majid issued the Gülhané decree, establishing a just system of imposing and collecting taxes, provided for equality of civil rights between members of the different religious communities and extended the obligation of military service to all alike.' The facts are that in 1839 Sir Stratford Canning was not British Ambassador at Constantinople, that he became Viscount Stratford de Redcliffe only in 1852, and that there is no mention in the Gülhané decree of the extension of military service to non-Muslims.

In pointing out this example I naturally lay no claim of immunity from error. Without, however, excluding the possibility of human error, I venture to vouch for the factual accuracy of this book. Therefore I beg those accustomed to some other versions and those with preconceived notions to take note that every new fact has a warrant in the sources, even where no footnote is given, and that every conclusion is preceded by supporting facts.

Several of the important original sources are specifically mentioned and quoted in the text. Others are cited in the Notes, which I could have easily multiplied as in previous works. I relax this custom slightly, not because I subscribe to the maxim ascribed to Grotius that 'it is a scandalous practice in authors to put notes to things that deserve no notice', nor because I find it convenient to agree with the British historian A. J. P. Taylor – himself an adept in the art of using and dispensing with notes – who said that 'If the reader does not accept my credentials, he will not be induced to do so by a display of the sources from which my plumes are borrowed.' But because of considerations of space I regard the Notes, with their grouping in the Bibliography, as sufficient for the purpose of this book.

It is, I think, important to call attention to the fact that a great many of the native chroniclers, as well as modern writers in Arabic, English and French, are Lebanese. Every one of them has his good qualities and some were or are distinguished men. But most if not all of them tend to idealise their small portion of the Syrian fatherland, and in the process to minimise the role of the rest of the country and its inhabitants. Quite often their patriotism appears to surpass their historical accuracy.

The substance of Chapters 7 and 9 has been published in the *Islamic Quarterly* and of Chapter 8 in the *Middle East Forum*.

A. L. T.

Part One

UNDER OTTOMAN SULTANS

'A land of the past, it has a future. . . . There is literally no limit that can be laid down to the mother-wit, to the ambition, and the intellectual capabilities of its sons; they are the most gifted race that I have, as yet, ever seen. And when the curse shall have left the country – not the ban of superstition, but the bane and plague-spot of bad rule – it will again rise to a position not unworthy of the days when it gave the world a poetry and a system of religion still unforgotten by our highest civilisation.'

Richard Francis Burton (31 December 1871), in the Preface to his *Unexplored Syria.* (Burton was British Consul in Damascus 1869–71, but his fame rests on his unexpurgated translation of the *Arabian Nights*, published in 1885–8.)

1

The False Dawn – The Era of Jazzār and Napoleon

I

In history 'Syria' signified different political or administrative entities at different times. This book is concerned with geographical Syria known to medieval Arab authors as *ash-Shām*. It is the land mass lying between the Taurus mountains and the Sinai desert and between the Mediterranean and the Arabian and Syrian deserts. Roughly its length is 500 miles and its width 100 miles.

The country thus defined has four distinct natural divisions that run parallel to the Mediterranean coastline. The first is a coastal plain which narrows in places almost to the point of vanishing and reaches its greatest width in the south in Palestine. The second is the western range of mountains, with Mount Lebanon in the centre, broken in places by lowlands and pierced by at least two famous rivers: al-'Āṣi (Orontes) and al-Līṭāni (Leontes).

The third natural division is a central plain, various in width and elevation, which ends in the depression of the river Jordan valley and the Dead Sea several hundred feet below sea-level. Another chain of mountains forms the fourth natural division of Syria and includes the Anti-Lebanon and the highlands of Transjordan. These highlands slope southwards to merge with the steppe country of north-west Arabia, while the whole chain slopes eastward to merge with another steppe and finally with the desert.

Syria has since antiquity formed an important link in the trade routes between the Far East and the Near East and between the latter and the whole Mediterranean world and Europe. It possesses the entire eastern Mediterranean coast, joins Asia to Africa and has easy access by sea to Europe.

Placed at the intersection of so many land and sea routes, Syria's strategic position was early recognised by the ancient empires in Mesopotamia and Egypt, and the rulers of these countries fought many a battle for its possession. Throughout recorded history, the country was a great battlefield and an indispensable passage for armies of many nations.

But Syria's claim to a special place in history rests primarily on other grounds. Both Judaism and Christianity were born in the southern extremity of the country. Islam, born in adjoining Arabia to the south, came to Syria after the Arab conquest in the seventh century. Jerusalem and Damascus each possess in the traditions of Islam a holy character which is second only to Mecca and Medina.

None of the vicissitudes of Syria's long history had more lasting influence than the Arab conquest. It gave the country its predominantly Arab-Muslim character which neither two centuries of occupation by European Crusaders nor four centuries of Turkish domination could alter. During the early Arab period the foundations of Syrian glory were laid. For nearly a century down to A.D. 750, Damascus was the capital of the Umayyads whose dominions stretched westward to Spain and eastward to India.

The Umayyad Caliphate was a Muslim state ruled by an Arab aristocracy, but in conformity with the Koran and the practice of the Prophet and his early successors, provisions were made for non-Muslim communities, notably Christians and Jews, in this Arab-Muslim empire. This early recognition of the 'people of the book' guided the practice of successive Muslim rulers from the Umayyad Arabs to the Ottoman Turks.

At the end of the eighteenth century, the approximate starting-point of this history, Syria had been an Ottoman dependency for nearly three centuries. Its population was then as now predominantly Muslim, with a mosaic of religious and other minorities. Arabic was the spoken and literary language not only of the Muslim majority but also of practically all the minorities. There is no official Turkish estimate of the population at the time. Napoleon's estimate in 1799 put the total population at two and a half million, including 320,000 Christians and 120,000 Druzes.[1]

The relative numerical strength of the communities, if so classified by religion as indeed they were under Turkish rule, is not in doubt. The dominant Muslim majority was spread fairly evenly all over the country with the exception of Lebanon. It constituted the core of the inhabitants of the cities, most of the villages, almost all the beduins, and included two racial minorities of Turks and Kurds. The Muslim majority owned most of the land, monopolised the civil service and controlled much of the commerce. It alone was called upon to serve in the imperial army and the local militia.

Most of the Muslims of Syria were Sunni, but there were among them pockets of different shades of Shiʿa, the most important being the Nuṣairiyyah mostly in the mountainous region east of Latakia, the Matāwilah in the hinterland of Tyre and elsewhere, the Druzes mostly in south Lebanon and in the highlands now bearing their name in the eastern chain of mountains. The Ottoman government accorded to none of these dissident Muslim minorities full sectarian rights. Legally they were all Muslims, subject to the jurisdiction of the Sunni *qāḍi*, though in practice they were allowed some latitude.

It is not so easy to give as neat a classification of the Christians in Syria. In 1800 as now the majority were Orthodox, spread all over the country in towns and villages within the territories of the ancient patriarchates of Antioch and Jerusalem which corresponded roughly to the limits of geographical Syria. The next largest Christian denomination was the Catholic, the Catholic church having been first established in Syria on the capture of Jerusalem by the Crusaders in 1099. It was then that some connection was established with the Maronites in Lebanon. In the early eighteenth century the connection was formalised by a concordat according to which the Maronites accepted the supremacy of the Pope but retained their own liturgy and priesthood. Other and smaller Uniate churches were formed in Syria, and Rome took an early interest in their religious education.

Lesser Christian denominations need not be mentioned in this place, nor the small native Protestant community which was to be formed in the course of the nineteenth century through Anglo-American missionary work. But it deserves mention that all Christian communities enjoyed autonomy in religious and personal affairs under the Turks. This was in accordance with the organisation of non-Muslims into religious communities. The internal affairs of each community (*millet*) were managed by its spiritual superiors who were responsible to the government of the land.

On the whole, native Christians differed little in occupation or social behaviour from their Muslim compatriots, despite certain restrictions which were gradually removed. Those who lived in villages engaged in agriculture and those in the cities paid special attention to commerce and certain crafts. Contact with foreign merchants who enjoyed certain extra-territorial privileges was practically a Christian monopoly. As a result a small but influential class of protected native Christians was created. Foreign consular or commercial agents contrived to extend their own privileges to this class of Christian Ottoman subjects.

Of the still smaller religious or racial minorities mention may be made of the Jews, not on account of their numerical strength which at the time was negligible but because of their subsequent recognition as a *millet* in the Ottoman Empire. Despite the destruction of their national life in Palestine and their dispersion, a few pious men clung to such centres as Tiberias, Ṣafad and Jerusalem, even in the darkest moments of their history. Some of those expelled with the Arabs from Spain eventually reached Palestine. Except perhaps for these, surviving Jews in Syria-Palestine became in the course of time Arabic-speaking or bilingual. In the nineteenth century we frequently read of a number of them employed in local government service as accountants and wielding considerable influence. Others engaged in commerce, especially in connection with foreign merchants. Still others enriched themselves by lending money with interest in a society where charging interest was illegal. The majority of the pious, however, lived on the charity of rich Jews resident abroad.

The reference above to foreign merchants must be a little amplified. These merchants lived either in such inland trade centres as Aleppo or more usually in seaports such as Alexandretta, Latakia, Tripoli, Beirut, Sidon, Acre and Jaffa. It was in these ports that foreign powers or large European commercial companies maintained consular agents and where a few others of their nations resided. Christians and Jews were their middlemen, and as indicated above their services were rewarded not only by material profit but also, in a number of cases, by their removal from Ottoman jurisdiction.

2

When Salim I conquered Syria in 1516 he confirmed an established order which was in essence feudal. The sultan was content with the acknowledgment of his sovereignty and overlordship by local chieftains, and the payment to the state treasury of a stipulated amount of the revenue. The sultan's representative was responsible for this payment, and in their turn local chieftains, Muslims as well as non-Muslims, were responsible to the sultan's representative for agreed payments and certain services.

This system remained substantially unaltered till the closing decades of the eighteenth century and well into the nineteenth. About the year 1800, Syria was divided into four administrative divisions or provinces, with ill-defined and shifting boundaries. Known first as *iyālah* and later as *wilāyah* (hence the Turkish *vilayet*), each province was administered by a pasha (hence the term *pashalik*) as the sultan's representative. The rank of a pasha of a province was usually that of a minister.

The four provinces in question were those of Aleppo, Damascus, Tripoli and Sidon (or later Acre). The province of Aleppo extended from the Mediterranean north of the Orontes to the Euphrates. For a long time it had closer connection with Mesopotamia and Anatolia than with the rest of Syria. It had powerful minorities of Armenians, Kurds and Turks, and its northern parts merged imperceptibly with predominantly Turkish districts.

The province of Damascus, of which the provinces of Tripoli and Sidon on the Mediterranean littoral were offshoots and upon which at times they were dependent, embraced the rest of geographical Syria. Though strictly part of the province of Damascus, Palestine, southwards from the northern areas of Jaffa, was in the early 1780s 'a district independent of every pashalik, and sometimes had governors of its own who resided at Gaza under the title of pashas'.[2]

This administrative anomaly was a result of the assignment of

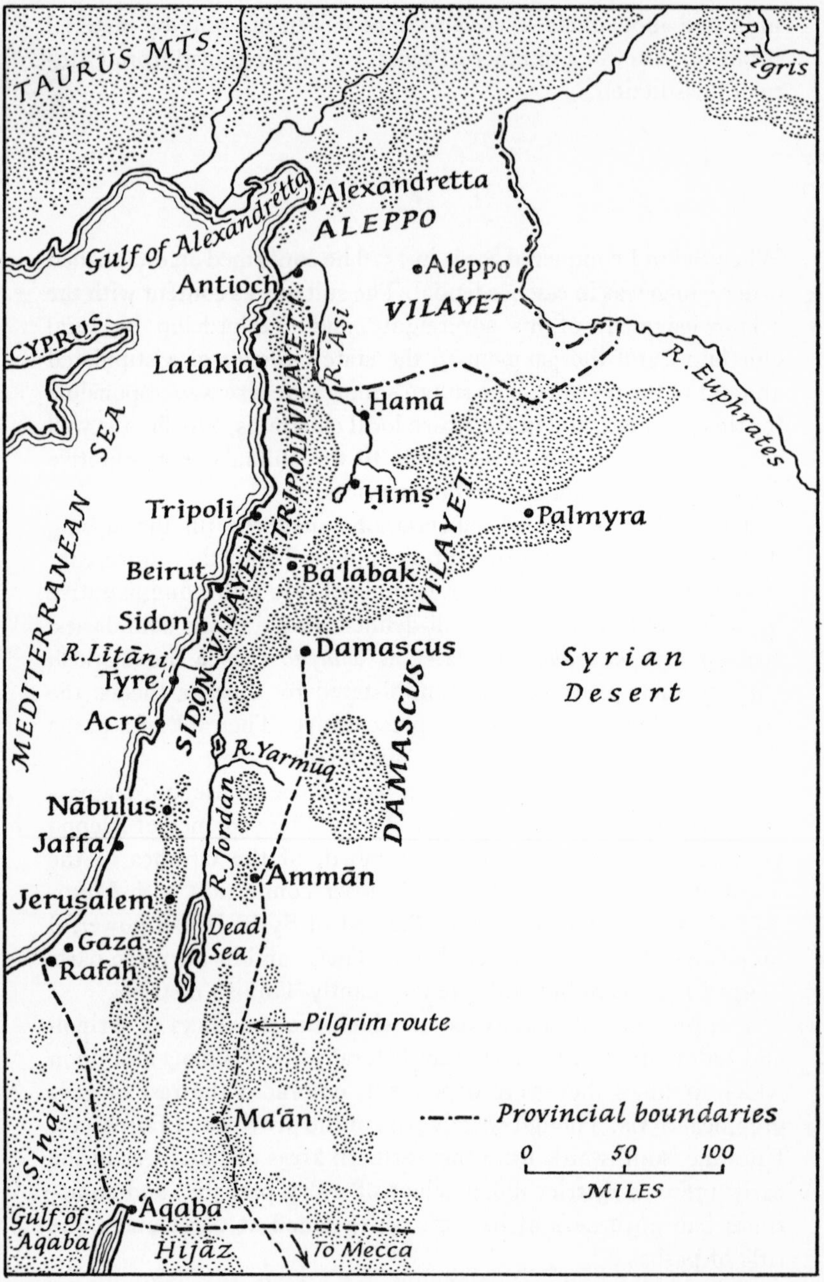

I Geographical Syria – administrative divisions, *c.* 1800

the revenue of Jaffa and its district to the Sultana Mother and that of Palestine south of ar-Ramlah to the Admiral Pasha. Each of the two holdings was accordingly farmed to a local chieftain who remitted the dues not to the governor of any province but directly to the feudal lady or lord concerned. Sometimes the pashas of Gaza extended their sway to embrace Jerusalem, depending on their own strength or the weakness of the pasha of Damascus or on both; sometimes Jerusalem itself was the seat of a pasha. But it may be safely stated that Palestine up to the Egyptian border was more often dependent upon Acre or Damascus than independent on its own.

The taxes expected, though not always received, by the imperial treasury from Syria were comparatively moderate. But intermediary agencies – pashas, local chieftains and tax-collectors – had gradually become corrupt and the actual incidence of taxation increasingly oppressive. In the closing decades of the eighteenth century the annual sum expected from the province of Aleppo was 800 purses (about £40,000), from each of Tripoli and Sidon 750 purses, and from Damascus only 45 purses because of the expenses of the pilgrim caravan.[3] But in addition to these specified amounts, unspecified quantities of provisions were collected from the provinces in kind, also for the pilgrim caravan.

According to custom, pashas seeking office had to give 'presents' to their patrons who were more often than not ministers. Whatever expenses a new pasha incurred in this way he recovered, often redoubled, from the income of his provinces as well as from 'presents' which he in turn expected, nay demanded, from chieftains over and above the official tax. Napoleon's estimate was that only one-fourth of the total revenue was sent to Istanbul. The rest was left in the hands of pashas as personal income, expenses on the pilgrim caravan and such public service as fell within a governor's province and outside that of religious foundations.

Each of the four capitals of the provinces of Syria, as well as of the district of southern Palestine, was either an ancient market town or a prominent station on trade routes by land or by sea. All the four or five seats were moreover the economic centres of their respective agricultural surroundings. As seats of provinces and seaports, Sidon and Tripoli each had a small colony of European merchants and commercial agents of large chartered companies such as the (English) Levant Company. Alexandretta served as the port of the inland trading city and market town of Aleppo, and as such had some resident European merchants in it. But among the capitals of the four provinces the city of Damascus had the added distinction of being the starting-point for the departure of the pilgrim caravan which left every year for Mecca. The governor of the province of Damascus was responsible for the safety of the highway down to Mecca. He maintained small forces in forts on the route and subsidised local shaikhs to enlist their co-operation or employed them as suppliers of mounts for the pilgrims.

Damascus was the rendezvous for all pilgrims coming from the Asiatic and European parts of the Ottoman Empire as well as from other parts to the east and north. In 1812 Burckhardt estimated the cost of hiring a camel from Damascus to Mecca and back and the expenses of one pilgrim on the way and in Hijaz at £125.

The pilgrims often included merchants who sold or exchanged their goods on the way to or from Mecca. To the city of Damascus and the stations on the route, the pilgrim traffic was an economic asset of great magnitude. By the sultan's orders inns and security posts were established on the route, especially near wells.[4] Hence the special importance of whoever held the post of pasha of Damascus. He was invested with the dignity of *amīr al-ḥajj* (commander of the pilgrimage) because he rode at the head of an army with the caravan.

But speaking in general, a pasha of a province was a virtual viceroy acting in the name and with the authority of the sultan. The Ottoman government was careful to appoint governors only for short terms, sometimes as short as one year. But the eighteenth century witnessed several governors of local extraction who remained in office in Damascus, Tripoli and Sidon for several years, and were allowed moreover to pass on their office to relatives or protégés. In the early nineteenth century governors who remained long in office were seldom of local extraction.

To keep local chieftains loyal, public highways open and to remit to the imperial treasury the assigned annual sum were the chief functions of a governor. He farmed the taxes of the province to local chieftains or minor officials who in turn farmed them to smaller tax-collectors. The yield at each level was greater than the amount ultimately remitted to the imperial treasury. The beneficiaries were members of the feudal hierarchy of all communities, at the head of which stood the governor himself. The sufferers of all the communities were the taxpayers, farmers, merchants and artisans.

Each governor had under his orders a garrison in the capital of the province composed of units of the regular army or Janissaries. These had long ceased to be recruited from the children of the Christian subjects of the sultan. Some of the units that served in Syria were of the imperial corps, but most of the other forces were local recruits who followed their professions until they were called for duty. Hence the custom of their carrying arms wherever they went, and hence also the temptation for some of them to take the law into their hands and tyrannise over the population in their immediate surroundings. They had in fact very little of the qualities or discipline of a regular army. But in an emergency the governor also summoned to his aid feudal contingents which local chieftains had to contribute. Beside the Janissaries and feudal forces, the governor had his own private army of mercenaries composed of men with no local ties such as the Maghribis (men from the Arab West, i.e. North Africa).

The numerical strength of these forces in relation to the extent of a pasha's territorial jurisdiction was in peacetime not considerable, but their fighting qualities were excellent as their resistance to Napoleon demonstrated. At the beginning of the nineteenth century, security in the cities and on the main highways was comparatively satisfactory on account of the extreme severity with which offenders were punished. Some serious breakdown in security was partly due to beduin raids and partly to the indiscipline of the corps of Janissaries who, when their pay was in arrears or when they sought to wring a concession from the governor, vented their wrath on the civil population by resorting to plunder and extortion.

But even when their discipline was at its best the forces of law and order were on several occasions powerless to protect caravans, the livestock and agricultural produce of exposed villages or merchandise exhibited in small market towns, from surprise raids by armed beduin horsemen.

Not all the beduin tribes in Syria were confined to the deserts on the 'fringes of the sown' to the south and east of the country. Indeed, some of them camped right in the midst of fertile and cultivated areas or near market towns. But these semi-sedentary tribes were not less contemptible of authority, of cultivators of the soil and of town dwellers than their desert brethren. They all regarded raiding as a legitimate means of livelihood. Some strong tribes demanded and received tolls for the safe conduct of caravans through their preserve or for peaceful coexistence with their rural and urban neighbours. Banū Ṣakhr and the ʿAnazah tribes were notorious for their daring raids and their skill in evading punitive expeditions.

Thus only the settled population was under government control and only against them could punishment be meted out. Governors and local chieftains had the power to imprison offenders, to impose collective fines and, in extreme cases, to confiscate property. Another method of punishing a chieftain or a locality was the cutting down of fruit trees, the burning of crops in the fields and the destruction of dwelling houses. This method was used by governors and chieftains alike. It was also extended to feuds among all sections of the population, whether these feuds were a legacy of the tribal division on Qais and Yemen lines or were rooted in religious division as were the feuds between the Druzes and the Maronites.

It is often stated that the Ottoman authorities tended to fan the fires of these feuds for political ends, but there is no convincing evidence that this was their decided policy. They had on several occasions to employ imperial forces in Syria, involving considerable expenditure and loss of men and revenue, in order to uphold law and order. To them, as indeed to any other government, the stratagem of 'divide and rule' was no substitute for the exercise of power. The Ottoman government, in the days of its decline, was known to maintain a skilful balance between stratagem and the employment of force.

3

On occasion a governor of a province did, like his master the sultan, act arbitrarily, but he was not, again like his master, above the law. Istanbul was very sensitive to complaints against governors from local notables, and not a few lost their posts, if not their heads, as a result of such complaints. In the provinces, as in the capital, members of the learned profession were the recognised guardians of Islamic law, the *Sharīʿah*. It was an established custom for an advisory council of notables, including men learned in the law, to act as advisers to the governor.

On this council sat the *mufti* of the capital of the province, whose office was as a rule hereditary and whose function was to pronounce on the legality or otherwise of any measure. Apart from the governor himself who was the *ex officio* chairman of the council there were two imperial officers in charge of the administration of justice and finance respectively. They were independent of the governor, and each within his own competence exercised some check on the governor's powers. The military commander, if he happened to be a person other than the governor, was not always a member of this advisory council. The first of the two imperial official members of the council was the *qāḍi*, the judge of the capital whose jurisdiction was all-embracing in so far as the Muslims were concerned. Even the governor and the other high officials were subject to his supervision. He appointed subordinates in smaller towns and through them controlled all religious foundations, schools, markets, weights and measures, customs dues, contracts and public morality in general.

Non-Muslims, even those who were Ottoman subjects, were outside the *qāḍi's* jurisdiction unless a Muslim was involved. This latitude is the practical application of the *millet* system guaranteeing autonomy in religious and personal matters to Christians and Jews.

Resident or visiting Europeans were subject to the jurisdiction of their own consular courts and not to the Muslim courts, again unless a Muslim was involved. The origin of this privilege is that at the height of their power and glory Ottoman sultans granted, as a logical application of the *millet* system, certain extra-territorial concessions to friendly nations, largely to facilitate trade. The concessions were enshrined in chapters (*capitula*), better known as the Capitulations which acquired such a bad name in their later history.

The other imperial official member of the council was the

defterdar, the treasurer whose main duty was to ensure the dispatch to the state treasury of the stipulated annual tax. Contrary to popular belief this amount was a small proportion of the revenue, the greater part of which was supposed to be spent in the province on the administration, the armed force and public utilities. The treasurer had the power, with the *qāḍi*, to demand from retiring pashas proof that they did not appropriate any public money for themselves. The property and wealth of a pasha who died in office was subject to confiscation by the treasurer for the state if it was shown that the wealth was acquired while in office.

Decentralisation of provincial administration and devolution of authority in non-Muslim religious affairs were then the two bases of the Ottoman system. Once an evidence of confidence, the system had now become a sign of decline. It worked very smoothly, and on the whole to the advantage of the government and its subjects, while the Empire was mighty and universally respected. Its risks became apparent only in the era of weakness and decadence. One of these risks was the abuse of power by provincial governors, local chieftains and certain ecclesiastical authorities. For it must not be supposed, as a chorus of hostile European writers would wish us to believe, that the Ottoman officials were alone responsible for abuses, or that their victims were invariably Christians. Muslims no less than Christians, Jews, Druzes and others were not spared. A great deal of the oppression which the population of all faiths suffered was from their immediate feudal lords who exercised wide executive and quasi-judicial powers which sometimes amounted to the power to exact the death penalty. Christians and Jews suffered at the hands of their own superiors as their immediate controllers and the actual collectors of the capitation tax, just as the Muslims suffered from the greed of their local tax-farmer. In neither case was the Ottoman governor directly responsible except as the ultimate authority for the action of his subordinates.

Another risk of decentralisation was the usurpation by some provincial pashas of the sultan's authority and the attempts by some local chieftains to renounce the pasha's control. As a result the political and administrative conditions were in virtual chaos in the closing decades of the eighteenth century. These conditions provided a fertile soil for rivalry and personal ambition. We frequently read of one pasha fighting another, and like their superiors the chieftains took advantage of the weakening of the central and provincial authority to assert their independence to the extent, in one or two instances, of treating with foreign powers. Nor is it rare to find in the chronicles accounts of a chieftain in revolt against his pasha or another chieftain refusing to pay the annual tributes.

The Ottoman government regarded these wars and insubordinations as petty disturbances. They took notice only when the authority of the sultan was seriously in question. Otherwise they waited for the parties to resolve their own differences. They even agreed, in certain cases, to postpone payment of the tribute or to reduce its amount. On the whole, even when imperial forces had to be employed, the sultan's pardon was just as easily given, or bought, as his vengeance was tardily meted out.

The catalogue of petty wars between the feudal lords or between the pashas or between the lords and their pashas fills the pages of native chronicles almost to the exclusion of everything that interests the modern historian. These wars are now of little significance and will on the whole be excluded from this book, no matter how much space they still occupy in the accounts of some modern writers.

Nor is there any advantage in citing long lists of pashas who governed in Syria. Most of them, generally known only by their personal names with no identification other than the title of pasha, are mere ghosts to us, if they were anything else in their own times. There is no intention to resurrect them here. There are, however, notable exceptions to which we shall occasionally refer, beginning with one straight away.

Out of the prolonged and confused turmoil of the last decades of the eighteenth century Aḥmad Pasha, better known by the nickname of al-Jazzār, emerged as the dominant power in the provinces of Sidon and Damascus. At one time or another his authority extended also north to Tripoli and south to the Egyptian border. The Ottoman government confirmed him in office for an exceptionally long period because he succeeded in asserting its authority effectively over recalcitrant chieftains, in stamping out lawlessness in the countryside, and in exacting the dues and remitting fairly regularly the stipulated share to the imperial treasury. He was the first pasha to drive the chieftains inland and to place such seaports as Tripoli, Beirut, Sidon and Acre under direct government control.

Jazzār made his seat in Acre which he fortified and embellished with a mosque, a public library and a public fountain attached thereto, a covered bazaar and an official residence for himself. While he was undoubtedly ruthless, tyrannical and extortionist, much of the stories about his cruelty is exaggeration and lost nothing in the telling. He showed a marked ability as an administrator and soldier. He formed a mobile police patrol to intercept and punish brigands, and never hesitated to impose collective fines on unruly districts and to collect the fines without mercy. He kept the feudal lords in his province, including the Amīr Bashīr Shihāb in Lebanon, under strict control. He subdued all the rebels with the exception of the Jarrārs in Nābulus district in Palestine. His most spectacular sucess, however, was the defence of Acre against Napoleon in 1799.

4

Ever since Sulaiman the Magnificent granted to Francis I the privileges enshrined in the Capitulations of 1535, French monarchs had been the friends, if not the allies, of Ottoman sultans. Nothing of great importance disturbed their harmonious relations for nearly three centuries. In 1789, Salim III became sultan and the French Revolution broke out. In less than two years the French Republic was at war with the Ottoman Empire.

But meanwhile the Revolution made no difference to Franco-Turkish relations. If anything, Ottoman ministers first regarded it as a heaven-sent scourge for the chastisement of their enemies in Europe. They realised that the conclusion of the war which Russia and Austria had waged against the Ottoman Empire in the Balkans for nearly five years was due in no small measure to the preoccupation of the powers with revolutionary France.

Even before succeeding to the sultanate, Salim exhibited keen interest in French culture, and exchanged letters with Louis XVI. The lessons of the war with Russia and Austria which clouded the early years of his reign were not lost on Salim. Not unnaturally he turned to France for advisers in order to modernise his army and to introduce other reforms. In 1793 he received in Istanbul the first resident ambassador from France. Three years later one of the first ambassadors ever to be sent from the Ottoman Empire to Europe was accredited to the French Republic.

But hardly a year had passed when ominous clouds began to appear on the horizon. By acquiring the Ionian islands and other territories formerly belonging to Venice, revolutionary France suddenly became Turkey's neighbour. Not only did the French Embassy in Istanbul not lose any time in exhibiting the symbols and the sentiments of the Republic, but enthusiastic Frenchmen took it upon themselves to spread republican ideas among the Greek subjects of the sultan in adjacent territories.

The powers opposed to revolutionary France were quick to point out these dangers to the sultan and to invite him to join their ranks. An appraisal of the situation by a senior Ottoman minister left little doubt that Franco-Turkish friendship was on the point of a breakdown. Branding the intellectual forerunners of the Revolution as heretics, atheists and materialists and the Revolution itself as evil, sedition and wickedness, the minister added that revolutionary France had published its rebellious ideas in the 'Rights of Man' and translated it into different languages in an attempt to instigate the peoples to rise against their legitimate kings.

A few months later General Bonaparte removed all doubt from the minds of the Ottoman ministers and put an end to the speculations in the chancelleries of Europe. The destination of the expeditionary force assembled in Toulon was not Ireland but Egypt. On 1 July 1798 the expedition reached Alexandria. By next morning the French, who had landed to the west in the night were, in the words of a native contemporary historian, surrounding the city 'like swarms of locusts'. Before noon it fell into their hands.

Napoleon had already issued a proclamation to his army in which he stated his aim: to inflict damage on British interests in a sensitive spot. At the same time he required his troops to show all respect to the Muslim faith and not to offend against the laws and customs of the Egyptians. To the Egyptians he issued another proclamation which opens with the conventional phrases and koranic verses which only a Muslim ruler would use on such an occasion. In defective Arabic which is supposed to have been written by the orientalist Jean-Michel de Venture who accompanied the expedition, Napoleon stressed his respect for the Prophet and the Koran, and went on to the extreme of asserting that the French were sincere Muslims and true friends of the Ottoman sultan. Hence villages submitting to French forces were required to fly the sultan's flag side by side with the tricolour.

But revolutionary France had wrongly assessed the sultan's reactions to an unprovoked assault against one of his dominions by a friendly power. At first the Ottoman government hoped that Paris would disown Napoleon, but they were disappointed in their expectation. Accordingly the sultan concluded an alliance with 'his respected brother the exalted sultan of the English'. A proclamation with this news was conveyed to Syria by the English squadron under 'our beloved signor Sidney Smith'.

It seems that the French or at least Napoleon had entertained some vague hopes that once they were established in Egypt and once an end was put to Mamluk misgovernment, the sultan might acquiesce in a French occupation on favourable terms. Careful reading of Napoleon's proclamations and the repeated mention of French friendship to the sultan suggest that it was not all bluffing or propaganda; it suggests that France might have recognised the sultan's sovereignty over French-occupied Egypt. The spectacle of Napoleon acting as a vassal of Salim III would have been very interesting indeed!

The French had almost at once been cut off from supplies by the destruction of their fleet by Nelson and the placing of Egypt under a British blockade. But it was also necessary for the sultan to counteract Napoleon's pretentions in his proclamations among the people of Egypt and Syria. Accordingly the Ottoman government issued a long circular in Arabic warning the Muslims that, according to documents intercepted by Ottoman spies, the secret design of the French was the destruction of Islam and the acquisition of its lands. The circular begins:

> In the name of God, the Merciful the Compassionate. . . . To the community of Muslims who believe that God is one: Know that the French nation, may God destroy their country and humble their flag, are impious infidels and iniquitous libertines.

They do not believe that the Lord of heaven and earth is one. . . . Nay, they have forsaken all religions. . . . They have confiscated the riches of their own churches and stripped them of their crosses and attacked their priests and monks. They claim that the [holy] books which prophets brought to mankind are manifest falsehood; that the Koran, the Torah and the Gospel are nothing but perjury; that Moses, Jesus and Muḥammad and others made false claims to being prophets. . . . [They assert] that all men are equal in humanity . . . and none has any merit or distinction over any other. . . . By their wrong-doings the rest of the European nations have been plunged into disturbance. . . . And now their mischief and evil intention have reached the Muḥammadan nation. . . . Then all you Muslims who believe in God and His Messenger . . . rise to fight this French nation . . . and God's help is with you. . . .[5]

In Syria Jazzār was the first to match words with action. He closed the Syrian ports to foreign ships, confiscated the property of French merchants in these ports, ordered the strengthening of their fortifications and the removal to the interior of some Christians. A strong detachment of his troops was sent to occupy the fortress of al-ʿArīsh, strictly in Egyptian territory and belonging neither to the province of Damascus nor even to the district of Gaza which Jazzār seems to have now annexed. Jazzār's action was in anticipation of the dispatch of two imperial armies which were to be supported by British and Russian sea power. But Napoleon acted more promptly than the Turks. In February 1799 he launched an attack against southern Syria.

Egypt's defence has always been linked with Syria or at least the southern part of it. Seldom has a major power taken possession of Egypt without seeking to protect its hold on the country by occupying Palestine or the whole of Syria. Napoleon proved to be no exception. Once a formal declaration of war on France was made by the Ottoman government, Napoleon's sense of strategy decided his first move: to attack before he was attacked. Like former military rulers in Egypt, he saw the necessity of either annexing adjacent territory in southern Syria or at least scattering the forces then massing in it for the recovery of Egypt.

In a proclamation to the religious leaders and all the people in southern Palestine, Napoleon claimed that he was provoked by Jazzār who had sent his troops as far as al-ʿArīsh in Egyptian territory with warlike intentions. Napoleon promised peace and protection of life and property to all the population and added: 'We desire all the *qāḍis* to continue in office and to perform their duties as hitherto, and we desire in particular the religion of Islam to remain glorious and respected, and mosques full of believers for prayer. . . .'[6]

5

Napoleon launched the Syrian campaign with some 13,000 handpicked soldiers.[7] His first obstacle was the fortress of al-ʿArīsh, with a garrison of about 1500 men, including some Mamluks who had fled from Egypt. Much to Napoleon's surprise the fortress withstood the siege for ten days. On 18 February it surrendered on terms: the men to retain their arms and go free, but not to serve Jazzār again for a year. But Napoleon disarmed the Mamluks among those who surrendered and sent them to Egypt under escort where they were set free.

Gaza was taken a week later without resistance, so was ar-Ramlah another week later. The French then marched towards Jaffa on the sea which they besieged on 3 March and took by storm four days later. If Gaza was looted, Jaffa was sacked and its population suffered the horrors of a town taken by storm.

Over 2500 soldiers who had taken refuge in the citadel offered to surrender if their lives were spared. Two of Napoleon's aides accepted the surrender on this single condition. But the general was dismayed; he saw the difficulties of guarding or feeding or releasing so many men. His decision to order their massacre has since been a subject of debate between those who defend and those who condemn him. His own contention that some of the men released on parole at al-ʿArīsh were found among the Jaffa prisoners is surely no excuse. If he was right, why did he order the shooting of all the Jaffa prisoners and not only those among them who allegedly broke their promise?

To the surviving people of Jaffa it must have seemed divine retribution itself that almost instantly the French camp was struck by bubonic plague. On a single day, while the massacre was still in progress, thirty-one soldiers were admitted to an improvised hospital and fourteen others died. The general appointed by Napoleon as administrator of ar-Ramlah and Jaffa held his office for only one day; on the second he was dead.

It was a plague-stricken army that marched under Napoleon to Acre. On the way the French were harassed by feudal levies from the Nābulus area and they had to fight minor battles at Wādi ʿAzzūn and near Qāqūn, in one of which General Junot with a corps of 1500 men was defeated. But that did not hold the advance to Acre. As soon as the news of Napoleon's advance from Jaffa had reached Sir Sidney Smith, who had been appointed in command of the British squadron guarding the approaches to Alexandria, he hurried to Acre. Some of his gunboats, with an Ottoman flotilla, were left cruising off the Palestinian coast. They intercepted nine French vessels of which they captured six with most of Napoleon's siege artillery on board – a crippling blow for a general proceeding to attack a fortified city.

Acre was a triangular city with two sides facing the sea which Smith controlled. Round the other side there were thick walls with towers and a castle which Jazzār used as a palace. He had an ample supply of guns, cannon balls and gunpowder, and the English supplied him with more.

By the middle of March the French had taken position near the walls and their engineers began preparations for the assault. At the same time detachments of the French army penetrated deep into Galilee as far north as Ṣafad and east as Tiberias. Receiving no response to his repeated overtures to Jazzār, Napoleon sought to enlist local support by rousing sectarian and factional groups. He assumed that the Maronites would rally to him as they had done to the Crusaders. He tried not without success to rouse the Matāwilah in Galilee and south Lebanon.

Napoleon's call was not unheeded by the Christians in Galilee and by some Maronites. Ṣāliḥ, son of Ẓāhir al-ʿUmar, accepted appointment as shaikh of Ṣafad where his father had ruled before Jazzār put an end to his career. The Druzes absolutely refused to play Napoleon's game. Bashīr Shihāb of Lebanon adopted a neutral attitude. He refused Napoleon's invitation to call upon him, but he also refused to give any material assistance to Jazzār.

Meanwhile Jazzār had strengthened Acre's defences. English marines were landed to reinforce his gun crews, and the captured

French guns were placed in position against their former owners. Several hundred Turkish gunners, trained by French instructors, arrived from Constantinople to take part in the defence.

Napoleon did not reckon with a long siege. He ordered several assaults but all failed to capture the fortress. Reports of massed forces coming from Nābulus and Damascus reached the French general. Scouts warned him of the approach of forces commanded by the pasha of Damascus. Some of these forces had actually encircled a smaller French force under General Kléber near Nazareth. With lightning speed Napoleon himself led a relief force which plucked victory from certain disaster. The victory was celebrated that night in Nazareth amidst local Christian rejoicing.

But when yet another of those desperate attempts on the walls of Acre failed, Napoleon decided to retreat. Shortage of supplies and the plague were among the compelling reasons for retreat. To make the maximum use of his heavy artillery which had to be abandoned and to cover the impending retreat, Napoleon ordered all the guns at his disposal to pound the city continuously for four days. On 20 May the retreat began. The siege had lasted exactly two months. So short of transport was the army that officers, including the commander-in-chief himself, chose to walk in order to spare mounts for the sick and wounded.

Back at Jaffa Napoleon once more tarnished his reputation. He ordered, or at least suggested, the poisoning of some fifty plague patients in the hospital who were unfit to be carried in litters. The retreat was at all stages very humiliating, but it was stage-managed as a victory. The army reached al-ʿArīsh at the beginning of June and entered Cairo two weeks later. Napoleon saw to it that those who marched behind him through the Gate of Victory (Bāb al-Futūḥ) were in good shape.

The Syrian campaign was very costly indeed. About one thousand soldiers were killed in action, another one thousand died of the plague and over two thousand returned sick or wounded. The army had lost at least one-third of its initial strength.

Napoleon's loss was Jazzār's gain. His prestige with the Ottoman government was greatly enhanced, so was his appetite for power. He began at once to settle accounts with traitors and waverers. In particular he accused Bashīr Shihāb of Lebanon of collaboration with Napoleon by not taking part in the defence of

Acre and by contributing no forces to fight the French elsewhere. Forced by Jazzār's displeasure to give up his position, Bashīr sought Sidney Smith's assistance to present him to the Grand Vizier Yūsuf Ḍiya Pasha who was marching at the head of an army through Syria to oust the French from Egypt. Having given assurances of his 'servitude to the exalted Ottoman government', Bashīr was summoned by Jazzār and restored to his position. The son of Ẓāhir vanished and the Christian collaborators were cowed.

The damage done by the French in Syria was greater than is generally recognised. The destruction of cities, the loss of human life and the looting of private property was indeed great. But greater was the damage to society by the fanning of religious antagonism. Napoleon's profession of love for Islam was taken seriously neither by the Muslims nor by the Christians in Syria. Thus the shaikhly families in ar-Ramlah withdrew before his arrival, but nonetheless he was warmly welcomed by the Christians of the city. Many Christians in Galilee acted as scouts or spies for the French. Indeed, it was native Christian scouts who warned Napoleon of the plight of General Kléber and the advance of the pasha of Damascus.

Such open cleavage between the Christian and Muslim population forced to the fore by French presence proved to be a prelude to the sharpening of religious animosities and strife in the next two generations. And yet we are continuously told that the Napoleonic invasion of Egypt and Syria was the herald of a glorious Arab renaissance. In this belief the French invasion is held to mark the close of medieval times in the Arab Near East. Those who still cling to this erroneous assumption may pause to reflect. The stream of history flows relentlessly and all barriers across it can only be artificial.

There is really no decisive point at which we can say that the old world changed itself into the new world in the Near East or elsewhere. Long before 1798 the movement that is variously called modernisation or reform was under way in different parts of the Muslim world. Long after 1798 'medieval' ideas held undisputed sway and their supremacy was not fundamentally in question. The change, modernisation, reform or renaissance was first inspired by native and internal forces; only its more obvious and later development was in response to foreign or external challenge.

2

Administrative Anarchy – The Sublime Porte, Pashas and Feudal Lords

I

ONE of the two Ottoman armies mobilised for the recovery of Egypt landed near Alexandria in July 1799 and was decisively beaten by Napoleon. About two weeks later he was on his way to France and ultimately to the imperial sceptre. Kléber was left in command of the French army, as well as in charge of the negotiations which Napoleon had initiated with the Grand Vizier then in command of the other Ottoman army marching on Egypt by land through Syria. The French were ready to evacuate Egypt on honourable terms, but the British government repudiated a preliminary agreement signed in January 1800 by the French and the Turks. In consequence fighting was resumed and a British expeditionary force had to be sent to Egypt. The way to peace was thus long and bloody. Not till 1801 did the French finally go; the English not till 1803.

In Syria the havoc caused by the French campaign had aggravated already existing administrative difficulties. It is true that as a stabilising influence Jazzār was then at the zenith of his power. But he died in 1804 and the greater part of Syria over which at one time or another he ruled returned to chaos. His protégés as well as others sought to profit from the anarchy. But we do not propose to go into details, and a few instances must suffice to illustrate the state of affairs.

In 1807 when the governor of Damascus was away with the

pilgrim caravan open fighting broke out between the Janissaries and the local militia in which many were killed. But the trouble was not confined to the citadel; it embraced the whole city which suffered much destruction and looting. The chronic chaos in Aleppo is symbolised by the circumstances of the entry of the new governor of the province into the city in 1811. He had to negotiate with and seek the agreement of the Janissaries before assuming office.

In Tripoli, Muṣṭafā Agha Barbar had been recognised as deputy governor (*mutasallim*) for some time. He was very ambitious, recalcitrant and often refused to pay taxes. His removal was ordered more than once by higher authorities. Two pashas of Damascus had each led an expedition against him. In 1809 he was besieged in the citadel for several months until forced to surrender on lenient terms and allowed to seek refuge with the pasha of Acre, only to rise again to the same eminent position shortly after.

While he was in Syria, the grand vizier had appointed Muḥammad Abū Maraq in Jaffa as deputy governor for southern Palestine and invested him with the title of pasha. But Abū Maraq proved too ambitious for Jazzār, who led an expedition against him and forced him to flee. Another *mutasallim* of Jaffa deserves mention. He was Muḥammad Agha Abū Nabbūt. It was he who in 1812 received the eccentric Lady Hester Stanhope and eased her passage to Jerusalem. But he too was removed by a mild successor of Jazzār, and had to seek refuge with Muḥammad ʿAlī in Cairo. Abū Nabbūt had obliged Muḥammad ʿAlī by recovering from some beduins in Gaza district the loot of an Egyptian caravan.

To these and similar internal disorders there was now added a new external danger. The appointment and dismissal of governors in Syria was for several years after Jazzār closely connected with the rise of the Wahhābi power in Arabia, which after its extension to Hijaz constituted both a challenge to the authority of the sultan and a menace to the security of Syria.

The princely house of Saʿūd in Najd had in the middle of the eighteenth century allied themselves with a fervent preacher of moral and spiritual regeneration named Muḥammad Ibn ʿAbd al-Wahhāb. Educated in the Ḥanbali rite, the strictest of the four Sunni schools, the preacher sought to rid Islam of all innovations and to restore its original purity. The house of Saʿūd undertook to support him even to the point of imposing his reforms by the force of arms.

By 1805 the Saʿūdi forces had occupied Mecca for the second time and forced the Sharif of Mecca to accept the Wahhābis as his overlords. The pilgrims from Syria, Egypt and other parts of the Muslim world had to pay taxes to the new masters and to submit to their system while in the Hijaz. Confident of their power, the Wahhābis made it known that they would oppose by force the entry of the traditional *maḥmal* (a litter covered with a cloth richly embroidered with gold and bearing the cipher of the sultan) and armed troops that usually accompany the pilgrim caravans from Syria and Egypt.

In 1807 ʿAbdullah Pasha al-ʿAẓm, scion of the family that provided Syria with a number of governors in the eighteenth century, was governor of Damascus. He led the Syria caravan, with litter, soldiers and all to the Hijaz. But the Wahhābis had placed a force north of Medina to prevent his entry. The evidence is contradictory whether ʿAbdullah did put up a fight or not, but all accounts agree that he and the Syrian pilgrims had to return. It was a great humiliation to the sultan who prided himself on being 'the guardian of the two noble sanctuaries' of Mecca and Medina. It was also a personal humiliation since, according to a report, either a daughter or a sister of the sultan was among the disappointed pilgrims.[1]

ʿAbdullah was promptly dismissed, and Kanj Yūsuf Pasha appointed in his place. While this governor proved an energetic and able administrator he was not very successful against the Wahhābis, even in his own province. Emboldened by success, and probably also impelled by hunger, the Wahhābis raided deep into fertile Hawrān in 1810. The pasha marched at the head of an army against them up to Muzairib, the administrative capital of the area, but he does not seem to have made actual contact with them. Nor did the forces commanded by the pasha of Acre, supported by a contingent from Lebanon under Bashīr Shihāb, go farther than Tiberias in their attempt to meet the invaders.

There was much burning, destruction and pillage. In addition the Wahhābis levied the *ʿushr*, the legal tenth of the income of the people who were temporarily at their mercy. It is not clear whether their withdrawal was due to the thunder of the pasha's artillery or to their encumbrance with rich spoils. Indeed, the Wahhābi raid came at the height of a prolonged drought all over Arabia. For six years beginning in 1805 the beduins suffered famine and serious loss of livestock.

But this is not to underestimate the religious zeal of the Wahhābis, a zeal which shines in the correspondence between Saʿūd Ibn ʿAbdal-ʿAzīz and the pasha of Damascus. The letters from the former contain much that was needless to address to fellow Muslims, and the little they contain on Wahhābi reforms is ill-expressed and lacks precision. But while these letters are polite in tone, the pasha's retort is very much less so. It appears that Kanj Yūsuf Pasha had sent with 'unofficial' pilgrims a message to Saʿūd. The latter's reply claims that the pilgrims were well received and that they saw how the Wahhābis were upholding Islamic law and the traditions of the early community, removing oppression and establishing justice.

Saʿūd goes on to explain his mission. Its basis is absolute monotheism and the worship of God alone without any associates or intermediaries. For to seek help except from God is to the Wahhābis tantamount to polytheism, and carries with it penalties: 'He who seeks God's help alone and is sincere in worshipping Him and performs his duties to Him is our brother Muslim. . . . But he who does not heed this call and persists in his polytheism we will declare infidel and will fight him. . . .'

Another letter from Saʿūd and one from the commander who led the raid into Syria were sent to the pasha. The commander denies that his aim was war and proposes a religious discussion between representative Syrians and Wahhābis. He adds to Saʿūd's letter further specific objections to what he regarded as polytheistic practices including sacrifice other than to God, erection of edifices over tombs, belief in the intercession of prophets, martyrs and saints.

But beneath this reforming zeal is concealed a desire to reap the economic benefits of the resumption of the pilgrim traffic. By its suspension the people of Mecca and Medina as well as the beduin and settled population on the pilgrim route had been deprived of their main source of income. So were the Saʿūdi overlords in Hijaz and their helpless vassal, the Sharif of Mecca.

The ʿAnazah shaikhs, who had almost monopolised the supply of camels for hire to the Damascus caravan, became restless and their friendship with the Saʿūdis was cooling. Small wonder if the Wahhābi threat of war is now tempered with an offer for calm negotiation. The commander wrote:

> . . . If you have a desire to despatch the pilgrim [caravan] let us know so that we can confront you with Saʿūd [in conference]. Then we will follow what true religion demands . . . we beseech you by the Creator of heaven and earth to spare Muslim blood. Let the learned decide between us, and send your representatives.

By the time this letter reached Damsacus, Sulaimān Pasha had succeeded to the inheritance of Jazzār in Syria. He replied to Saʿūd as follows. Direct your preaching Islam to non-Muslims; discussion conducted with you on several earlier occasions revealed truth from falsehood' and there was nothing to be gained by its renewal. Then referring to the Wahhābi boast that they were *aʿrāb* (beduins), like the Prophet and his companions, the governor quotes the Koran IX, 98: 'The beduins are more stubborn in unbelief and hypocrisy, and apter not to know the bounds of what God has sent down on His Messenger.' He brands the Wahhābis as virtual heretics and concludes:

> If your aim is to uphold Islam . . . then fight its enemies the infidels, not the Muslim community. . . . What greater evil and what grosser transgression than [your] fighting the Muslims, plundering their property, violating their women, killing their livestock and burning their villages in parts of Syria? . . . Go back to your country . . . and remove your evil. . . . Otherwise we shall put you to the sword. . . .

2

It was all very well for the pasha to utter this threat. Neither he nor the Ottoman government was yet in a position to do much. In Istanbul the will to act was atrophied by revolution and counter-revolution. In 1807 Salim III was deposed, Muṣṭafā IV proclaimed sultan only to be also deposed, and Maḥmūd II finally recognised as sultan in the following year. Next to Salim, he was the second of the reforming sultans. He was determined to assert his authority and to curb the powers of rebellious pashas and mutinous soldiers.

The recovery of Hijaz was one of Maḥmūd's first ambitions. But since at least three of the pashas in Syria had failed to open the way to Mecca, the sultan decided to appoint Muḥammad ʻAli, the strong pasha of Egypt, as commander of a special expedition to the Hijaz. As a result Mecca was recovered in 1813, the pilgrimage resumed and eventually the Saʻūdi empire in Hijaz and Najd destroyed.

But external dangers, whether from the French invasion or the Wahhābi raids, produced little more than a suspension of the chronic disorders in Syria. Mutinies in the armed forces remained as frequent as ever. Local chieftains and factions returned to their intrigues and rivalries. Pashas resumed their mutual jealousies and quarrels. And the Sublime Porte shifted its support from one side to the other with remarkable ease. A classic example is provided in the events of 1821–2. When the rivalries between Darwīsh Pasha of Damascus and ʻAbdullah Pasha of Acre led to open conflict the Porte sided with the weaker of the two. ʻAbdullah was dismissed and Darwīsh was appointed his successor. But the former refused to obey the order and open war between the two pashas broke out in which Bashīr Shihāb took the side of ʻAbdullah. Thereupon the Porte ordered the pashas of Aleppo and Adana to join forces with Darwīsh in an attempt to defeat ʻAbdullah. But when the combined forces failed, after a nine months' siege, to take Acre, the Porte was gracious, on Muḥammad ʻAli's intercession, to order the lifting of the siege and to pardon ʻAbdullah who promised to pay 25,000 purses as war indemnity!

To go into more details would not deepen our knowledge either of the Ottoman system or of its operation in Syria during the first two or three decades of the nineteenth century. In the words of a native chronicler, it would merely 'bore the reader'.

So from the squabbles of pashas and chieftains we turn to consider an aspect of the administration which has given rise to some misconception. This aspect is the employment by governors of Christians and Jews, the former generally as secretaries and the latter as accountants. The custom was so widespread in the period under review that practically all clerical and financial posts in the provinces of Damascus and Sidon (or Acre) were occupied by Christians and Jews. Gradually these posts became the virtual monopoly of certain Christian and Jewish families. So established was the practice that it applied to pashas and their subordinates alike. Thus Abū Nabbūt had for secretaries at ar-Ramlah and Gaza members of the Christian family Jaḥshān, just as his master Sulaimān Pasha had the Christian Ḥannā al-ʿAwrah as his chief secretary.

The employment of non-Muslims in such key positions in an administration professedly based on Islamic law requires an explanation, especially because it gave rise to some misunderstanding. First of all, the practice had a long history that goes back to the Arab conquest. Not only did the conquerors not fill subordinate posts with Arabs, but for more than a century they suffered the records and accounts to be kept by the officials of their predecessors in their own languages.

Secondly, other considerations became operative in modern times. By the nature of their education, eligible Muslims tended to prefer work as secretaries and financial administrators in the *qāḍī*'s department rather than in that of the governor. This preference was not due to lack of qualifications for the corresponding posts under the governor, but largely to religious scruples of the ulema as a class. There is no question that the standard of a shaikh's Arabic composition as seen in the records of a religious court at the time is higher than the semi-colloquial product of a Christian clerk in a governorate. Nor were the shaikhs as a class less qualified in mathematics, since as administrators of religious foundations and assessors of inheritance, which according to Islamic law could be very complicated, they required sound knowledge of higher arithmetic. A simpler knowledge – little more than manipulation of the four rules – was required by the governor's clerks for the compilation of lists of districts with amounts due from each.

A Christian or a Jew was more likely to act according to the whims of a governor, even if the action was illegal. He had none of the scruples of a pious shaikh. He would more readily be his Muslim master's servant, if not slave, and would not dare question his actions, no matter how illegal. In this manner these officials, especially the accountants, wielded great influence and amassed huge fortunes while they were in favour. If they lost favour their lot was not an enviable one. Some of them suffered imprisonment and confiscation of property, some loss of an eye and even death at the hands of their masters.

This is particularly true of the Jewish accountants. They were envied and hated by Christians and Muslims alike, the former largely because the Jews had taken what was once a Christian monopoly, the latter because Jewish accountants either through members of their families or their agents practised usury on a large scale among the peasants, the city merchants and even the pilgrims. To gain and retain favour with the authorities they entertained lavishly and were generous with 'presents' to successive governors.

There is no doubt that the accountants were efficient. Their efficiency was, however, tempered with cunning, and their cunning enabled them to engage in the intrigues of their time with telling results. The following story may be spurious, but it shows the typically sound if cynical advice which Ḥayyīm Fārḥi is supposed to have given Jazzār on a very delicate matter.

The pasha had once offered as an excuse for the delay in sending the annual tribute to Istanbul the extraordinary expenses he incurred in subduing Mount Lebanon, inhabited, as he stated with gross exaggeration, by 20,000 Christians and 60,000 Druzes. Little did the pasha expect that Istanbul would reassess the amount of the capitation tax according to this inflated figure. Fārḥi's advice was that the tax should be paid, according to the new assessment, from the pasha's own resources, but that soon afterwards he should announce the news that the Christians had embraced Islam and therefore were no longer subject to this tax.[2]

Jazzār's successors, both in Acre and in Damascus, continued to employ members of the Fārḥi family, despite public protest and accusations of usury, malpractices with the currency and embezzlement of public money. Governors, let it be remembered, were ephemeral; the accountants with their 'presents' were permanently there. Nor did they spare any expense to get unfriendly pashas removed. A member of the Fārḥi family was entrenched as chief accountant (*ṣarrāf-bāshi*) in Istanbul itself. He too used the methods successfully employed by the other members of the family.

But somehow protest was at last heeded in Istanbul. The Jewish accountants in the capital and those in Syria lost favour with the authorities. Twenty-nine account books were sent to the capital from Syria for inspection. A Christian government official in Damascus reports that the Fārḥi family had to pay to the treasury a fine of five thousand purses. (In 1812 Burckhardt estimated Ḥayyim's wealth alone at £300,000.)

Another fine, whatever its amount was, seems to have been at once an atonement and a fee for recovery of office. Rafael Fārḥi who had been replaced as an accountant in Damascus by a Christian from Ḥimṣ, spent several hundred purses in a successful attempt to get both the offending pasha replaced and himself reinstated. At long last a petition was sent to the sultan himself who ordered that Jewish accountants be dismissed. But a practical difficulty was immediately discovered. For self-preservation, Jewish accountants had kept their records in Hebrew and, moreover, in handwriting which amounted to secret codes. The story is succinctly well expressed by the poet Amīn al-Jundi, a native of Ḥimṣ, in a long poem addressed to Sultan Maḥmūd II in which 'praiseworthy' is the meaning both of the proper noun and adjective *maḥmūd*:

O most pious of sultans, praiseworthy are your deeds,
And with glory and victory you are blessed.
To your Highness I submit a grievance from
Your subjects, their patience at an end:
In Syria a weak group has assumed too much power:
They cast their spell over governors and were given a free hand.
How often they beguiled the innocent,
And betrayed many a pasha to justice inclined?
For three score years and ten they are the accountants,
One generation goes and another follows.
Hebrew is the language of their registers,
Not in our tongue – hence their secret unknown.
By their usury they ruined many a native of the country
And out of their way he was removed
Till God guided His caliph to uproot them,
And with this uprooting their evils effaced.[3]

3

Native chroniclers as well as modern writers, both in Arabic and in European languages, tend to forget that besides pashas, chieftains and tax collectors, Syria was inhabited by a great multitude of peasants in the countryside and a considerable number of merchants and artisans in the cities. The existence of these is seldom noticed except in connection with the actions of their masters. And yet they were the backbone of the country's economy, the actual taxpayers and the source of the wealth that the country's rulers enjoyed.

In the early nineteenth century the peasants in Syria were of three types. Two types lived in more or less permanently established villages: those who cultivated their own small plots and those who were tenants of absentee landlords. The third type were the semi-nomads who lived either in tents or in ramshackle huts near the land they cultivated for a season or more. The ephemeral nature of such settlements and the habits of the settlers seem to account for the misleading reports of European travellers which mention the 'disappearance' of incredible numbers of 'villages'.

In theory all land was the sultan's property; the landlords as well as the cultivators were his tenants. They were all subject to the payment of the *mīrī* tax i.e. rent of what may be termed crown land. In practice however, the farmer who cultivated his own small plot, and more specially the semi-nomad who cultivated where he happened to settle temporarily, were on the whole beyond the reach of the tax collector. The former could easily hide the produce which was seldom in excess of his needs, and the latter could even more easily dismantle his hut or 'fold his tent . . . and silently steal away'. It was on the cultivators of larger plots and on tenants of extensive properties in well-established villages that the burden of rural taxation fell.

The *mīrī* as 'permanently' fixed by Sultan Salim I was indeed moderate. But gradually the manner of its collection by a hierarchy of chieftains and other tax-farmers gave rise to abuse and increasing oppression. Two contrasting examples must suffice. During the period under review, the *mīrī* for Mount Lebanon was 530 purses, and for Nābulus district in Palestine 600 purses. But whereas in the former Bashīr Shihāb was always not only willing to collect the tax but also eager to enrich himself and his family in the process, the Jarrārs and their allies in Nābulus district had since the days of Jazzār been accustomed to resist the extortions of the pasha and even the tax itself by the force of arms, so much so that the governor of Damascus had once to represent that to collect the 600 purses from the district an expedition costing nearly the same amount would be required. Hence Nābulus was detached from his jurisdiction and placed under that of the pasha of Acre. But he too had to send an expedition in an attempt to levy the tax, and the result was fighting, burning of villages and destruction of wells, but little or no tax.

Similar circumstances led to a revolt in the city of Damascus in 1831, just a few months before the Egyptian invasion. The cause of the revolt was an attempt by a new governor to impose a new tax on houses and shops in the city. The people resisted, and to subdue them the pasha ordered the guns of the citadel to shell the bazaar. In the confusion that followed he himself was intercepted by a few ringleaders and murdered. Istanbul's preoccupation with Muḥammad ʿAli's invasion of Syria saved the Damascenes from a punitive expedition.

Nowhere in Syria was the imposition and collection of taxes easier than in Mount Lebanon, thanks to the heavy hand of Bashīr Shihāb. Not only did he collect the taxes payable to the pashas of Tripoli and Acre, but also sufficient amounts to meet their demands for 'presents' and his own expenses and the needs of members of his family. According to Burckhardt who travelled and lived in Syria in 1812:

> the Emir often exacts five or six *mīrīs* in the year. . . . Last year many peasants were obliged to sell a part of their furniture to defray the taxes. It may easily be conceived therefore in what misery they live: they eat scarcely anything but the worst bread, and oil or soups made of the wild herbs of which tyranny cannot deprive them. Notwithstanding the wretchedness in which they are left by the government, they have still to satisfy the greediness of their priests, but these contributions they pay with cheerfulness.[4]

It is clear that Bashīr maintained himself in office at the expense of his people of all faiths. He was as extortionist and oppressive as any of the native rulers or Ottoman pashas. There is little or no evidence to support the contention of some modern Lebanese writers that Bashīr was an independent ruler, or that in his days Mount Lebanon was an oasis of freedom and prosperity in a surrounding desert of oppression and poverty.

How far Bashīr was independent in Lebanon may be deduced from his frequent removal, and on occasion even long imprisonment, by the pashas. More than once he had to go into 'voluntary' exile awaiting the return of his master's favour. This is not to say that he was not an able ruler, who very skilfully and on the whole successfully maintained a balance between the Christians, Druzes and Muslims. His contemporaries, including European travellers, ascribed his reported conversion to Christianity to an administrative or political necessity. They pointed out that other members of his family, his rivals to power, remained openly loyal to Islam.

As to freedom under Bashīr, Lebanon like the rest of Syria had little or nothing of it. Much has been made of the fact that some individuals or groups sought refuge under Bashīr's protection. But surely this was not peculiar either to him or to Lebanon. All the chieftains, and the pashas themselves, followed this ancient custom. The pasha of Egypt was perhaps the most generous in granting asylum, but he was, like Bashīr, an exploiter of the peasantry and his measures were equally oppressive. As to prosperity, the available evidence leaves no doubt that the lot of peasantry in Lebanon, as in the rest of Syria, was very wretched indeed.

Speaking of Syria as a whole, the peasants were not much better than serfs, not so much because of limits set upon their freedom to desert their landlords as by the misery of their circumstances. The implements and methods they used were primitive, and their annual produce was barely sufficient for their needs and commitments to their landlords. Oppressed by rulers and fleeced by tax-collectors, those who cultivated land in exposed areas were frequently plundered by beduins, and those who needed capital to purchase animals or seeds had to mortgage their crops to moneylenders at ruinous rates.

For the small farmer, land tenure was precarious and its security not very desirable. Unless he farmed his plot surreptitiously and managed to evade the tax-collector, he was more often than not within the jurisdiction of a town notable who had contracted with a chieftain or directly with the pasha to collect the taxes of a group of villages for an agreed aggregate sum. Although, as stated above, the whole country was in theory a state domain some individuals or families had, either by purchase or by long and continued possession, acquired certain rights over considerable land properties. In order to keep this property under their control in perpetuity they legalised the possession as a form of religious foundation (*waqf*). They were thus enabled to administer it partly for their own profit and partly for the support of religious and charitable institutions. This was an extension of the system of public foundations, embracing very extensive land and other properties, administered by public bodies exclusively for the support of religious and charitable institutions such as mosques, schools and hospitals, in Syria and also in Hijaz. Such properties were exempt from the payment of the *mīrī*.

Public foundations are quite familiar and need no illustration here. For semi-public or family foundation one example must suffice. The right of collecting the revenue of the town of Idlib to the south-west of Aleppo, as well as that of some fifteen villages in that district up to the course of the Orontes, was vested in an Istanbul family. Each year they sent more than a third to Mecca and Medina, and in addition they defrayed the expenses of hospital-hostels they established for the poor of the area where food was provided gratis. The surplus was enjoyed by the family as personal income.

A great many villages were, however, exploited for private gain. Let us cite as an example the Catafago family who had long settled in Aleppo as Frank merchants. A member of this family, Louis, born in Aleppo, hence his surname al-Ḥalābi, had later made Nazareth his residence and engaged in commerce, moneylending and tax-collecting. In the second decade of the nineteenth century he had bought for £3000 a year the right to collect the taxes of some dozen villages in the neighbourhood. Like the rest of the tax-collectors he made handsome profits at the expense of the peasants, and his wealth encouraged him to meddle in local politics and intrigues.

It is surprising that despite such discouraging political and fiscal conditions Syria's agricultural economy did not collapse.

Miraculously the country was comparatively prosperous. The agricultural produce then included grain of different varieties that was grown in the plains. On the mountains and elsewhere fruit trees abounded. The most precious was the olive tree, the oil of which was, next to wheat, the staple food of the majority of the population. Mulberries were grown both for their fruit and for sericulture. Apricots, figs, peaches, pomegranates, vines, oranges and lemons were grown in different parts of the country. Other agricultural produce included cotton, tobacco, sesame (a kind of grain with oily interior), pistachio nuts, water-melons and various kinds of spring and summer vegetables. The rural and nomadic population were engaged in rearing cattle and employed for their purposes such domestic animals as the horse, the camel, the ox, etc.

The lot of city merchants was far better than that of the farmers. Trade routes through Syria by land followed their ancient course. Caravans converged on Aleppo from Mesopotamia, Armenia and Anatolia and thence to Alexandretta on the Mediterranean. Another major artery of trade was along the famous pilgrim route from Damascus to Mecca. A third channel was the caravan route from Egypt to Palestine which diverged at Gaza to join the pilgrim route at Maʿān.

Christian pilgrims to Jerusalem and Bethlehem followed two main routes. By land from Russia and Armenia to Aleppo and then along internal caravan routes, and by sea from the Greek islands and European provinces of the Ottoman Empire, mainly to Jaffa. This traffic was, on a smaller scale, as profitable to the economy of the country as the traffic of Muslim pilgrims to Mecca. It brought alms to the poor, donations to the churches, fees to the government, tolls to the chieftains, employment for many guides, and boosted the native trade in souvenirs.

In addition to the main routes there were lesser internal highways along which smaller caravans plied between the cities and seaports. The ports themselves were the termini of merchandise from the hinterland as well as the marts for the transit or exchange of foreign goods. The caravan trade was almost entirely in the hands of Muslim merchants. Foreigners and native Christian merchants were confined to seaports and internal commercial centres such as Aleppo, Nazareth and ar-Ramlah. Before Napoleon's attack on Syria, French commercial interests predominated over all other foreign interests. As a result of the attack this predominance was lost. There is no evidence to support the assertions of some European travellers that Syria's trade was exclusively in the hands of Franks and Levantines.

Domestic trade was largely by barter, and even some of the exports were bartered for imported goods. But on the whole imports for local consumption, as distinct from articles in transit, were limited to such articles as shawls from India, indigo dye, sugar and hardware from Europe, and coffee from the West Indies. (This coffee was offered at prices competitive with the mocha from Arabia.) Exports included sweetmeats and conserved fruit from Damascus to Anatolia, raw or spun silk from Tripoli and Mount Lebanon to France. Soap manufactured at Nābulus and Tripoli was exported from the latter to Anatolia and the Greek islands; beads, rosaries and crosses made of wood and cloth embroidered with souvenirs from Jerusalem and Bethlehem to Italy and Spain, and tobacco from Latakia to Egypt where it was bartered for rice.

Merchants were comparatively less oppressed than the peasants, though, again comparatively, not less taxed or exposed to exactions and hazards of various kinds. Long-range caravans had to buy peace at a high price from beduin tribes on their way, and to provide and pay for armed escort through both friendly and hostile territory. On internal routes there were, if not toll bridges, at least some chieftains who exacted such tolls for safe conduct. To these expenses were added the official customs dues payable both on imports by land and sea and on merchandise in transit. Finally the unpredictable expense of compulsory 'loans' and 'presents' to pashas. But even after these considerable expenses some merchants made handsome profits and grew rich.

The economy and the country as a whole suffered from the frequent visitation of the plague and locusts. While the epidemic affected villages less than congested towns, the devastation left by locusts was ruinous for an essentially agricultural economy. A contemporary source reports that the 1813 plague which raged all over Syria carried away nearly a fourth of the population. The locust invasion thirteen years later was particularly devastating.

It is a singular paradox that in an agricultural country merchants should on the whole have considerable public facilities at their disposal while peasants had practically none. The reference here is not to services which the merchants themselves provided for the protection of their merchandise, but to such public facilities as inns. The size and amenities of an inn (*khān*) varied according to its location. But essentially all inns were similar: around an open courtyard reserved for the animals there were apartments for lodging and stores, and all round the front of the apartments there was a covered area. The courtyard contained either a well over a natural spring or at least one cistern in which rain water was stored. Some inns, especially those on the pilgrim route, had watch-towers manned by armed guards, temporary or permanent. Other inns in the cities were the centres of commercial houses, native and foreign.

The bazaars were built in internal market towns and seaports, according to the same pattern: two parallel rows of small shops on both sides of a roofed way with vents to let in light and air. Such bazaars can still be seen in the major cities. But in addition to bazaars as permanent markets there were held, usually once a week, open-air markets in towns with a dependent rural population. Here the peasants marketed their produce, sold or bought animals, bought cloth from the bazaars and visited their disguised enemy, the town moneylender.

Even communal amenities were more for the benefit of the merchant than the farmer. These included the public guest-house (*maḍāfa*) and the private guest-house (*manzil*). At the first, shelter and food were given gratis to travellers by the well-to-do members of the community in rotation. At the second, the same hospitality was given in private houses on routes constantly used by travellers. Householders who thus provided hospitality were given an allowance which was made by deduction from the tax due from them. A landlord with heavy calls on his hospitality was not only exempted from paying the tax but was given an allowance from the total collected in his village. 'The establishment', says Burckhardt, 'of these public *manzils* which are general over the whole country to the south of Damascus does great honour to the hospitality of the Turks (i.e. Muslims).'

It now remains to say a word on artisans. Although comparatively few in number, a great many of them had the benefit of a long tradition of corporate organisations. Muslim artisans had long been organised into guilds and closely associated with sufi orders or also with certain military units. In this way members were protected against abuses and the system helped to maintain recognised professional and ethical standards. Non-Muslim artisans had no comparable affiliations.

By the nineteenth century, however, the corporate structure of Muslim artisans was not as strong as it had once been. Its weakening was perhaps due to a change within the sufi movement and in the Ottoman army organisation. But the resultant comparative relaxation of guild rules did not entail individual enterprise or inventiveness. Indeed, the artisans were on the whole even more conservative in their methods and techniques than the farmers. From generation to generation son followed father in the same profession with little or no change in the quality or quantity of the articles produced.

Artisans here as elsewhere tended to assume descriptive names connected with their professions; hence the weaver (*ḥā'ik*), earthenware-maker (*fakhkhār*), jeweller (*ṣā'igh*) etc. Most of the products were for the local market, rural and urban. Every village of considerable size had its own craftsmen in addition to cottage industries. The womenfolk spun wool and wove cloth for garments and rugs; mats and baskets were made from straw and reeds. Their other limited needs, such as cotton cloth and hardware, villagers sought in market towns.

Town artisans were naturally more sophisticated and their products more varied. Silk was spun into cloth in Lebanon, Damascus and elsewhere, both for the domestic market and for export. Cotton was spun in all parts of the country since the cloth was used for garments by the great majority of the population. Volney mentions five hundred looms in Gaza alone. Gaza with Nābulus and Tripoli were famous for the manufacture of soap both for the domestic market and export. Weapons, copper articles and utensils and carved and inlaid wood were and still are specialities of one or the other of Damascus, Aleppo and Jerusalem. Earthenware was made almost everywhere because of its extensive use for plates, pitchers and jars. Glassware was also made for use as containers for medicine, perfume or other liquid. Hebron remains famous in this ancient industry to this day. Every city had a corner in its bazaar where the jeweller was not far away from the moneylender, if the two were not one and the same person.

But this section on economic conditions would be incomplete without a brief reference to the subject of monopolies. The idea seems to have originated in the mind of Ibrāhīm Ṣabbāgh, the Christian secretary of Ẓāhir. For it was he who began the practice in the province of Acre of monopolising for his master the sale of essential local products including wheat and cotton as well as such imports as sugar and indigo.

Jazzār made the practice more comprehensive. Once he had paid the annual tribute to Istanbul, he regarded all the resources of his province as under his personal control. Not only did he farm the taxes of agricultural land but he also took possession of some land and put farmers on it to exploit it for his own profit. Not only did he farm the customs, but thereafter he pursued the merchants and artisans and shared their profits, real or imaginary, under all sorts of pretexts.

Nowhere in Syria was monopoly so exacting and ruthless as it was in the province of Acre under Jazzār. His successor Sulaimān Pasha, though depicted in native chronicles as *al-'ādil* (the just) continued the practice with varying degrees of severity. He did not hesitate to enrich himself at the expense of his subjects by the practice of monopoly. This is clear from a contemporary Lebanese estimate:

> Sulaimān Pasha's rule in Acre was just and his time peaceful. The Matāwilah returned to their district, regained possession of their land and felt safe as regards life and property. In Ṣafad area the number of the population and the farmers increased, and the land yielded more produce. Sulaimān Pasha's income was thus increased and his riches multiplied. From the people of the Druze Mountain [i.e. Mount Lebanon] he had no trouble at all – The Amir Bashir was obedient to the pasha's orders and rendered to him the *mīrī* taxes every year as usual.[5]

4

Before bringing this narrative to the turning point of the Egyptian occupation of Syria in 1831 it is convenient to sum up here the achievements of the first three decades of the century in public works, a subject which continues to be misunderstood by writers who generalise from limited evidence. Then we propose to single out for some consideration a few significant episodes in the history of Syria before the Egyptian occupation. In chronological order these episodes include the arrival of Protestant missionaries in Jerusalem and Beirut, the impact of the Greek revolt, and the consequences of the use by pashas of armed men from Lebanon against rival pashas and Muslim chieftains.

European travellers followed by more scholarly writers have repeatedly stated that little or no public works had been undertaken in Syria during the period under review, and moreover that ancient buildings had been suffered to decay. There is a measure of truth in this statement, but it is not the whole truth. In every civilisation there is an era during which architectural monuments of special distinction are erected, and future generations fail to emulate them. Thus Jerusalem has nothing to match the mosque of the Dome of the Rock just as London has no church equal to St Paul's.

It is no doubt true that many ancient buildings in Syria were for a variety of reasons neglected or suffered to decay. But it is also true that no great public monument suffered this fate. In 1817 an Ottoman minister at the head of a special commission visited Jerusalem for the sole purpose of initiating repairs at the mosques of al-Aqṣā and the Dome of the Rock. Besides, erection of new mosques all over the country never ceased, even in villages. The erection of Jazzār's mosque in Acre was by no means an exception.

Jazzār's other public works in Acre have already been mentioned. His successor, Sulaimān Pasha, had equally respectable achievements in this field. But let us take for another example a lesser governor, Abū Nabbūt at Jaffa. Not only did he repair the damage done by Napoleon to the city's walls and towers, but he also repaired the great mosque, completed the building of the bazaar near it and built a new water fountain between them. Furthermore he cleared some rocks from the approaches to the port and built a breakwater and promenade all along the sea front. Outside the city, on the way to Jerusalem, he built an inn which still bears his name.

Reference has been made above to the building of public inns on pilgrim and caravan routes. Chieftains built for themselves houses of such solid and elaborate structure that they served in times of trouble as forts, such as the fort of Ṣānūr in Nābulus district and that of Abū Ghosh near Jerusalem. Even disregarding these and the more ostentatious palaces of the ʿAẓm family in Damascus, of Jazzār at Acre and Bashīr Shihāb at Bait ad-Dīn as not strictly falling within the category of public buildings, we still have instances of pashas and chieftains building mosques, roads and bridges. Thus according to a native chronicler, in 1814 'Sulaimān Pasha ordered the Emir [Bashīr] to build a bridge over the River Dāmūr near the sea. . . . Two hundred and fifty masons were employed and the work was completed in two months' time at a cost of one hundred thousand piastres which the pasha reimbursed the Emir.'[6]

Nor were all the cities as ugly or insanitary as European travellers make out. Here again it is a question of untenable generalisation. While conditions in the cities left much to be desired, at least one of them contained amenities which should serve as correctives to sweeping assertions. In 1812 Burckhardt found Tripoli well built and 'much embellished by gardens which are not only attached to the houses in the town but cover likewise the whole triangular plain lying between it and the sea'.

Protestant missionaries from Great Britain and the United States converged on Jerusalem in the early 1820s almost simultaneously. But while the English had at this stage the sole aim of converting Jews, the Americans had in addition to this aim that of converting those who were 'Christian in name'. Since Christian missionary work among Muslims in the Ottoman Empire was illegal, and since foreigners including even diplomatists were not yet permitted to reside in Jerusalem, English and American missionaries had to confine themselves to what was legal and possible. The English bided their time until they could settle in Jerusalem during the Egyptian occupation. The Americans took the plunge in 1823 when two young missionaries were established in Beirut as a preliminary step towards Jerusalem.

The positive educational and philanthropic work of English and American missions is not in question. But here we are merely concerned with its negative results in arousing religious controversy and upsetting the sectarian equilibrium. The Jews were a small and closed community. Their rejection of missionary overtures was unequivocal and on the whole effective. But it was not so with the more numerous Christians and their various sects. From these, Anglo-Saxon missions could in the course of time, but in the teeth of fierce opposition, make enough converts to create eventually a native Protestant community.

But the price of this achievement was very high. Protestantism, even in its American form, was associated in the minds of Syrian Christians with 'English' power. The ecclesiastical authorities considered it as foreign intrusion; some opportunists as entailing material advantages and prestige. If Napoleon's play with sectarian politics was the first European interference with the religious equilibrium in Syria at the beginning of the nineteenth century, Protestant missionary work from the 1820s onwards may be regarded as the second. The first created new tensions in the relations between Christians and Muslims; the second introduced unrest and further division among the Christians themselves.

Religious tensions in Syria were further increased by the outbreak of the Greek revolt in 1821. The insurgents in the Morea and elsewhere began their struggle by a massacre of the Muslim population. Sultan Maḥmūd II took what military measures were within his power, but he also proceeded to penalise individual Greek notables in his capital suspected of sympathy with the revolt. Both the Greek dragoman of the Sublime Porte and the Greek patriarch of Constantinople, himself a native of the Morea, were executed. But not till the arrival in 1825 of an Egyptian expeditionary force commanded by Ibrāhīm Pasha, son of Muḥammad ʿAli Pasha, did the tide begin to turn against the Greeks.

And yet in the following year Greek armed vessels could reach Beirut, shell it from the sea, and land men in an attempt to scale the walls and capture the city. The small garrison was more than a match for them. According to the American missionaries who witnessed the engagement, the Greeks gave up the struggle some ninety minutes after its commencement, and were content to pillage the houses outside the city walls. The Americans were saved from molestation by declaring themselves English. This was technically correct since they enjoyed British consular protection.

A relief force sent from Acre arrived after the Greeks had withdrawn. Another force under Bashīr Shihāb came to within 'an hour's distance' of the city. According to the American mission, it was not certain 'whether he will assist the Greeks or the Turks'. Similar doubts troubled the minds of the Muslims in Beirut. 'Native Christians', wrote a Maronite historian, 'were accused of collusion with the Greeks'.[7]

The panic experienced by the Muslims during the Greek attack was surpassed by similar panic among the Christians after its defeat. Some of them fled to the mountains, others were arrested and still others suffered some loss of their goods in the confusion. But on the orders of the pasha of Acre normal conditions were restored without penalising anybody.

It is difficult to establish how effective the pasha's order was, but to judge by subsequent events it is fairly certain that the fire of religious antagonism thus kindled continued to smoulder. Apart from Greeks domiciled in Syria and Syrians of Greek origin, it would be surprising if there was not among the Christians in general more sympathy with the Greek cause than with that of the Turks. At that time the bonds of religion were unquestionably stronger and more intelligible to Christians and Muslims alike than loyalty to a dynasty or a fatherland, unless the one or the other was identified with religion. To the Muslims, the Ottoman Empire was *dār al-Islām* (i.e. land of Islam) and the Ottoman dynasty was its guardian. To the Christians neither concept evoked any sense of loyalty.

Hence it was reckless of the pashas of Acre to include occasional contingents from Lebanon under Bashīr Shihāb in the armies which they used both to fight their rival pashas or to suppress revolts by Muslim subordinate chieftains. In both cases the experience, even more than foreign intervention, produced religious antagonism. Two examples must suffice.

In 1810 Sulaimān Pasha of Acre marched an army, supported by a contingent under Bashīr, ostensibly to help Yūsuf Pasha of Damascus repel the Wahhābi attack. But in Yūsuf's absence, Sulaimān with Bashīr marched on Damascus with the secret design of executing an order from the Sublime Porte to oust Yūsuf and install Sulaimān in his place. Yūsuf got wind of the plot and hurried to the capital. But after a struggle, in which Bashīr's force took part, Yūsuf was defeated. He fled to Cairo where Muhammad 'Ali gave him asylum.

More serious was the employment of Bashīr's forces against the wholly Muslim population in and around the fortress of Ṣānūr in the Nābulus district. Ever since the days of Jazzār the chieftains in this area had been in rebellion, refusing to pay taxes. At the end of 1829 the impetuous ʿAbdullah Pasha decided to send an expedition, supported by 2000 men under Bashīr Shihāb, to take the fortress at all costs. According to a native Christian historian there was in Bashīr's entourage a Maronite bishop, Jubrā'īl al-Nāṣirī.[8] The fortress was besieged but the Jarrār chiefs inside and their allies in the countryside put up a heroic fight. Even women took part; chroniclers mention that they soaked bedcovers with oil, set them on fire and dropped them outside the walls, so that their men could shoot accurately at the besiegers.

From all over the district horsemen came to help the besieged and several small but bloody engagements followed. Worse than the siege and fighting was the ruthless burning of villages, 'the slaughter of men like sheep', the looting of private property, the burning of fruit trees and the blocking up of wells. The siege, fighting and devastation continued for three months. In the end capitulation was arranged in Acre not on the battlefield. ʿAbdullah guaranteed the Jarrār chieftains and their allies safety of life and property, but insisted on demolishing the fortress. The fortress was partially demolished, but a bitter feeling against Christians and Druzes lingered in the memory of the people of the district till comparatively very recent times.

ʿAbdullah's own days at Acre were numbered. In less than two years after the capitulation of the fortress of Ṣānūr that of Acre, with ʿAbdullah inside, was once more under siege. The Egyptian conquest of Syria had begun.

3

The Dawn of Modern Times – The Egyptian Occupation

I

OUT of the confused state of affairs in Egypt following first the French and then the British withdrawal, a Macedonian Turk, an officer in the Ottoman army named Muḥammad ʿAli, emerged as the dominant figure in Cairo. By 1805 the Sublime Porte recognised him as governor of Egypt. Apart from consolidating his political position the new pasha had to find enough money to keep his troops loyal and to maintain a rudimentary administration. His trading background must have indicated to him the advantage of striking a bargain with English merchants eager to supplant the French in Egyptian trade. The pasha began by monopolising the grain crop and selling it at great profit to the English for cash, munition and commodities. His next move was to expropriate wide areas of land and set farmers to cultivate it for his own profit.

Until now Muḥammad ʿAli's army had not differed from the armies of other pashas. But after the Wahhābi campaign a French officer, Colonel Joseph Sèves, known after embracing Islam as Sulaimān Pasha al-Faransāwi, was engaged to modernise the Egyptian army. Together with that of a group of European instructors, Sèves's work proved highly successful. The war against the Wahhābis was the first occasion for building transport ships and then armed vessels, the nucleus of a navy.

An army reorganised on modern lines required ancillary services such as schools, arsenals, workshops and shipyards, all of which were established by the pasha. But these projects required money.

Hence Muḥammad ʿAli's intensification of the system of monopolies till he became the principal farmer and the chief merchant of the country. He controlled its agriculture and commerce just as completely as he utilised all its manpower.

The new military power proved its worth in the 1820s both in Crete and the Morea, where the pasha was called to his master's aid against Greek uprisings. Nothing stood between the Egyptian army and final victory except the intervention of the major European powers. In 1827 the combined Egyptian and Ottoman fleets were virtually destroyed in Navarino Bay by the British and French fleets, and after a futile war with Russia the sultan had to reconcile himself to an independent Greek state.

Muḥammad ʿAli's resources had been greatly strained in the service of his master, and he naturally expected to be rewarded for his efforts. He needed to enlarge his 'farm', to augment his income, to obtain such raw material as timber for the rebuilding of his fleet, and to find fresh recruits for his armed forces. Disappointed that the Sudan did not measure up to his expectations he turned his covetous gaze in the direction of Syria.

Like previous masters of Egypt from the Pharaohs to Napoleon, Muḥammad ʿAli saw in Syria an obvious shield for Egypt's defence. It is difficult to give a precise date, but there is good evidence that as early as 1812 he coveted Palestine,[1] and equally good evidence that he desired the whole of Syria as early as 1825.[2] He had indeed been cultivating pashas and chieftains in Syria for a long time. He gave refuge to Yūsuf Kanj Pasha, Muḥammad Abū Nabbūt and Bashīr Shihāb. With the last he is supposed to have made a secret agreement. Muḥammad ʿAli was always ready to intercede with the Porte to secure a pardon for such pashas or chieftains in disgrace who sought his good offices. Perhaps his most conspicuous intercession was on behalf of ʿAbdullah Pasha, governor of Acre, whose province Muḥammad ʿAli now coveted.

The exploitation of the Egyptian peasants by their pasha was oppressive enough, but they detested conscription even more than economic exploitation. A few hundred of them fled to Palestine to escape conscription, and ʿAbdullah Pasha refused his benefactor's request to repatriate them, presumably because according to custom such refugees were entitled to protection, and its denial would have been shameful. But ʿAbdullah is reported to have made a provocative comment: the Egyptian refugees did nothing illegal; they simply moved from one Ottoman territory to another. It is also reported that Muḥammad ʻAli was angered by ʻAbdullah's alleged interference with Egyptian commercial traffic in the Gaza and Sinai region and the excessive tariffs he levied from Egyptian merchants.

Muḥammad ʻAli's real grievance was, however, against the sultan who turned a deaf ear to the pasha's repeated petitions to grant him the Syrian provinces. Whether Syria, or parts of it, was definitely promised to Muḥammad ʻAli is not very important. There is no doubt of his ambition to add Syria to his dominions and of the disappointment of this ambition. He chose a most suitable time to take by force what he failed to get by diplomacy. The sultan's military and naval resources after Navarino and the Russo-Turkish war were in bad shape, barely enough to cope with a revolt in Bosnia and disturbances elsewhere. Apart from the fortress of Acre, ʻAbdullah Pasha commanded far fewer troops than did Jazzār a generation earlier. Every major European power was busy either with internal problems or with problems affecting its relations with the other powers after the 1830 upheavals.

In October–November 1831 Muḥammad ʻAli's forces, commanded by his son Ibrāhīm Pasha, opened the offensive. The war was carefully represented as one between two pashas similar to those wars familiar in the annals of the previous decades, and as such did not involve the sultan's authority. Muḥammad ʻAli even took the strange course of sending a special emissary to Istanbul to inform the Sublime Porte of the attack! The Porte replied by sending a special emissary to the pasha with the strong advice to desist and to submit the dispute to the Porte's arbitration. The emissary was to point out that war between the two pashas would disrupt communications and might prevent the dispatch of the pilgrim caravan. But it was all to no avail. The pasha's forces had already occupied Gaza and advanced as far north as Jaffa.

On his own initiative ʻAbdullah issued circulars to the notables in Jerusalem, Nābulus and Damascus declaring Muḥammad ʻAli a rebel against the sultan, even though the august master was still hoping to bring his rebellious vassal to the fold of legality. In a firman to the authorities in Tripoli and Sidon provinces, the sultan mentions the war between the two pashas and merely reminds his subjects of their duty to obey him in accordance with the Koran: 'O believers, obey God, obey the Messenger [of God] and those in authority among you.'

A little later, when all efforts to restrain the ambitious vassal had failed, the sultan issued another firman stating that Muḥammad 'Ali had refused the mediation of the Sublime Porte, that the war between the two pashas was shedding Muslim blood contrary to the sacred law, and that therefore Muḥammad 'Ali was a transgressor who must be punished. The firman goes on to specify the forces mobilised for this purpose and to name their commanders.[3] War between vassal and suzerain could no longer be disguised.

The Egyptian expedition advanced by land and sea. To begin with, the land force was not greater than the army with which Napoleon invaded Syria, but the Egyptian forces were augmented by landings first at Jaffa and finally at Haifa. The naval force consisted of twenty-three armed vessels and seventeen transport ships. Ibrāhīm himself came by sea directly to Haifa after only a brief halt at Jaffa. Siege artillery and supplies were landed at Haifa which became the general headquarters. On 26 November Acre was besieged by land and sea.

'Abdullah relied mainly on the strength of the fortifications which had withstood for nine months a siege by the combined forces of three pashas. His army consisted of some five thousand men with plenty of guns and ammunition. He was encouraged to expect imperial reinforcements by land and sea. But the speed of Ottoman mobilisation of land forces had not greatly improved since the days of Napoleon. While Muḥammad 'Ali lost no time in rebuilding his fleet after Navarino, the sultan did little to match his vassal's efforts in this or any other matter. As a result, 'Abdullah was virtually left to defend Acre alone, and he proved a most tenacious and heroic fighter.

Meanwhile deputations of notables called on Ibrāhīm and offered their submission. The interior towns of Jerusalem, Nābulus, Janīn and Tiberias were thus taken without fighting and occupied by token Egyptian forces. So were the coastal towns north of Acre up to Tripoli. But when Ibrāhīm's summons to Bashīr Shihāb was ignored, Muḥammad 'Ali was furious: here was another ungrateful protégé. Accordingly he warned Bashīr that any further delays in joining Ibrāhīm would bring military devastation on Mount Lebanon and the destruction of Bashīr's own home, and 'the planting of fig trees on the site', to use the colourful phrase of the native Lebanese chronicler. Bashīr had no alternative. After this he unreservedly placed himself, members of his family and the resources of Mount Lebanon at the disposal of the Egyptians. He was handsomely rewarded by increased powers and privileges bestowed upon him and members of his family.

The Egyptians were now very deeply committed in Syria, even though they had not yet engaged any imperial forces. Muḥammad ʿAli was indeed perturbed by the sultan's firmans declaring him a rebel and a virtual infidel. He wrote to his son that he was just as capable as the Sublime Porte of invoking religion in his cause. He asked Ibrāhīm to write to, among others, the Mufti of Marʿash whom he had met at Mecca, that Aleppo was about to be conquered 'because it is part of the holy Arab land which must be delivered from tyranny and misrule. Explain to him that the Exalted [Ottoman] government has gone contrary to religion and Islamic law.'[4] To the Porte, however, Muḥammad ʿAli was still pleading. Have they forgotten his service to Islam in Arabia and to the Ottoman state in Greece? Will they even now change their policy and confer upon him the province of Syria?

The Porte, however, was no longer in a conciliatory mood. When the customary annual appointments and reappointments were announced early in 1832 the posts of governors of Egypt, Jiddah and Crete were declared vacant until Muḥammad ʿAli and his son 'end their rebellion'. Ibrāhīm's reply was the intensification of the assaults on Acre. A *fatwā* was issued declaring Muḥammad ʿAli and his son 'traitors of the state and apostates from the religion of the [Islamic] community'. Not to be outdone, Muḥammad ʿAli obtained a counter *fatwā* from the Sharif of Mecca declaring the sultan an 'infidel' and unworthy of his office on account of the innovations he introduced contrary to the sacred law and of his imitation of the ways of the infidels. By implication this pronouncement conferred some religious sanction on Muḥammad ʿAli's venture in Syria. The breach between sultan and pasha was now complete and recourse to the sword was inevitable.

The first Ottoman military effort was an unsuccessful attempt to capture Tripoli. Ibrāhīm was quick to sense the danger of such attempts from the north. He swiftly moved to the scene and easily defeated the loyalists at Zarrāʿah. He then stationed a strong force astride the lines of communications with Aleppo and Damascus and hurried back to Acre. On his way he had to deal with the first attempt by the Druzes at revolt.

Bashīr had stripped some of the Druze shaikhs of their power and appropriated their property some time before the Egyptian occupation. Once he had sided with the Egyptians, discontented Druzes inevitably supported the Ottoman cause. There were minor clashes between Druzes and Christians at Dair al-Qamar and elsewhere. Bashīr feared the consequences and submitted the matter to Ibrāhīm, who took Druze hostages and ordered the confiscation of the property and the burning of the houses belonging to those Druzes who defected to the Ottoman side.

About a month later, on 27 May 1832, Acre fell after six months' siege. That sealed the fate of Damascus. An imperial army commanded by the pasha of Aleppo was defeated near Ḥimṣ. This victory opened the gates of Aleppo to the victor. Another imperial army was defeated at the strategic Bailān Pass, and this victory secured Alexandretta, Antioch and Latakia. Then Ibrāhīm rounded the Gulf of Alexandretta and occupied Aḍana. The Egyptian army had thus reached the natural boundaries between Asia Minor and Syria.

Once more Muḥammad ʿAli sought the Porte's acquiescence in his conquests and the sultan's agreement to appoint him governor of the Syrian provinces. But Istanbul was not yet ready to accept defeat. A third imperial army commanded by the grand vizier himself was then marching to punish the invader. Late in December 1832 Ibrāhīm engaged it in battle near Kūniah and defeated it, taking the grand vizier prisoner. This latest victory had more serious consequences. The way to Istanbul lay open to the Egyptian army, and Muḥammad ʿAli toyed with the idea of marching on it and deposing the sultan. Ibrāhīm had reached Kutahiya before he received his father's order to halt the advance.

The conflict between sultan and pasha had now assumed international significance. At least three major powers were interested. Russia desired to increase her influence in Istanbul and to prepare for the seizure of the lion's share of the inheritance of the Sick

Man of Europe. Great Britain sought to maintain the integrity of the Ottoman Empire both to check Russian ambitions and to safeguard her communications with India. France likewise wished to maintain the integrity of the Empire and was jealous of Russian ambitions. However, French public opinion rejoiced in the Egyptian victories as due to French instruction and discipline, and French official quarters hoped Muḥammad ʿAli would gather the fruits of his victory.

It was therefore natural for Maḥmūd II, having previously refused French mediation, to turn to Great Britain with a request for naval intervention. When this was refused, the sultan was compelled both to send a commissioner to negotiate with Muḥammad ʿAli, and to accept a Russian offer of naval and military assistance. The news of impending Russian intervention and the call of a Russian emissary on Muḥammad ʿAli were both responsible for the order to Ibrāhīm to stop the advance. In Istanbul even the rumour of agreement with Russia caused a great stir. So great was public consternation that the ulema submitted a written protest against seeking help from the traditional enemy.[5]

Louder and more effective was the protest from Great Britain and France, following the landing in February 1833 of Russian troops on the Asiatic side of Istanbul and the appearance of Russian warships in the waters of the capital. In order to allay the alarm of the Porte and to remove the cause for the Russian presence, the two powers called on Muḥammad ʿAli to withdraw from Asia Minor and threatened to blockade Alexandria unless he complied .There was no need for that, for the negotiations with the pasha had led to the conclusion in May of the so-called Kutahiya agreement, by virtue of which Muḥammad ʿAli was granted, in return for his withdrawal from Asia Minor, not only the governorship of Egypt and Crete but also the four Syrian provinces and the region of Aḍana, and his son Ibrāhīm was reappointed governor of Jiddah and 'tax-collector' of Aḍana. The war was over.

2

Long before the end of the war the enterprising Muḥammad ʿAli had begun combing Syria for raw materials and useful products.

His correspondence with his son dwells on these matters almost as frequently as on political and military affairs. Timber was in immediate demand. The pasha's supply from Austria was not as assured as it had been before the war. A special official was in charge of the timber resources of the conquered territories. Cut timber was immediately sent to the ports for transport to Egypt, and the process continued throughout the period of the Egyptian occupation.

A special expert in mineralogy was in charge of searching for and exploiting whatever the Syrian subsoil contained in the way of coal, iron and other minerals. Coal was known to exist near Qarnāyil and iron ore near Shuwair in Lebanon. The Egyptians exploited these limited resources at once, using almost forced labour at reduced wages. Transport was expedited by new roads built by the army.

The entire silk crop was bought by the Egyptian government. To the protests of foreign merchants, Muḥammad ʿAli replied that he had not actually monopolised the commodity. But all the same he was in a position to get it at more favourable terms. Wool was likewise bought for the Egyptian government who used it to manufacture blankets and other articles for the army.

Nothing was too small for the pasha's enterprise. Hides were bought to make shoes and brief-cases for the army. Even the rind of pomegranates was wanted for use in dyeing cloth manufactured in Egypt; so were the galls of a Syrian variety of the holm-oak for use in dyeing the felt from which fezes were made.

No doubt these activities and demands created employment for many Syrians. But the Egyptians were strict employers and hard bargainers: labour was often exploited if not actually cheated by the local authorities. Muḥammad ʿAli himself was very generous with presents to superiors and assistance to protégés or friends. Thus he never forgot that Abū Nabbūt had once helped Egyptian merchants to recover plundered merchandise. On his personal orders Abū Nabbūt's widow was paid a pension.

On the whole his dealings with the Syrians were more business-like than paternal. When Jerusalem experienced shortage of food on account of the war and disrupted communications, and the *qāḍi* wrote to the pasha requesting one thousand measures of corn to relieve distress in the city, he was probably expecting a bounty from the new ruler. But the reply was characteristic: corn was scarce in Egypt; one thousand measures of rice would be sent for sale at market price, the money to be paid to the army cashier. Later on rice was a regular item of Egyptian exports to Syria, sold on behalf of the pasha and for his profit.

The increase of civilian activities prompted Ibrāhīm to recommend the appointment of a civil administrator. Ultimately a governor-general (*hukmdār*) was appointed for the whole of Syria with headquarters in Damascus but still subordinate to Ibrāhīm. As usual in senior military or civil appointments under Muḥammad ʿAli, the governor-general, Muḥammad Sharīf Bey (later Pasha), was a relative of the family. The civil administration under Sharīf was simple in structure. There was an Egyptian *mudīr* (governor) or a Syrian *mutasallim* (deputy governor) or both in the main cities or districts. In each of the major cities a consultative council (*majlis shūrā*) was constituted. Where applicable non-Muslims were represented on these councils for the first time. The deliberations of the councils, mainly concerned with financial and local affairs, were recorded and submitted for scrutiny by higher authorities.

Actual financial and clerical administration was entrusted to Ḥannā Baḥrī, a Greek Catholic already in the service of Muḥammad ʿAli. He was Syrian by origin, his family being from Ḥimṣ. Although he made Damascus his headquarters, Ḥannā had a roving commission all over the land. All accounts and records of the councils were submitted for his inspection. He had his brother, Jirmānus, stationed in a similar though subordinate position in Aleppo. At Sharīf's recommendation the financial and clerical system was Egyptianised and a corps of clerks were introduced from Egypt for this purpose.

Ibrāhīm made his headquarters at Antioch but also sometimes at Aḍana close to Anatolia in order to watch Ottoman developments. His military sense told him that the peace was not permanent. Accordingly he reported to his father all suspicious movements. But he soon found out that internal dangers were greater and more immediate. In less than a year after Kutahiya, Ibrāhīm was heavily engaged in fighting first the Palestinian peasantry, then the Nusairiyyah, and then the Druzes.

The cause of the discontent, which cost the Egyptians in men and treasure more than defeating the Ottoman armies, was Muḥammad ʿAli's obstinacy in applying in Syria measures he had easily applied in Egypt: monopolies, heavy taxation, *corvée* and above all disarmament and conscription. Ibrāhīm began well enough in Syria, and the series of revolts might have been avoided had his father given him a free hand. Two of his early measures may be noted here.

With European public opinion in mind, and in an obvious attempt to win the sympathy of European consuls in the Levant, Ibrāhīm issued an early order to the civil and religious authorities in the province of Sidon and the chief cities in Palestine concerning Christian and Jewish pilgrims proceeding to Jerusalem. Collection of any taxes or fees from them was strictly prohibited both on their way to and while in the Holy City.

A few months later another order was issued to the deputy governors of, among other large cities, Jerusalem, Tripoli, Antioch and Aleppo. The commander-in-chief expressed his concern for the welfare of the people in view of the hardship they had endured under the previous administration in the matter of taxes. Accordingly he ordered that nothing more than the fixed *mīrī* was to be collected by any civil official. As for soldiers, they were strictly forbidden to take food or fodder unless it was against payment.[6]

The first order may have won Ibrāhīm the sympathy of the European consuls and the approval of public opinion in Europe, but it antagonised, among others, a powerful Muslim feudal lord, Ibrāhīm Abū Ghosh, whose family had by an established custom the right to collect tolls from foreigners passing through their district on the way to Jerusalem. Abū Ghosh, indeed, was among the first to revolt against Eyptian rule. But Ibrāhīm's order had also distressed those ecclesiastics and native Christians who had always charged fees from foreign pilgrims for facilitating visits to the holy places and other services.

Ibrāhīm's second order was nullified by his father's decision to introduce a new tax, over and above those which had been levied under Ottoman pashas. The new tax (*al-Fardah*, pronounced either with a soft or strong 'd') was a kind of income tax payable by all males of all communities between the ages of fifteen and sixty at the rate of 12 per cent of the income. The minimum payment was 15 piastres and the maximum 500. This tax must not be confused with the statutory *per capita* tax which only Christians and Jews were required to pay under Ottoman rule. They still had to pay it to the Egyptians over and above the new tax.

An anonymous Christian contemporary writer states that this new tax had greatly annoyed the Muslim majority,[7] which was already uneasy about the Egyptian introduction of Christians and Jews to the consultative councils if not also the removal of certain social restrictions such as distinctive dress. Muḥammad ʿAli and his son, it was whispered, were no more than rebels against the legal Islamic government in Istanbul. Their rebellion had certainly resulted in the suspension of the pilgrimage to Mecca. Ibrāhīm in particular was accused of being a Christian simulating Islam.

But probably neither their toleration of non-Muslims nor their taxation would have been enough to damn the Egyptians in Syrian eyes. It was the policy of introducing conscription and disarmament which roused all sections of the population, Muslims, Christians, Druzes and others. Perhaps the earliest rehearsal for introducing conscription was staged only a few days after the fall of Acre. Ḥannā Baḥri wrote to the Maronite patriarch that Ibrāhīm was marching on Damascus and that he had ordered Bashīr Shihāb 'to collect all armed men, Christians and Druzes in Mount Lebanon and to send them in the noble service of His Excellency [Ibrāhīm Pasha]'. His Beatitude was requested to lend his support to the summons, which he did without any hesitation.

This Lebanese contingent was, however, little different from the customary contributions which Lebanon, Nābulus or other districts had made before to the forces of their pashas. Hence the men marched under a son of Bashīr, not as a unit of the Egyptian army. Ibrāhīm was quite satisfied with the arrangement. He advised his father not to introduce conscription, and it was because of his strong objections that it was postponed for a year. But when the order was finally made in the spring of 1834, Ibrāhīm had no hesitation in insisting on its execution.

There was an immediate revolt in the Nābulus region under the leadership of Qāsim al-Aḥmad of the Jarrārs who had been a thorn in the side of Ottoman pashas. The standard of revolt was next raised in the Jerusalem district by Abū Ghosh. His men cut off communications between the Egyptian garrison in Jerusalem and

Jaffa, defeated a relief force and killed its commander. Jointly with the rebels from Nābulus, they overwhelmed the garrison in Hebron, and then turned their fury on Jerusalem, where only the citadel remained in Egyptian hands.

Muḥammad ʿAli, with a fresh army, arrived by sea at Jaffa to relieve his harassed son. Combining promises with threats the two pashas won Abū Ghosh to their side. His son, Jabr, was soon appointed deputy-governor for Jerusalem. But the Egyptians failed to win Qāsim who returned to Nābulus to continue the fight alone. Ibrāhīm pursued him literally with fire and sword, but Qāsim was a very brave and elusive fighter. Ibrāhīm's 'scorched earth' tactics drove Qāsim from one village to another till in the end he withdrew with his men and a few allies to Transjordan. Ibrāhīm pursued them first to Karak and then Ṣalt, until finally they took refuge with the ʿAnazah beduins in the Syrian desert. How this strong tribe could violate the code of honourable conduct and hand over refugees is not clear. Qāsim and other leaders of the revolt were executed by Ibrāhīm.

The news of Ibrāhīm's trouble in Palestine stiffened the resistance to his orders elsewhere. There were minor disturbances in Aleppo, Antioch and Beirut but these were quelled by force. In Damascus, Sharīf feared a large-scale rising, and had to be content with 700 enlisted men and a few thousand surrendered muskets and swords. In Tripoli and the countryside to the north resistance was nipped in the bud with extreme severity. Some notables were imprisoned, others banished to Cyprus and about a dozen executed.

But no sooner had the Palestine revolt been put down when another not less serious flared up in the Nuṣairiyyah mountains. It began by inflicting a crushing defeat on an Egyptian regiment and occupying Latakia and besieging its deputy-governor. Ibrāhīm ordered the commander of the artillery division to mount a punitive expedition, and Bashīr Shihāb to contribute an auxiliary force under one of his sons. In the Nuṣairiyyah mountains as in the Nābulus mountains the Egyptians burnt villages, cut down fruit trees, destroyed wells, and pillaged. Not before December 1834 could they gain the upper hand.

With the subjugation of the Nuṣairiyyah nine months of continuous fighting came to a temporary end. At great cost Ibrāhīm had completed the disarming of the coastal regions and the imposition of conscription. He tried to mitigate its severity by the appointment of sons of chieftains as officers and by granting favours to their fathers. Lebanon was excepted, obviously because it had always obeyed the summons to contribute contingents, but the exception was only temporary. During most of the year 1835 Ibrāhīm was in Egypt. Immediately on his return in September he began disarming first the Druzes and then the Christians in Lebanon. Several of the Druze chiefs were then in exile. Only those subservient to Bashīr remained, and these were powerless to resist, after disarmament, the forceful enlistment of several hundred of their men.

Comparative peace had at long last been achieved throughout Syria. Before it was shattered by renewed revolts, the Egyptian civil administration had assumed final shape. It is convenient to examine its operation more closely in the next section.

3

The most striking achievement of the Egyptian administration was its eclipse of the feudal hierarchy. Local chieftains were stripped of their independence and of their function as tax-farmers. Most of those who survived the change became deputy-governors with salaries paid by the administration. Subordinate officials down to the village controller (*nāẓir*) were likewise paid servants. At the head of the new hierarchy was the governor-general, acting with the authority of the commander-in-chief and finally that of Muḥammad ʿAli. Below the governor-general were Egyptian and Syrian governors and deputy-governors.

The Egyptians continued the Ottoman system of frequently changing deputy-governors. Even those who came from families loyal to the Egyptians were not excepted. Thus the early appointment to Acre of Ḥusain ʿAbdul-Hādi, the chieftain in Nābulus district who declared for the Egyptians soon after its conquest, did not last long. Ḥusain himself was pensioned, but members of his family were given appointments in their own area and elsewhere. Similarly the early appointment of sons of Bashīr Shihāb to the coastal towns was terminated when the area was placed under Sulaimān al-Faransāwi. Based on Sidon, he was charged with the task of dealing with European merchants, consuls and others.

Bashīr Shihāb himself was a conspicuous exception. He retained his post and functions as a tributary to the government. In return for his ready obedience to their orders, the Egyptians allowed Bashīr to enrich himself and members of his family, both at the expense of the Druzes and of the population of Mount Lebanon as a whole. His income under Egyptian rule was, after payment of the tribute, several times more than it was during the Ottoman period.

Little visible change was made in the judicial system. The *qāḍi* continued to perform his usual functions, though some of them seem to have been assumed by the consultative councils. The Egyptian authorities dealt with criminal cases very harshly, although capital punishment was in theory subject to ratification by the commander-in-chief. The consultative councils were allowed, within their limited province, quasi-judicial functions in that they decided minor questions of local taxation including assessment of the *Fardah* and the controversial innovation of a Muslim government licensing and taxing taverns.

Egyptian taxation was more comprehensive than the Ottoman. Ibrāhīm's earlier promises of requiring no more from his subjects than the fixed *mīrī* were soon forgotten. New taxes of various descriptions were imposed on urban and rural areas alike. Much of the injustice attending the imposition or assessment of taxes was perpetrated by overzealous officials with Ḥannā Baḥrī at their head. They knew that their master had not found Syria the profitable farm he expected it to be, and that he was eager to compensate himself for the heavy military expenditure he incurred in suppressing the Syrian revolts. They tried to curry favour with him by squeezing the taxpayer. Native chroniclers relate how villagers were led by unscrupulous officials to expect relief if they declared all the extras they paid over the fixed tax to the Ottoman officials. The result was assessments which included the tax *and* the extras, sometimes raising the amount of the legal tenth (*'ushr*) up to a fifth of the produce. None has described this misfortune more aptly than the Egyptian poet, Ḥāfiẓ Ibrāhīm, protesting nearly a century later against other injustices:

> The oppression we suffered before was chaotic
> Now it is refined and well-organised.

Well-organised and all-embracing indeed were Muḥammad ʿAli's measures to exact the maximum taxes from the Syrians. The most comprehensive new tax was the *Fardah* mentioned above. Then there were other new taxes. Family properties registered as charitable foundations were, as already explained, exempt from taxation under Ottoman rule; now they were taxed. The revolt of the Damascenes against the Ottoman governor who attempted to impose a new tax on shops and houses has been mentioned. Muḥammad ʿAli had stronger forces to impose such a tax on the whole country. He also collected taxes on fruit trees in urban and rural areas, as well as on cattle, beehives, flour-mills, public baths and taverns.

During the Ottoman period customs tariffs were chaotic, largely because under the Capitulations different European powers obtained different rates for their merchants, and these rates were in turn different from those paid by native merchants. Muḥammad ʿAli could not materially alter the Ottoman system, nor improve the lot of native merchants who had to pay as high a rate as 12 per cent compared to the maximum of $3\frac{1}{2}$ per cent paid by foreigners. Small wonder if many native merchants found it more profitable to trade for foreign merchants than on their own account. In this way they escaped not only the higher import tax, but an additional tax payable on merchandise, whether imported or locally produced, transferred from one district to another within the country. Officials in foreign consulates, in alliance with natives enjoying consular protection, abused consular privileges and enriched themselves by trading in imported articles on which low tariffs were paid as well as in transferred local products which were exempt from tax.

The above account indicates that Syria escaped the rigorous monopolies applied in Egypt, but that it did not escape certain measures which were akin to monopolies. Thus certain articles like silk, and a number of foodstuffs required by the army, had to be sold to government agents at prices fixed by the agents. Suppliers were moreover compelled to transport the required goods to specified centres at costs fixed by the authorities. Occasionally men and their animals were impressed into government service, especially in building fortifications and barracks or transporting timber and coal. The services of artisans were sometimes requisitioned at reduced pay and not always near their homes.

But despite heavy taxation and direct and indirect exploitation of natural resources and manpower, Syria was on the whole a burden on Muḥammad 'Ali's treasury. This was not so much due to the tribute he agreed at Kutahiya to pay the sultan at the rate of £175,000 per annum, as it was to the extraordinary cost of a standing army in Syria, and its frequent and heavy losses of men and material in fighting rebels.

Nor were these losses cut down after the defeat of the Palestinians and the Nuṣairiyyah. Their defeat gave Ibrāhīm only two years of comparative peace. In 1837 the news of Ottoman preparations to regain Syria became more persistent, and on his father's orders, Ibrāhīm made fresh demands for conscripts. The demand was resisted this time by the Druzes in Ḥawrān. They had emigrated from Lebanon to this remote and sparsely inhabited district to escape, like beduins, direct government control. The Egyptian demand for 170 conscripts was moderate, but the Druzes claimed exemption similar to the beduins living in their neighbourhood. The Egyptians were adamant, little anticipating that they would have to face a bloody revolt which would last for nearly nine months.

The story of the Druze revolt is another demonstration of the ineffectiveness of regular troops and the uselessness of their superior armour when fighting smaller mobile groups of brave men in a rugged country. Ibrāhīm himself was then in the north watching Ottoman movements. When a small force sent by Sharīf was defeated, a large expedition of several thousand commanded by the inspector-general of the Egyptian army in Syria was sent, only to meet with an even greater disaster. The third expedition commanded by Muḥammad 'Ali's minister of war fared even worse.

Druze victories reverberated throughout Syria and delighted Istanbul. Emboldened by success, Druze horsemen roamed the villages round Damascus inciting the people to rise and release the conscripts from the city barracks. 'Seditious talk', wrote Ḥannā

Baḥrī to Ibrāhīm, 'is now widespread and continuous in Damascus, and signs of disorders have begun to appear also in villages. Some outlaws . . . have cut off the road to Beirut. . . .' The disorders were more serious than Baḥrī represented. Ibrāhīm decided to intervene. After the failure of the first expedition, the issue was no longer the eight-score conscripts; it was the challenge Ḥawrān presented to the Egyptian army.

Ibrāhīm with Sulaimān al-Faransāwi mounted another expedition. The regular forces were supported by Kurdish irregulars and an Albanian contingent under the governor of Crete. The initial setbacks also met by this expedition prompted Ibrāhīm to adopt the long-term strategy of controlling the springs and destroying the wells near the rebel hideout in the Lajah district. He is even reported to have ordered the placing of poison in drinking water not under army control. As usual the Druzes fought bravely in the battle for water and inflicted heavy losses on the Egyptians. But time was against them, so to relieve pressure in Ḥawrān they decided to open a new front nearer their original home.

With some two hundred horsemen, Shibli al-'Uryān escaped from the Lajah to south Lebanon. He overran Rāshayya and, supported by disaffected Druzes, scored several minor victories. Ibrāhīm hurried to this second front. But here he and his father committed a political blunder which Bashīr Shihāb was powerless to avert. Bashīr was ordered to mobilise several hundred Christians and march them under one of his sons against 'the treacherous and infidel Druze sect'.[8] The seeds of future enmity between the two communities were thus sown.

Even with the superior forces ranged against them, the Druzes fought bravely and in the end even desperately. But the Egyptians won a decisive victory which led to the end of Druze resistance. When Shibli surrendered, those in the Lajah were persuaded to do likewise. Ibrāhīm offered them very lenient terms: a few hundred muskets and the captured Egyptian arms to be surrendered, and no conscription. Shibli was appointed commander of a unit of irregulars attached to the Egyptian army. By August 1838 the revolt was over.

Here it is pertinent to explain the obstinate resistance to conscription of brave men, such as the Palestinian and Druze mountaineers undoubtedly were. Their resistance was not due to cowardice; it had deep social and economic motives. Armed men were accustomed to march behind their own leaders who were often members of their family, clan or tribe. They fought to defend property or to vindicate honour or in answer to a call by an ally or an overlord. But they did so in their immediate neighbourhood for a day or a few days, and returned after the completion of the task to their homes and their normal occupations. Their arms were personal property which they displayed, if they did not always use them, to ward off an aggressor and to assert their independence and power. An unarmed man was indeed a novelty.

At best the Syrians owed no allegiance to the Egyptian government; at worst they regarded it as a rebel authority against the legitimate sultan. Military service under the Egyptians was for a minimum of fifteen years, and involved absence from family and home in distant lands and risk of life and limb in pursuit of aims with which the average Syrian had no sympathy. If the conscript happened to be the bread-winner, his removal meant personal loss and economic ruin to his family. A family in this situation, with no male protector, was a humiliation no Syrian of that period could bear.

Muḥammad ʿAli had misjudged the Syrian character and did not realise how different it was from the Egyptian. He paid very dearly for his miscalculation. In 1836 when conscription was finally imposed Ibrāhīm estimated that 20,000 Syrians were already enlisted. Some estimates put the losses in men killed in fighting rebels as high as that figure, but even if it were half or a quarter of it the loss is still very great indeed. The cost in money cannot be estimated, but its extent can be gauged from the strained finances of Egypt and Syria from 1836 till the end of Egyptian rule in the latter country.

Nearly three years after the instalment of Sharīf as governor-general and Baḥrī as director of financial affairs, Ibrāhīm was constrained to complain to his father of their maladministration. Sharīf neglected to consult the commander-in-chief, meddled with matters outside his jurisdiction and did not check the danger of bribery. Bahrī left the management of his affairs to assistants imported from Egypt, and these accepted bribes and were guilty of other offences. Both Sharīf and Baḥrī and a number of others, including army officers, were allowed to hold real estate in Syria with special privileges. Such holdings were bound to be distracting, if not corrupting. So perhaps Ibrāhīm and his father are not entirely blameless.

Ibrāhīm's reports of maladministration did not disturb Muḥammad 'Ali as much as other reports that consuls of foreign powers were sympathetic to the complaints of the Syrians against taxation and conscription. Accordingly Ibrāhīm was instructed to do his best to appease the consuls. The task had already been entrusted to Sulaimān al-Faransāwi. But Ibrāhīm did not leave it at that; he was determined to expose abuses of consular privileges. In an order of the day he denounced the practice of native merchants and others who sought foreign consular protection in order to evade taxation. This practice must have been more prominent in Beirut than elsewhere, since Ibrāhīm's order was addressed to the people of that city. But Muḥammad 'Ali would not relax his taxation. He had every reason to apply even stricter measures of collection. Finding Syria less profitable than he had expected, he insisted that it should be self-sufficient and not a burden on Egypt. But even this limited aim was in the end unobtainable. The failure was to a great extent due to a near collapse of the system modelled on the Egyptian in collection and accountancy.

Once more it was Ibrāhīm who exposed the rot. After personal inspection he wrote to his father bitterly criticising maladministration, misappropriation of public money and the negligence or corruption of officials. Sharīf he considered as a lazy governor-general who was inclined to dissipation. Baḥrī he accused of dereliction of duty. It is typical of Ibrāhīm's military methods that, on finding that the consultative council in Damascus had done no work for eighteen months, he ordered the 'imprisonment' of the members in the council chambers till they had settled all outstanding cases. But in addition he recommended the dispatch of an inspector from Egypt to investigate the whole state of affairs. When he eventually arrived and submitted his report, his accounts did not tally with those of Baḥrī.

Baḥrī's own explanation, however, confirms Ibrāhīm on one important matter. Two years' taxes were in arrears and the books were in a chaotic condition. No doubt the illiteracy of village controllers suddenly saddled with the task of book-keeping and accountancy, the inexperience of new district officers in the same field, the incompetence and corruption of Egyptian and Syrian clerks, and the increasing evasion by taxpayers, all contributed to the muddle. Even a man of Baḥrī's ability was overwhelmed. He had a corps of 408 clerks and asked for some fifty more. Ibrāhīm does indeed blame the difficulty partly on Baḥrī's 'sleep'.

Things became so bad that army officers were employed to collect taxes and keep records. It is surprising how various and increasing were the non-military tasks required of an army officer. He was employed to teach reading and writing to illiterates in his unit, to fight locusts with his men and to supervise works in mines. Now he was to act both the tax-collector and the book-keeper.

One of the consequences of this state of affairs was the inability of the administration to meet its obligation: salaries of civil servants and the pay of army officers and men were several months in arrears. Muḥammad 'Ali ordered more severity in the collection of taxes and economy in the services. It seems that a cut in army rations resulted from this order. Ibrāhīm was informed that his men were served boiled rice, not as hitherto treated with butter or olive oil. He vented his fury on the governor-general and the director of financial administration.

To the former he wrote: 'Why is the rice served to soldiers not treated with butter or olive oil, both of which are plentiful near Damascus? Do you pay the cost out of your own pocket?' To Baḥrī he was even more stern: 'By God, O Ḥannā, your end will be bad! On the receipt of this letter you must . . . prepare the required amount of butter and send it quickly.'

4

It was Ibrāhīm's habit to minimise the impact of his forceful interventions in civil affairs by dwelling on his preoccupation with military affairs. His stricture of Sharīf and of Baḥrī followed the same pattern, but this time the excuse was genuine. He had to face an imminent Ottoman attack with a new army. Sultan Maḥmūd who had been smarting under the humiliation of Kutahiya was now determined, contrary to the advice of the major powers, to punish his rebellious vassal. Ibrāhīm met the Ottoman army at Nezib (Naṣībīn) on 24 June 1839 and inflicted a crushing defeat on it. Less than a week later Maḥmūd died. A few days later still the Ottoman fleet under its admiral defected to Muḥammad ʻAli. Almost simultaneously an emissary from the grand vizier arrived to inform the pasha of the accession of Sultan ʻAbdul-Majīd, and that the new sultan had pardoned Muḥammad ʻAli and granted him the hereditary governorship of Egypt.

Nothing was said about Syria. But while at his insistence the Porte was about to meet Muḥammad ʻAli's demands, the major powers intervened. A joint note presented by Great Britain, France, Austria, Prussia and Russia advised the Porte to take no action without their concurrence. The Porte accepted the note and communicated it to Muḥammad ʻAli. The next eighteen months or so saw him lose the game. It took nearly a year to formulate a policy; another six months to put it into action.

The prolonged uncertainty increased the difficulties of the Egyptian administration. Ibrāhīm's grip on the military situation remained firm. He intensified his defensive measures, especially in the coastal towns and on the borders with Anatolia, and called more local recruits to the colours. On the other hand, the administrative and financial difficulties, already acute before Nezib, were rendered more so by clandestine interference by Ottoman and European agents actively inciting the people to revolt against their Egyptian masters. Secret agents distributed first money and then arms, till finally naval forces supplied by Great Britain, Austria and the Ottoman Empire appeared in Syrian waters. Ibrāhīm's remaining days in Syria were numbered.

It is therefore appropriate at this juncture in the narrative to sum up the Egyptian achievements in Syria and set them against the shortcomings. Perhaps the greatest achievement was the successful establishment of law and order throughout the country. Security in the towns and villages and on the highways had never been better. Special efforts were made to tame the beduins and encourage them to settle on the land. Offenders were impressed into the army, and uncooperative shaikhs were banished to Egypt. Only two years after the occupation, the practice of paying 'protection money' to the ʻAnazah, Bani Ṣakhr and other tribes was discontinued at Muḥammad ʻAli's orders. But while the proud ʻAnazah could be intimidated to hand over to Ibrāhīm a rebel who sought their protection, other and smaller tribes were more defiant. Some openly sided and fought with the Druze rebels in the Lajah; others attacked the official mail and the governor-general himself between Jaffa and Gaza.

Next to improving security, the Egyptians made special efforts to gain favour with the Christians of the country and, as recorded above, to conciliate public opinion in Europe by easing the reception of Christian visitors and pilgrims. For native non-Muslims removal of such restrictions as discriminatory dress was no doubt welcome, but more important was the representation of Christians (and Jews) on consultative councils in those towns where their numbers justified such representation. It must not be forgotten that the head of the department of finance was a Christian, and that he imported many Copts from Egypt and recruited many more local Christians for work in his department. Ibrāhīm's policy of winning the Christians to his side is well expressed in an order he issued in 1832 to the deputy-governor of Latakia: 'Muslims and Christians are all our subjects. The question of religion has no connection with political considerations. [In religious matters] every individual must be left alone: the believer to practise his Islam and the Christian his Christianity. But no one to have authority over the other. . . .'

These sentiments were not entirely inconsistent with Islamic theory and past practice, but they were contrary to Ottoman practice in Syria and elsewhere, and Muslim public opinion was not yet ready to change that practice. Hence any popularity that the Egyptian administration may have enjoyed was confined to the Christian minorities. The Muslim majority was on the whole hostile. There were, however, certain matters concerning Christians and Jews where Islamic practice was followed by the Egyptians just as strictly as by the Ottomans.

Muslim jurists are agreed that under Muslim sovereignty old churches and synagogues may be repaired, but entirely new ones may not be erected. Muḥammad 'Ali adhered to this ruling with scrupulous care. Thus despite repeated requests he refused to allow, without the sultan's sanction, the erection of a new English Church in Jerusalem. With the same firmness he refused a request from foreign Jews to buy land in and near the Holy City. (Foreigners were still debarred from acquiring real estate in any part of the Ottoman Empire.)

More important for future history, he refused a request from the Jews in Jerusalem to pave the ground close to the walls of the Ḥaram area on which stood both the Aqṣā and the Dome of the Rock mosques. The ground in question was part of the property of an adjacent *waqf*, being the traditional spot where Muḥammad tethered his mount before ascending to heaven. To allow the Jews to pave the ground would have constituted a recognition of their title to its ownership. But the Jews were permitted, without ostentation or raising their voices, to visit the place as hitherto for meditation. For to them that part of the wall, commonly known as the Wailing Place of the Jews, was the only surviving remnant of the Temple.

Public security and toleration encouraged foreign merchants, missionaries, pilgrims and travellers of all sorts to come to Syria in greater numbers than they ever did before. The cities of Damascus and Jerusalem, hitherto denied for permanent residence even to diplomatic representations, opened their gates to receive them. Here again Muḥammad ʿAli waited for the sultan's recognition of the appointed consuls before admitting them. Great Britain was a pioneer in sending consuls to these difficult centres. A British consul was appointed for Damascus before the Egyptian occupation, but he had to bide his time in Beirut for nearly four years.

In 1833 he entered Damascus in procession. The Egyptian army provided a colourful and impressive escort both on the way and through the city of Damascus to the consular residence. The demonstration appears to have been designed to strike awe into the hearts of the Damascenes, unaccustomed as they were to witness Christians on horseback, and to curry favour with the British government. A native eyewitness says the consul rode a well-bred horse and wore a hat 'studded with diamonds and topped with white and red feathers'. The entry of the first British vice-consul into Jerusalem in 1838 was a similar break with tradition, but it was attended with no special ceremony.

Promotion of commerce was the primary reason given for the establishment of consuls in Damascus and Jerusalem. But at the insistence of missionaries interested in the conversion of the Jews the functions of the consulate in Jerusalem were enlarged to include the protection of Jews. Jerusalem was not the trade centre that Damascus was. During the Egyptian occupation neither city had special significance to British commercial interests equal to that of Beirut. This city had gradually become the chief port of Syria, and the greatest number of foreign merchants had adopted it as the centre of their business with the interior.

Domestic commerce in essential commodities was almost entirely in the hands of government agents. Although there were strictly no monopolies, foreign merchants found it more profitable to concentrate on imports. There was an increasing demand for, among other commodities, paper from France and glassware from Austria and, above all, for cloth from Great Britain. Machine-made cloth was offered at comparatively low prices, and its popularity had a most damaging effect on the traditional cloth industry in Damascus and Aleppo. At least for this reason the opening of Syria to more foreign enterprise was not in the best interests of native industries. Their protection was difficult because of the terms of the Capitulations which, in this case, permitted English merchants almost free and unrestricted trade. Such loopholes as existed under this system were sealed off by the Anglo-Ottoman commercial convention signed in 1838.

But the Egyptians made special efforts, despite their preoccupation with external wars and internal revolts, to promote agriculture, to open a few new schools, and to undertake some public works not directly required by the army. These are aspects of their administration which are either unknown or known imperfectly and thus incorrectly assessed. It is therefore important to establish briefly the precise contribution in each of the three fields.

Mention has been made above of the fact that in their fight against rebels the Egyptians deliberately destroyed villages, cut down fruit trees, burnt the crops in the fields and demolished wells. Against this destructive record must now be set a record of reconstruction: peasants and beduins were encouraged to settle in villages and to reclaim and cultivate waste land. Those who co-operated with the authorities were exempted from taxes for the first three years and from military service for an unspecified time, and were given loans to buy seeds and tools. The Egyptian authorities recognised that to increase the country's yield of grain was a form of military service, since the army was, next to the native population, the greatest consumer of grain. But we must not be deceived by statistics. A 'village' revived or even established meant little more than a few farmers with their families living in primitive and improvised dwellings. In 1837 Ibrāhīm reported to his father that the total number of villages in Syria was 1008 and that 237 were 'under reconstruction'.[9]

Nor was Egyptian interest confined to the growing of grain. Their record in encouraging the planting of trees, especially olive and mulberry, is indeed respectable. Apart from their commercial interest in the silk produced in Syria, they encouraged the planting of mulberry trees and sent great quantities of the silkworms that fed on these trees to Egypt for experimenting with the introduction of sericulture in that country. Egyptian motives in promoting the planting of olive trees was likewise utilitarian. Next to grain, olive oil was required by the army in great quantities. But considering the fact that it takes several years for the olive tree to bear fruit, the Egyptians must have been optimistic when early in 1833 they encouraged the planting of 150,000 saplings in the hinterland of Acre alone.

Such encouragement was not always due to selfish ends. For there is good evidence that it was a general policy. Thus in answer to 'the order concerning reclamation of waste land and the planting of trees', the *qāḍi* of Jaffa acquired a plot outside the city walls and began in 1837 to work it. The deputy-governor, backed by the consultative council, objected, probably on security grounds, that trees would obstruct access to some of the towers on the city wall. The *qāḍi* appealed to the commander-in-chief. Ibrāhīm issued orders that the *qāḍi* must be allowed to proceed with his project.[10]

A Christian Arab physician had a less happy story to tell: 'My losses were so great that I nearly became destitute. I had taken from the government land in Ayyib village in the Lajah district in order to bring it under cultivation. I employed farmers for this purpose, but in the second year outlaws plundered it and destroyed it. The same happened in the two villages of Khuraibah and Manṣūrah in the Ḥūlah district. The crop was plundered from the threshing floor and the animals stolen.'[11]

With regard to education the Egyptian contribution was limited to three boarding schools in Damascus, Aleppo and Antioch designed as preparatory establishments for future army officers. The pupils were taught by army officers and others, dressed in military uniform and enlisted as soon as they could read, write and reckon. At the height of the financial difficulties in 1838, Ibrāhīm wrote to his father offering to abolish these schools. They had then a total of under one thousand pupils.[12] But despite the deficiency in the Syrian budget Muḥammad 'Ali continued to pay, as under the Ottomans, the salaries of such Muslim religious teachers as the *mudarris* and the *imam* as well as to compensate officials for what income they lost from foreign pilgrims.

In the literary field the Egyptian impact was more profound. Preserved in the Egyptian archives are cumulative lists of books printed in Cairo and supplied to various centres in Syria. They tell a most illuminating story and provide a better indication of literary tastes and the availability of books than the surmises of even the most acute of foreign observers. The lists include books on science, mathematics, medicine, theology, mysticism, language, history, geography and travel. They were ordered not only by civil servants, physicians, chemists and army officers, but also by religious functionaries, members of consultative councils, notables, teachers and private individuals of all communities, Muslim, Christians and others.

Otherwise the Egyptians left the educational situation of the majority of the population much as they had found it on succeeding the Ottomans. Traditional Islamic schools supported largely by religious foundations, native Christian schools belonging to the various communities, and private Jewish schools, all existed before the influx of foreign missions in the early nineteenth century, and continued to develop thereafter. Foreign missions were debarred from teaching Muslims, and their activities had to be confined to those Jews and Christians willing to listen. Roman Catholic missions in Syria antedate all other missions, and they had moreover a point of anchor in the native churches that had accepted the supremacy of the Pope. The task of Protestant missions, begun in the 1820s, was harder in that they had, with the assistance of a handful of native converts, to create a new Protestant community through teaching and preaching.

Security and tolerance enjoyed by the natives and foreigners under Egyptian rule were favourable to all foreign missions. It was during the Egyptian occupation of Syria that American and English missions were finally established in Palestine and Lebanon.

During the same period old Catholic missions were revived and greatly extended all over Syria. Rivalry between Protestant and Catholic missions became henceforth a familiar feature of Christian education in Syria.

It now remains to say a brief word on public works undertaken by the Egyptian administration, excluding those directly required by the army such as barracks, workshops and military roads. Repairs of great mosques remained, as under the Ottoman government, the ultimate responsibility of the ruler. There is a record that the great mosque in Aleppo was repaired at government expense with Ibrāhīm's approval. But apart from this specific mention of the government assuming direct responsibility, funds of religious foundations were as usual used for repairs to mosques, schools and public inns. There are other projects of a different nature which the Egyptian administration financed from public revenue. They established a quarantine in Beirut and constructed water sewerage in Damascus. Three larger projects may also be mentioned. The drainage of swamps and the consequent reclamation of land near Alexandretta, the repair of the hot mineral water baths at Tiberias and the bringing of drinking water from the river Sājūr to the town of Aleppo. This last project, reviving an old water supply system, was undertaken about the date of the battle of Nezib, when it seemed that with the defeat of its army, defection of its navy and death of its sultan the Ottoman Empire was at the mercy of Muḥammad ʿAli had he decided to follow his advantage: occupy the capital, supervise the investiture of the new sultan and name the grand vizier he favoured. But it was not to be.

5

Following the joint note presented by the five powers to the Porte, Syria's fate and indeed that of the Ottoman Empire was to be decided neither on the battlefield nor in Cairo nor in Istanbul. It was in fact decided in the chancelleries of Europe, and more precisely the Foreign Office in London with an appearance of association and consultation with the Porte. In the words of a native Syrian chronicler, 'the box was in Istanbul but its key was in London'. Palmerston had finally made up his mind that to check the growth of Russian influence in Istanbul was to check and reduce Muḥammad ʿAli's power. But while the powers deliberated the pasha was sternly warned not to take any military action.

It took nearly a year for four of the five powers to come to an agreement, France abstaining. During that year the Egyptian administration had still to cope with financial difficulties. More serious, however, were the difficulties created by Ottoman and English agents who were busy inciting the people to revolt. While this subversion was mounting, an internal incident caused much embarrassment. A Capuchin padre, long resident in Damascus, entered the Jewish quarter of Damascus one day and all traces of him vanished.

The disappearance of the padre was connected with the belief then common in the Near East, as it had been common in medieval Europe, that the Jews murdered Christians in order to mingle their blood with the unleavened bread of Passover. Details of the case, which assumed international significance, have often been related and need not be repeated here. But the crime was one of robbery followed by murder of which a Jewish barber and his assistant were accused, duly tried and condemned. The British consul Werry, himself sympathetic to the Jews, testified that the promptness of the Egyptians in taking action saved the Jewish community in Damascus from a general massacre.

According to Mīkhā'īl Mishāqa, a respectable Christian physician then resident in Damascus, who personally knew the padre and some of the Jews questioned, the leaders of the Jewish community made the mistake of overpleading the innocence of a few scoundrels in their community. In this way they compromised themselves and brought unnecessary accusations and suffering on themselves. Mishāqa adds that Sir Moses Montefiore was so moved as to seek an audience of Muḥammad ʿAli. He is reputed to have given him a present of 60,000 purses and 3000 purses to the secretaries, in return for obtaining a pardon for the Jewish leaders but not a declaration of their innocence.[13]

Scarcely had this incident been settled when the Syrian question was brought to the fore by more serious internal and external developments in quick succession. Muḥammad ʿAli had expected the worst from the joint note presented by the five powers, but he calculated that all the five could not agree on one course of action. He was encouraged to expect at least moral support from France, and could not believe that Russia would act contrary to her interests by bolstering the sultan. He thought that either or both powers would neutralise any action that Great Britain might desire to take.

At the same time he prepared for war. Among the measures he adopted was the demand for the surrender of the arms given to the Christians of Lebanon two years earlier to fight the Druze rebels. Lebanon was the only district in Syria which had not revolted against the Egyptians. But now, fearful of conscription and increased taxation, and expecting nothing from Bashīr Shihāb but subservience to the Egyptians, sections of the population decided to resist, taking care to enlist the support of some of the disaffected Druzes. Foreign agents played a great part in bringing about what turned out to be the last revolt against the Egyptians in Syria.

At first Ibrāhīm was conciliatory. He denied solemnly that conscription was contemplated and assured the Christians that government arms only were to be collected for use in the emergency and that no general disarmament was intended. It was to no avail, since much of the discontent was directed more against Bashīr than against Ibrāhīm. This is clear from the testimony of a contemporary witness who states that Bashīr 'had impoverished the people and suppressed them' to such an extent that they could bear it no longer, and so revolted as one man and with great ferocity against him, with the result that his own position was ruined.[14] This is also clear from the demands of the rebels near Beirut. They asked Bashīr to establish a consultative council representing all the communities. Lebanon was the only place where such a council was not established. They also asked for the amount and time of collecting the *Fardah* tax to be fixed and the practice of levying this tax from the relatives of those who died to be stopped, as also the practice of holding the relatives of a defaulting debtor responsible for his debts.

The rebellion began to spread to other parts, but the Egyptians with force and Bashīr with negotiation succeeded in subduing or intimidating the rebels. Arms began to be surrendered and over fifty rebel leaders, including some of the Shihāb family, were captured and exiled to Egypt. That might have been the end had not the rebels been provided with concrete evidence of impending intervention by the powers. Early in July 1840 a squadron of the Royal Navy commanded by Sir Charles Napier appeared before Beirut, but only as a demonstration at this stage.

About the same time the second dragoman in the British Embassy in Constantinople, the Roman Catholic Richard Wood, who had a few years earlier been in Lebanon to learn Arabic, arrived secretly with vague instructions to act on behalf of the Ottoman government. Sheltered by his brother-in-law, Noel Moore, the British consul in Beirut, Wood began an active campaign of subversion. Among other activities he encouraged the despatch of petitions to the Porte and to the British and French Embassies complaining of Egyptian oppression. From now on the written demands of the rebels were presented in a more systematic way which suggests that a European mind may have inspired them.

Almost simultaneously with these developments in Syria the four powers and the Porte signed the London agreement on 15 July 1840. Under its terms the sultan offered to grant Muḥammad ʿAli the hereditary governorship of Egypt and the governorship of an enlarged province of Acre for life provided he accepted the offer within ten days. If he accepted it within twenty days he would receive only Egypt. If he refused altogether the powers would blockade Syria and Egypt, and would act jointly if he moved in the direction of Istanbul. All offers were conditional on the return of the Ottoman fleet.

In adversity Muḥammad ʿAli lost none of his resourcefulness. On hearing the news of the London agreement he asked his son to proclaim to the Syrians that the Ottoman ministers had accepted bribes from the infidels, agreed to the dismemberment of the Empire and signed away Syria to Great Britain and Istanbul to Russia. So far as can be discovered there is no record that Ibrāhīm did launch such a propaganda offensive. It would have made little difference anyhow.

The old pasha did refuse the offer, and the sultan dismissed him from all his appointments. In August, Napier issued circulars to the Syrians informing them of the decision of the powers, in alliance with the Porte, to end Egyptian rule. In September, British marines and Ottoman soldiers were landed north of Beirut, and the distribution of arms to the rebels began on a large scale. Bashīr Shihāb must have now reckoned that he was doomed. Another member of his family, Bashīr al-Qāsim, arrived at the allied camp and the Ottoman commander recognised him as the new governor (*ḥākim*) of Lebanon. The old Bashīr surrendered to the British navy and was exiled to Malta, carrying with him a fortune estimated at between eight and eighteen thousand purses.

The allies confined their military operations to the coastal towns and on the whole did not venture beyond the range of the guns of their warships. They never engaged Ibrāhīm in any major battle or interfered seriously with his movements. He too was careful to regroup his forces in the interior and to avoid close contact with the enemy. The coastal towns including Acre fell one after the other after what seemed only token Egyptian resistance. Ibrāhīm was no doubt waiting for his father to reach a political solution with the allies. The uncertainty was resolved when Muḥammad ʿAli agreed to withdraw his forces from Syria, restore the Ottoman fleet and beg the sultan to reappoint him hereditary governor of Egypt. The old fighter had finally capitulated.

Ibrāhīm's feat of successfully withdrawing an army estimated between sixty and eighty thousand, often through hostile territory, must be reckoned among his brilliant military achievements, perhaps not far less so than his victories against Ottoman armies. Nor did he leave chaos behind. He met the notables in Damascus and made them elect a temporary civil governor pending the arrival of one appointed by the sultan. He issued a stern warning that any disturbance of the peace would cause him to return and punish the offenders. It took two months of hazardous marches to complete what was on the whole an orderly withdrawal. At the end of January 1841 Ibrāhīm reached Gaza. About three weeks later the Egyptian occupation of Syria passed into history.

4

Official and Actual Reforms – The First-Fruits of the Tanzīmāt

I

ONLY in a political sense is it correct to say that Egyptian influence in Syria came to an end in 1840. Much of that influence had in fact survived. A centralised administration was too precious a prize to be given away, since it fitted very well with the policy of Maḥmūd II and his successor. It was also convenient for Ottoman pashas to have found the powers of feudal lords drastically curbed. With the blessing of the Sublime Porte they continued and on occasion even accelerated the process. Nor, contrary to a current assumption, was the Porte intent on reversing the Egyptian liberal policy towards non-Muslims. For this policy was the keynote of ʿAbdul Majīd's decree, the *Hatti Sharīf* of Gülhané, which ushered in the formal era of reform known as *Tanzīmāt* (reorganisation).

The decree was issued in 1839, some four months after the new sultan's accession. It has been suggested, even by respectable historians, that the decree was a diplomatic gesture designed more to gain European favour than to introduce genuine reforms, and that its ultimate inspiration was foreign not Ottoman. These assertions ignore the trend in Ottoman political thought since the reign of Salīm III if not earlier. Related to this thought, the decree must be regarded as a culmination of a long period of deliberation. The decree might indeed have been issued by Maḥmūd II had he been spared the series of internal revolts and external wars. The timing of the promulgation of the decree was no doubt a shrewd move on the part of Rashīd Pasha, the minister for foreign affairs, but there is little justification for suspecting the intentions behind the decree simply because it was not fully implemented.

That some of its principles bear resemblance to their counterparts in European thought and practice is self-evident. But it is noteworthy that some of these principles were not foreign to the best Islamic tradition and had already been practised by the Egyptian administration in Syria, particularly in regard to the treatment of non-Muslims. The sultan's decree was in effect an endorsement of this practice, announced with a flourish of trumpets. But this is not to say that the decree contained little that was new. The fact is that, beneath pious protestations and flowery phraseology, the decree was for its time revolutionary in one important matter.

It was not revolutionary in that it proposed the introduction of new regulations or codes (*qawānīn*), since sultans had done so before partly to avoid encroachment on the fundamental law of the Empire, Islamic law. Nor was it revolutionary because the regulations it proposed included such welcome guarantees as security of life, property and honour, limiting the term of military service, replacing tax-farming by fixed dues, and prohibiting the punishment of offenders without due trial. It was revolutionary because, after enumerating these reforms, the decree states: 'This royal favour is to embrace all subjects of our sultanate, Muslims and [followers] of other religions without any exception.'

A breach with tradition, if not also an infringement of the fundamental law, was now contemplated. Non-Muslims under Muslim sovereignty had long enjoyed tolerance, protection and a large measure of communal autonomy. At the very beginning, non-Muslim communities became separate and distinct from the community of Islam by their own choice. In the course of time this separateness had been emphasised until it became an institution which like most formalised institutions was very difficult to change radically. The sultan might attempt to do so by decree, but tradition and public sentiment was against change.

'Beware, beware, of the dangers of misunderstanding!' Thus is the warning contained in the instructions following the text of the decree. It occurs in an Arabic version addressed to Muḥammad 'Ali and duly registered in the *qāḍi*'s court in Jaffa, some four months after the proclamation of the decree. It is addressed to the pasha, the religious and civil officials under him and the notables of the land. Although Muḥammad 'Ali was among the few pashas who could appreciate the decree, he received it with great reserve, possibly because it condemned monopolies. Its application, he said, was extremely difficult even for him who had spent forty years introducing reforms. He hoped it could be applied in Egypt after forty years; in Istanbul and its neighbourhood after a hundred.[1]

That there were powerful elements in the state, both at the centre and in the provinces, opposed to the spirit of the decree is not in doubt. But that the decree had at the beginning been intended as a guide for provincial administrators is clear from its circulation to governors. How far were its provisions acted upon in Syria after the Egyptian withdrawal? To the important province of Damascus, the Sublime Porte sent Najīb Pasha who had some time previously served Muḥammad 'Ali as official agent in Istanbul. Najīb's administration may be taken as an indication that the implementation of the imperial decree depended more on the character of provincial governors than on paper guarantees or popular displeasure.

Najīb brought from Istanbul his own treasurer, but appointed 'Abdullah Nawfal, a Christian from Tripoli, as chief clerk and restored to the post of accountant Raphael Fārḥi, a member of the Jewish family that had long served former pashas in this capacity. Najīb's first order was for the city to be cleaned of rubbish. He reconstituted the consultative council and required all officials to swear, 'the Muslim on the Koran, the Christian on the Gospel and the Jew on the Torah', that they would not deviate from the way of justice and would not accept bribes. (Bribery was one of the abuses strongly condemned in the sultan's decree.)

However, official action was one thing, and popular reaction quite another. The Damascenes accepted Najīb's measures in the same way that they had accepted Ibrāhīm's – with passive docility. But a mere rumour that taxes were raised in Aleppo caused a stir in Damascus and evoked longing for the Egyptians. Some Christians in Damascus had more tangible cause to miss the firm hand of Ibrāhīm when they could wear white turbans and ride horses without fear of molestation. Now some of the common people in the city began to make a sport of ruffling the white turbans worn by Christians. Some of those against whom complaints were made to the governor were punished, even though the complaints are reported to have been made to the British consul in the first instance.[2]

Najīb needed no prodding to check beduin incursions; the military commander in the province had an army of 5000 infantry and three regiments of cavalry. But it is difficult to reconcile the reports of Richard Wood, now British consul in Damascus, with the pasha's actions. The reports accuse him of being a fanatic Muslim who was hostile to Christians, natives as well as Europeans. But there is little or nothing to substantiate this accusation against a pasha who had taken Christians and Jews on to his staff, who had appointed Christians and Jews as members of the consultative council, and who had moreover punished Muslims accused of molesting Christians.

An explanation of Wood's ill-concealed bias against the pasha is not hard to seek. During his secret mission in Lebanon, before the end of the Egyptian occupation, Wood made much of his rôle as an agent not of the British but of the Ottoman government. On becoming British consul in 1841 he acted and wrote as if he still held a special position in the Ottoman system. Hence his frequent meddling with provincial administration and his wide and intimate contacts with notables, Christians, Druzes and Muslims. Even the British consul in Jerusalem complained to the ambassador of Wood's meddling in religious affairs in the city and his misrepresenting the Roman Catholic church as '*the national church* of Great Britain'.[3]

Such proceedings must have caused much irritation and resentment to such an able administrator as Najīb. A clash of personalities was the inevitable result. Wood's attitude to Najīb is in sharp contrast to that of his predecessor in the consular office. The following passage is at once a report on the reception of the sultan's decree in Syria and on Najīb's own attitude to it:

> I have to observe to your Lordship that in all the communications I have had with the pashas and authorities since my return to Damascus, they not only seemed doubtful of the possibility of carrying into execution the new system, but I discovered in them a distaste for it. But there is every appearance that Najīb Pasha does all in his power to carry it into execution. . . .[4]

Najīb's actual measures cited above leave little doubt that he was in earnest. Diminished enthusiasm for the execution of the imperial decree as regards non-Muslims and other matters was not due to men like Najīb. The change of attitude began in Istanbul when a weak sultan conceded the conservative contention that the provisions of the decree went too far. When Rashīd fell from power less than two years after the issue of the decree, many observers thought that was the end of the matter. It was not so for reform continued sporadically in the spirit of the decree until it culminated in the constitution of 1876.

In Syria some of the provisions of the imperial decree had been anticipated by the Egyptians whose measures were substantially continued by the restored Ottoman administration. At the centre of power in Istanbul the conservatives were fighting a losing battle; the process of reform was slow but it was not stifled. Rashīd regained his position at the helm of the movement, and he and his disciples like 'Āli and Fuād began to realise that an educated society was the basis of all effective reform. A small beginning was made, but it took more than a quarter of a century for the new educational system to be extended to Syria.

To this important subject we shall return in due course, but for the purpose of this chapter a word is essential on the provincial organisation in Syria. Not because the Ottoman and after it the Egyptian system was radically changed, but in order to point out its continuity with only minor adjustments after the restoration of Syria to the sultan. Aleppo, Tripoli, Damascus and Sidon (or Acre) continued to be the capitals of provinces. In the city of Beirut, however, a provincial administration was set up, similar to that maintained by the Egyptians, and concerned mainly with the affairs of Mount Lebanon. But this administrative arrangement was not tantamount to the creation of the province of Beirut which had yet to come.

Otherwise it is surprising how much of the Egyptian apparatus and even personnel was retained. Two examples must suffice. Sulaimān 'Abdul-Hādi, who held the post of deputy-governor in the Nābulus district under the Egyptians, was confirmed in his post by Najīb, the pasha of Damascus. On Sulaimān's death his brother Muḥammad was appointed by the same pasha. The pasha of Aleppo likewise confirmed 'Abdullah al-Bābinsi in the position of deputy-governor which he also had held under the Egyptians.

2

Mount Lebanon was the district where radical administrative changes were made. Bashīr al-Qāsim proved a dismal failure. He antagonised all sections of the population, and when the Druzes challenged his authority the Christians gave him little help and the Ottoman government was quick to exile him and introduce direct rule.

Until the Egyptian period, Mount Lebanon was known very loosely as *Jabal ad-Durūz* (the Mount of the Druzes), probably on account of the predominance of the Druze feudal lords. However, the country of the Druzes was actually the south of Mount Lebanon; the north was the country of the Maronites and other Christians. In the seventeenth century the Maʿn family, Druzes from the south, extended their control also over the north, and thus began the peculiar Druze-Maronite relationship. The Maʿn's were succeeded in the eighteenth century by the Shihābs who were Muslims. The conversion to Christianity, political or otherwise, of members of this family increased the sectarian complications in a tiny country.

Sectarian divisions were aggravated by social, economic and political changes. Maronite peasants and artisans from the north had for generations been migrating to the Druze south in search of work and better living conditions. The effects of this movement of population, at first welcomed as cheap labour by the Druze nobility disdainful of manual work, was ultimately to influence the shift of power from the Druzes to the Christians. By the time of Bashīr the balance began to tilt in favour of the Christians and at the expense of the Druzes. Not only did Christians increase in numbers but Druzes began to decrease on account of mass migration from Lebanon to Ḥawrān promoted by a desire to escape oppression or to avoid local factional quarrels. The decline of the Druze power was followed by their eclipse during the Egyptian occupation. Their leaders had either to flee the country, go underground or suffer Bashīr's excessive taxation and Ibrāhīm's conscription. Bashīr had then nearly dealt the death-blow to the Druze power by wholesale confiscation of property and destruction of family seats.

With the fall of Bashīr and Ottoman restoration, Druze chiefs loyal to the sultan returned from exile to a much changed Lebanon. By an imperial order confiscated property was to be restored, but no order could restore all property and produce immediate wealth. The Druzes could not forget Bashīr's assaults against their privileges and wealth. Nor could they forget that under Bashīr's banner the Maronites fought against them both in Ḥawrān and in Lebanon. They were accordingly determined to make it impossible for a Shihāb to govern in Lebanon, and in this they were successful. Bashīr al-Qāsim was the last of the family to hold office.

The Ottoman governor of Lebanon was the renegade 'Umar Pasha an-Namsāwi, the surname indicating his former Austrian nationality not his family. Immediately he was faced with conflicting consular policies which were reflected in the different attitudes of local communities. For ever since the powers intervened to restore Syria to the sultan, major political developments in the country were seldom settled by the Sublime Porte without diplomatic interference by Europe.

As a result of such intervention 'Umar was withdrawn and Lebanon was divided into two administrative districts, roughly along the Beirut–Damascus highway. The Maronites to the north were placed under a Maronite district officer and the Druzes to the south under a Druze district officer, both answerable to the pasha of Sidon. Neat on paper, this plan was far from working smoothly in practice. It did not remove the cause of Druze-Maronite antagonism which had already in 1841 led to the first armed clash between the two communities.

In 1845 the second and more serious clash erupted. It was the Christians who opened hostilities. To put an end to the fighting was of great and immediate importance, but to pacify the country was the ultimate aim and of greater importance for the future. Accordingly the sultan appointed Shakīb Efendi, minister for foreign affairs, as special commissioner and sent him to Lebanon with military reinforcements. Before leaving Istanbul the minister informed the heads of European diplomatic missions of his commission and insisted in no uncertain terms that the consuls in Beirut must stop meddling and must not interfere either directly or indirectly with his measures.

Among these measures was the occupation by Ottoman troops of the main mountain villages and the disarming of the population of all communities. To forestall any resistance influential leaders of the two main communities were placed under arrest, and to prevent any means of foreign communication with the villages all foreign residents, even missionaries, Catholic, Protestant and others of all nationalities, were temporarily removed to Beirut.

The political solution imposed by Shakīb virtually confirmed the administrative division of the country as before into a Druze and a Maronite district under a Druze and a Maronite district officer respectively, both holding office at the pleasure of the pasha of Sidon. The only innovation was the formation of an appointed council of salaried members in each of the two districts representing the various communities and not only the Druzes and Maronites. The functions of this council were analogous to those of the advisory council established by the Egyptians all over Syria with the exception of Lebanon. With Shakīb's arrangement Lebanon had now been brought under complete and direct Ottoman control.

The application of the Gülhané decree increased Ottoman control and centralised administration in Syria as a whole. It coincided with increased European influence, political and economic, religious and educational. The three powers with major interests were Great Britain, France and Russia. The interests of one power seldom harmonised with those of the other two, with the result that their rivalry in Syria was a mark of the two decades between the end of the Egyptian occupation and the outbreak of the civil war in 1860. As well as exercising pressure to further its ends in Istanbul, each power sought to achieve these ends locally by an alliance, open or secret, with one of the religious communities in the land.

But each power already had rights and privileges secured by treaty. The first power to obtain such rights and privileges was France. In 1535 Sulaimān the Magnificent granted commercial and other privileges to the subjects of Francis I. Apart from guaranteeing French nationals freedom to profess and practice their religion in the sultan's dominions, the sultan granted extra-territorial rights to French nationals trading or residing in the Ottoman Empire and virtually removed them from the jurisdiction of Muslim courts to that of their consuls.

Although preceded by similar privileges granted to Italian cities, the French privileges became the model for future 'Capitulations', at first begged and later exacted from Ottoman sultans. In 1580 Queen Elizabeth secured similar Capitulations from Murād III which he clearly calls privileges. In giving these the sultan's tone was still one of condescension. The English monarch was given what 'we have given and granted' to the French, the Venetians and other kings and princes.

Russia's rights and privileges were obtained about a century later, following an Ottoman defeat in war. In 1774 the treaty of Kutchuk Kainarja was signed with two articles which proved of direct bearing on the history of Syria in the nineteenth century. Ottoman practice had long been to sanction the erection of chapels in the official residences of the Christian diplomatic missions in Istanbul and consuls in large cities. But now under articles seven and fourteen, Russia secured new privileges. She was permitted to erect a new Orthodox church for public worship in the Galata quarter of Istanbul, to place this church under her protection and to make representations concerning it to the Sublime Porte. Upon this limited concession Russian diplomacy and Russian arms sought in the nineteenth century to establish a protectorate over the Orthodox church in the Ottoman Empire and even over the Orthodox subjects of the sultan with results that will be apparent later in this chapter.

Analogous French claims in respect of the Catholic church in the Empire were traced by French publicists to the era of the Crusades, if not to the days of Charlemagne and Hārūn ar-Rashīd. Relations had indeed been established with the Maronites in Lebanon during the Crusades, but following expulsion of the Crusaders from Syria these relations had lapsed till the seventeenth century when Catholic missions began to operate in the Near East. Since then France as the foremost Catholic power had assumed the rôle of protector of Catholic interests. Close relations with the Maronites and other Uniate Christians were established and developed.

Great Britain, on the other hand, made no formal alliance with any religious group in the Ottoman Empire. But she did uphold the cause of Christians in general especially after the issue of the Gülhané decree. Then responding to powerful evangelical pressure groups, Britain afforded, through the newly established consulate in Jerusalem, some protection to the Jews. For a similar reason British consular officers throughout Syria afforded a large measure of protection to American and English missionaries operating on behalf of voluntary societies among Christians and Jews.

But Great Britain did not remain without a 'client nation' in Syria. In 1841, the more France appeared to incline towards supporting the Maronite cause the greater became the Druze desire for a British alliance. In that same year the Roman Catholic Richard Wood, then consul in Damascus, suggested to Palmerston the expediency of reducing the Maronite patriarch's authority and showing a 'degree of countenance' to the Druzes. Henceforth there was an informal alliance between them and British agents in the Near East.

Thus each of the three powers had at least one local party in Syria. While Russia confined her interest to the Orthodox and France to the Catholic, Great Britain's clients were aspiring minorities: the Druzes, the Jews and the new converts to Protestantism from all these communities. The following section is devoted to the activities of each of the three powers in Syria up to the Crimean War. Political and commercial activities were naturally the concern of diplomatic representatives, while religious and cultural activities were carried out by organisations enjoying official or unofficial backing.

3

French commerce enjoyed a predominant position in Syria before the Napoleonic invasion; it lost that position gradually to British merchants. By comparison Russian commercial interests were negligible except in connection with the transport of pilgrims to and from the Holy Land. An Anglo-Ottoman trade convention was signed in 1838, and though it was intended to undermine Muḥammad 'Ali's monopolistic practices he was so anxious to conciliate Great Britain that he raised no objection to its operation in Syria.

British trade continued to expand, and most of it passed through

Beirut. According to a consular report no fewer than sixty-eight English vessels called at the city in 1843.[5] With the exception of four vessels which brought coal for use by foreign merchants in the city, the rest brought manufactured goods, chiefly cloth and hardware, and colonial produce, chiefly sugar. French merchants were still bartering sugar made from beetroot for local produce such as silk, but the sugar marketed by English merchants was preferred.

In 1851 the correspondent of the *New York Daily Times* in Istanbul reported that the value of imports via Beirut was five million dollars and of exports half that amount.[6] In 1858, a local newspaper described Beirut as the entrepôt of Syria and Palestine.[7] Through it cloth from Manchester, manufactured goods from Birmingham, silk cloth from France, arms from Belgium and paper from Austria were distributed as far inland as Baghdad. Within Syria itself the goods reached Damascus and Jerusalem inland and Tripoli, Jaffa and Gaza on the coast. Among the exports the paper mentions olive oil and raw silk.

There was an imbalance of trade. In Syria as in the rest of the Ottoman Empire foreign trade enjoyed under the Capitulations and other instruments privileges which proved damaging to native industries and commerce. From about mid-century the Ottoman treasury found it increasingly difficult to balance income and expenditure. The difficulty was partly remedied during the Crimean War by foreign loans, but these had the ultimate effect of increasing Ottoman financial embarrassment and European penetration.

Trade was the ostensible purpose of the opening in 1838 of a British consulate in the non-trading city of Jerusalem. Before then Muḥammad ʿAli refused to accept even a vice-consul in that city without the sanction of the legal sovereign, the sultan, since, as the third holy city in Islam, Jerusalem was still closed to foreigners for permanent residence. The British consulate was the first to be established by a European power, but Russia and France were quick to establish their consulates afterwards. To judge by the correspondence of the British consulate alone, political and religious affairs were paramount among the interests of the three consulates. The British consul was assiduous in his reporting on the activities of his colleagues among the Orthodox and Catholic communities just as he was in reporting on the activities of English and American missionaries, his unofficial protégés.

Catholic missionary work in Syria antedates the Protestant by more than a century and a half. From the beginning it was mainly concerned with the religious education of native Catholics, but it made occasional forays into the Orthodox camp. The Anglo-American missions began with attempts to convert some of the few Jews in Jerusalem and elsewhere, but gradually they shifted their attention to converting Eastern Christians, both Orthodox and Catholic, to Protestantism. Thus by their zeal European and American missionaries created new tensions among the local communities, complicated their interrelations and confronted the three interested powers with new difficulties.

The Maronite hierarchy was vehement in its protest against the first Protestant missions in and near Beirut. This local reaction is very clearly reflected in French consular reports which suspected a political design behind religious missions. As seen through French consular eyes the secret aim was to form a 'party' of natives favourable to Great Britain, even when the agents were American. In one of his searching reports, a French consul stresses the urgent need to 'uphold our holy religion and our incontestable privilege to protect all those who practice it in the Levant'.[8]

The call was not unheeded. The 1830s witnessed a vigorous Catholic missionary effort. In 1831 the Jesuits returned to Syria, and together with the Lazarists, the Sisters of Charity, the nuns of St Joseph and other agencies, covered the country with schools for boys and girls. Although members of these agencies were of different nationalities, they all tended, together with those who were French, to look to France for protection and to the local French diplomatic agent for immediate assistance.

English missionary enterprise in Palestine and American enterprise in Lebanon had also been established by then, though on a smaller scale. American and English missionaries were at this stage under unofficial, but not less effective, British consular protection. The two camps, the Catholic and Protestant, viewed each other with intense hostility, and they were bound to be rivals. But while Catholic missionaries found ample scope for work among their own communities, their Anglo-Saxon rivals had to create the scope themselves. In the attempt to do so they created political complications for their protectors who either did not anticipate or otherwise minimised the significance of the complications.

Thus following the restoration of Syria to the sultan's authority, English missionaries began to agitate for concessions in recognition of British efforts in that direction. Through powerful patrons, they exercised pressure on the British government and persuaded even Palmerston to further their aims. They wanted to build a new church in Jerusalem even before they had a congregation. Furthermore, it was decided to establish a missionary bishop in the Holy City within the ecclesiastical jurisdiction of *the* Bishop of Jerusalem, the Orthodox patriarch. Palmerston's power to obtain concessions from the Porte was at the time very great, but he failed to obtain a licence to build a church, and the Porte withheld recognition of the bishop who was appointed and sent without prior Ottoman approval.

The Anglican bishop took up residence in Jerusalem at the beginning of 1842, still without Ottoman recognition of his ecclesiastical dignity. Despite this fact his arrival alerted both the Orthodox and the Catholic camps. The Orthodox patriarch of Jerusalem, who had hitherto resided at Constantinople, was persuaded to return to occupy his seat among his flock. The Pope revived the Latin Patriarchate of Jerusalem which had ceased to exist *de facto* on the fall of the last crusading stronghold in the Holy Land in 1291. As the new patriarch the Pope sent a zealous prelate and an accomplished scholar.

But neither Russia nor France had as direct a hand in these developments as had Great Britain in establishing the Anglican bishop in Jerusalem. When Russian and French direct involvement followed soon afterwards, it was largely as a result of developments in Syria, not in St Petersburg or Paris. In 1842 the patriarch of Antioch sent an ecclesiastical delegation to Russia to seek material and moral support against the tide of Protestant and Catholic missions. Two years later the American missionaries in Beirut succeeded in converting to Protestantism a section of the Orthodox population of the village of Ḥāṣbayya in south Lebanon. American missionary sources state that the Russian consul-general lodged a protest with the Ottoman governor of Damascus. 'We have the rights', he is reported to have said, 'of protecting the Greek [Orthodox] Church in the Ottoman dominions.'

To complicate an already complicated situation the old dispute between the Orthodox and the Catholic communities over their respective rights in the Holy Places in Palestine flared up again in 1847–8. According to the reports of the British consul in Jerusalem, there were serious skirmishes between the two parties inside the Holy Sepulchre, and the Ottoman governor of Jerusalem had to place over three hundred soldiers on guard inside and outside the sanctuary. In the Church of the Nativity actual hand-to-hand fighting took place in which a bishop was wounded. Crosses and candlesticks were used for weapons when monks fought monks. The occasion was the disappearance from the Church of the Nativity of the Latin silver star marking the traditional birthplace of Christ.

Russia and France were quickly involved in the dispute which ultimately led to the Crimean War. The claims which each of the two powers made in support of its right to intervene are obscured rather than clarified by the treaties, decrees and ministerial orders on which they are professedly based.

Reduced to its simplest form, the French case rests on capitulatory rights enshrined in the treaty of 1740. By virtue of this treaty French religious orders, who had been the custodians of the Holy Places, were given the privilege of repairing the fabric of these places. These privileges were in the course of time undermined by decrees and orders issued in favour of the Orthodox patriarch, during periods of Ottoman hostility to France or French indifference to religious affairs in the Near East.

Russia had no comparable claims. Its case rested on the limited stipulation of the Kainarja treaty of 1774. But this treaty gave Russia none of the rights she now claimed to protect the Orthodox Church and even the Orthodox population of the Ottoman Empire. Russian anxiety to clarify the position was however justified. It happened quite often that what the sultan granted by a decree or the Porte by an order was revocable. The Orthodox prescriptive right had just been reduced by these means.

In 1808 the Church of the Holy Sepulchre was destroyed by fire. On this and on subsequent occasions the Ottoman authorities allowed the Orthodox to rebuild the church. Either through fire or rebuilding or both much of the Latinity of the church which goes back to the days of the Crusades was lost.

The consolidation of the Orthodox position received a strong emphasis by increased Russian interest in the Holy Land. From the 1830s the number of Russian pilgrims and the amount of Russian cash contributions to the Confraternity of the Holy Sepulchre began to increase. After careful investigation, a Russian ecclesiastical mission was established in Jerusalem in 1847 with the revival of Orthodoxy as its general aim. Thus before mid-century there was, as well as the Anglican bishop and the Latin patriarch, a Russian archimandrite who was not invested with the dignity of bishop out of consideration for the Orthodox patriarch.

During this Orthodox ascendancy in the early nineteenth century, France seems to have forgotten the Holy Land, possibly as a result of the Revolution. In 1799 Napoleon was marching on Acre, and when he reached ar-Ramlah some thirty miles to the west of Jerusalem he did not so much as cast a glance in the direction of the Holy City. In the two or three decades after him the number of Latin or French pilgrims was smaller than that of the Orthodox. Revival of French interest in Syria and the Holy Land in the 1830s was largely due to missionaries and partly to poets and romantics like Lamartine and Chateaubriand. The crisis over the expulsion of Muḥammad ʿAli from Syria awakened the politicians to France's self-imposed task as protector of Catholics in the Levant, and this awakening was reflected in a sharp increase in French monks and nuns in the Catholic missionary establishments throughout Syria.

When the Catholic-Orthodox quarrel flared up in 1847–8 the Ottoman authorities appointed a committee of enquiry, representing all the communities concerned, to study the various claims and to submit a report. Following this enquiry the Porte granted a measure of redress to the Catholics. It had a disastrous effect in the Orthodox camp, but did not wholly satisfy the Catholics.

4

Immediate attention to these affairs in southern Syria was distracted by the revolutions of 1848 in Europe. Louis-Philippe was swept away and Louis Napoleon emerged eventually as the Emperor of the French. Tsar Nicholas I was firmly on his throne and hardly affected by the convulsions to the west of his empire. Both Nicholas I and Napoleon III became involved in the dispute over the Holy

Places and regarded its outcome as of great importance to personal and national prestige. Napoleon's aims were comparatively modest, consisting mainly of the restoration to the Catholics of their lapsed rights, but meanwhile insisting on the execution of what had been conceded. On the other hand, the Tsar sought not only the restoration of the *status quo* as it was before the latest Ottoman award which was somewhat favourable to the Catholics, but also its solemn guarantee in a treaty which would have the effect of placing the Orthodox church and the Orthodox population in the Ottoman Empire under Russian protection.

Each of the two emperors staged a warlike demonstration in order to intimidate the Porte. Great Britain, who had no direct interest in the Holy Places, was still pursuing the policy of maintaining the integrity and independence of the Ottoman Empire. Whatever happened in Palestine must not give either Russia or France a preponderant influence in Constantinople. Hence a British reply to increased Russian threats to the Porte was a naval demonstration just outside the Dardanelles. As a last resort the Tsar sent Prince Alexander Mentschikov to Istanbul as a special envoy to press the Russian demands. This bombastic soldier had had no training in diplomacy and his methods of negotiation were a mixture of open threats and secret offers of alliance. His mission failed. In July 1853 Russian troops crossed the Pruth, and in October the sultan declared war on Russia. Thus began what is known in history as the Crimean War.

How Great Britain and France entered the war on the side of the sultan is not of direct concern here. It is important, however, to point out the ascendancy which British diplomacy gained over the Ottoman conduct of affairs. But the indication of evidence of this ascendancy will largely be restricted to Syria in the decade preceding the outbreak of the Crimean War. During this period British consuls assumed considerable influence over provincial administration and over local affairs in general. They had direct access to governors; their subordinates, including native staff, supplied reports on local politics, religious quarrels and commercial activities.

More often than not native consular staff were Christians and Jews of Syrian or Levantine origin. They were seldom popular, for they tended to enrich themselves by dealings with commercial interests and to assume an air of superiority. In 1845 the interpreter of the British consulate in Beirut applied for confirmation in his post. He frankly wrote that without his consular appointment he feared the animosity of the local authorities and his own countrymen, for in the discharge of his duties, he says, he had to 'maintain a bearing towards them suitable to my functions'.

If British consuls dabbled in provincial affairs, the ambassador gained an overpowering influence over the sultan's ministers in Istanbul. Whether this informal British protectorate over the Ottoman Empire proceeded from a concern to preserve it as in the best interests of Great Britain, or from a genuine zeal for the prosecution and success of the reform movement, or from the ambitions of the persons concerned, is difficult to establish. What is clear from the diplomatic and other correspondence of the period is that practically all British diplomatists desired the sultan and his servants not to forget that Syria was restored to him largely through British diplomacy and arms and that gratitude was due and must be shown in yielding to British pressure. A few illustrations of British demands must suffice.

Richard Wood's meddling with provincial administration has already been mentioned. More than ten years after the events he claimed that while holding the office of British consul in Damascus he was

> likewise directed by the Turkish government to report on the state of Syria, and to assist its officers in the establishing of a regular form of administration, in regulating the system in the Lebanon, in proclaiming and establishing the *Tanzīmāt* and in fixing the taxes, etc.[9]

No trace of any document conferring such sweeping powers by the Porte on a foreign diplomatist could be found in the diplomatic and consular papers of the period, either in the Public Record Office in London or in the Ottoman Archives in Istanbul. The only evidence bearing on this subject is a report by Wood himself that in December, 1841 he received, through the governor of Damascus, a snuff box with the sultan's cipher on it, in recognition of his past services during the eviction of the Egyptians.

Be that as it may, the Ottoman governor of Damascus was removed from office in 1847, not because his government was dissatisfied with his administration, but because of adverse British consular reports. The British Embassy demanded the governor's removal with pressure exercised both on the sultan and the minister for foreign affairs. In the end not only was the pasha removed but the minister promised to consult the Embassy before providing the new pasha with instructions.

Equally serious was British consular influence in the appointment and dismissal of Muslim religious functionaries. In 1852 a Catholic mob attacked the new Protestant school in Nazareth and maltreated the missionaries. The British consul in Jerusalem went to investigate the incident. He seems to have acquired a reputation for effective intervention in the appointment and removal of Muslim religious functionaries. For although there was no charge that the *qāḍi* of Nazareth had a hand in the riot, the small Protestant community seems to have had another grievance against him. They seized this opportunity to petition the consul to secure the *qāḍi*'s removal.

In 1853 a mob attacked the newly established Protestant missionary school in Nābulus. The same consul held an enquiry, and in his opinion the *mufti* of the town was among the instigators. Accordingly he reported that he was recommending the removal of the 'fanatical' *mufti* and the appointment in his place of 'a good friend of the Protestants'.

More serious were the interventions of the ambassador Sir Stratford Canning, later well known as Viscount Stratford de Redcliffe. That part of his instructions directly bearing on the subject under discussion is twofold: render friendly advice to the Porte to act in the spirit of the Gülhané decree, and encourage no section of the Christian population to look for British support more than the other sections. The instructions as a whole were signed by Lord Aberdeen, then Foreign Secretary.

That was the official British policy; unofficially, however, Canning was overwhelmed by advice and demands. Not the least among the demands was one for a new Protestant church in Jerusalem which the Porte had for years persistently refused to sanction. Lord Shaftesbury, the patron of most Protestant missions, was at the head of a pressure group which sought the ambassador's assistance. Shaftesbury himself was satisfied that Canning went out 'in a high sentiment for the cause, politically and even religiously'.

From being the concern of a small missionary society the building of a church in Jerusalem had become a national concern. A memorial signed by the president of the society, and countersigned by the Archbishop of Canterbury, 137 peers and dukes, 1428 clergymen of all ranks and 14,083 citizens from all walks of life, was submitted to Aberdeen. This was the second memorial of its kind to be submitted to the Foreign Secretary three months after another equally representative one. In another three months Stratford Canning secured the sultan's approval. But the ingenious Ottoman bureaucracy wrote in the sultan's firman a 'consular chapel' not an 'independent church'. After further correspondence between the ambassador the grand vizier and the governor of Jerusalem the practical difficulty of adhering to the letter of the decree was resolved: the church and consulate, already in close proximity, were to be within an English enclosure protected by the consulate.

A curious interpretation of this diplomatic victory was made by the handful of new Protestant converts. They had already, and without official approval, been calling themselves 'English'. In a country where the people were accustomed to classify themselves on religious or sectarian lines, each sect identifying itself with a foreign protecting power, the new Protestants were accordingly called, nay they called themselves, 'the English party'. Contemporary sources leave no doubt that almost all Jews and Christian Arabs who became Protestant believed that they had also become English. Agents of English missionary societies did little to discourage this belief until they were forced to do so by consular advice.

Nevertheless the British ambassador was regarded by all Protestant missionaries in the Ottoman Empire, English, American and others, as their patron and protector. He unwittingly played into their hands by championing their cause on the question of apostasy though he may have been moved by humanitarian sentiments. The occasion for his intervention was that first an Armenian and later a Greek had each embraced Islam and had then apostatised and been executed. Although the executions were in both cases according to the law, such cases were by no means common.

Protestant missions were encouraged by the British ambassador's stand. They had been taunted for their conversion of other Christians and their lack of success among non-Christians, notably Muslims. They had two standard answers to this taunt. From long observation of the idolatrous practices of Eastern Christians, they explained, the Muslims had become contemptuous of Christianity itself and confirmed in the belief of the superiority of Islam. It was therefore necessary first to reform the Eastern Christians who in God's good time would seek to convert the Muslims. The other missionary answer was that in any case there was an insurmountable obstacle to the conversion of individual Muslims, since the punishment for apostasy was death under Islamic law and Ottoman legal practice.

It was precisely this law and practice that the British ambassador sought to change. Having failed to persuade other European envoys to make with him a joint attack on the Porte, he himself pursued the matter by the most undiplomatic means, including the threat to insist on the dismissal of the minister for foreign affairs who resisted the demand. Rif'at Pasha's reply to the threat was a protest that the ambassador's demand amounted to the abandonment of divine law. It was 'neither [a question] of policy nor of administration, but of religion'.

But the ambassador was convinced that to overcome the Porte's 'scruples' on this matter would promote the Ottoman moral and political standing. He pressed on the mild Aberdeen the idea that the sultan could dispense with the law as an act of state, and the 'dreaded' possibility that a British subject, not an Eastern Christian, might some time be involved. But the ambassador was either misinformed or trying to mislead – the sultan had no power to dispense with *religious* law, and Rif'at Pasha left no doubt that if called upon to make a public declaration the Porte had no option but to assert the supremacy of that law.

What was in the end obtained was one of those obscure Ottoman pronouncements which can mean different things to different people. It was an unsigned *note verbale* consisting of one sentence: The Porte undertakes not to execute the Christian who is an apostate. The words 'Islam' and 'Muslim' are carefully avoided in this sentence which is clearly concerned with the Christian who embraced Islam and then returned to Christianity. The British ambassador does not seem to have perceived that it did not cover the case of the Muslim who might have embraced Christianity. From a missionary point of view the concession was therefore useless. From a humanitarian point of view, its restriction to Christians vitiates its moral value. It says nothing, for example, about a converted Jew who apostatised.

Indeed, the British ambassador's concentration on Christians, and more particularly Protestant Christians, raises some doubts as to his wisdom in forcing a general ruling rather than pleading individual cases as they arose. Next to the church in Jerusalem and the question of apostasy, he was instrumental in forcing the Porte to recognise the native Protestants as a religious community in the Empire. In 1850, when recognition was given, the total number of the new Protestant *millet* was a few hundred, mostly in Armenia. In Syria there were only a few score of them, mostly in Lebanon and Palestine.

The recognition of the Protestants as an independent religious community was of great service to the missions in that it facilitated conversion. A Jew or an Eastern Christian who became Protestant could now afford to ignore religious excommunication and social ostracism. The mission church provided him with a spiritual shelter, the mission often found him employment, and the local head of the community gave him civil and legal protection.

Any foreign intervention in fundamental religious beliefs and practices was bound to cause resentment and reaction, and in the end defeat its purpose. As will be shown later on, this was the ultimate outcome of what the British ambassador had temporarily achieved. It is idle to speculate, but the ambassador might have served his country, the Porte and the cause of humanity better had he adhered to his instructions and insisted on the enforcement of the Gülhané decree for the benefit of *all* Ottoman subjects. For the beginning of his embassy had coincided with the eclipse of Rashīd and the virtual shelving of the decree.

5

It is true that the Gülhané decree was shelved, but it was not really abandoned. There were indeed formidable obstacles to its enforcement, both internal and external. Ottoman public opinion, in so far as it was expressed by the ulema and conservative elements, was against it. The very administrative machinery of the

Empire was still too primitive to supervise its orderly application.

The liberal revolts of 1848 in Europe had little or no echo in Russia and only a temporary effect in Austria. The sultan's autocratic neighbour to the east remained suspicious of the possible repercussions of Ottoman reforms on his empire. The sultan's other autocratic neighbour to the west withdrew in 1849 a liberal constitution granted less than a year earlier. On both sides of his dominions the sultan was not in strange company. European convulsions and the reactionary regimes at their doorstep reinforced the opposition of Ottoman conservatives to the Gülhané decree. The sultan himself is reported to have had second thoughts.

But despite all difficulties and misgivings some beginning was made in the spirit of the imperial decree. The foundations had actually been laid by Maḥmūd who had proclaimed his desire to see equality between all his subjects and to eradicate abuses in administration and taxation. It was he who created a judicial council through which all new codes were to pass. After the proclamation of the Gülhané decree selected non-Muslims were invited to serve on this council. In 1840 a penal code (*qānūn*) was passed confirming the Gülhané on the equality of *all* Ottoman subjects before the law. Under a commercial code tribunals were later formed to deal with matters affecting foreigners, and therefore non-Muslims were represented on them.

Like the Gülhané decree itself all the new codes and measures that proceeded from it were issued as instructions to the provinces. How many of these were enforced in Syria and how many of them remained pious pronouncements on paper is a question whose answer is not to be found in the form of any conspicuous results, for none were to be found perhaps anywhere in the Empire. The results were indeed very small, but they were symbolic and as such significant. In 1846 the British consul-general in Beirut went out of his way to emphasise that following Shakīb's pacification of Lebanon the Christian population had the privilege, enjoyed nowhere in the Ottoman Empire, of having their evidence accepted by tribunals.[10]

The Porte's earnestness is shown by the new practice, common since the end of Egyptian rule, of sending to the Syrian provinces the most able and experienced of its pashas, some of whom had been grand viziers or rose to that rank later on. In the first place, the country had various communities with conflicting interests and was by no means easy to govern; in the second place it had several and increasing European interests, religious, cultural and commercial. The interested powers, Great Britain, France and Russia, matched the Porte's action by sending as diplomatic representatives to Syria men of great ability and experience, some of whom rose later to very high ranks.

But the Crimean War, like all wars between the Ottoman Empire and any Christian power, created conditions both favourable and unfavourable to progress. As allies who came to the aid of the sultan, Great Britain and France used their good offices with his government to honour the solemn promises of the Gülhané decree. But as regards its Christian subjects, the Porte was then in a dilemma: they wished to favour Catholic and Protestant interests, but, with an eye on the peace that was ultimately to come, they did not wish to undermine the cause of the Orthodox over which Russia went to war. According to the Anglican bishop in Jerusalem the war contributed to soften Muslim prejudice, to rouse the anxiety of the Orthodox clergy and laity and to elate the Catholics 'to an intolerable degree'.

Nor was it easy, despite official pronouncements, to proceed with measures calculated to ameliorate the status of Christians (and Jews) in general. For on the outbreak of the war with Russia, public excitement throughout the Ottoman Empire was great. In Jerusalem, for example, there was anxiety lest native Christians be exposed to attack. The British consul had in mind the standard remedy of the time when he suggested that the presence of an English or French warship in Palestinian waters would prevent disorder. It was, however, Muslim notables who prevented disorder. They knew that although the sultan was fighting Russian Christians, English and French Christians were fighting with him. 'The more ignorant', wrote the same consul, 'were pleased at the ready obedience of the English and French to the sultan's orders'.[11]

This story may be spurious, but in commenting on the same subject an American missionary journal published in Boston struck a characteristic note in a front page editorial:

> Britain and her ancient rival forgot their traditional enmity in their desire to rescue a Mohammedan state from its Christian

invader. What a spectacle have we seen within the last few weeks! . . . Once it was 'the Cross against the Crescent'. Now it is the Cross shielding the Crescent from the Cross. . . .[12]

It was for such considerations that the Porte was not insensible to the dangers of communal disturbances in Jerusalem or anywhere. Thus following the formal declaration of war on Russia, a firman was publicly read by the governor of Jerusalem which assured the Christian subjects of liberal treatment and protection. It was now even more expedient to impress the two allies, and to make safeguards in order to defeat the ambitions of the enemy. Apathy was abandoned and Ottoman policy began to show a trend towards reviving and even reinforcing the Gülhané decree.

A supreme council for the application of the *Tanzīmāt* was established under 'Āli Pasha. But he and other Ottoman ministers had now summoned enough moral courage to resist English and French representations on behalf of the Christian subjects of the sultan and to insist on their master's sovereign prerogative to be the sole guardian of the welfare of all his subjects. Ottoman ministers were, however, open to friendly suggestions if they fulfilled this condition. They had in fact co-operated with the British, French and Austrian envoys on the draft of a new decree confirming and enlarging the liberties granted by that of Gülhané, in preparation for the peace conference.

For following the fall of Sevastopol to the allies a conference was convened at Paris. But before it met, the sultan issued the decree known as the *Hatti Humāyūn* on 18 February 1856. It reiterated the equality of all Ottoman subjects, reaffirmed their security of person, property and honour, confirmed the privileges and immunities granted to all Christian and other non-Muslim communities, guaranteed freedom of belief and worship to all sects irrespective of numbers of adherents, opened the civil service and the army to non-Muslims, confirmed mixed councils and mixed tribunals, and promised gradual substitution of direct taxation to tax-farming.

Representatives of the powers assembled in Paris expressed their great satisfaction with the decree officially communicated to them by the Ottoman delegation. The powers signified this satisfaction by writing into the peace treaty: (1) the admittance of the Sublime

Porte to that discordant system called 'the Concert of Europe', (2) the guarantee of the independence and territorial integrity of the Ottoman Empire, (3) the reference of any future dispute between the Porte and one or more of the signatories to the Concert for mediation before any resort to arms, and (4) that the terms of the *Hatti Humāyūn* precluded any right of the powers, either collectively or separately, to interfere between the sultan and his subjects or in the internal administration of his empire.

Simultaneously a treaty was signed by Great Britain, France and Austria guaranteeing the independence and integrity of the Ottoman Empire, and undertaking to consider any infraction of the terms of the peace treaty as *casus belli*. The Paris conference was thus a marked victory for the sultan and an equally marked defeat for the Tsar. It must have been due to 'Āli's skill and foresight that the peace treaty included safeguards against his allies as well as against the enemy. Great Britain and France had now solemnly renounced any right to interfere on behalf of the Christians or to dictate to Ottoman provincial officials.

Meanwhile the new imperial decree was circularised to the provinces including those in Syria. Its reception was on the whole just as unfavourable as that accorded to its forerunner. Muslims and non-Muslims alike found objections to one or other of its provisions. Thus Christian and Jewish ecclesiastical authorities resented the reduction of their power and material gain by the stipulation requiring each community on the one hand to reform its internal organisation in consultation with the Porte, and on the other to abolish all dues hitherto collected by these authorities and to assign fixed salaries to ecclesiastics according to rank.

Lay Christians and Jews in general were equally dissatisfied. They and their European mentors wished to remove the humiliating implication of having to pay the poll-tax. The tax was considered at the time to be in lieu of military service to which only Muslims were subject. Equality of rights entailed equality in bearing the burden of duties to the state. It transpired that what non-Muslims wanted was prosperity without risks, privileges without responsibilities. They resisted the notion of military service, and availed themselves of obtaining exemption by payment of a tax, and ended by paying the poll-tax under another name and by another method.

As for Muslim reaction to the new imperial decree, one or two illustrations must suffice. News of the issue of the decree reached Jerusalem before the decree itself. It was the practice, before giving effect to such an important document to have it read publicly by the governor in the presence of notables, dignitaries and foreign consuls. But the Anglican bishop did not wait for this ceremony. He proceeded at once to Nābulus, had a new bell hung on the school building, which served also as the Protestant mission house, and had the bell rung loud and clear.

Two days later the birth of the Prince Imperial of France was celebrated in Nābulus by the hoisting of French and English flags on the French and English consular agencies in the city. Now by an ancient custom no foreign flags were allowed to be hoisted and no church bells pealed in this predominantly Muslim city. Public indignation was mounting when by a coincidence an English missionary passed through the city on horseback and armed with a gun. At the gates he was beset by a beggar, and either the gun was accidentally discharged or the Englishman lost his nerve and fired it, and the beggar was instantly killed.

The riot that followed was a climax of mounting provocation. The missionary was arrested pending trial. But the bell and flags were dragged down, the English mission house wrecked and the houses of the handful of Protestants sacked. A Syrian Christian who had studied medicine in London and had been appointed British consul in Jaffa by Palmerston reported on the riot. In his opinion it was due 'to the roused anger of the Muslims in consequence of the Christians taking their liberty by virtue of the late firman of reform . . . the Muslim population of this country are not favourable to the new order of things. . . .'[13]

Eventually the decree arrived in Jerusalem and was ceremonially proclaimed by none other than the future Ottoman statesman, Kāmil Pasha. According to the same consul resentment was great at Gaza when the decree was read in Arabic. The annual report of the Church Missionary Society states that the decree provoked 'fanaticism and violence'. Despondency among the Muslim population was heightened by the news of heavy casualties. For the first time since the end of Egyptian rule, the Ottoman ministry of war could enforce effective conscription in Syria. According to the wife of the British consul in Jerusalem, villages were drained of able-bodied men some of whom were marched off manacled like criminals.[14]

To cite more evidence is rather unnecessary. But here is a story which may be taken to represent Christian and Muslim feelings alike. When the Metropolitan of Ismid heard the 1856 decree read and then saw it replaced, in accordance with protocol, in its envelope of crimson satin, he exclaimed: 'Pray God it may remain there.'

5

The Civil War and its Aftermath

I

In 1837 Sultan Maḥmūd was called *giaour padishah* (infidel sultan) to his face by a bold dervish in a public place in Istanbul. In 1856 'Abdul-Majīd was condemned in his absence by his Muslim subjects in Jerusalem as *khā'in* (betrayer of trust). The son even more than the father introduced innovations repugnant and incomprehensible to the majority of his subjects, Turks and Arabs alike. That part of the *Tanzīmāt* which had been applied in Syria created new tensions among the communities and, in the long run, destroyed the established social equilibrium which regulated their relations.

Twenty years of the new order were enough to show the Muslims that it was primarily for the benefit of the non-Muslim minorities. Apart from membership of advisory and administrative councils, non-Muslims had acquired the right of equality with Muslims before the law. The new obligation of military service they could escape by the legal means of paying for exemption. Furthermore, they could, according to a new procedure, repair old places of worship and establish new ones where their numbers justified it. Lastly they could establish community schools subject to some control over the curriculum and the appointment of teachers by a mixed education council. Restrictions concerning dress and mounts were forgotten without need for legal provisions. All these improvements in the civil, social and religious conditions of the Christians and Jews contributed to an increase in their material and educational conditions.

But it is noteworthy how little attention was shown by Europeans who championed the cause of Christians to the fact that the sultan had other and more numerous non-Christian subjects in Syria. It is true that the Jewish minority was sometimes grudgingly mentioned along with Christians, but little or no concern was shown for the Muslim majority. If the Ottoman system was according to European standards oppressive, it was indiscriminate in application, and the relatively heavier burden was borne by the Muslims: they paid the greater part of the taxes and they alone were the cannon fodder, with consequent social and economic losses. Unlike Christians and Jews, the Muslim had no recourse to consuls of the Christian powers with just and unjust complaints and claims. Small wonder if they felt betrayed and frustrated by their rulers and angered and humiliated by foreign influence.

Signs of discontent and unrest were visible all over Syria just before the end of the Crimean War and immediately after it. Unrest and discontent were manifested in different forms, but it would be rash to assume direct connection in every case with the order of affairs proclaimed in the sultan's decree. It would not, however, be sheer speculation to assume some connection between the decree and some of the disturbances before the major eruptions in 1860.

For five years before 1860, the country was seized by sporadic convulsions from one end to the other. In Palestine a new eruption of the old Qais and Yemen feud, in the Nuṣairiyyah region another bloody revolt against the government; in the city of Aleppo tension between Muslims and Christians which very nearly led to violence when a native Catholic stood up in the bazaar fully armed and 'loudly called on the Christians to attack the Mussulmans':[1] while in the city of Damascus similar tension was mounting, for in their impotent rage against foreign Christians the Muslims vented their ill-feeling on native Christians.

News from other parts of the Empire, all telling the same story of Christians rising against Muslim rule and of the sultan yielding to Christian pressure and compromising Islamic principles, tended to aggravate an already grave situation. The serious troubles in Crete and with Montenegro were bad enough, but they aroused public indignation less than the bombardment of Jiddah, the port of Mecca, by a British warship, following a riot in which the British and French consuls were murdered. There is evidence that in both Aleppo and Damascus the news created great consternation.

The outbreak of a peasant revolt in 1857 in a Maronite district of north Lebanon is of a different order. The peasants, supported by the clergy who were themselves of peasant stock, rose against their feudal lords. The sultan's decree is specifically quoted in their demands which included equality before the law, representation on the district council and equitable distribution of the burden of taxes. Soon to be led by the semi-literate Ṭānyus Shāhīn, the peasants actually drove out of the district the Khāzin shaikhs and seized and shared their property. The peasants continued in virtual control till the general Lebanese settlement in 1861.

The most serious of all civil disturbances was, however, the third Druze–Maronite war which broke out in 1860, although it had long been in the making. Native chroniclers possess that rare gift of tracing major and tragic events to trivial and comic origins. Just as the first war in 1841 began with a Maronite shooting a partridge on a Druze property, so the 1860 war began with a quarrel between a Druze driving pack-animals and a Christian driving another pack in the opposite direction (or was it a quarrel between a Druze boy and a Maronite boy?).

There were of course deeper causes for the conflict. Occasional reference has been made in the preceding chapters to the factors that cumulatively contributed to its climax in war. From the final disruption of the alliance between Bashīr Shihāb and foremost Druze chief, Bashīr Janbalāṭ, symbolised by the murder of the latter in Acre prison at the instigation of the former, ultimate conflict was inevitable, especially since the Maronites continued to gain in numbers, power and wealth at the expense of the Druzes. Besides, Druzes never forgot that the Maronites had taken up arms against them in the pashas' armies.

Bit by bit the stoking of the furnace of war continued. The Egyptians left the Maronites with their arms almost intact. The arms liberally distributed in 1840 by British agents were never recovered. While a measure of disarmament was enforced by the Egyptians on the Druzes in Lebanon, those in Ḥawrān were never effectively disarmed. Thousands of Druzes who had been enlisted in the Egyptian army returned without arms, but with modern military training. Immediately after the first clash in 1841, Druzes and Maronites began to rearm. The quantity of arms that cleared the customs in Beirut in the three years preceding the war in 1860 was estimated at over a hundred thousand rifles, excluding large quantities of revolvers. The shooting of a partridge or the collision of two pack-animals or the quarrel of two boys could have been no more than a spark that set ablaze this pile of explosive material.

Most of the accounts of the war were written by Lebanese Christians or by other Christians in sympathy with them. In these accounts the Druzes and the Ottoman authorities are almost always condemned unheard: the former as murderous aggressors, the latter as connivers and even participants. Some accounts even accuse the 'British government' of being the accomplice of the Druzes. While it is no part of this history to sit in judgement on any of the parties concerned, a brief account of the opening phase of the war is indispensable.

Several weeks before the outbreak, predominantly Christian villages witnessed what amounted to a mobilisation: in every village or group of villages a small unit of men was formed under an officer; the men were put in some sort of uniform and provided with arms if they did not possess them already. These small units with their officers were placed under the orders of a higher commanding officer. Some of the units were allowed to march with their arms from one village to the other calling for the extermination of the Druzes. The Maronite bishop of Beirut himself organised such an armed group in the city. Wealthy Maronites vied with one another in contributing money towards the purchase of arms.

Nor did the Druzes remain idle, but unlike the Christians they made their plans in secret. Discipline and solidarity were among their qualities which had stood well the test of wars against Ottoman and Egyptian pashas. The seasoned fighters in Ḥawrān were valuable reserves, while those trained in the Egyptian army were to serve in the front line. Nevertheless the prospect was grim: at best the Druzes could muster a maximum of twelve thousand men to the advertised Christian figure of fifty thousand.

Before fighting broke out Druzes and Christians in mixed villages began to leave their homes and remove their modest belongings to safer neighbourhoods. This movement exposed a considerable number of people from both sides to attacks followed by counter-attacks in which men were robbed or killed, and property was stolen or set on fire. The gathering storm broke in the last week of May 1860 at 'Ain Dārā in the Druze district where the first battle was fought with 'regular' forces. Here a Druze force of a few hundred repulsed and routed a Christian force five times greater in number.

What happened in the next three weeks or so has often been told with varying degrees of objectivity; it need not be retold here. Suffice it merely to quote, on this first phase of the war, from some contemporary reports by foreign observers.

On 24 May 1860 the British consul in Beirut wrote that hopes for peace were fading and that 'large bodies of armed men, Christian and Druze, are assembling at different points preparing for the conflict which indeed is said to have already commenced near Andara ['Ain Dārā]'. On 30 May he wrote: 'Civil war has just broken out in Mt. Lebanon between Christians and Druzes. The villages, Christian and Druze, within view of Beirut are at this moment in flames. . . . The Pasha has proceeded with a detachment of troops and irregulars to the Mountain.'[2]

More colourful, if less objective, is a report dated 1 June 1860 written by an American missionary then living in Beirut:

> Civil war has actually commenced in all its fury. The Druzes and Maronites have plunged into deadly strife. . . . The war has been actually raging some four days, and during this brief period, thirty or forty villages have been burned, the country laid waste, an immense amount of property destroyed, and men, women and children butchered. . . . The whole district of the Matn, directly east of Beirut, is in desolation. The Druzes, who are a race of warriors, have driven the Maronites before them nearly as far as the Dog River, and their track is marked by smoking villages and desolation in every form. Hitherto, in the wars of the Druzes and Maronites, women and children have been spared, but now no one is spared. . . . In view of the fact the Greek [*sic*] and the papal ecclesiastics have been stirring up their people to a war of *extermination* agianst the Druzes, it would seem as though the reverses and defeats are a just punishment. . . .[3]

2

Various accusations ranging from conspiracy with the Druzes to personal hatred of Christians have been levelled against Khurshīd Pasha, the governor of Sidon. These accusations have never been judiciously investigated by an historian. While this is not the place to go into great details, some unknown or hitherto unused evidence is offered below as a contribution towards a revision of current views based on little more than suspicion. Early in May 1860, the British consul in Beirut sent his native dragoman to Khurshīd to request help for those Khāzin notables humiliated by peasants. Khurshīd's reply, faithfully reported by the dragoman, is as follows:

> . . . He has been long trying to induce his government and the serasker [commander-in-chief] at Damascus to put at his disposal a military force for the coercion of the Kisrawanites. . . . But His Excellency stated that no troops can be spared for that service, that his government is withdrawing almost all the troops from the pashalik of Damascus to Constantinople and that the serasker has applied to him, Khurshīd Pasha, to send to Damascus a battalion of troops from the very limited garrison of Beirut which request H.E. refused to comply with. Khurshīd Pasha said that under these circumstances order cannot be maintained in this pashalik, and that he never before governed a district without a sufficient military force to carry out his orders, and that therefore his position has become very degrading to his government and to himself. He said he is weary of his present position and that he had sent his report to the Porte explaining at length the state of the pashalik and offering his resignation, as he finds it more creditable to leave the country in its actual state than in a worse one. H.E. finished by desiring me to convey officially the above to you with a request that you will have the goodness to report the same to Her Majesty's ambassador at the Porte.[4]

Nine days later the British consul reported that Khurshīd had sent a detachment of irregulars to the Druze district and 400 regulars to the Christian village of Dair al-Qamar. A few days later still, Khurshīd sent his chief clerk to the consul to convey the pasha's opinion that responsibility for the disorders lay with the Maronite bishop of Beirut and the committee working under him. On 30 May the pasha himself proceeded with regular and irregular troops and placed himself between the Druzes and the Maronites on the Beirut–Damascus road.

From that strategic position he intimidated or persuaded the victorious Druzes not to carry the war to north Lebanon. Likewise he turned back a token force under Ṭānyus Shāhīn which was all the Maronite north could muster to help fellow Christians in the south. Failing enough military forces to occupy villages in all the troubled areas, Khurshīd seems to have done the next best thing: a show of strength in one Druze stronghold and in one Christian stronghold, then the placing of his main troops between the combatants and call for peace. But hardly had both sides agreed to sign the peace agreement Khurshīd proposed, when the city of Damascus fell victim to mob frenzy on 9 July and the following four days.

In the Druze–Maronite civil war many atrocities were perpetrated and thousands of innocent lives were lost apart from great destruction of property. In Damascus the Christian population was attacked by bands of villains and thousands were massacred in cold blood, their property looted or destroyed. The Damascus mob was largely Damascene Muslim but included Druzes, Matawilah, Kurds, beduins and others.

As the British consular report quoted at length above clearly shows, the governor of Damascus had even fewer troops than his colleague Khurshīd. This report from Beirut is amply confirmed by another from Damascus itself. In May the British consul wrote that 'there are very few troops here, the greater portion having been recalled to Constantinople. Our pasha is therefore powerless.' Despite this the pasha increased the guards in the Christian quarter at the beginning of June, according to the same consul.

The governor, Aḥmad Pasha, held the military rank of *mushīr* (field-marshal) and had a distinguished record in the Crimean War. He and the commander-in-chief must have felt even more than the less senior Khurshīd the humiliation of having to maintain law and order without adequate forces. Consular reports indicate that they had to rely upon irregulars and local militia, an embarrassing necessity to professional soldiers. However, Aḥmad is blamed in these reports for 'inaction' and 'loss of nerve', but not for any dishonourable 'contrivance'. Here again his case awaits judicious scrutiny.

The Damascus carnage might have been even worse had not prominent Muslim notables risen to the occasion, not only by checking the mob but also by protecting and giving shelter to as many Christians as they could. The Algerian Amīr 'Abdul-Qādir with his retainers took a leading part in restoring order and saving the lives of many Christians. The efforts of this noble knight were seconded by those of Maḥmūd Ḥamzah, Salīm 'Aṭṭār and others.

Doctor Mīkhā'īl Mishāqa, the distinguished native Protestant convert, was in 1860 United States vice-consul in Damascus. Here is his report of his treatment at the hands of the Matawilah:

> They attacked our house and looted all they could find in it. . . . I was hit on the head by an axe. . . . But then one of my friends, al-Hāj Muḥammad al-Suṭari, came with some Algerians and rescued me and took me to his house: bare-footed, bare-headed and [almost as] naked as God had created me. He also brought my family, and has since been keeping us. Some Muslims sent us clothes and money.[5]

Such acts of humanity shine the brighter in contrast with the dark barbarism of mob violence and greed. Much more has been written on the latter than the former, and very little on the origins of the outbreak. The fact that the Jews in Damascus escaped unharmed calls into question a current view that the Muslims were animated by a spirit of fanaticism against non-Muslims in general. What probably saved the Jews was that they offered less provocation and showed less signs of gaining new influence by foreign intervention.

Colonel Charles Henry Churchill, who lived in Lebanon at the time, wrote that, encouraged by the French consul-general, the Christians irritated the Ottoman authorities and the Muslim population in general by their haughty and arrogant conduct and by their 'sense of self complacent security and even superiority'.[6] Writing some sixty years later, the President of the Arab Academy says that Muslim resentment at the sultan's decree of 1856 was the root cause of the trouble in Damascus. He adds that dissatisfaction with Ottoman rule had increased so much since the decree that some Damascenes opened unsuccessful negotiations with Cairo with a view to restoring Egyptian rule. 'The Christians in this country, especially in Lebanon', he wrote, 'have since the Crimean War assumed airs of superiority.'[7]

But as already pointed out the war in Lebanon had somewhat different causes. There is little connection between it and the massacre in Damascus. It is, however, on record that Druze agitators from Lebanon and Ḥawrān went round to Damascus and other places in Syria inciting Muslims against Christians. 'We have done our part of the job', they are reported to have said, 'when are you going to do yours?' In the smaller cities, where notables had stronger control over the people, the agitation, whether of local or Druze origin, did not lead to violence. Even so the war in Lebanon and the massacre in Damascus engendered a feeling of insecurity among the Christians everywhere in Syria. 'We had to go through the same ordeal of danger and panic', wrote an English missionary commenting on the arrival of refugees from Lebanon in Nazareth.

3

With the signing of the peace terms proposed by the Ottoman governor, the Druze–Maronite war came to a formal end, and by controlling the mob violence in Damascus the carnage was terminated. In Lebanon and in Damascus law and order had been restored, but immense problems of restitution were created. These problems were tackled on three levels in Beirut, Istanbul and the chancelleries of Europe.

In Beirut the consuls were inhibited in the political field by the terms of the 1856 Treaty of Paris. But the city was inundated with refugees whose relief was an urgent necessity. It was a mark of their divided counsels that instead of forming a joint relief committee the consuls formed two: the one under the chairmanship of the British consul and the other under the French consul; the former acted through American missionaries and native Protestants and the other through Catholic missionaries and native Catholics. Muslim notables, including ʿAbdullah Bayhum and Muḥammad Barbīr, had already organised relief for the refugees from the mountains while the war was still raging.

In Istanbul the sultan appointed Fuād Pasha, minister for foreign affairs, as extraordinary commissioner and sent him in a frigate with military reinforcements to deal with the Syrian crisis on the spot. He arrived after the war in Lebanon had ended in a peace treaty and Damascus had been rid of lawlessness.

In the chancelleries of Europe there was meanwhile great activity. Napoleon III was for immediate intervention, but the Porte and Great Britain feared possible French designs of annexation or the proclamation of a protectorate. In the end general agreement was reached in the form of a solemn declaration that no territorial or other advantages were to be sought by intervention. This was embodied in a protocol signed in Paris on 3 August 1860, which provided for not more than twelve thousand European troops to be sent to Syria 'to contribute to the restoration of tranquillity'. France sent half that number. The other powers sent no troops, but together with France undertook to maintain certain naval units on the Syrian coast. The officer commanding the French troops was, in accordance with the protocol, to co-operate with Fuād in Syria.

Since his arrival in Syria Fuād had worked feverishly to forestall active European intervention. What he and the other Ottoman ministers feared most was the danger of foreign troops in Damascus. After a brief stop at Beirut, where he assured the Christians of protection and ordered the immediate distribution among them of relief from government funds and stores, he hurried to Damascus. He had been invested by the sultan with unlimited powers, and he used them ruthlessly and arbitrarily, often with little regard to the due processes of the law. Hardly anyone accused by foreign or local Christians escaped summary and speedy punishment.

By Fuād's orders over a hundred regular and irregular soldiers including three officers were shot, some fifty civilians hanged, a number of notables banished, a collective fine of £200,000 imposed on the city (plus £160,000 inexplicably on the province), and all eligible men in Damascus were immediately enlisted in the army. Much of the looted property was recovered and restored. Homeless Christians were put in Muslim houses or public buildings, and relief in the form of money and provisions was distributed from government funds and stores. A committee to assess damage and award compensation was set up. 'Abdul-Qādir was decorated. But the governor, Aḥmad Pasha, was secretly executed, only to be acclaimed by his men as well as by Syrians as *shahīd* (martyr). The appellation is still attached to his name in history books. There is no evidence that he was tried by any civil or military court. At any rate there were no soldiers equal or senior to him in rank who could have formed a court martial.

Fuād's expediency was clearly calculated to gain political advantages. He had a full month to settle in his own way the affairs of Damascus before the French expedition landed in Beirut. He himself returned to Beirut to deal with the Druzes and Maronites, to agree with the French officer commanding the expeditionary force on the employment of its officers and men, and soon to preside over an international commission, with representatives of Great Britain, France, Russia, Austria and Prussia, which was set up to investigate the disturbances and to recommend a new administrative system for Lebanon.

By his return to Beirut, Fuād's fury had been spent. His measures here bore little resemblance to those he adopted in Damascus. Khurshīd and three of his senior subordinates were first placed under arrest, but later transferred outside Syria. The district officer in the Druze district was replaced by an Ottoman official; the officer in the Maronite district by the temporary appointment of Yūsuf Karam. Of the Druze chiefs who did not flee to Ḥawrān, about a dozen, including the foremost chief Sa'īd Janbalāṭ, were tried and sentenced to death, the sentences being later commuted to life imprisonment. Several scores of lesser Druze notables were banished from Syria. Then Fuād charged a committee of Christians to submit names of Druze offenders. But when those Druzes whose names were listed appeared before a special tribunal, no Christian, not even the members of the committee that prepared the lists, came forward as a witness.

In all these proceedings no Christian was punished. This is another example of Fuād's expedient action or rather inaction. But beneath the surface he did not in fact regard the Christians in Lebanon in the same light as those in Damascus. In this he was supported by Lord Dufferin, the British member of the international commission. Dufferin thought it was wrong to describe the war in Lebanon as an aggression against innocent Christians.

The French expedition proved far less of a menace than was first feared. After encamping for some time near Beirut with nothing to do, the officers and men were moved to the devastated Christian villages in the Druze district, where they had to 'beat their swords into plough-shares and their spears into pruning-hooks'. Their occupation was relief, helping villagers to rebuild their homes and their farms. No reparations were exacted from the Druzes, but Fuād promised that the Porte would bear the cost of rehabilitation and reconstruction.

Fuād's main task was completed in less than two months; seven were required for the international commission to produce its report. On its basis the Porte, with the diplomatic respresentatives of the five powers concerned, formulated in Istanbul the *Règlement organique* for Lebanon which was signed on 9 June 1861. Four days earlier the French expedition left Lebanon.

Under the *Règlement*, Mount Lebanon was to be administered by a Christian district governor (*mutaṣarrif*), appointed by the Sublime Porte, in consultation with the signatories and, like a governor of a province, directly responsible to the Sublime Porte. There is, contrary to popular belief, no provision for autonomy, and the word itself does not occur in the statute. There is, on the contrary, a clear provision in article fourteen that the administration of Lebanon was to be like that of any other district (*sanjaq*) in the Ottoman Empire.

Thus in accordance with the administrative practice established in Syria after 1840, the governor was to be assisted by a council representing all the communities. But feudal privileges were specifically abolished and equality before the law was guaranteed. Provision was made for mixed courts and for a local mixed police force (except that for a time the Beirut–Damascus road and Sidon–Tripoli road were to remain under the control of imperial troops, and that more troops could be called in by the governor in case of emergency). The annual tribute of 3500 purses (about £15,000), which could be doubled when circumstances permitted, was to be spent on the administration and public services, the surplus going to, and deficit made good by, the imperial treasury. The first governor was the Armenian Catholic, Dāwūd Pasha, who possessed wide experience in the Ottoman diplomatic and civil service.

Apart from causing an appalling loss of life and the destruction of the homes and means of livelihood of several thousands, the disturbances in Syria brought about an immediate stagnation in trade and a considerable loss of income through the decrease in the number of pilgrims and foreign visitors. Of the less tangible and more lasting ill-effects, the most serious was the rise of a new spirit of religious antagonism among the native communities, the sharpening of a feeling of hatred among the Muslims towards Europeans, and the beginning of signs of Arab Muslim discontent with the Ottoman Turks. These are some of the results of the policy of reorganisation begun in 1839.

Seldom has alien innovation been forced upon a traditional way of life without causing a strain both in the institutions and the human society concerned. In their attempt to reshape their Islamic tradition after a European image, Ottoman statesmen had in two decades introduced enough innovations to create such a strain. In Syria the strain resulted in the various explosions described above. Encouraged by official pronouncements, some native Christians, with European support, sought to abolish centuries of history in a decade or two. Little were they aware that even in Europe religious equality was not then universal. Not before 1829 were the native English Roman Catholics emancipated in Great Britain; not before 1858 could native English Jews sit in Parliament.

And yet it was European encouragement and instigation which pushed some native Syrian Christians to extremes. They were encouraged to combine communal autonomy and the new right of equality with insistence on virtually complete exemption from duties to the state. It was a striving towards a status not dissimilar to that enjoyed by European Christians under the Capitulations. The more organised and modernised the Ottoman system became the more it was expected to make concessions calculated to free Ottoman subjects from their obligations. Even laws introduced according to European models were irksome. Before these laws were introduced the Ottoman system was condemned as chaotic and oppressive, after their introduction it was assailed as intolerant and fanatical. Native officials of an English missionary society were forbidden to serve on local administrative councils to save them from the risk of 'loss of spiritual life.'

After 1856 Christians in Syria could with good reason look forward to an improved status and lighter burdens, the Muslims to a diminished status and increasing burdens. It was a process of levelling up for the minority, levelling down for the majority. The two imperial decrees of 1839 and 1856 embodied noble principles of social justice, but even their partial application brought about social unrest and contributed to disorders and caused bloodshed. Even so the process of change was now irreversible. It could be slowed down, but it could neither be stopped nor abandoned. The men of the *Tanzīmāt* had in a generation become truly like the crow of the fable who tried to imitate the walk of the grouse only to find that his legs became crooked and that he was unable either to learn the new walk or resume his own.

Such was the predicament which was seemingly solved by a pretence of maintaining two parallel systems, officially in harmony but actually in deadly conflict. Nowhere was the divorce between theory and practice more pronounced than in the two important departments of education and justice. It was Maḥmūd II who began the duality in education, continued and extended by his successor ʿAbdul-Majīd, but it was the latter who created definite duality in the laws of the Empire and the courts that applied them.

Maḥmūd began the establishment of schools modelled on European patterns parallel to the traditional Islamic schools. The new schools were intended to train officers for the sultan's new army and officials for his new centralised administration. In some of the new schools European teachers were employed and French was taught, both for the first time. A ministry of public instruction was created under ʿAbdul-Majīd in 1847 to administer the new system of education. From then until the issue of the education law in 1869, a fully-fledged new school system was established. Though intended to supplement the traditional system it began henceforth to undermine and finally to supplant it.

The province of Islamic law suffered a similar invasion. It began immediately after the Gülhané decree when a new penal code and later a commercial code and other laws were promulgated. They resulted in the establishment of civil courts, outwardly parallel to the Islamic courts, but in reality diminishing their jurisdiction. The models for the new laws were, like the models for the new schools, European. In both cases the new system was established at the expense of the old.

In Syria the application of the new systems was felt first in the legal and then in the educational field. Mixed courts and commercial tribunals made their appearance before the state began to establish new schools beside the old. Perhaps the earliest of the new schools in Syria was the *Rushdiyyah* established in the city of Aleppo about 1861. Aleppo was nearer than any large Arab city to the Turkish areas where the new measures were first applied, and a good number of Turks, or Turkish-speakers, were among its inhabitants. In the following years more state schools were established in Damascus, Beirut, Tripoli, Jerusalem and elsewhere. But the movement did not get into its stride till the 1880s.

4

The dawn of a brighter day began to break in Syria after the dark night of 1860. Pacification was slowly followed by reconstruction and reconciliation in Damascus and Lebanon. The signing of the statute regulating the administration of Lebanon was one of the last acts of ʿAbdul-Majīd's reign. He died a few days later and was succeeded by his brother ʿAbdul-ʿAzīz. Compared to his predecessor, the new sultan was reactionary, but it was too late even for him to reverse the trend towards modernisation by decree or otherwise.

Its signs in Syria became increasingly apparent. In 1862 a lighthouse was erected at the harbour in Beirut. Two years later a landing place and a lighthouse were constructed at Jaffa. Almost simultaneously work began on the construction of the Alexandretta–Aleppo, Beirut–Damascus and Jaffa–Jerusalem carriage roads, which had hitherto been little better than earth tracks. These major ports and large cities were in the early 1860s connected by telegraph with Istanbul and Europe. According to reports from Jerusalem, published in an English missionary annual, steamers of two English lines called at Jaffa monthly, in addition to French and other steamers, and a postal service to Europe was available at the French consulate in Jerusalem three times a month at 8*d* per quarter ounce.[8]

A history of Aleppo by a native Aleppine contains vivid details, rare in works of its kind, of similar developments and how they were received by the different classes of people in the city. The first novelty the author mentions is the rolled cigarette which began to replace the pipe. Until then Aleppo craftsmen made elegant pipes for tobacco smokers and those made for the rich were three cubits long, with mouthpieces studded with precious stones. Another novelty was the use of kerosene and lamps instead of olive oil and wicks. At first the people thought the smell of burnt kerosene harmful to the chest and the brighter light of the lamp bad for the eyes.

When work on the Alexandretta–Aleppo road began, the authorities required villages to contribute four days' labour per able-bodied man and to plant fruit and other trees on both sides of the road. The governor of Aleppo at the time was none other than Jawdat Pasha, the famous Ottoman historian and jurist. He had the main streets of the city paved, the heaps of rubbish near the citadel cleared and a public garden planted on the site. The postal service between the city and Alexandretta which had been in the hands of the French consulate was now taken over by the government.[9]

In 1875 Beirut was supplied with water from Nar al-Kalb (the Dog River). According to reports from the city published in a missionary annual, branch roads to connect with the three main highways from the coast to the interior were under construction in 1868. Garrisons were placed in newly constructed forts or old castles on the highways or in strategic places, especially in the interior along a line running from the Dead Sea to Palmyra. English engineers were then investigating on the spot the possibility of a railway from Tripoli to the Euphrates valley and Baghdad as an overland link between the Mediterranean and India.[10]

The improvement in communications rendered centralised administration a more practical proposition. Increased security on the roads revived trade and encouraged more pilgrims and travellers to come to the country. The garrisoned forts on the borders of the desert were intended to reduce the danger of beduin raids or to induce beduins to adopt a more settled life.

A measure of success was scored in the north-eastern corner of Syria. Here force and persuasion were employed to form a special beduin district based on the mean village of Dair az-Zūr. One of the methods employed is noteworthy. Wealthy shaikhs from different tribes were kept under arrest in the village until each had a stone house built for himself. But taking the measure as a form of taxation, shaikhs quickly returned to their camps as soon as the houses were erected. In 1871 troops had to be used to suppress a beduin attempt to get rid of the new government administrative offices and all the measures they represented.

Taming the beduins was one of the aims of the new administrative measures. In 1864 the Vilayet law was promulgated, and Syria was divided into two large provinces, Aleppo and Damascus. The first extended well into Anatolia but gained no territory in the south. The second resumed its control over its former dependencies, Tripoli and Sidon (or Acre) and henceforth became more known as the province of Sūriyya (Syria). As we have seen, Lebanon was in 1861 detached from the province of Sidon and constituted as a special district. A similar treatment was now accorded to Dair az-Zūr. It became the second special district in Syria, and its governor, like that of Lebanon, was directly responsible to Istanbul. In the former district it was the religion of the majority of the population, in the latter their nomadic character which decided the special treatment.

At last the Ottoman authorities began to perceive the futility of punitive expeditions against beduins who raided merchant caravans or carried away the farmers' cattle and produce. But without abandoning such measures, the authorities began to try others as well. Settlement on the land, enlistment in the army and participation in local government were among the inducements now used to civilise the nomads. They met with very little success. However, the improvement in communications placed more and more of the country under direct government control, and ultimately the nomads were at least contained, though still virtually beyond reach.

The peasants, on the contrary, were now almost completely tamed. They submitted to conscription and paid the taxes with but little violent resistance. Conscription had, since the end of Egyptian rule, become a regular imposition, accepted just as was the payment of taxes. British consular reports regarded the taxes as 'light as compared with most European countries', not more than 10 per cent on agricultural produce. This produce was still, in quantity and quality, much the same as it had been a generation or two before. The Syrian farmer had not in the meantime improved his methods of cultivation.

What was crippling for the farmers was not the burden of taxation, but the ruinous rate of interest charged by city moneylenders. It is therefore a sorry spectacle indeed to find the efforts of a newer type of Ottoman governor towards freeing the peasants from the yoke of moneylenders being frustrated by a British consul. In 1862 the governor of Damascus revived an old firman and instituted a commission to examine the account books of moneylenders and to reduce the rate of interest, which was at times as high as 4 per cent per month, to 8–12 per cent per annum. The consul wrote to the ambassador requesting him to obtain an early ministerial order to exempt British subjects and protégés (native Christians and Jews) from this measure. In a meeting which the governor had with all the consuls of the powers on this subject, the French consul, perhaps mischievously, suggested that the governor's duty was to apply the sultan's firman. The British consul replied that the high rates were 'accepted by custom' and that the firman was disobeyed by local authorities. To the ambassador he disclosed the fact that 'the claims of British subjects and protégés on the villagers amount[ed] to more than the claims of all the other nationalities put together.'[11]

Next to the moneylender the peasant's worst enemy was the beduin. Surprise raids in the harvest season discouraged large-scale cultivation of land away from the immediate neighbourhood of populated villages. Hence much fertile soil was left uncultivated, for neither small farmers nor absentee landlords were willing to risk the loss of livestock and crop. Although they did their best to protect the farmers from beduin raids, and even from money-lenders, the Ottoman authorities were less enterprising than the Egyptians had been in promoting agriculture. After the Egyptians there was little or no attempt to exploit the forests, mines and fisheries.

Native crafts, much more than agriculture, were undergoing change, largely on account of the importation of cheap machine-made goods and partly because of the dislocation of the civil war. Native industries were even less taxed than agricultural products, only 8 per cent on raw material or manufactured articles. But as elsewhere in the world, the handloom proved a poor competitor with the mill. In the summer of 1860 most of the cotton looms in Damascus stopped working. Many of the master weavers were Christians, and those who survived the massacre moved to Beirut.

Trade suffered more general dislocation, and the dislocation was aggravated by the American civil war and the Austro-Prussian war which caused a general rise in prices. In 1863 the American consul in Beirut reported that 'machinery for the washing and pressing of wool has been placed here to advantage by a Boston firm which deals in Syrian wool'. But apart from this, American trade with Syria was at a standstill. In 1866 the American missionaries reported the disastrous effects of the war in Europe on Syria: 'Many of the Beirut merchants became bankrupt; such a scarcity of money had not been known before'.

European mercantile houses that had supplied the Syrian market with goods and credits were alarmed by the civil war and stopped practically all dealings with the country. But native Syrians who had settled in London, Manchester, Liverpool and Marseilles took advantage of the withdrawal of Europeans. They began to forward goods on their own account to their partners and relations in Syria. In this manner much of the import trade passed from foreign to native hands.

The export trade was hardly affected. While the silk crop of 1860 was practically lost through the war in Lebanon, merchants still found it profitable to export wool, sesame oil, gall nuts and wheat. In the circumstance of diminished international confidence in the Syrian market, export was the most practical and profitable means of remitting money to Europe. But the pacification of the country, the improvement in internal security and communications, the end of the wars in America and Europe, and the opening of the Suez Canal all contributed to the restoration of confidence.

Another important factor in restoring confidence and promoting general progress was the improvement in the quality of Ottoman governors. Reference has already been made to the concern shown by the governor of Damascus for the welfare of the farmers and by that of Aleppo for general civic development. Two other pashas are praised by British consuls, something very rare in the preceding decades. Kāmil, who served as governor in Jerusalem, Beirut and Aleppo after the 1856 decree, was described by one consul as 'an upright, intelligent, educated and energetic public servant'. Of Rashīd, who held the post of governor in Damascus for the unusually long period of five years, the British consul-general wrote in 1871: 'within my knowledge no governor general has left Syria so sincerely regretted by all classes'.

By 1871 governors had a more elaborate administrative machinery to serve them. In addition to the old secretarial and financial departments, there was now a department of police as distinct from the army. A whole Ottoman army formed the garrison of Syria under a commander-in-chief based on Damascus. Seldom in peacetime had the post of civil governor been combined with that of commander-in-chief, even when the governor happened to have held high military rank. Division of functions is further to be seen in the creation in the capital of every province of a new council (*dīwān*) for judicial affairs side by side with the original council which continued to be concerned with administrative affairs. The governor was the *ex officio* chairman, with Muslim and non-Muslim official members. The same pattern was followed in the capitals of districts except that a council was here called *majlis*.

Apparently commercial tribunals did not give full satisfaction to demanding foreigners. Take for example the tribunal in Aleppo which in 1871 had four Muslim members including the chairman, four native Christians and four Europeans. The British consul complained of its 'inefficiency' and, despite a clear Christian majority, complained that Islamic law was a great hindrance to its operation.[12] The truth is that from the Crimean era onwards, British consuls in Syria began to show a prejudice against the ulema as a class. They favoured their replacement on provincial and district councils and commercial tribunals by business men who, it was assumed, would be more pliable.

Most of the ulema at the time came from influential and wealthy families. It was not practicable to deprive them of their prestige in the community, for whether appointment to positions of responsibility was by selection or election they were bound to secure most of the vacancies. This proved the case when under the amended *vilayet* law municipal councils were established in the larger cities soon after the issue of the law of municipal election in 1875. The majority of members in such cities as Aleppo, Damascus, Tripoli and Jerusalem turned out to be of the ulema class.

5

In the decades following the civil war, Syria experienced a great educational and literary movement which had been gathering momentum for a generation or two. Unfortunately both the character and the forces that contributed to the rise of the movement have long been obscured by partisan or uncritical presentation. By some writers the rise and development of the movement is ascribed exclusively to Protestant or more particularly American missionary effort; by others to Catholic missions, by most to Christians to the exclusion of Muslims, but by none to a combination of native development and foreign efforts. Very few indeed recognise that the influence of foreign missions was confined to the Christian minorities to the exclusion of the Muslim majority. A section of a chapter is not adequate for the removal of such misconceptions and the establishment of all the facts. But a minimum of the relevant facts is indispensable for a correct understanding of the intellectual life in Syria during the coming decades.

Syria was not a country rescued from the fetters of ignorance by foreign missions. Native Christian schools existed before the arrival of the foreigners who for decades in the nineteenth century did little more than build on native foundations and with native personnel. Nor was the printing press first introduced by the Americans and Jesuits, for native convent presses were already in existence and employed, like the foreign presses in their early history, for the production of religious literature.

Traditional Muslim schools were beyond foreign Christian influence. They were in due course either modernised or superseded by modern schools established by a Muslim state. As to the printing press, Arabic books were printed in Istanbul from the beginning of the nineteenth century. From 1820 more Arabic books were printed in Cairo at the Būlāq press established by Muḥammad ʿAli. During the Egyptian occupation of Syria, much of the product of this press was circulated to all classes of readers in Syria.

While most of the product of the Cairo press was acceptable to all Syrian Arabs, Christians and Muslims alike, the product of the American and Jesuit presses remained till the last quarter of the nineteenth century religious or even sectarian in character, and hence not universally acceptable to all Christians, let alone Muslims. It is only when missionary presses began to produce scientific and literary works that their usefulness became more widespread. But clearly they were not pioneers. In certain departments they were actually overtaken and outstripped by native development.

In the late 1850s, when both the American and Jesuit presses were still engrossed with purely religious literature, native Syrians began the introduction of the 'secular' printing press. They printed school books, trade and official circulars, literary works and newspapers. The press established by Khalīl al-Khūri in Beirut in 1857 is noteworthy, because from it he issued in the following year *Ḥadīqat al-Akhbār*, 'a civil, scientific, commercial and historical journal', the first of its kind in Syria. Other presses and journals followed in quick succession, private and official, Christian and Muslim.

But this is not to belittle the American or Jesuit contributions to the educational and literary revival in Syria. The purpose of the discussion is to relate these contributions to facts. Without therefore extending the discussion to other foreign missions, a glance at American and Jesuit work must suffice for our purpose.

About the middle of the nineteenth century the Americans had some 500 pupils, including 150 girls, in seventeen primary village schools taught by as many native Syrian teachers. There was also a higher boarding school with a dozen boys established at ʿAbeih in 1846 and a less stable girls' school with ten pupils in Beirut. The boys were taught more systematically than the girls in general subjects with strong emphasis on the Bible, by native and American teachers through the medium of Arabic. English was not taught except to individual pupils selected for future employment by the mission.

At approximately the same time Catholic missions had at least five times as many pupils in their schools as had the Americans. The Capuchins, Lazarists, Franciscans, Jesuits and Sisters of Charity covered the country from Aleppo to Jerusalem and from Damascus to Beirut. Not only were primary schools for boys and girls established but also higher boarding schools at important centres. For example, the Capuchins had such a school at ʿAbeih, close to the Americans, the Lazarists another at ʿAntoura and the Franciscans another at Ḥarīṣa, and the Sisters of Charity several schools all over the country. More important for the future than all these schools was the Jesuit school at Ghazīr, established in 1844. Apart from Arabic and general subjects, all these schools taught at least one foreign language: French, Italian or Turkish.

In Beirut and on Mount Lebanon the Americans soon felt the competition very strongly, not only because of Catholic superiority in resources and personnel but also because of the marked difference in curricula. In particular the teaching of foreign languages was a great attraction in Jesuit schools and its lack a deterrrent in American schools. Even sons of native Protestants who had been taught in primary schools controlled by the Americans began to enrol in Jesuit higher schools. Their parents wished them to prepare for professional careers or for business, and foreign languages were an indispensable preparation in the growing importance of Beirut and its neighbourhood.

By the order of their superiors in Boston, the Americans were debarred from teaching foreign languages, even English. This was one of the considerations which led the American mission in Beirut to seek the establishment of a Protestant high school independent of Boston's control. The result was the establishment in 1866 of the Syrian Protestant College, now the American University of Beirut. In 1875 the Jesuit school at Ghazīr, which meanwhile became a fully-fledged seminary, was transferred to Beirut as the Jesuit College, later known as the Université Saint-Joseph.

The difference between the two institutions was more than sectarian. The Protestant College emphasised its missionary character, and for some time taught literary subjects and medicine through the medium of Arabic. The Jesuit College also emphasised its missionary character, taught all subjects through the medium of French, but gradually developed a department of Arabic studies with first-rate scholars. There was little or no contact between the two institutions which viewed each other with belligerent jealousy.

Associated with each of the two colleges was a mission press for printing in Arabic. The American one came to Beirut in 1834, and specialised in the production of missionary literature and a few school books. Its greatest undertaking was the printing of a new Arabic translation of the Bible. After the establishment of the Protestant College a few textbooks, mostly on science and medicine, were printed. There is no evidence of the printing, under American or Jesuit auspices, of any of the Arabic classics; there is under native auspices. Thus in 1860, Buṭrus al-Bustāni edited the *Dīwān* containing al-Mutanabbi's collected poems and had it printed at Khalīl al-Khūri's press. One of the earliest books published by Yūsuf Sarkīs's press established in 1876 was the *Prolegomena* to Ibn Khaldūn's famous history.

Neither the American nor the Catholic press was as yet interested in such classics. The Catholic press was established in 1848 and performed functions for the Catholic mission and the Jesuit College not dissimilar to those performed by the American press for the American mission and the Protestant College. It is a mark of the antagonism between the two sides that their respective presses engaged in printing their polemics. Some of the Catholic polemics were against the Protestant translation of the Bible. This was a preliminary to taking positive action. In 1876 the printing of a new Catholic translation of the Bible began. Just as the Americans employed Buṭrus al-Bustāni to assist them in their translation, the Jesuits employed Khalīl al-Yāziji to assist in theirs. According to its introduction, the Catholic translation sought to counteract 'the omissions and distortions' perpetuated by the Protestant 'heretics'.

It must be acknowledged that both sides contributed to the sharpening of controversy and the increasing of sectarian division, to the neglect of constructive tasks. Thus up to the proclamation of the Ottoman constitution in 1876 neither Americans nor Jesuits made significant contributions to the Arabic language and culture, still less to the history of Islamic civilisation. By then Cairo had printed al-Ghazāli's *Iḥyā'*, al-Aṣfahāni's *Aghāni*, al-Maidāni's *Amthāl*, and al-Maqrīzi's *Khiṭaṭ*, to name only four of the standard classics.

But the Americans were at this stage more instrumental than the Jesuits in the development, by native writers under their influence, of a new Arabic style suitable for textbook exposition and newspaper reporting. The first generation of these writers was educated in native schools. American influence over their literary output was more by way of creating a demand for it in their schools than by actually providing the models. It is important to distinguish between this generation represented by men like Buṭrus al-Bustāni and the next represented by men like Ya'qūb Ṣarrūf.

The new style emerged gradually, and was to start with simple, almost semi-colloquial language. Small wonder that it was frowned upon by the purists, Christians as well as Muslims. It was unacceptable to them partly because of genuine concern for classical standards and partly because of the purists' ignorance of foreign languages. Take as example the two contemporaries, Buṭrus al-Bustāni, the Maronite convert to Protestantism, and Nāṣīf al-Yāziji, the Greek Catholic linguist. Both helped in the American translation of the Bible, the first actively because of his knowledge of languages, the second only to eliminate linguistic and grammatical mistakes because he knew only Arabic. At a lower level Yāziji could produce only grammar textbooks for schools; at a higher level philological works, ornate prose according to classical models, and some conventional poetry. Bustāni's product was more varied: it included simple textbooks in Arabic grammar and arithmetic, a simplified Arabic dictionary, an encylopedia of general knowledge, and three journals. The contrast between their works is great, both in content and literary style.

Taking into consideration the above facts concerning education and the printing press, the claim made by Protestant missionaries, and propagated by their Lebanese Christian admirers, that the missionaries were instrumental in the 'rediscovery' of the Arabic literary heritage, is untenable. The heritage was of course never lost, and anyhow those who claim to have 'rediscovered' it can never specifically point out any Arabic classics they have revived, edited, printed, or at least taught in their institutions.

This fantastic claim gained wide currency through uncritical quoting and requoting, and was reinforced by another not less extravagant assertion that the literary revival was almost entirely due to the effort of Lebanese Christians. To say this is to disregard entirely the prior revival in Egypt. There is no need to cite distinguished names in Egyptian literary history in the first half of the nineteenth century. Syria could boast of no equal, neither Christian nor Muslim, to Ḥasan al-ʿAṭṭār or ʿAbdu'r-Raḥmān al-Jabarti. But limiting the discussion to Syria itself, it is astonishing how outstanding Muslim literary figures are neglected. Writers who seem to have never heard of Aḥmad al-Barbīr (d. 1811), ʿUmar al-Bakri al Yāfi (d. 1818) and Amīn al-Jundi (d. 1841) lose no opportunity to remind us of the mediocre Nicola at-Turk (d. 1825), 'the court poet' of Bashīr Shihāb.

Muslim scholars and men of letters of the next generation do not fare better at the hands of writers who seldom mention any scholar without emphasising some foreign connection, no matter how trivial. Thus Maḥmūd Ḥamzah (d. 1887) is more remembered as the recipient from Napoleon III of a gilded gun in recognition of help rendered to the Christians of Damascus in 1860 than as the jurisconsult of the city, an author of several works including an exegesis of the Koran, a member of the provincial council, and chairman of the provincial education council.

Then Yūsuf al-Asīr (d. 1889), who was instrumental in 'the diffusion of Arabic and Islamic sciences amongst the Christians in Beirut and Lebanon'[13] is accused by some reckless writers of having fallen under the influence of American missionaries simply because, for generous fees, he polished their Arabic translations of the Bible and other works. He had already held a high post in the ministry of education in Istanbul and taught Arabic at the higher training college in the capital before returning to Syria and settling in Beirut where he devoted himself to teaching and study. He wrote on jurisprudence and published a volume of his poems.

Ibrāhīm al-Aḥdab (d. 1890) was even more prolific as a poet and author of books on grammar, rhetoric and literature. He edited for some time with 'Abdul-Qādir al-Qabbāni the newspaper *Thamarāt al-Funūn*, established in 1874, and was elected member of the new education council for Beirut. While Ḥusain Bayhum (d. 1881) is well known as a merchant, high Ottoman official, and member of the first Ottoman parliament, little is known of his reputation in the literary field both as a poet and a patron of learning. He became president of the Syrian Scientific Society after the death of its first president.

Such men, jurists, linguists, poets and educationists, were the guardians of Arabic and Islamic tradition, and the transmitters of culture and promoters of learning in general. Their time can boast of only three figures of similar stature among the Christian Arabs, namely Fāris Shidyāq, Buṭrus al-Bustāni and Nāṣīf al-Yāziji. The first, born Maronite and converted to Protestantism, outwitted both the American and English missionaries. After working for them as translator and editor, he embraced Islam and finally settled in Istanbul where he established in 1860 the newspaper *al-Jawā'ib*. His works are linguistic in substance, but while engaged in journalism he edited at least three classical texts.

Bustāni, too, was disenchanted with the American missionaries, but there is no evidence that he renounced the Protestant faith. After close collaboration he followed an independent line, established an interdenominational school on patriotic lines (*waṭaniyya*), wrote books acceptable to all communities, and wholeheartedly supported the Ottoman system.[14] But neither Shidyāq nor Bustāni was educated at a foreign institution. They both received their education at the Maronite seminary of 'Ain Warqa. Yāziji was even more native in education and tastes. He was just as fanatic an upholder of classical standards as any Muslim scholar of his time, for his learning was entirely derived from, and based upon, the classics. He had studied and memorised the Koran, in addition to great quantities of poetry.

Enough has been said above to dispel the double misconception that foreign missions in Syria 'rediscovered' the Arabic heritage and that Lebanese Christians made more contributions towards the literary revival than Christians and Muslims in the rest of Syria and even in Egypt. There is no concrete evidence to support either contention for the period ending with the proclamation of the Ottoman constitution in 1876.

6

Divided Loyalties: Ottoman, Muslim, Christian and Arab

I

REFORM or reorganisation in the Ottoman Empire had always been conceived by the ministers concerned as acts of favour by a sovereign solicitous of the welfare of the state and his subjects and not as deliberate steps towards limiting the powers of an absolute despot. Indeed, men like ʿĀli and Fuād, who presided over the application of reform after Rashīd, were convinced that the sultan's subjects were unfit for the exercise of representative government in the European sense. Nevertheless they continued to introduce what they thought was conducive if not to a representative, at least to a better government.

By 1871 both Fuād and ʿĀli were dead. Within the next five years the Empire was shaken by internal and external crises. Extravagant sultans, the cost of the Crimean War and a chaotic fiscal policy landed the state in foreign debts. The financial difficulties had become so grave that the imperial treasury was forced to repudiate half the interest on the public debt. At the same time unrest in the Balkans was followed by Ottoman repression which in turn created a danger of European intervention.

Ottoman liberals, who had been critical of the extravagance at the palace, the autocratic ways of the reformers and the inefficiency in the administration, now feared the consequences of active European intervention and sought to forestall it by the standard modern Ottoman remedy: more measures towards a greater resemblance to Europe. They rallied round Midḥat Pasha, a disciple of ʿĀli and Fuād, but with more positive convictions on the efficacy of constitutional government. Midḥat, together with powerful allies, played a major part in the deposition of the extravagant ʿAbdul-ʿAzīz. Some three months later the new sultan himself had also to be deposed on account of mental derangement and his brother installed as ʿAbdul-Ḥamīd II.

Though the two depositions of 1876 were both backed by a legalisation from *Shaikh al-Islam*, the initial decision on both occasions was taken by ministers. The lesson was never lost on ʿAbdul-Ḥamīd. If he had any leanings towards despotism he took some time before he showed his hand. To start with he was careful to honour a promise he made before his accession to grant a constitution, the draft of which was shown to him by Midḥat, who was soon appointed grand vizier. With much pomp and ceremony the constitution was proclaimed on 23 December 1876, as a command from the sultan to Midḥat. It reaffirmed the principles of previous decrees and promised to all Ottoman subjects of all communities liberty (*ḥurriyat*), justice (*ʿadālat*) and equality (*musāwāt*).

The proclamation was timed to coincide with the opening of a conference of the European powers in Istanbul on the Balkan question. When salvoes of artillery fire were heard in the conference hall while the head of the Ottoman delegation was delivering the opening speech he made a dramatic pause to inform puzzled delegates that the Empire had at that moment received a new constitution. But it would be a mistake to regard the proclamation of the constitution as a mere device for the gratification of European taste, or simply designed to gain political or diplomatic scores. For it was, above all, a culmination of the long process of grafting Western upon Islamic ideas of the state and sovereignty. Apart from the decrees of 1839 and 1856, its principles were propagated by a group of publicists and intellectuals known as the Young Ottomans.

In the constitution sovereignty was still vested in the sultan, who was caliph, protector of Islam and enforcer of the provisions of the sacred law (*sharīʿah*). He rendered account for his actions to none, and his ministers, including the grand vizier, held office at his pleasure. The constitution provided for a general assembly composed of an appointed senate and an elected chamber of deputies. In the first session of the chamber of deputies, Syria was represented by nine men: four (three Muslim Arabs and one

Christian Armenian) from the province of Aleppo, four (two Muslim Arabs and two Christian Arabs) from the province of Sūriyya (the old province of Damascus), and one Muslim Arab from the district of Jerusalem.

The deputies came from well-known families. Among the Muslims there were Nāfiʿ Jābiri (Aleppo), Khālid Atāsi (Ḥimṣ), Ḥusain Bayhum (Beirut), and Yūsuf Ḍiya Khālidi (Jerusalem). Among the Christians there was the Maronite Nicola Naqqāsh (Beirut) and the Orthodox Naufal Naufal (Tripoli). They all distinguished themselves, and Jābiri and Khālidi in particular made most favourable impressions on foreign observers by their integrity and courage. Jābiri made history by being the first deputy to question ministers, and his questions were concerned with the budget and the poor performance of the navy in the war with Russia which began in April 1877, barely five weeks after the opening of parliament. Khālidi was even more intrepid in challenging the unconstitutional appointment by the sultan, and not by the chamber, of its speaker.

Jābiri and Khālidi, together with a few other Arab and Turkish deputies, formed what might be considered as the opposition. But the Syrian deputies do not appear to have formed any bloc, Syrian, Arab or Muslim. Little or nothing of the affairs of Syria was raised by them. When, however, an amendment was moved by a Greek deputy to delete from the law governing provincial administration the provision for *muftis* to sit as members of provincial and district councils, two prominent Syrian Muslim deputies rose to defend the practice. This occasion was perhaps the first in Ottoman history where official defence, nay justification, of Islamic practices had to be offered to newly emancipated non-Muslim subjects.

Bayhum argued that attendance of shaikhs, *qāḍis* and *muftis* was by virtue of their character as representatives of the *sharīʿah*, not merely as religious leaders. Religious leaders including Christians were anyhow called in whenever a matter affecting their religion was under consideration. Jābiri added that *muftis* were elected by the people in their locality and not appointed by any authority in Istanbul and hence must not be deprived of their representative character. On the other hand, Khālidi is reported to have supported, among measures of economy, the cessation of the payment by the state of the salaries of mosque *imams* and *khatibs*.

The chamber as a whole proved more independent and less subservient to the executive than was expected. Members showed themselves jealous of their new rights and responsibilities and perhaps overzealous in demanding from the Porte full information on a variety of subjects including the delicate peace negotiations with Russia. Though the chamber acted strictly in accordance with the constitution, some deputies appear to have given unnecessary provocation not only to the Porte but also at a critical moment in Russo-Ottoman relations to a sultan not yet accustomed to the new order. At a special council held at the palace to consider the crisis, attended by ministers, dignitaries and a few deputies, a Turkish deputy from Istanbul rather rudely addressed the sultan.

An already irritated ʿAbdul-Ḥamīd now became angry. Henceforth, he declared there and then, he would govern like his grandfather Maḥmūd through royal prerogative and not as intended by his father ʿAbdul-Majīd through liberal institutions. True to his word, on the next day, 14 February 1878, he prorogued the second session of the chamber of deputies *sine die*, some eleven months after its inauguration. Midḥat had already been dismissed, even before the first meeting of parliament. For the next thirty years the chamber remained technically prorogued, and the constitution the law of the land, though the sultan was as autocratic as any of his ancestors had been.

Immediately after prorogation the police served notice on the ten deputies who had been outspoken critics of the government and of the sultan, to leave the capital forthwith.[1] The ten included Jābiri and Khālidi as well as two new Syrian deputies elected for the second session of the chamber, ʿAbdur-Raḥmān Badrān and Khalīl Ghānim. A fifth non-Arab deputy from Aleppo was also among the ten thus disgraced. Their protests were to no avail; without ceremony they were put on board a ship and sent to their homes.

2

Barely two weeks after the dissolution of the chamber, the Porte signed humiliating peace terms with Russia at San Stefano. But once more the Ottoman Empire was rescued by British intervention. Great Britain, who had recently purchased the Khedive's share in the Suez Canal Company, was more than ever suspicious of any increase of Russian influence in the eastern Mediterranean. Russia's acquisition, under the peace terms, of considerable Ottoman territory in north-east Anatolia was regarded as a prelude to a drive to the Syrian coast at Alexandretta. Accordingly Russia was told that the peace settlement was the concern of all the major powers and not only of the two belligerents.

The peace treaty of July 1878 hammered out at the Congress of Berlin saved the Ottoman Empire, but the Empire emerged from it with a reduced international status. Apart from loss of territory in Europe and Asia, the Porte was demoted from the position of an equal under the Paris Treaty of 1856 to that of an inferior and even suspect. While the new treaty paid lip service to the Porte's spontaneous declarations on religious liberty and reforms, it specified in detail what was to be done. With regard to provinces inhabited by Armenians, the reforms were to be introduced 'without further delay', the Porte to inform the powers periodically of progress and they to 'superintend' the application of reforms. Though Syria is not specifically mentioned, the province of Aleppo, which extended well into Anatolia and had a considerable Armenian population, was involved.

But all of this was better than the treaty of San Stefano, which assigned to Russia considerable territory in north-east Anatolia and left Constantinople itself threatened by Russian occupation. British intelligence then predicted a possible uprising against the sultan in the capital, and friend and foe reckoned the Ottoman Empire was about to collapse. Under these circumstances, Great Britain began to search for a strategic base in the eastern Mediterranean both as a check against Russian ambitions and a protection of its sea communications through the Suez Canal. As will presently be shown, Syria figured prominently in this preliminary search, but in the end Cyprus was chosen as likely to arouse the least jealousy and as conveniently near Asia Minor and Syria.

'Propose to the sultan', began the instructions to the British ambassador who was to offer British military support against further Russian attack in Asia in return for British occupation and administration of Cyprus. 'Press immediate acceptance with all the energy in your power', the ambassador was told. He was to say that it was necessary to exercise 'vigilance over Syria and Asia Minor . . . [and] to frustrate attempts to excite rebellion' in both areas, and that the presence of British troops in Cyprus would 'strengthen the sultan's authority in Syria . . .'.[2]

A harassed sultan had no hesitation in accepting the British offer, formalised in a convention only a few days before the Congress of Berlin. When the terms of the convention became known, it was suspected that Great Britain intended to place the Asiatic provinces of the Ottoman Empire under a protectorate. These suspicions were reinforced when it transpired that Great Britain was the only power who chose to exercise the right of superintending the application of reforms. The Marquis of Salisbury lost no time in appointing an inspector-general of reforms for Asia Minor and special military consuls to obtain first-hand information on the spot.

Before the Cyprus convention or the Treaty of Berlin was signed, while the fate of the Ottoman Empire hung in the balance and the San Stefano agreement was still in force, the proposal of a British occupation of Syria was secretly under consideration. Two confidential political reports dealt with the matter in an adroit and forceful manner. One report dwells on Syrian and especially Muslim discontent with Ottoman rule and on a general Syrian feeling that, after acquiring major shares in the Suez Canal, Great Britain was on the way to occupying Egypt. According to this report the Syrian desire to be annexed by Egypt was strengthened by the expectation of falling under British rule and deriving therefrom the same benefits as derived by the Muslims in India. The report contained this cancelled passage: 'Should the course of events render expedient for H.M. Govt. to act in the same sense as the wishes of the Syrian population and were they to occupy Syria with a military force, it is my impression that they would be received by the population with open arms.'

The second report confirms the conclusions of the first. Provided no enemy other than Ottoman troops is encountered, the occupation of Syria could be effected without difficulty and without opposition from the Syrians. Only a small occupation force would be required, and for internal security a local militia of 20,000 could be raised with ease. But 'if H.M. Govt. contemplates eventually an occupation of

Syria I suggest that one or even two small vessels of war should be sent to the [Syrian] coast'.[3]

Just as the possibility of a British occupation of Syria was conceived as a check against Russian expansion, so the choice of Cyprus was prompted by a desire not to provoke Russia and probably also France by an immediate occupation of Syria. But this country did not cease to excite British interest. In 1879 Sir Henry Layard, the British ambassador at Constantinople, made a pompous tour of the country. He arrived on board H.M.S. *Antelope* and visited among other places Jaffa, Jerusalem, Beirut and Damascus. His reception everywhere was little less than that reserved for royalty. Everywhere the civil, military and religious authorities, Muslim and Christian, turned out to welcome him. He was obviously more than a traveller, for he inquired into the operation of the administration, listened to reports on governors and even complaints against the Porte.

The governor of the province of Syria was then none other than Midḥat Pasha, the former grand vizier. He too spared no effort to impress the ambassador and to fill his ears with complaints against the Porte and the Palace. A general impression was created by the visit that it prepared the way for a British protectorate. The Druzes and the small native Protestant community, and even some American missionaries, were convinced that the proclamation of a protectorate was impending. The ambassador lent colour to such speculations by ignoring the advice of the governor of Lebanon, and visiting the Druzes at al-Mukhtāra, the seat of the Jānbalāṭ chiefs. This fact, and their traditional leaning to France, accounted for the cool reception the Maronites showed to the ambassador.[4]

3

Midḥat Pasha was not new to the province when at the end of October 1878 the sultan commanded him to take up the post of governor. His son and biographer states, but gives no dates, that his father had served for two years as a civil servant in Damascus (this was probably just before 1849) and later as a commissioner to investigate administrative and financial problems in the provinces of Aleppo and Damascus (and this was probably soon after 1851).[5] Since then he had held various senior posts and proved remarkably successful as governor of the Danube province and to a lesser degree as governor of the province of Baghdad.

Scarcely had Midḥat completed the first year in Syria when he submitted his resignation on account of 'physical and mental fatigue and old age' (he was then only fifty-seven). He begged the sultan to allow him to live in retirement in Constantinople or 'in some habitable district of the Syrian coast'. 'Abdul-Ḥamīd had reason to be suspicious. He refused to accept the resignation and began to ask his former grand vizier very serious questions. He even invited him to communicate directly with the palace.

Midḥat's reply was full of complaints but contained no recommendations. He described as disorderly the administrative machine in the province, the population on the coast as under foreign influence and in the interior as disaffected because of the manner of the application of reforms. He further pointed out that while responsibility for security was the governor's it was actually in the hands of the commander-in-chief in the province.

These points were elaborated and supplemented in communications to the grand vizier. Midḥat referred to the rivalry between England and France and their respective protection of the Druzes and Maronites, to the schools established by American missionaries for the Nuṣairiyyah, to the German immigrants and their new colonies in Palestine and to other foreign enterprise as producing 'the very worst effect on the country'. Having done nothing to change these conditions, the central government was obliged, because of the war with Russia, to ask for more men and money from Syria, only to increase the discontent of the people. Corruption in the civil service was rife, security was in a sorry state, and the turbulent Druzes in Ḥawrān were again giving trouble. The introduction of paper currency had the effect of reducing the revenue to one half, and army depredations made matters worse. These chaotic conditions might be exploited by the interested powers to impose foreign supervisors on the country.

There was a measure of truth in all of Midḥat's points, but he purposely exaggerated them. He apparently could not forget that the governorship of a province was too insignificant for a former grand vizier. His demand for unlimited powers exposed him to the charge that he wanted to prepare the way to declare himself an autonomous ruler on the Egyptian model. That did not endear him to the sultan, nor did his outspoken criticism of the Porte and the Palace freely given to foreign diplomatists, most of which was relayed to ʿAbdul Ḥamīd.

However, Midḥat's claim, reproduced uncritically by his admirers and printed by his son, that all his efforts to put matters right in Syria were thwarted by the Porte and sultan does not sound well founded when considered together with the achievements of the first year in the province. According to the British ambassador's report these achievements included the organisation of a gendarmerie force under a Polish or Hungarian renegade, the construction of several new roads and the beginning of a project for a tramway in Tripoli. Furthermore, under Midḥat's influence Muslims and Christians joined together and established a chamber of commerce and the organisation of a bourse in Beirut.

Since the ambassador, who was very favourable to Midḥat, makes no mention of the new schools in the city of Damascus and elsewhere it must be assumed that they were established during the second year of Midḥat's tenure. To the second year, or rather nine months before his transfer, must also be assigned the project of a public library in Damascus, better known through the efforts of Shaikh Ṭāhir al-Jazā'iri as al-Maktabah aẓ-Ẓāhiriyyah, as also Midḥat's encouragement of the foundation of a Muslim benevolent society known as al-Maqāṣid al-Khairiyyah, principally concerned with the opening of schools in Beirut and other centres.

A renewed request for permission to retire was met by further attempts by the palace to discover Midḥat's real reasons.[6] His replies dwell more on criticising existing conditions than on suggesting remedies, even after the sultan had opened yet another channel for Midḥat to communicate with him through a messenger of his own choice. Indeed Midḥat's reticence with his master contrasts sharply with his outspoken manner with foreign diplomats. One complaint he made more or less clear, thereby increasing the sultan's suspicions: the ultimate control of the army in the province was not in the governor's hands. But this was in accordance with established Ottoman practice in Syria, and hence there is no reason to regard the system as specially devised to rob Midḥat of authority, though it may have suited ʿAbdul-Ḥamīd to maintain central control by playing the military authority against the civil in the province.

However, Midḥat's criticism of the application of the new laws is noteworthy. The British ambassador reproduced this criticism more explicitly and clearly in these words: 'I was assured that the new regulations for the reform of the judicial tribunals had produced general confusion and had rendered the administration of justice more unsatisfactory and more corrupt than it had been before their promulgation.' The evil was no doubt the outcome of duality in the law and the courts that applied it. It was one thing for ministers and jurists in the capital to adopt or adapt European civil codes; it was quite another to find the judges with the education, nay inclination, to apply them, in the face of Muslim hostility. Reform was clearly needed first in the personnel and then in the measures.

Midḥat himself was soon to suffer from this dichotomy when he with others had to face trial on a charge of regicide. He could easily show that even judges of a high court were either ignorant or feigning ignorance of the new criminal code. And when Midḥat and the others were sentenced by the court and the sentence referred to the religious authorities for confirmation, the Mufti Emimi refused to do so for this reason: 'The men had been tried and condemned by a civil tribunal, according to laws and a procedure with which we have no professional acquaintance. If we are to give a decision, the case must be tried again according to the procedure prescribed by the Sacred Law.'

Despite his ultimate misfortune under the new laws, Midḥat's sympathies were with the new order, not with the old, and despite a persistent tradition his popularity in Syria was not universal. Even such an admirer as Sir Henry Layard, the British ambassador, was constrained to concede the existence of 'a small fanatical party' ranged against Midḥat. Probably the adjective 'fanatical' simply meant Muslims who disliked the new order. How small or large their number was, it is now very difficult to establish, but that a shaikh could be given the facility to publicly denounce Midḥat in the Great Mosque in Damascus as 'an unbeliever' seems to indicate that the party enjoyed wide support.

It is not certain that ʿAbdul-Ḥamīd was influenced by this

demonstration against Midḥat in Damascus. But the sultan was at least as well informed about Syria as Midḥat and the foreign diplomats he sought to impress and use as channels to air his grievances. Rumours of Midḥat's ambitions circulating freely in Syria and in the foreign embassies in Constantinople must have decided the sultan's next move. He neither permitted Midḥat to retire to the capital where he might intrigue, nor to a place on the Syrian coast where he might plot to achieve his reported ambitions in the province. On 4 August 1880 the pasha was transferred to be governor of the province of Smyrna. His governorship in Syria had lasted some twenty months.

4

Syria had been accustomed to the sudden departure of Ottoman governors. But Midḥat's claim for further attention after this rests on the fact that his name had been associated with one of the first concrete expressions of Syrian discontent with Ottoman rule and the assertion of Arab rights and aspirations. Reference has been made in the last chapter to signs of unrest in Syria and their first manifestations. These included a purely Muslim hatred of the new order and of the European Christians who inspired or dictated it. They also included a Syrian Arab discontent with Ottoman rule.

Each of the two kinds of dissatisfaction, ever present since the end of the Crimean War, began to be more pronounced soon after the collapse of the experiment in parliamentary government. The Muslim Arabs sincerely mourned the diminished rule of the *sharī'ah*. They blamed this result first on European Christians who applied pressure to bring it about, then on native Christian Arabs who were the beneficiaries, and finally on a Porte no longer worthy to be called sublime. From 1860 there appeared a few Syrian Arabs, both Muslims and Christians, who reconciled themselves to the new order, but desired to secure a measure of decentralised administration for their country and more official recognition of the Arabic language.

The Muslim Arabs alone had some vague aspirations of reviving Islam under an Arab caliph. But they shared with the Christian

Arabs a romantic enthusiasm for past Arab glory which they demonstrated by cultivating the study of Arabic literature. ʿAbdul-Ḥamīd was soon to rally most of those with an Islamic 'programme' to the cause of pan-Islamism and to the support of his own claim to be caliph of all Muslims. But as we shall point out he did not neglect those who had a Syrian or Arab programme.

The earliest solid evidence of Muslim Arab aspirations seems to go back to 1858. It is reported by the British consul in Aleppo as follows:

> It is worthy of remark that the hatred felt by the Arab population of this part of Syria for the Turkish troops and officials in general, whom they regard as degenerate Mohammedans, is little less violent than their fanaticism against the Christians. . . . The Mussulman population of northern Syria hope for a separation from the Ottoman Empire and the formation of a new Arabian state under the sovereignty of the sharif of Mecca. . . .[7]

After 1860, however, hazy ideas of common interests binding Muslim Arab and Christian Arab began to be formed by a few men of letters. To start with, the Arabic language was a common bond and an object of love and pride. Then there grew the notion of a regional fatherland (*waṭan*) as distinct from the larger and universal Ottoman Empire. Namik Kemal's famous forecast that, although possessing racial and territorial homogeneity, the Muslim Arabs were not likely to harbour separatist ambitions because of Islamic ties with the Turks and loyalty to the sultan-caliph, was falsified by history. As the above consular report shows the Muslim Arabs began to shift their loyalty from an Islamic empire to a regional fatherland.

By mental attitudes the Christian Arabs were even more ready for such a shift. The Ottoman Empire and what it stood for meant less to them. While it is true that many of them would have preferred some European Christian government to Ottoman Muslim rule, some of their thinkers reconciled themselves to a Muslim government that guaranteed religious equality. Indeed, collaboration between Muslim Arab and Christian Arab under such a system was increasing after the application of the reform edicts. There was evidence of collaboration in commerce, industry and above all in cultural pursuits. Of these pursuits the formation of literary associations was one of the most significant, for it was in the bosom of such societies that a pioneer historian of the Arab national movement sought to establish its origin.

But there is no convincing evidence that such early literary societies as were established in the thirty years preceding the reign of ʿAbdul-Ḥamīd had any political aims. A brief mention of the aims of the most prominent of these societies will confirm this statement. The first to be established was *Majmaʿ at-Tahdhīb*, in Beirut. It held its first meeting either late in December 1845 or early in January 1846. Its aim was 'the cultivation of the mind and the acquisition of useful knowledge', but it excluded politics and religious controversy. Its secretary was Buṭrus al-Bustāni, and Nāṣīf al-Yāziji was one of its fourteen initial members. Except for two American missionaries the members were then all native Protestant converts or Christians in friendly relation with the American mission. According to a senior American missionary the initiative in forming the society was native not American. This society remained in existence for about five years, but the circumstances of its disappearance are obscure.

Two other early societies deserve mention. In 1849 the Jerusalem Literary Society was established by the British consul, James Finn, for the literary and scientific investigation of the Holy Land. Its members were exclusively Protestant, foreigners and natives. Here also politics and religious controversy were expressly excluded. The other society, *al-Jamʿiyyah ash-Sharqiyyah*, was established in 1850 in Beirut by native Catholics, under Jesuit guidance, with aims and membership analogous to those of Bustāni's society.

Such was the sharpness of the sectarian spirit before 1860 that even literary and scientific associations had more or less to be established on sectarian lines. But thanks to the spread of education and the official recognition of religious equality that spirit was gradually mellowed. Thus when in 1868 *al-Jamʿiyyah as-Sūriyyah al-ʿIlmiyyah* was founded in Beirut as a successor to another society bearing a similar name, its membership included Christians, Druzes and Muslims. The Ottoman authorities recognised the society under its first president the Amīr Muḥammad Arslān, and distinguished Ottoman statesmen like Fuād Pasha and other prominent men in Damascus, Cairo and Istanbul enrolled as honorary members. This society perhaps more than any of its predecessors stressed the historic contributions of the Arabs to arts and sciences and urged their descendants to emulate them in the establishment of schools and learned societies.

Neither this society, however, nor any of its predecessors can be regarded as a platform, still less an agency, of the first call for Arab political emancipation. The late George Antonius greatly dramatised and exaggerated the significance of the recitation at one of the society's meetings of the ode ascribed to Ibrāhīm al-Yāziji as well as to an unnamed Muslim shaikh, beginning 'Awake ye Arabs and recover'.[8] Prior and more conclusive evidence was apparently unknown to that pioneer historian of the Arab national movement. Our discussion of the application of Ottoman reforms will have shown that Muslim Arab discontent developed into a separatist tendency with the aim of creating an Arab Islamic state long before any Christian Arab had any notion even of autonomy.

As will soon be pointed out, the existence of these discontents and aspirations was not unknown to Midḥat Pasha when he was governor in Syria. He appears to have exploited them to secure wider powers if not permanence in office. He may have toyed with the idea of becoming ultimately an autonomous ruler of the country, possibly under or with British protection. His request to be allowed to 'retire' somewhere on the Syrian coast must have sounded suspicious to a sultan well informed of the rumours concerning Midḥat's ambitions. His son, however, states that the rumours were propagated by his father's enemies.

Some three months before the end of Midḥat's governorship in Syria, the military attaché of the French Embassy in Constantinople visited Jerusalem. In a conversation with the British consul in the city the Frenchman is reported to have said that he was 'very unfavourably impressed by Midḥat Pasha, whom he accused of plotting to secure for himself eventual supreme independent domination in Syria'.[9] The attaché was, according to another British consul, gathering evidence to prove Midḥat's disloyalty to the sultan. The French Embassy had been suspicious of British moves in Syria and of Midḥat's intrigues since Layard's visit to the country. It is claimed that French representations to the sultan had material influence on Midḥat's recall.

Layard's successor as British ambassador is not as laudatory of Midḥat. Only five days after the pasha's transfer to Smyrna the new ambassador made a reference to the 'intrigues on the part of

Midḥat Pasha in Syria' and commented that 'whatever view may be taken of Midḥat Pasha's reform capacity and merits in past times, I am bound to say that much evidence is produced to shew that he has somewhat degenerated. Ḥamdi Pasha [his successor in Syria] is said to be both an able and an honest man.'[10]

That there was a party opposed to Midḥat in Syria has already been mentioned. But there was another party of admirers who asked Sir Henry Layard to exert his influence with the sultan to keep the governor in Syria and invest him with wider powers. Had Midḥat allied himself with the moderate malcontents who would have been satisfied with local autonomy? In Beirut the voice of the business community was heard by Sir Henry Layard. Members of the chamber of commerce

> expressed in very decided terms and unanimously the determination of the Arabs of Syria, without distinction of creed, not to be governed as they had hitherto been from Constantinople. They gave me to understand that if Midḥat Pasha, with whose administration and desire to promote the welfare of the province they said they were highly satisfied, were removed, the feeling of discontent and hostility to the Turkish authorities might show itself in a very serious manner.

This was a demand for decentralised government, not for independence. It can be safely assumed that it was made with Midḥat's approval. But he knew much more of the wishes of the Syrians and the agitation among them than he cared to disclose to the sultan. Layard, however, was told everything. The information he elicited from Midḥat is so important and of such direct bearing on the movement for Arab independence that it deserves to be reproduced *in extenso*. Sir Henry wrote:

> I asked His Highness whether he had any information with respect to a Mussulman, or Arab, conspiracy, the centre of which was said to be at Medina or Mecca, one of its objects being to dethrone the present dynasty and to establish an Arab Kingdom or Empire. I told His Highness that, from official reports which had reached me, it appeared that agents had been sent amongst all the Mussulman population of the Turkish Empire, and even to Algeria, to prepare them for insurrection.
>
> His Highness admitted that facts had recently come to his knowledge which confirmed this information. He had learnt that a certain Sheikh Ali, a native of the Hidjas, and probably one of

the agents to whom I alluded, was secretly enrolling persons in Syria in a kind of brotherhood, that he had even succeeded in doing so amongst the troops, and that secret committees had been formed in some of the principal towns. It had been stated to him that there were already no less than a hundred thousand persons in Syria who had enrolled themselves, but this number was probably exaggerated. He intended, he said, to go to Acre, in the neighbourhood of which Sheikh Ali was residing, to investigate thoroughly the whole affair, which he considered one of great importance. I told him that on my return to Constantinople I should probably mention the matter to the Sultan, and he expressed a wish that I should do so.

Consul Henderson . . . refers to secret committees as existing in Aleppo, and I heard that similar committees have been established in Damascus, Beyrout, and other places. But it is possible that they may have no relation to the conspiracy referred to by Consul Zohrab(?) in his despatch to Y[our] L[ordship] secret & conf. of the 12th March last which appears to be exclusively Mussulman and to be directed against Christians. I am assured that the secret committees in Syria were composed of Mohammedans and Christians alike, and that their object was to bring about a movement to free the province from the misgovernment of the Porte, and to establish some kind of Arab autonomy.

5

Syrian Arab independence, or even autonomy, was a contingency abhorrent to the Ottoman authorities. This is clear from their reaction to the appearance in the major cities of Syria in the last weeks of Midḥat's governorship and for some time after his recall, of anonymous handwritten placards asserting some fundamental Arab rights. The authorship of the placards has been assigned to a secret society, and the credit for founding the society has been given to five Christian Arabs educated at the Syrian Protestant College. We are told that 'after some time' the five enlisted some twenty-two other members, including Christians, Druzes and Muslims, and that branches of the society were organised in Damascus, Tripoli and Sidon.

These assertions do not stand the test of examination in the light of all the available evidence cited above, nor even in the light of the actual texts of the surviving placards. So far as could be discovered, three were preserved thanks to the foresight of the British consul in Beirut who saved one in the original and copies of the other two. His colleague in Damascus preserved none although in reporting on the placards he states that one was fixed on his own door. Under a sketch of a drawn sword, the first placard reads:

> By the sword lofty aims are attained,
> Then use it if you are to succeed!

> O sons of Syria! Moses rose as a reformer (*muṣliḥ*) but the Egyptians said he was possessed by the evil spirit; Socrates rose as a reformer but the Greeks killed him; Jesus rose as a reformer but the Jews said he was possessed by Satan; Muḥammad rose as a reformer but the pre-Islamic Arabs said he was mad. You may say that the writer (or rather writers) of this notice is intoxicated and that his words are delirium. But if he is mindful of your affairs then he is better than your rulers who do not care about your welfare nor uphold your honour. Would that you were all intoxicated [like the writer].
>
> We [the writers] spend the night awake with thought and the day with diligence in understanding events and news. But for our moribund condition we would not be the slaves of the degraded Turks; but for our dissension the Franks would not consider us insensible. Where is your Arab pride? Where is your Syrian zeal? O people! Return [to your past glory] while it is opportune! Do not despair of the mercy of your Lord! The [light of the] moon cannot be obscured, and he who lives will see.

The second placard, preserved in the original, has a sketch of a drawn sword coloured with red ink to contrast with the black ink of the text, which reads:

> O sons of Syria! Reform of [or at the hands of] the Turks is impossible. Otherwise why did they not reform [or introduce any reforms]? They have given countless pledges of honour to their subjects concerning reform [but did nothing]. So what do you expect from them?
>
> Despite their deep-rooted corruption, extreme ignorance and effeminacy, the Turks have continued till now to rule, with two millions of their number, over thirty-five millions of the servants of God. Are there not among our wise men, sons of our fatherland and guardians of our pride some men who are able to assume management of our affairs, who are jealous of our honour and

[mindful] of uplifting our fatherland, though we are only two millions, sons of one fatherland? Does your great understanding prevent you from doing that?

As for ourselves we have dedicated our possessions and our lives for the redemption of the fatherland – neither belong to us any longer, but to the fatherland. By the Great God we shall awaken you from your present repose of death even if we meet our death [in the attempt]. And he who lives will see.

The third placard has the Arabic for the word 'woe' written between two drawn swords pointing downwards to the text which reads:

O people of the fatherland! You are aware of the injustice and oppression of the Turks. With a small number of themselves they have ruled over you and enslaved you. They have abolished your sacred law (*sharīʿah*) and despised the sanctity of your revered books [? possibly singular in the original and then the meaning would be 'your revered Koran']. They have even passed regulations to destroy your noble language. They have closed before you the doors of success. They have taken you as slaves and as if you were devoid of human feelings. But you were the rulers in the past. Among you were raised the men of learning and virtue. With you the lands [of Islam] were populated and through you the wide [Islamic] conquests were achieved. And your language contains the principles of the caliphate which the Turks had stolen from you. Look how [at present] your men are sent to the battle field and exposed to death and what [ill-] treatment they receive. Then look at your religious foundations (*awqāf*) how they are managed and in what manner [their income] is spent.

But now, and after consultation with our brethren in all parts of the country it was resolved and decided to make the following demands before calling the sword as an arbiter. If your demands are met we will return to manage our [own] affairs. Otherwise,

Our aims by the sword we shall seek,
By it none of our aims can fail.
And we shall leave the uncouth Turk
To bewail the punishment of iniquity.

The demands which our council decided to make are as follows: First, autonomy [not independence here for the Arabic *istiqlāl*] which we share with our Lebanese brethren, while our common interests bring us all closer together. Secondly, recognition of the Arabic language as official (*rasmiyya*) in the country and of the right of those who speak it to complete freedom in publishing their thoughts, books and newspapers, in accordance with the demands of humanity, progress and civilisation. Thirdly, the employment of soldiers recruited from among us in the service of [their] fatherland only and to rid them of servitude to Turkish officers.

Then there are other indispensable improvements and concessions the discussion of which we leave for another occasion.

> Awake ye Arabs and recover!
> For you are knee-deep in adversity.
> Why entertain vain hopes
> While you are captives of armed force?
> You have neither government to give you strength
> Nor a helper upon whom to lean in distress.
> Have you not blood to boil one day,
> And remove this shame when it does boil?
> He who lives will in future days see
> And glean wonders in their events.[11]

In the three documents the stress is on the regional Syrian Arab fatherland whose inhabitants, proud of their descent from conquerors and men of learning, had two main demands: autonomy and recognition of Arabic. Apart from the general complaint of Ottoman oppression and injustice, the three documents contain specific grievances of the greatest importance: the Turks usurped the Arab Caliphate, disabled the sacred law, mismanaged the religious foundations, degraded the Arabic language and debarred the Arabs from a share in the government.

The specific demands constitute what might be considered as the 'national' programme, common to Muslims and Christians. Except on the score of Arabic, the general grievances were the concern of the Muslims alone. Hence the citation of these grievances is not followed by suggested remedies. There is no mention, for example, of a Syrian Arab desire, such as had been reported in 1858, of linking independence or autonomy with a plan for the restoration of the Caliphate under the Sharif of Mecca or any other leader. The concrete demands were restricted to Syria and no external movements or personalities were invoked. Behind the façade of rhetoric, therefore, the demands sound more moderate than appears on first consideration.

What reliable and contemporary eyewitnesses thought of the

origin, content and aims of these placards is of greater importance to the historian than the deductions, based on insufficient or incomplete evidence, of an author who wrote some sixty years after the event. Therefore the assessments written within days of the event by two British consuls and a report by a native Christian employed as dragoman in the British consulate in Beirut must have prior claim on our attention. Equally noteworthy is the action taken by the Ottoman authorities.

The two consuls agree that the placards had very little or no effect and that there was no party of sufficient strength to answer their appeal. The two consuls and the native dragoman trace the placards to Muslim rather than Christian origin. Basing themselves on reports then current among Muslims and Christians, the two consuls mention Midḥat Pasha as an instigator. The existence of a secret society or societies dedicated to the cause of Arab autonomy is acknowledged, as Midḥat had already disclosed to the British ambassador.

The Ottoman authorities did not take the placards very seriously. Nevertheless consular reports state that two Christian suspects were arrested in Damascus and banished from the country, and a few other suspects were arrested in Sidon and sent to prison. But the most drastic action was taken in Beirut. A Christian from Sidon, whether in self-defence or out of malice, wrote to the authorities that the Muslim Benevolent Society in Beirut was responsible for the placards. The authorities must have had other evidence to support this accusation, for they proscribed the society and transferred its educational function to the official board of education in the district.

That the sentiments expressed in the placards were confined to a few individuals with little popular support is unquestionable. But the sentiments of the few were important as a basis for the wider and more sustained action of the next generation of political leaders. Indeed the programme contained in the placards remained substantially the maximum Arab demand within the Ottoman system down to the outbreak of the First World War. However, the publication of the placards at a time when their ideas could command no effective popular support had one unfortunate result. It alerted the Ottoman authorities and produced tight controls of the press, book production and school curricula.

6

The stories about Ottoman censorship under ʿAbdul-Ḥamīd must not all be taken literally, nor should all the abuse heaped upon the sultan by a chorus of authors. In reality he was as favourable to the introduction of reform as his father or grandfather had been. His misfortune was that he chose to rule personally a weakened empire whose finances were unsound, whose Christian population was in actual or potential revolt, while every major European power was acting as self-appointed adviser if not instructor. The methods he used were repugnant to European public opinion and ultimately doomed him in the eyes of his subjects.

But except for these methods and his utter dislike of limited constitutional rule, ʿAbdul-Ḥamīd was as enlightened in accepting and applying reform as any of his predecessors had been. With all its dark aspects his reign witnessed the fruition of the schemes of reform which he did much to consolidate and extend. Syria in particular reaped much of the fruits of reform in many directions, particularly in education. Here again except for the sultan's dislike of the separatists, the Syrians enjoyed a measure of prosperity under him seldom enjoyed by any other part of his empire, not excepting the Turkish provinces.

By the end of the first half of ʿAbdul-Ḥamīd's reign, the provisions of the education law of 1869 were almost completely implemented in Syria. Modern state schools at every level, *Subyāniyya* (lower elementary), *Rushdiyya* (higher elementary), *Iʿdādiyya* (lower secondary) and *Sultāniyya* (higher secondary), were established in the principal cities, soon to be followed by a few technical schools, schools for training teachers and preparatory military schools. A great many of the traditional schools in the smaller towns and vlliages, managed by local committees, were placed under government control. Private schools, controlled by natives or foreigners, had to submit to official supervision.

In state schools the pupils were still predominantly boys, but the number of schools for girls was increasing. Though the schools were legally open to the children of all Ottoman subjects irrespective of creed, the number of non-Muslim pupils in state schools was still small. An increasing number of Syrian pupils who completed the higher secondary schools in their neighbourhood were selected for further study in Istanbul. They were enrolled in the *Mulkiyya* high school or in the *Harbiyya* high school and trained for the civil service or the army respectively. A few others were admitted to the Imperial School of Medicine. Many of the future leaders of the Syrian Arabs after independence were thus educated. In addition to Turkish they learned some French but little or no Arabic. Their deficiency in literary and even spoken Arabic contrasted with the proficiency of those Syrian Arabs, Muslims and Christians, who had received their education at native private schools or other non-government schools.

It became a universal practice in native as in foreign schools to teach foreign languages. But foreign schools also taught, and at a higher level, natural sciences, much to the enrichment of a literary tradition. This was particularly true in Beirut of the Syrian Protestant College and the Jesuit College. In 1883 the latter was extended by the addition of a medical department, thanks to French support. By then France had more than doubled the number of scholarships it made available to Syrian students and the amount of French aid to native Catholic schools. Besides, the number of French schools, hospitals and other establishments had multiplied in almost every major centre.

On the other hand, Arabic and Islamic studies in Beirut had at that time received a great fillip during the enforced sojourn in the city of Muḥammad ʿAbduh. Not only did he teach Arabic at the new *Sulṭāniyya* school, but he held a circle in the great mosque devoted to Koranic exegesis. His well-known *Risālat at-Tauḥīd* is a revised and final version of what he first taught at Beirut. He also edited, with extensive commentaries, the two classics of *Nahj al-Balāghah* and *Maqāmāt al-Badīʿ*.

In addition, he submitted a memorandum to the governor of Beirut on the subject of education. In an introductory note he denied that the inhabitants of Syria had any ambition to be independent of a state identified with the Caliphate. The idea had been entertained only by a few people 'of no account in the community'. Hence he deplored the action of the Ottoman authorities who had proscribed the Muslim Benevolent Society whose schools had saved Muslim children from exposure to missionary influence or to foreign loyalties fostered by foreign schools. To safeguard against these dangers, Muḥammad ʿAbduh recommended more state schools for all parts of Syria. In particular he wished to see established in Beirut a central boarding high school teaching through the medium of Arabic (state schools were then teaching through the sole medium of Turkish). At this school Turkish and French were to be taught as foreign languages, but the whole curriculum was to be designed for 'the revival of religion and love of the [Ottoman] state'.[12]

That was precisely according to the needs of the moment, and fitted very well with ʿAbdul-Ḥamīd's new policy. His empire, the last survivor of the great Islamic empires, had done its best and worst to Europeanise its system only to be disillusioned by the model. Not only had the process of Europeanisation produced discontent among the Muslims, and not only had it failed to satisfy the Christian minorities whilst sharpening their appetite for more privileges and even independence, but it also proved no check on European Christian aggression. Within five years of his ascending the throne ʿAbdul-Ḥamīd had to witness a major Russian attack that threatened his very capital, a French seizure of Tunis when it was still technically part of his dominions, and a British occupation of Egypt, an autonomous province of his empire.

He suspected a united European Christian front ranged against his Muslim empire, and sought to counteract it by what the British ambassador called 'a Mussulman league to be constituted with a view to resisting the union of the Christian nations against the Turkish Empire.' On the occasion of the first of Ramaḍān in 1880 ʿAbdul-Ḥamīd held a private meeting with the leading ulema and concerted plans for the prosecution of the new policy. His agents had already established contacts with Muslims under British, French, and Russian rule, in India, Algeria and Turkestan. The vague hopes of reviving the Islamic caliphate had now found a leader with plausible credentials. His staunchest supporter was the jurist-mystic Syrian, ash-Shaikh Muḥammad Abul-Huda aṣ-Ṣayyādi.

Nor did ʿAbdul-Ḥamīd neglect to surround himself with Muslim thinkers and notables from other countries within and without his dominions. In 1892 he invited the campaigner for another form of

Islamic unity, Jamāl 'ud-Dīn al-Afghāni, to Istanbul where he remained as an honoured guest until his death. About the same time, Ḥusain Ibn 'Ali, later the Sharif of Mecca, was more or less 'exiled' with his family to Istanbul, where he remained an equally honoured guest till 1908. To keep the former at his court was good publicity for the sultan-caliph; to keep the latter was a form of check on Arab claims to the Caliphate.

In Syria the sultan-caliph's call for pan-Islamism had the immediate effect of drowning, for the time being at any rate, the feeble voices calling for Syrian or Arab autonomy. A movement of turning away from Europe to Islam was unmistakable. Its slogan was 'combat Europe with its own weapon'. Learn the science of war, establish more schools and develop the resources of the country, but in doing so adopt European ideas and techniques only where they agree with the spirit of Islam and promote its strength, physically and morally.

There is no question that in the 1880s this Islamic movement had a stronger appeal to the majority of Syrians than any regional, racial or national movement that may then have been in the making. How strong this appeal was, and how wrong the British report of 1878 that the Syrians, particularly the Muslims, welcomed a British occupation proved to be, may be demonstrated by the Syrian reaction to the British occupation of Egypt. A British consular report mentioned hostility to Great Britain in southern Palestine and traced the cause to 'the war with 'Arābi Pasha'. An American missionary reported demonstrations in Tripoli in sympathy with Egypt. American and English missionaries made matters worse by publicly speaking of the British occupation of Egypt as 'another phase of the great, inevitable conflict between Christianity and Mohammedanism'.

Henceforth European, and in general foreign Christian, activities in Syria had to be conducted in conformity with this new trend in Ottoman policy and Muslim public opinion. While the country remained open to foreign enterprise, official control became tighter and the application of the law stricter. This was resented by some Anglo-Saxon educational and similar agencies. Their sponsors mounted a powerful campaign in England and elsewhere accusing the Ottoman authorities of 'fanaticism' or 'bigotry'. But when specific cases were investigated by the British ambassador they were found to rest on no foundation of fact, but rather to be a cover for refusal to obey the law.

None of the other large foreign agencies made such complaints. The largest foreign cultural interests in Syria were at the time French and Russian. The French ambassador, the patron of French and French-speaking institutions in Syria, agreed on behalf of his protégés to comply with the requirements of Ottoman law. There is no evidence of Russian resistance even at the height of Russian activity in the two patriarchates of Jerusalem and Antioch. The brief mention of the beginning of these activities in Chapter 4 now requires a supplement in order to bring the history of Russian cultural work into juxtaposition with other such work.[13]

Soon after the Crimean War a Russian ecclesiastical mission under a bishop arrived in Palestine and made Jerusalem the centre of its activities. These were aimed at the revival of orthodoxy and the counteracting of Protestant and Catholic missionary work among the native Orthodox. At the same time a voluntary society, patronised by the Tsar and subsidised by the Russian government, began operations in the Holy City. An area of over thirty acres was acquired outside the city walls on which were quickly erected a cathedral, a consular house, a residence for the ecclesiastical mission, a hospital and two hostels for male and female pilgrims. Experimental work in education began through native agents and by subsidising existing schools.

Russian activities were consolidated after 1882 by the Imperial Orthodox Palestine Society. Several archaeological researches were conducted under its aegis. It erected new churches, monasteries and schools. Above all it created a complete educational system comprising primary, secondary and teachers' seminaries. The schools were for boys and girls, in towns and in villages. They were first concentrated near Jerusalem and in Galilee, but soon other schools were also opened in Lebanon and other parts of Syria. Instruction was through the medium of Arabic, and this language was taught very thoroughly throughout the system. Russian was taught only as a foreign language. Promising students were sent to Russia for further training. The most famous of these is Mikhā'īl Nuʿaimah.

An English missionary stationed in Nazareth complained to his society in London that the opening of Russian schools had caused the closure of Protestant missionary schools in Nazareth and the neighbouring villages through the withdrawal of Orthodox children. It was at this moment that Protestant missionaries in Syria complained of Ottoman 'intolerance'. Were they seeking scapegoats? Otherwise why did the same missionary lament the decline of British influence at Constantinople and wonder whether the matter could not be pressed further?

7

If the Ottoman system was really as intolerant of non-Muslim foreigners as we are so often told, how can we account for the flow of refugees from the tolerant Christian west to the 'intolerant' Muslim east, and not vice versa? From the 1840s, if not earlier, the Ottoman Empire, and Syria in particular, began to receive non-Muslim refugees, at first in small numbers but gradually the numbers became greater, particularly of Jews.

In 1841 Palmerston lent his support to an Anglo-Prussian scheme of settling 'European Protestants' in the Ottoman Empire, but it was John Bowen, the English missionary, who revived interest in the project in the 1850s. He tried to instruct Arab peasants near Nābulus in the use of the English plough and an improved oil press. He dreamt of seeing farming colonies 'of Protestants only' established in the Plain of Esdraelon. His dream was realised about a decade later. In 1868 a group of American Adventists settled outside Jaffa, but soon it was apparent that their love of the Holy Land was greater than their ability to cultivate its soil. They gave way to the German Community of the Temple who, after a struggle, succeeded in establishing agricultural colonies near Jaffa, Haifa, Nazareth and elsewhere. These are the colonies of which Midḥat Pasha complained as one evidence of foreign influence in Syria. He did not realise that the German colonists were the first pioneers of modern agriculture in Palestine, for it was they who first introduced European methods of cultivation, implements and seeds.

After the Treaty of Berlin, Syria received more immigrants. 'Abdul-Ḥamīd deliberately encouraged the transfer of Muslims from the Caucasus and adjacent territories conquered by Russia.

They were settled on the eastern fringes of Syria, mostly in the land east of the river Jordan. ʿAmmān, the present capital of the kingdom of Jordan, began its modern existence as a Circassian colony. At the same time Muslim Bosnians (*Bushnāq*) were transferred to Syria on the occupation by Austria of Bosnia and Herzegovina. They were settled in the half-ruined Caesarea on the coast of Palestine and given land to own and cultivate.

Earlier Muslim immigration into Syria is also noteworthy. From the days of al-Jazzār, mercenary troops from al-Maghrib (Arab North Africa) were employed in the private armies of pashas. And yet the earliest and the most enduring of the Maghrib's connection with Syria was purely religious. It dates from Saladin's time when his son al-Afḍal dedicated as a religious foundation (*waqf*) the land outside the south-west corner wall of the Aqṣā Mosque in Jerusalem for the benefit of their pilgrims and scholars. In 1320 another bequest was made by Shuʿaib Abū Madyan, a Maghribi divine, for erecting dwelling-houses and a *zāwiyah* (a retreat for mystics) on the land. Since then the area became the Maghāribah Quarter of the city.

Since the Egyptian occupation, small numbers of Jews began to settle in the cities of Jerusalem, Ṣafad and Tiberias out of religious motives. In 1840 the total number of Jews in the historic Holy Land was about ten thousand; by 1880 it had risen to about thirty-five thousand. Two years later Jewish refugees from Russia and Poland came in greater numbers following the pogroms. The main stream of refugees went to western Europe and America, but a trickle reached Palestine. Hitherto the Jews had been animated by religion; they went to the Holy Land 'to pray and to die and be buried in its soil'. Now a new motive was added; a group of dreamers desired to establish agricultural colonies similar to those of the German Templars.

The first attempts were on the whole unsuccessful, but the endeavour was rescued by the philanthropy of Baron Edmond de Rothschild who took under his patronage the first two or three colonies. The Ottoman government was, as hitherto, tolerant in welcoming the refugees. But soon other considerations dictated caution. For one thing, they disliked the greater opportunity now provided for Russian diplomatic and consular missions to interfere on behalf of so many people who were still, and were likely to remain for a long time, Russian subjects. For another, the Ottoman authorities were always anxious to maintain the sectarian equilibrium, especially in Jerusalem. A great increase in the number of Jews was undesirable from both a Christian and a Muslim point of view. Accordingly stricter regulations concerning the entry, residence and purchase of immovable property were introduced. But like most Ottoman regulations they were never fully applied.

There was as yet no political element in Jewish immigration. But it was soon introduced by a new nationalist wing inside the Jewish communities in Europe. In 1897 the first Zionist congress was held at Basle, and it definitely gave Jewish immigration a political character. According to the new ideology, immigrants went to the Holy Land not merely to die and be buried in its soil, but also 'to create a home for the Jewish people'. A year earlier Theodor Herzl the Zionist leader sought to secure ʿAbdul-Ḥamīd's approval of such a scheme. He failed largely because of the influence of Syrians like Abul Huda and ʿIzzat al-ʿAbid. The sultan spoke through a Polish intermediary. 'Advise Herzl,' ʿAbdul-Ḥamīd said, 'advise him not to go a single step further in the matter. I cannot sell even a foot of land, for it does not belong to me but to my people. They have won this Empire and fertilised it with their blood. . . . I can dispose of no part of it. The Jews may spare their millions.'[14]

While by the immigration of Maghribis, Circassians, Bosnians and Jews the population of Syria was becoming more varied, a great internal movement of population and emigration was taking place. From 1860 onward the Druzes began to move from Lebanon to Ḥawrān till this district became their greater home. In the last quarter of the nineteenth century increasing waves of emigrants, mostly Christians from Lebanon and the Jerusalem district, left to seek their fortunes in America and elsewhere. After the British occupation of Egypt a good number of Syrians, again mostly Christians educated at American or English schools, emigrated to that land which had greater opportunities either in the service of the English or in private enterprise, especially journalism.

The immediate effect of emigration was a social and economic loss, since the emigrants were the younger and more educated members of the communiiy. The economic loss was more than offset in a decade, for many of the emigrants either returned with capital or sent remittances to their relatives. Much of the money was invested in building new houses, buying land or cultivating family holdings with vine, mulberry and olive groves. An American medical missionary reported that in certain Lebanese villages three-quarters of the new houses were built with money earned in America. An English missionary made a similar observation on the new prosperity in the Christian villages round Jerusalem.

That was only one evidence of the material prosperity around 1890. It is true that until then native agriculture had made little headway except in an increase in the area brought under cultivation. Peasants were still using the same methods and implements to extract from the soil the bare necessities for their existence. They were still the sufferers from chronic indebtedness and in consequence the victims of the city moneylenders. These and not the Ottoman authorities were the real oppressors of the peasants. Thus when a beginning at land registration (*ṭābu*) was made, some of the city merchants, moneylenders and absentee landlords sought to divert its benefits to themselves. They misrepresented the measure as a device both to register the men for military service and to increase the taxes. The peasants, who dreaded both contingencies, were easily persuaded to sell their prescriptive rights to the land they cultivated for nominal prices, to the rich who grew richer in the process. It was members of this rich class of absentee landlords who made large profits by selling to the early Zionists extensive lands acquired in this way or by other means.

Some of the native industries appear to have recovered from the shock of foreign competition. Take cotton cloth, used for dressing the greater majority of the population, as an example. The thrifty Syrian soon discovered that the local hand-made cloth, though more expensive, was superior in quality and more durable than similar cloth made in Manchester. This fact formed the subject of an inquiry conducted by British consuls in Syria. They were asked to send samples of the cloth in demand in the local market and to recommend ways and means for capturing it.

As usual the report from Beirut was the fullest.[15] It revealed that several Manchester firms had either branches or agents in the city to take note of the changes of fashion. They had already sent native patterns to Manchester where they were copied and cheap cloth produced and sent to Syrian markets. But a similar strategem was adopted by the large number of Syrians engaged in this trade. They

Al-Jazzār's justice as seen by a European contemporary (p. 32)

Sowing and ploughing, c. *1830* (p. 51)

Abū Nabbūt's bazaar and fountain, Jaffa, c. *1830* (p. 58)

The Fortress of Acre,
c. *1835* (p. 66)

A missionary sketch of the entry of the first Anglican bishop into Jerusalem (p. 106)

A Protestant mission house: church, school and parson's study, c. *1870* (p. 142)

The Amīr ʿAbdul-Qādir-Al-Jazā'iri (p. 127)

Buṭrus al-Bustāni (p. 144)

A Syrian gentleman with shamsiyyah, *or sun umbrella*, c. *1900* (p. 135)

A Syrian gentleman with pipe and inkwell, c. *1860* (p. 135)

Ḥusain Ibn ʿAli (p. 215)

Faiṣal Ibn al-Ḥusain (p. 284)

Sulṭān al-Aṭrash (p. 346)

Shukri al-Quwwatli (p. 372)

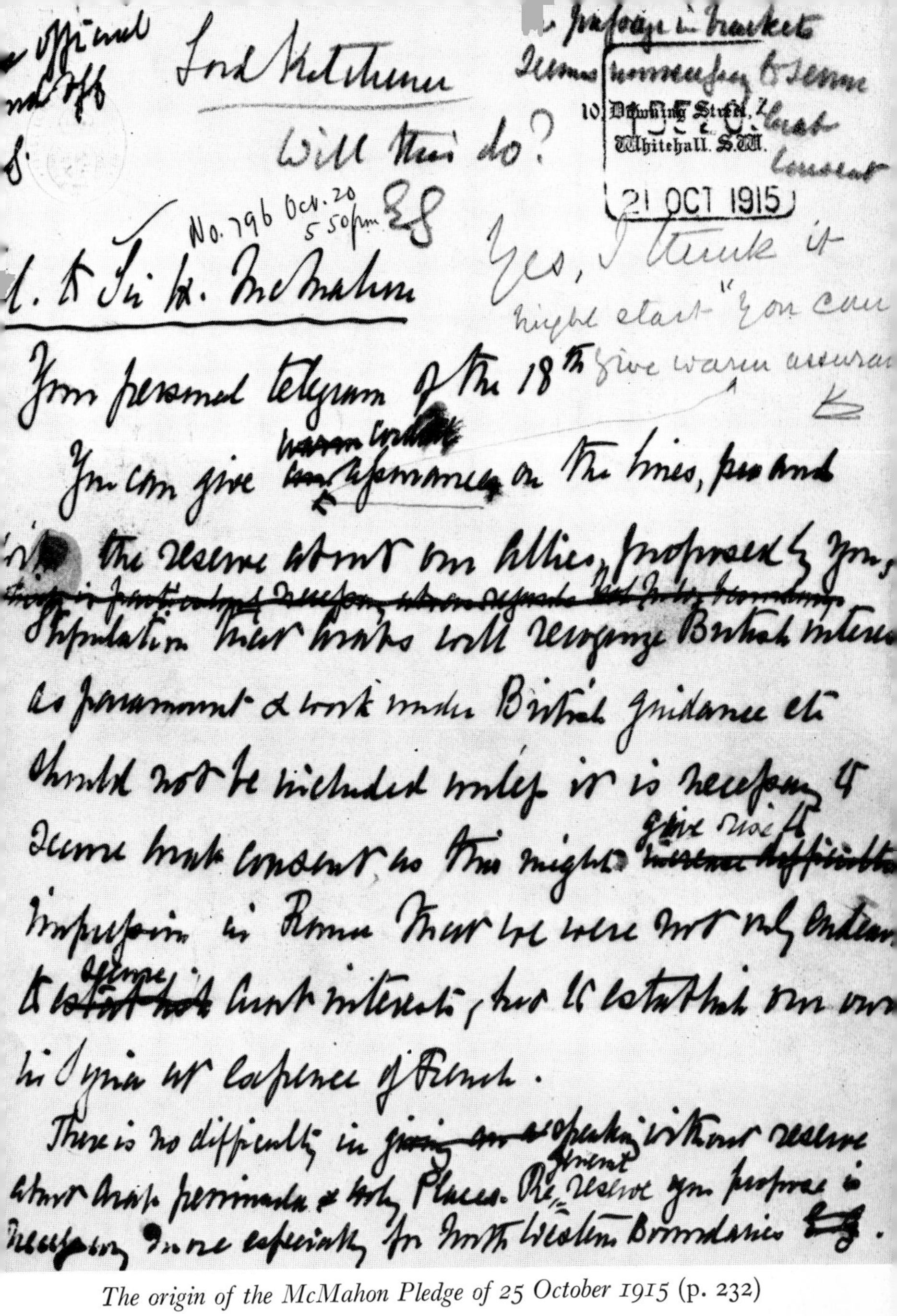
Lord Kitchener
Will this do? E.G.
... passage in brackets seems unnecessary to secure Arab consent
10 Downing Street, Whitehall. S.W.
21 OCT 1915
No. 796 Oct. 20 5 50pm
Tel. to Sir H. McMahon
Yes, I think it might start "You can give warm assurances" K
Your personal telegram of the 18th
You can give cordial assurances on the lines, and with the reserve about our Allies, proposed by you.
Stipulation that Arabs will recognize British interests as paramount & work under British guidance etc should not be included unless it is necessary to secure Arab consent, as this might give rise to impression in Rome that we were not only endeavouring to secure Arab interests, but to establish our own in Syria at expense of French.
There is no difficulty in speaking without reserve about Arab peninsula & Holy Places. The general reserve you propose is necessary more especially for North Western Boundaries.

The origin of the McMahon Pledge of 25 October 1915 (p. 232)

The Umayyad Mosque, Damascus

Above right:
A modern yarn and cloth mill near Damascus (p. 396)

Below right:
A group of folklore singers in traditional dress belonging to Ministry of Culture (p. 418)

A contemporary village scene in the Ghūṭah (p. 406)

imported the Manchester imprint and used it with such success that, because of native competition, the profit of the English firms was reduced to a minimum. Thus, concludes the consular report, neither were the native manufacturers driven out of the market nor was there much room for increasing the sale of the Manchester goods.

Beirut continued to grow in commercial importance, not only as a market for local and foreign goods but also as a port of call for foreign ships and for the export and import of the Syrian hinterland. Other Syrian ports to the north had comparatively declined; also those to the south with the sole exception of Jaffa which occupied a position in the southern part of Syria analogous to that of Beirut in the northern part. In the coastal plain near the city orange groves had been multiplying for decades. In 1890 about two hundred thousand boxes were exported. In the same year the value of imports through Jaffa was over a quarter of a million pounds sterling and the value of exports was about double that amount.[16]

As to the life of the people very little change occurred in the rural areas. In the larger cities and seaports, however, the change was revolutionary in housing, furniture, clothing and even crockery, cutlery and utensils. Beside the traditional Arab house with apartments opening to an enclosed courtyard and surrounded by a high stone wall, there sprang up new types of dwellings, with open front gardens, wide staircases, large colonnade verandahs, balconies, and floor-to-ceiling windows. These houses were furnished largely according to French or Italian styles. But ostentation produced endless incongruities in the salons of the rich: the imitation French gilded chair contrasted with the exquisite Persian carpet and the cheap Swiss silk prints with the Damascene brocade.

Men, and to a lesser degree women, had gradually adopted European clothes. The example had already been set by the Ottoman army, civil servants and rich merchants. For men nothing of the Oriental style remained except the fez, itself a comparatively new headgear. The turban had virtually disappeared except for religious leaders and teachers. The comic stories that are still related of the confusion caused by the introduction of forks and knives at banquets may be exaggerated, but they symbolise the struggle between the old customs and manners and the new. No ridicule was more seriously meant than that of the tendency of some westernised Christian Arabs to use foreign languages in their conversation at home. 'We have met', wrote the president of the Arab Academy in Damascus, 'men and women educated at foreign schools who became neither Arabs nor Europeans: they speak at home a language other than their own, and exhibit sentiments other than those of the Syrian, nay, they hate their own tradition and history and their country is black in their eyes. . . .'[17]

The westernisation in material life may be dismissed as superficial, but that in speech indicates mental attitudes built up through a long process of education in foreign schools, mostly American, English and French but now also Russian, German, Spanish and Italian. All these foreign influences tended to retard movements towards a Syrian Arab entity; they militated even more against any form of Ottoman unity. Within the Syrian Arab house foreign cultural influences heightened and aggravated religious divisions by giving them a cultural stamp. An observer who might have seen the country around the year 1890 thus tossed from one ideology to another could hardly have resisted asking the question: whither Syria?

7

‘Abdul-Ḥamīd’s Despotism in Syria – Light and Shade

I

‘ABDUL-ḤAMĪD is reputed on several occasions to have expressed his confidence that history would vindicate him. In this chapter we shall merely let the facts speak for or against him, without any attempt at vindication or condemnation. Taken as a whole, the facts concerning Syria do not only depict a sultan served by an elaborate net of spies and aided by a rigorous censorship of press and publications, or a sultan merely concerned with enforcing his personal rule and checking the development of all liberal thought and institutions. There are other aspects of ‘Abdul-Ḥamīd’s action in Syria which have hitherto received little or no notice. In their eagerness to stress the dark side even respectable historians have neglected to point out the light side. It is to redress the balance that this lighter and little known side receives more detailed consideration here.

There is abundant evidence to indicate that ‘Abdul-Ḥamīd paid special attention to the affairs of Syria and did his best to win the loyalty of the Syrians to his person and his policies. He continued the practice of sending very experienced governors to the country. Thus Ḥamdi Pasha who succeeded Midḥat had also been a grand vizier. The British ambassador described him as ‘both an able and an honest man’. Another British diplomatist spoke of the governor of Jerusalem as ‘an honest and well-intentioned man’. A third neutral observer described the governor of Latakia as a man ‘with drive and organizing ability’.

More provincial reorganisation was introduced in Syria under ‘Abdul-Ḥamīd, both to increase central control and to suit local

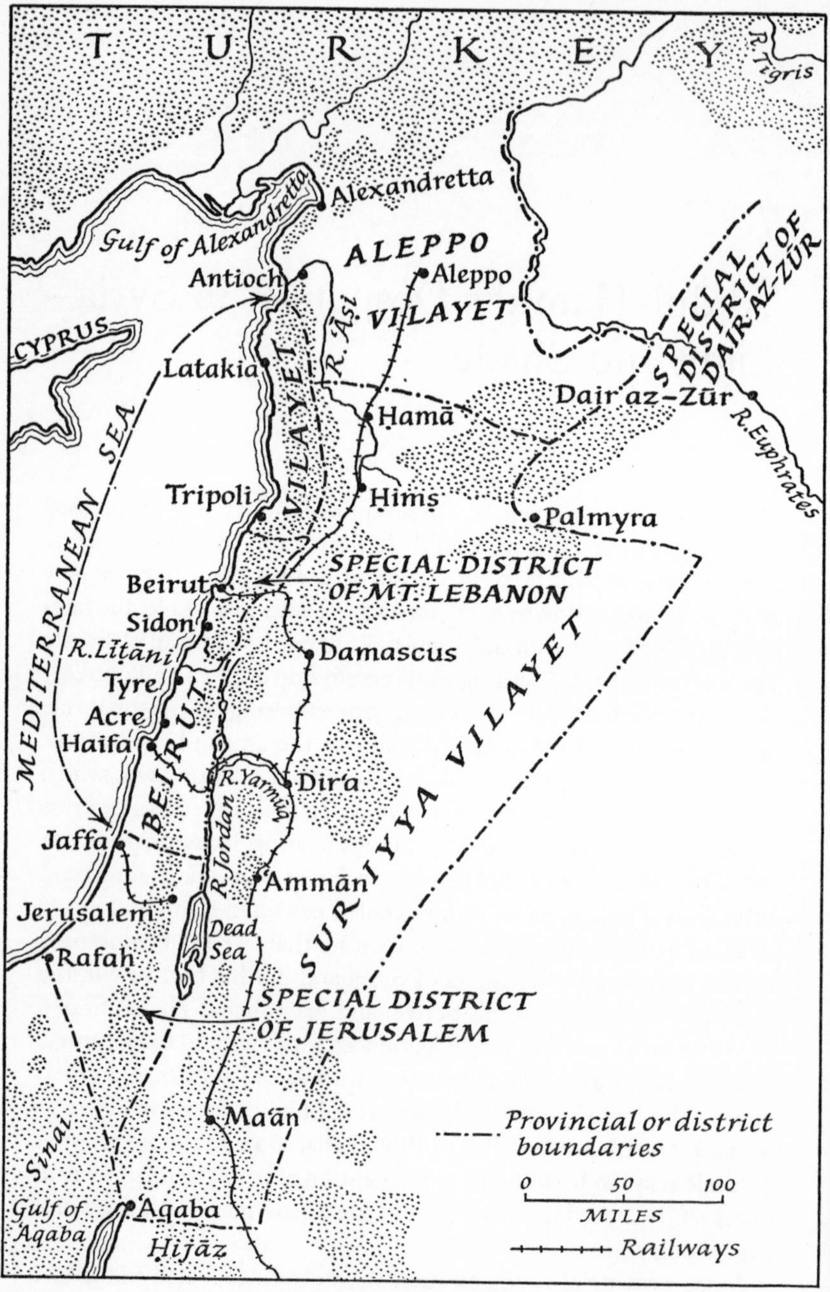

II Ottoman administrative divisions in 1914

conditions. In 1887 the southern and larger part of Palestine was constituted as a special district (*sanjaq*) based on Jerusalem with a governor directly answerable to Istanbul. The complicated religious character of the city and the increased foreign interests in it and in the district as a whole were among the considerations which brought about the change. Then in 1888 a new province based on Beirut was created out of the coastal regions from Tripoli to Acre. The arrangement was prompted by the growing commercial importance of Beirut and the increase of foreign interests, cultural and commercial, in the city and its dependencies. At this time the administrative machine in the capital of every province and district included a section for dealing with the affairs of foreigners.

By 1890 Syria had thus been divided into three provinces (Aleppo, Sūriyya and Beirut) and three special districts (Lebanon, Dair az-Zūr and Jerusalem). Lebanon enjoyed greater administrative decentralisation than any of the other five divisions, so much so that the placards of 1880 demanded similar treatment for the rest of Syria. Decentralisation was not, however, one of the aims of the new administrative reorganisation. It is true that pashas were allowed a larger measure of initiative in local affairs and made greater and more efficient use of local councils, but they had to refer all major questions to the capital.

The Porte was no longer satisfied with loose administrative control, and showed an increasing determination in enforcing centralisation. Accordingly the civil and military pashas in Syria were specifically instructed to deny the special privileges claimed by the Druzes in Ḥawrān and the semi-nomads east of the river Jordan. In 1893 the latter were persuaded or forced to accept direct government when the district of al-Karak was formed as the southernmost part of the province of Sūriyya. Three years later an expedition was sent against the Druzes in Ḥawrān which succeeded, though only temporarily, in subduing them. They, too, were forced to submit to government control after a bitter struggle and the banishment of several chiefs to distant Tripolitania.

Foreign residents, particularly diplomats and those engaged in cultural activities, are almost unanimous in their observation of an educational and religious revival in Syria inspired and encouraged by 'Abdul-Ḥamīd himself. The positive aim of the revival must not obscure its negative and not less important aim. 'Orders have been issued', wrote an English missionary from Nazareth in 1884, 'forbidding Mohammedan children from attending [foreign] Christian schools, and what is more, efforts have been made to establish Mohammedan schools for girls as well as for boys, not in towns only, but also in villages.'[1] According to a circular issued by the governor of Jerusalem to local councils and village headmen the orders on this subject were from the sultan himself.

Writing three years later the British consul in Damascus speaks of the animation of 'a Mussulman religious revival' and cites as evidence the repair of old mosques and the construction of new ones all over the country, as well as the new schools designed to promote 'Mohammedan education in accordance with the precepts of the Koran'.[2] An American missionary saw the same development in Beirut. He wrote that Syria's share of the new state schools was greater than any other part of the Empire, and added that on his own extensive properties in Syria the sultan ordered the construction of a mosque and a school in every village at his own expense. The missionary's opening sentences deserve to be quoted verbatim:

> It was asserted twenty years ago that Islam in Turkey is going to decay, and that not a new mosque could be seen in the land. From my window as I write I can see *five* new mosques built during the past twenty years, the minaret of the last one just now receiving its top stone. There is, no doubt, a Mohammedan revival. . . .'[3]

The revival was deliberately fostered by the sultan for political no less than religious considerations. While preliminary moves in this direction had been initiated by ʿAbdul-ʿAzīz, it was ʿAbdul-Ḥamīd who prosecuted the policy with persistence and vigour. From the beginning he enlisted a number of Syrian Arabs in support of the cause. The earliest to appear on the scene and to gain great influence over the sultan was ash-Shaikh Abul-Huda. He hailed from the Aleppo district and belonged to the Rifāʿi order of sufis and his family claimed descent from the Prophet. His views of the caliphate and the nature of political power were not strictly contrary to those held by other orthodox jurists in classical times, but their re-publication, with some stronger emphasis, was tantamount to an approval of ʿAbdul-Ḥamīd's despotism. For not only did Abul-Huda the Arab recognise the legitimacy of the Ottoman Turkish claim to the Caliphate but he regarded the reigning sultan as God's viceregent on earth obedience to whom was a duty incumbent on every believer.

The other Syrian Arab who exercised a great influence over 'Abdul-Ḥamīd was his second secretary, Aḥmad 'Izzat Pasha al-'Ābid. Educated at a Catholic mission school, he began his career in the commercial tribunals and rose to be judge in the tribunal at Istanbul. From that position he managed to bring himself to the notice of the sultan, or according to another report he was introduced by Abul-Huda. To start with, the two men appear to have worked well together, but soon they became rivals. Their rivalry was not apparently discouraged by the sultan. In practice, however, each had a sphere of influence as different from that of his rival as their respective educational backgrounds. Abul-Huda is now mainly remembered for the religious support he gave to the sultan's claim to be the legitimate caliph, while 'Izzat's reputation rests mainly on his part in the project for the construction of the Hijaz railway starting from Damascus.

Nor were these two men the only Syrians in the personal service of the sultan. The royal guards included units wholly composed of Syrian Arabs. Furthermore, 'Abdul-Ḥamīd had taken care not to forget the Syrian Christians, some of whom held high office in the ministries for foreign affairs, agriculture and public works. A Maronite was in charge of the secret police while outwardly holding a junior ministerial post.

Then the sultan through his numerous agents, and Abul-Huda and 'Izzat through their relatives and friends, won many influential religious leaders in the country for the sultan's cause. Some of the men were invited to the capital, others were placed in positions of responsibility in their own localities, and all were showered with favours. Among the men thus won were Yūsuf an-Nabhāni and Ḥusain al-Jisr. The first composed among numerous poems one in praise of Abul-Huda, while the second wrote a lengthy treatise on the Islamic faith entitled *al-Ḥamīdīyyah* after the sultan who is described as the protector of Islam, the support of its *sharī'ah*, the commander of the faithful and by the grace of God the caliph.

So much for those Syrians who played 'Abdul-Ḥamīd's tune. Their audience was probably the majority of the Syrian Muslims. But there was a significant minority of individual rebels who voiced their opposition in Cairo. Two of them deserve specific mention:

ʿAbdur-Raḥmān al-Kawākibi (Aleppo) and Muḥammad Rashīd Riḍā (Tripoli). Kawākibi's revolt had a beginning in petty local jealousies. Abul-Huda had a member of his own family appointed as head of that class of men in Aleppo recognised as descendants of the Prophet. But some of these and their allies, including the Kawākibi family, did not recognise Abul-Huda's claim to noble descent and naturally resented the appointment.

Riḍā's revolt also began as a quarrel with Abul-Huda, but this quarrel had fundamental causes. As an admirer of the strictest of the four schools in orthodox Islam, Riḍā had little respect for the sufis and their claims. Moreover he genuinely deplored the sultan's disregard of Islamic democracy, government by consultation (*shūrā*). These were compelling reasons which prompted Riḍā to go against the precepts of his master, Muḥammad ʿAbduh, and to first withhold support from and then oppose the despotism of ʿAbdul-Ḥamīd.

Kawākibi's treatise on despotism contains little or nothing which is not explicitly or implicitly enshrined in the Islamic tradition, or which has not been pointed out by earlier reformers from the authors of the Gulhané decree onwards. What is somewhat novel is an open call for the restoration of the Caliphate to the Arabs. Even this call was not new to the Syrians, some of whom had entertained such hopes a generation earlier. But it is singular that the call should have been made by one whose family was of Kurdish, not Arab origin. This fact lends colour to the suggestion that Kawākibi was an agent of the Khedive.

Riḍā's independence is, however, beyond question. Like his master he regarded the Ottoman Empire as the last surviving Islamic power and for that reason alone deserving of support. Neither he nor his master ever questioned the title of the Ottoman sultans to the Caliphate, nor did they support the call for an Arab Caliphate. Indeed they suspected the call to be inspired by foreign interests and designed to undermine ʿAbdul-Ḥamīd's claim. But Riḍā was definitely against the sultan for what he called 'manipulation' of the evidence in the authoritative sources on the creed, tradition and jurisprudence, and more particularly for the disregard of the principle of consultation.[4]

A third less well-known Syrian deserves specific mention. Shaikh Jamāl'ud-Dīn al-Qāsimi was the imam of the Sināniyya mosque in

Damascus during the last phase of 'Abdul-Ḥamīd's reign. Many of the future Syrian political and literary leaders were his disciples and admirers. He was twice questioned and his notes examined by the Turkish authorities who accused him of a tendency towards personal opinion (*ijtihād*) in religious matters, sympathy with Wahhābism and membership of an Arab nationalist association.

2

No serious criticism of 'Abdul-Ḥamīd's actions was published in Syria. But he took full notice of all criticism published in Cairo and Europe by exiles, Turks, Arabs and others as well as of foreign news reports. He employed methods fair and foul to reconcile some exiles; he did his best to inform the generally hostile European press of the constructive sides of his rule; and not infrequently he complained to foreign ambassadors of what he regarded as unfair criticism in their national press.

He felt increasingly isolated and friendless. After the *dictat* at the Congress of Berlin and the subsequent occupation of Ottoman territories by Russia, Austria, France and Great Britain, the sultan began to search for a dependable ally to take the place hitherto occupied by Great Britain. He was aware of hints Bismarck had made to the powers that Germany would not be a party to any coercion of the sultan in the matter of his Christian subjects. Germany was more interested in opening new markets in, and obtaining raw materials from, the Ottoman Empire than in the fate of its Christian subjects.

Count von Halzfeldt, the German ambassador, carefully represented his country to the sultan as the power least interested in territorial gains or interference in his internal affairs. Germany was only interested in developing trade. The *Drang nach Osten* began as a trade drive. In 1881 the French consul-general in Beirut reported on the activities and methods of a German trade mission. Its members included not only business men but also bankers, industrialists, engineers, architects and savants.[5] They offered long-term credits and competitive prices for raw materials in exchange for manufactured goods such as pharmaceutical products, hardware, hosiery, wool cloth and leather goods.

In 1883 merchants were followed by soldiers. ʿAbdul-Ḥamīd invited von der Goltz as an unofficial instructor to train the Ottoman army in modern methods. The rise of German influence thereafter is too well known to be detailed here. It paved the way for William II's first visit to the sultan in 1889, and the visit in turn opened up more opportunities for German trade and enterprise, including the concession for the famous Baghdad railway.

The construction of railways by foreign concessionnaires in the Ottoman Empire, and the Baghdad railway itself, fall outside the scope of this book, except where the Baghdad railway touches northern Syria at Aleppo. But to follow the chronological order of their construction, we must first mention a few railway lines completed before the turn of the century within Syria itself. They were built by foreign, principally French, companies registered as corporations under Ottoman law.

In 1892 the *Société du Chemin de Fer Ottoman de Jaffa à Jérusalem et prolongement* completed the construction of the line between the Holy City and its port. Three years later the Beirut–Damascus line was opened parallel to the carriage road which also had been constructed by a French company more than thirty years earlier. Other lines, particularly those connecting Damascus with Aleppo to the north and Ḥawrān to the south, and connecting Tripoli with Ḥimṣ, were partially or wholly completed within the next ten years or so.

It was an English idea to connect the Syrian Mediterranean coast with the Euphrates valley by a railway with a view to opening a short route to India via the Persian Gulf. The idea lost much of its attractiveness after the opening of the Suez Canal, but was revived a decade later on a grander scale, when it was projected to build a railway from Istanbul (already connected by the Orient Express with Vienna and Paris) to Baghdad and finally the Persian Gulf. This is the project in which German engineers and financiers, supported by William II himself, took a great interest. The concession was granted piecemeal, and construction met with formidable engineering and political difficulties, but the work continued down to the outbreak of the First World War. The railway did not reach Aleppo before the last year of the war. A projected branch from that city to Alexandretta was never constructed by the concessionnaires.

None of these lines, however, had greater significance for Syria than the railway projected and constructed between Damascus and Hijaz during the last eight years of 'Abdul-Ḥamīd's reign. The Hijaz railway was primarily intended to gain for the sultan the goodwill of his Muslim subjects, as well as of the Muslims all over the world, by reducing the hardship and cost of the journey to the majority of those who travelled by land. That the railway proved useful for the increase of the Ottoman hold on Hijaz and the regions near the line is probably an afterthought. To 'Abdul-Ḥamīd it was more important as an instrument of advancing his claim to be the caliph of all Muslims.

The idea of the railway is sometimes ascribed to 'Izzat Pasha especially because the sultan made him chairman of the board which controlled the execution of the project. Its cost was raised by voluntary contributions from Muslims all over the world. 'Abdul-Ḥamīd opened the list with 320,000 Ottoman pounds from the privy purse. The Shah of Persia, Indian Muslim princes and rich and poor Muslims from China to Transvaal sent their contributions. In 1900 the sultan celebrated the silver jubilee of his accession by the beginning of the construction of the Hijaz railway.

Its progress from Damascus southward was rapid, bringing prosperity and civilisation to the countryside. In four years the main line reached Ma'ān in Transjordan. Within the same period an important branch line was completed. This branch line was from Dir'ā westward across the river Jordan and through the fertile Marj Ibn 'Āmir to Haifa on the Mediterranean. (Beyond Ma'ān the line was strictly outside Syria; it reached Medina in 1908.) Of the incidental benefits of the railway mention may be made of the settlement of Circassians and beduins near the garrisoned stations. Security encouraged them to cultivate the land in the neighbourhood, and the farms thus cultivated ultimately grew into villages. Civil administration was greatly facilitated by all these developments.[6]

Unlike the other railways in Syria and the rest of the Empire, the Hijaz railway was an Islamic project in every sense. The necessary capital came from Muslims and the execution of the project was entirely in the hands of Muslims. German and Italian engineers were employed but primarily as consultants to Ottoman engineers, civil and military. The Ottoman army did most of the work aided by the free labour of the civilian population who often also provided free material. The railway was legally a religious foundation held in trust for the Muslim world. It belonged to no civil department of government and had a separate budget of its own.

Reliable statistics of pilgrims who used the Hijaz railway are very hard to find. For Christian pilgrims and travellers who used the Jaffa–Jerusalem railway a French consular report gives the numbers for the third year after the opening of the line. The report states that the well-known British travel agents, Thos. Cook and Son, were already utilising the railway for party travel to the Holy Land. Most pilgrims now travelled by rail to Jerusalem. In 1895 their total number was some fourteen thousand, including 8530 Russians.

3

Ottoman sultans tended to trust, if they trusted at all, only one European power at a given time. From 1882 it was increasingly evident that ʿAbdul-Ḥamīd placed greater trust in Germany than in any other power. Seldom had the growth of any European influence been less resisted in the past. It may even be said that the growth of German influence and enterprise was not unwelcome to the sultan. Though officially unconnected with the German government, the unobtrusive von der Goltz served to enhance German influence in the Ottoman army. Within a decade Germany enjoyed a virtual monopoly in the supply of arms, rifles from Mauser and cannons from Krupp. In 1898 the influential Turkish newspaper *Tarjumani Hakikat* wrote that German military discipline was a model which the Turks could emulate. 'The Turkish cadets', it wrote, 'who return from Germany with a complete military education are a source of inexpressible gratification to their countrymen.'

The special correspondent of *The Times* in Syria at the time remarked that English prestige had been almost 'annihilated', and English financial enterprise had been 'paralyzed'. A similar remark could be deduced from the reports of the French consul in Beirut, at least concerning French trade. Indeed, English and French sources agree that German trade was making headway to the top. The same English correspondent ascribed this to good reasons. 'The German commercial agent', he wrote, 'is ubiquitous – his linguistic acquirement, his readiness to suit all customers, his perseverance, his honesty and the cheapness of his wares enable him to distance most of his rivals.'

A living example of German enterprise was the agricultural colonies established by immigrants from Württemberg. Their success was largely due to their perseverance and adaptability. While clinging to their nationality and maintaining their separate identity, they quickly learnt Arabic and established friendly relations with their Arab environment. The colonies near Jaffa, Haifa and Jerusalem were model villages, self-governing communities each with its own church and school. They produced all the food they needed and soon had a great deal to sell not only in the local market but also for export. In a commercial report for 1896 the French consul in Jaffa stated that the German colonists exported wines worth 542,550 francs and eggs worth 67,000 francs.

Nor was German influence and enterprise confined to the army, colonisation and railway concessions. It began actually in the cultural field where German agencies were among the earliest cultivators. The movement began in 1841 when Frederick William IV came to an agreement with the Archbishop of Canterbury and the British government which resulted in the establishment of an Anglican bishopric in Jerusalem as a step towards a united Protestant church and ultimate church unity. From the beginning the German element in the bishopric was strong, and even English evangelical organisations associated with it availed themselves of the services of German missionaries.

In 1851 Prussian deaconesses arrived in Jerusalem, and in alliance with the second Anglican bishop established a small hospital and later on also a boarding-school. In 1860 the *Missionsgesellschaft für das Heilige Land* established the Syrian Orphanage in Jerusalem, probably the earliest modern trade school in the whole of Syria. Though its original founders were based on Basle the German element in the institution was preponderant. In 1871 the Berlin Missionary Society took over two Protestant schools in Bethlehem and Bait Jāla from the Anglican bishop and maintained them together with other new schools in the area.

By then German nationalism proved a stronger force than Protestant unity. The bishopric, which had been rent by internal

Cook's crusader, 15th October 1898

dissension and compromised by the second bishop's aggression against the Greek Orthodox communion, was gradually abandoned by the Germans. In 1869 the Crown Prince of Prussia visited Jerusalem and took formal possession of part of the site of the Hospice of the Knights of St John near the Holy Sepulchre, which the sultan had already made a present of to the king of Prussia. The British consul surmised correctly that the intention was to build a German church on the site, an indication of the impending end of the alliance with the Anglican bishopric. In 1887 the bishopric was reconstituted as a purely Anglican see, when the Germans definitely withdrew.

Interest in the Holy Land was not confined to German Protestants, for German Catholic organisations were equally active. A society based on Cologne took the initiative in establishing an agricultural settlement of Lazarist fathers at Tabigha, on the north-western shores of Lake Tiberias. In Jerusalem the Sisters of St Charles Borromeo established and maintained a hospice and a school; the latter became well known as Schmidt Girls' College. In addition to purely Catholic or Protestant institutions there developed also non-sectarian societies for biblical and archaeological studies, notably the *Deutsches Institut für Altertumswissenschaft* and the *Deutscher Palästina-Verein*.

There were thus considerable German interests in the Ottoman Empire and in Syria when in 1898 William II paid his second visit to 'Abdul-Ḥamīd. With him came an impressive entourage including the minister for foreign affairs, von Bülow, and a director of the Deutsche Bank. The latter wanted a new concession to enable his consortium to build the next stretch of the Baghdad railway beyond Konia. The Emperor was officially on his way to Jerusalem to open the new German church. His reception by, and secret negotiation with the sultan need not detain us; we are interested only in his visit to the Holy Land and Syria.

Escorted by German and Ottoman warships, the *Hohenzollern* with the Emperor and Empress on board appeared before Haifa on 25 October.[7] Elaborate preparations had been made for their reception by the Ottoman authorities, the German colony and an advance party of the imperial household in charge of the carriages, horses and baggage. Twenty-seven high Ottoman officials were in readiness to accompany the party and 600 picked troops to form the escort. The English travel agents, Thos. Cook and Son, provided a travelling camp, composed of some ninety sleeping, saloon and kitchen tents, and a large number of attendants, interpreters and servants.

On the brilliant afternoon of 25 October the Emperor and Empress landed and were given a royal welcome by the authorities. Apart from a ceremonial drive in the imperial carriage through the streets, with a strong escort of lancers, the Emperor confined his visits to the German church and school and replied very briefly to loyal addresses by his Protestant and Catholic subjects. Next day the imperial party left by carriage for Caesarea, preceded by the travelling camp and accompanied and followed by cavalry escort. On the way to Jaffa the governor of the province of Sūriyya and the governors of Jerusalem and Jaffa welcomed the Emperor and joined the imperial processoin.

In Jaffa as in Haifa the Emperor restricted his visits to the institutions of his subjects. He spent one night at a hotel in the German colony, and early next morning he left with the Empress both on horseback, for ar-Ramlah, some fifteen miles on the way to Jerusalem. The camp and the pompous trappings were all sent to Bāb al-wād where the Emperor planned to spend the night. Next morning, 29 October, he arrived at the main camp on the outskirts of Jerusalem.

Once his face had turned in the direction of Jerusalem, William II began to assume the character of a pilgrim. He proceeded from the camp to make a formal entry into the city. Attended by a cavalcade of knights wearing the mantle, he rode a charger and wore his service uniform and decorations under a white silk dust coat cut like a pilgrim's cowl. The Empress, attended by her ladies-in-waiting, drove in the imperial carriage. At Jaffa Gate the Emperor dismounted and the Empress alighted from her carriage. By the sultan's command the city wall to the right of the gate was knocked down so that his illustrious guest could enter the city through this wide gap and not through a gate.

Amid roars of guns from the citadel close by, the Emperor and Empress entered the city on foot and walked down to the Holy Sepulchre. Palm leaves were spread in their way and cobbled streets were covered with carpets. At the shrine the Greek Orthodox, Latin and Armenian patriarchs delivered speeches of welcome to which the Emperor replied. All the high ecclesiastical dignitaries of the other denominations were present.

The *Erlöserkirche*, the Church of the Redeemer, the ceremony of whose dedication William II came to witness, was built as already mentioned on the ground of which his father had taken possession in 1869. For the ceremony of dedication the Emperor entered the church to the strains of Handel's 'See the conquering hero come', and in his brief address he stressed Christian unity and prayed for world peace: 'As nearly two thousand years ago, so to-day, from this spot shall the cry resound throughout all the world, the expression of the ardent hope of all, "Peace on earth".'

On the same day the Emperor, attended by a company of marines, and in the presence of the Latin patriarch of Jerusalem, hoisted the German flag, on a plot of land on Mount Zion which he had received as a gift from the sultan, and officially handed it over to the representatives of the Cologne Catholic Society. On this spot, which is generally known as *La dormition de la Vierge*, there stood according to Catholic tradition the house in which the Virgin Mary lived and died, and on it stood the Church of the Apostles, the earliest Christian church. The German Catholics soon erected on the site a magnificent rotunda in the style of the famous church of Aix-la-Chapelle.

In addition to German institutions, the Emperor visited the Dome of the Rock and al-Aqṣā mosques, the Russian Church at Gethsemane and the Church of Nativity in Bethlehem. A special train took the imperial party to Jaffa. They sailed immediately and arrived at Beirut on 5 November. Two days later they left by special train for Damascus. The Emperor visited the Umayyad Mosque and ordered a wreath to be deposited on Saladin's tomb inscribed 'William II, German Emperor and King of Prussia, in memory of the hero Sultan Saladin'. Hitherto William II had said and done nothing of a political nature. But in his reply to the speeches of welcome at the Damascus banquet he said:

> I am under the influence of the thought that I stand upon the spot where one of the most chivalrous rulers of all time once dwelt, the great Sultan Saladin, a knight *sans peur et sans reproche*, who often had to teach his adversaries the true nature of chivalry. It is with these feelings that I joyfully seize the opportunity of thanking above all His Majesty the Sultan 'Abdul-Ḥamīd for his

hospitality. May His Majesty the Sultan, and may the three hundred million Mohammedans who, dwelling dispersed through-out the earth, revere him as their Khalif, rest assured that at all times the German Emperor will be their friend!

By his return from a visit to Baalbak, and before his special train took him back to Beirut, the Emperor knew that a translation of his Damascus speech had been printed in gold letters on handbills that were in circulation in Beirut and the rest of Syria. There was a great demonstration at the quay in Beirut when on 12 November the Emperor with all his party left Syria. Shore batteries and Ottoman warships fired salvo after salvo in salute as the *Hohenzollern* moved away from Syrian waters.

4

The German Emperor's visit, particularly his public declaration in Damascus, served ʻAbdul-Ḥamīd as a tonic. The comforting words, coming as they did from a powerful European monarch, contrasted very sharply with contemporary European hostility exhibited against the sultan during the troubles in Armenia and Crete and the war with Greece, and mitigated the sultan's political isolation on an international level.

There is little doubt, however, that ʻAbdul-Ḥamīd was popular with the majority of Muslims inside and outside his empire. His reign had lasted long enough for the majority of Syrians to become familiar with its vicissitudes of light and shade. Many of them not only did not regard his despotism as reprehensible but also thought that his rule was beneficial to their country.

Apart from the Hijaz railway with its religious and economic significance, perhaps the most important aspect of the Hamidian era was the expansion of the state educational system and the consequent social gain. New state schools were continuously opened so that at the turn of the century Syria was served by a wide, though by no means universal, elementary and secondary school system. At the secondary level the system was sufficiently diversified to embrace literary, technical (including crafts for boys and domestic science for girls) and teacher training. Under the general scheme of expanding military education, Syria's share was the establishment in 1904 of a military school in Damascus. A year earlier a school of medicine was established in the city by an imperial order. It was suggested at the time that the school was intended to attract native students who would have gone to the Syrian Protestant College or to the Jesuit College in Beirut. Later still a school of law and another for arts and sciences were established in Damascus, both destined ultimately to form the nucleus of a university.

But talented pupils continued as hitherto to be sent to Istanbul for further training as doctors, civil servants or army officers. From 1900 onwards they were sent also to *Dār al-Funūn*, the university which in that year had finally been well established in the capital. Here Syrian students could study law and engineering among other liberal subjects leading to professions. While the majority of pupils in the state schools in Syria continued to be Muslim, the number of Christian and Jewish pupils was steadily increasing. So also was the number of those non-Muslim students who went to Istanbul for further education, attracted particularly by the schools of law and medicine. Those who qualified served in the mixed courts or as army doctors respectively or practised on their own account.

A parallel though perhaps less spectacular development of independent schools, both native and foreign, is especially noteworthy. The education of the native Christians had never been a monopoly of foreign missionary or other agencies. Every community had its own schools which it continued to develop and modernise, irrespective of whatever foreign agencies had to offer. Thus in the last decade of the nineteenth century native Christian schools were not below similar foreign schools in efficiency. The teaching of science and languages in which foreign schools had had an initial advantage was now an accepted part of the curriculum of native Christian schools as well.

Similar developments are noticeable in Muslim education from the days of Midḥat Pasha onwards. Not content with the state system, benevolent societies and individuals assumed responsibility for opening modern schools. The curriculum of these schools was still essentially Arabic and Islamic in spirit and content, but it now included the teaching of science and foreign languages, as in the native Christian schools and the foreign schools. Of the modern Muslim schools which combined the traditional with a modern curriculum mention may be made of the National Muslim School maintained by Ḥusain al-Jisr in Tripoli and of the Ottoman Muslim College maintained by Aḥmad ʿAbbās al-Azhari in Beirut.

It is curious that a sultan who had done so much for the spread of education should have acquired a reputation for censoring the dissemination of knowledge. In most accounts of his reign, the operation of official censorship is marked as among the darker aspects. The censor is almost always depicted as ignorant and absurd, thereby implying that the adjectives could be applied to the master censor. That would be a travesty of the facts, for as he emerges at least from the reports of successive British ambassadors, ʿAbdul-Ḥamīd was neither ignorant nor absurd. While it is true that the Hamidian censorship, like most other censorships, had absurd aspects rendered obnoxious by overzealous and insufficiently educated officials, the sultan himself knew what he wanted.

He knew what information was likely to undermine the stability of his reign and therefore must be banned, and what information was conducive to stability and the advancement of learning and therefore must be freely diffused. But he did not initiate censorship; it was already in operation under ʿAbdul-ʿAzīz. The Hamidian censorship was, however, more comprehensive. At first only newspapers, but later on all printed matter was covered. The inspection of textbooks was provided for in the Ottoman education law of 1869. The purpose of the inspection is explicitly mentioned: 'to safeguard against any teaching contrary to the established moral and political order'.

To enforce censorship within the Empire was a relatively easy task; from force of habit it looked in the end as if it was self-imposed. But it was not easy to control matter printed abroad by exiles, for it often entered through a foreign post office operated by one or other of the European consulates. The censor had powers to inspect, seize or impound prohibited newspapers and books only if transmitted through the Ottoman post office.

The sole purpose of the Hamidian censorship was to combat sedition, not to prevent the diffusion of learning. Enemies of the sultan, Turks, Arabs and others, voiced their opposition from safe centres in Europe or nearer home in Cairo. Within the Empire, and in defiance of the censor, it was possible to publish only surreptitiously. Hence the anonymous handwritten placards distributed in Syria in 1880, and the leaflets printed more than a decade later on a hectograph machine by Armenian teachers in an American missionary school. Discoveries of such methods produced more stringent censorship.

It is important, however, to distinguish between censorship of this kind clearly designed to check sedition, and the 'censorship' of works of a literary character which meant little more than obtaining formal licence to publish in accordance with the provision of the law. One illustration must suffice. The publication of the classic, Ibn Khaldūn's *Muqaddimah*, had first to be licensed by the education department of the province of Sūriyya.[8] We cannot now know how long it remained under consideration, for that obviously depended on the diligence, intelligence and education of the official who had to examine the book and pass it as 'free from seditious matter'.

Another example of the watch over textbooks used in foreign schools and even over their extra-curricula activities is to be found in the demands made by the governor of Beirut in 1891 to the president of the Syrian Protestant College. The president was asked first to submit for inspection 'all textbooks used in all classes', no doubt in accordance with the provisions of the education law. The governor's other demand, based on an imperial order, required the president to submit for prior approval all orations to be delivered and all plays to be acted at prize-giving ceremonies. In both cases the governor politely explained that the demand was of general application embracing all schools.[9]

It would be a mistake, however, to assume that because of censorship the literary output was stifled. The facts point to an opposite conclusion. Careful scrutiny of bibliographies, lists of publishing houses and library catalogues is more indicative of the facts than the surmises of hasty or biased writers. Patient investigation of the lists will not fail to show that there was a constant flow of new books on traditional Arabic and Islamic as well as on scientific and modern scholarly subjects. It will also show a great variety of books printed for use in the new state and private schools. In addition there was a vast Christian and missionary literature for Catholic, Protestant and other denominations. There were also significant translations from foreign languages, dealing with science, history, drama and fiction. Although political criticism was banned, books bearing on political subjects are not entirely absent from the lists. Thus Naufal Naufal of Tripoli is listed as the translator into Arabic both of the Ottoman constitution and of the Rights of Nations.[10]

It would likewise be a mistake to credit ʿAbdul-Ḥamīd's censorship with success in sealing off his subjects in Syria from political enlightenment or from what he feared most, sedition. Well known periodicals as well as newspapers, published in Cairo by Syrian émigrés, were allowed free circulation in the country. While they were careful not to infringe the rules laid down by the censor they served to supplement the work of the schools in widening the intellectual horizons of the increasing number of literate Syrians. In addition foreign periodicals, in English, French and other languages, reached a good number of Syrians educated at foreign schools, either directly or through diplomats and missionaries.

Of course foreign periodicals and newspapers were not restrained in any way and they often carried items critical of the sultan and his government. Although the foreign press was scrutinised by the censor he had less power over its circulation, particularly if it came via diplomatic channels or through a foreign post office. Nevertheless his wrath was feared at least by the American mission in Beirut. One missionary advised against the publication of an article on Islam as likely to give offence. Another urged that the Board of Foreign Missions of the Presbyterian Church exercise care in what it published about Muslims since they received all the journals.[11]

From the facts discussed above emerges a conclusion about the Hamidian censorship contrary to current notions. It was not comprehensive and was not, where applied, as effective as we have been led to believe. But of course ʿAbdul-Ḥamīd was not the only autocrat who fought in vain against ideas. From his point of view, the ideas he fought so long were seditious, harmful alike to his own rule and to the society over whose interest he regarded himself as God's appointed guardian.

5

The ideas which the sultan feared most – and these were principally concerned with constitutional as opposed to absolute government –

could not be voiced publicly in the press or published in books within the Empire, but they were published abroad and often penetrated the censorship. Nor had the sultan any effective means of combating the secret expression and propagation of such ideas even in his capital. Simple in content and aim, these ideas presupposed that all the tribulations and humiliation of the state were due to the sultan's personal rule and that restoration of constitutional government held the master key to salvation and honour.

Hence all Ottoman liberals, in exile and in hiding at home, Turks, Arabs and others, never ceased to agitate for the restoration of the constitution and parliament. Not unexpectedly the agitation infected the sultan's own schools, civil and military, despite strict control of their curricula and textbooks. Thus about 1889 a few cadets under training at a military school in Istanbul formed a secret association to further the above-mentioned aims. They soon attracted other members from the other civil and military schools in the capital and furthermore succeeded in establishing contact with liberals in exile.

These furtive moves of the 'Young Turks' were organised for action in alliance with the Society or Committee of Union and Progress. Directed largely from abroad, the movement spread slowly from the capital to the provinces, especially after its members graduated and were posted as army officers or civil servants in centres as distant as Damascus and Salonika. In 1906 one of the earliest branches was formed in Damascus, the headquarters of the fifth army corps. Either simultaneously or a little later another branch was formed in Salonika, the headquarters of the third army corps. Both branches were strengthened by the recruitment of local members. Muḥammad Kurd 'Ali, the future president of the Arab Academy, was enrolled as a member in Damascus, through the more senior member, Rafīq al-'Aẓm.[12]

But it was from the Salonika branch that a revolution was proclaimed. In July 1908 the revolutionaries sent an ultimatum to the sultan: restore the constitution or face an army revolt. He chose the former alternative, and by the stroke of the pen the constitution of 1876 was restored, elections for a new parliament promised and the censorship lifted. Celebrating what they thought was a new dawn of liberty, the sultan's subjects of different races and creeds embraced and danced in the streets amid cries of joy. Writers and poets vied with one another in celebrating the occasion, condemning the old regime and eulogising the new. Colloquial singers were not far behind in their effusion. Below are the opening lines of a song by a Lebanese villager from Kisrawān:

O Muslims, O Christians! Hear the news proclaimed.
All the people of the land cry: long live liberty!

Refrain

O people of Kisrawān: say in one voice:
Long live the House of ʻUthmān, the prop of the sublime state
Long live Niyazi and Enver, and the imperial army.
'Crushed is the spirit of despotism' – proclaim it throughout the land,
The past will not return, the stars of tyranny are eclipsed.[13]

Niyazi and Enver were the two army officers who raised the banner of revolt in Salonika. But the revolutionaries had now become the power behind the government and the throne. Among the proclaimed aims of the revolution two deserve notice here: to ensure equality between all Ottoman subjects and to ward off the threat of foreign ambitions. It has been pointed out that one of the branches of the committee of Union and Progress in Syria had Arab members. The Salonika branch derived much of its strength from the support of an Arab general, Maḥmūd Shawkat Pasha.

The Syrian Arabs had therefore good reason to expect a fair deal under the new regime and within the Ottoman state. Together with other Arabs, the Syrians were quick to assert their right to equality with the Turks. The old Syrian demands were now revived: administrative decentralisation that gave the Arabs a share in managing their local affairs, and recognition of the Arabic language, in addition to Turkish, in official business and education. Since the Arab deputies in the parliament were a minority, the Syrain or Arab demands were also voiced through newly formed societies in the capital.

The first society to be formed, within a few weeks of the restoration of the constitution, was the Arab-Ottoman Brotherhood (al-Ikhā'). It hoped to further the Arab cause within the Ottoman Empire through constitutional means, but its hopes were quickly disappointed when external and internal developments led the

Committee of Union and Progress, within months of coming to power, to change its declared policy. In the first week of October 1908 Bulgaria, with the prior agreement of Austria, declared her independence. Two days later Austria announced the annexation of Bosnia and Herzegovina which had been under Austrian occupation since 1878.

When it became evident that the new rulers of the Ottoman Empire were powerless to take any counteraction, jubilation at the restoration of constitutional government gave way to frustration. The constitution was after all neither a talisman nor a substitute for strength, real unity and progress. The Committee of Union and Progress stood condemned by a dismal failure to maintain the Empire at least as well as 'Abdul-Ḥamīd did.

That shrewd calculator must have been mortified, but he seems merely to have utilised rather than engineered a counter-revolution by some army units which broke out in the capital in April 1909. Nevertheless the Committee held him responsible and decided to get rid of him. At the head of an army Shawkat marched on the capital ostensibly to restore order. Not without a struggle the mutiny was suppressed and martial law declared. A joint session of the chamber of deputies and senate passed a resolution deposing 'Abdul-Ḥamīd and proclaiming his brother Muḥammad Rashād as sultan. The resolution had already been legalised by Shaikh al-Islām.

These external and internal shocks silenced the liberals and strengthened the nationalist element in the Committee. It was obvious that Ottoman unity had failed to attract the Christians. To the Committee the Arab demand for decentralisation seemed to contain the seeds of a future separate existence. The Turks were the only loyal and reliable element in the state. Centralised administration and Turkish domination must therefore be strongly upheld.

The nationalist trend in the policies of the Committee became evident from the summer of 1909. The Arabs, who had hitherto sought nothing more than equality in a multi-national empire guaranteed by the constitution, became alarmed. A grave crisis in the relations between the two Muslim elements that formed the backbone of the Empire was rapidly developing. But there was as yet no evidence of Arab separatist tendencies. On the contrary prominent leaders of Syrian Arab thought were still solidly for loyalty to the Ottoman Empire.

Thus when in 1908 Muḥammad Kurd ʿAli returned from Cairo to Damascus and reissued *al-Muqtabas* it never, as he later insisted, 'called for separation from the Turks, but only desired the Arab rights to be respected within the larger Ottoman unity'. In 1909 Rashīd Riḍā visited Istanbul with two ends in view: to remove the 'recent misunderstanding' between the Arabs and the Turks, and to urge the establishment in the capital of an Islamic institution for the education of missionaries. With regard to the first aim he then wrote: 'It is well-known to us that Turkish statesmen fear the rise of an Arab state as an Arab caliphate in the Arabian Peninsula.' He assured the Turks that these fears were based on illusions, not facts.[14]

Nor was the striving towards Ottoman unity confined to the Muslim Arabs. For a number of influential Christian Arabs, inside and outside the Empire, were among its staunch supporters. In 1910 a farewell party was given by the Syrians in Cairo to Sulaimān al-Bustāni, the Christian Arab deputy for Beirut. When on that occasion Rafīq al-ʿAẓm complained that the Turks had denied the Arabs their rights and despised their language, Bustāni rejected both allegations. More important than this 'official' denial is the opinion of the independent Yaʿqūb Ṣarrūf who said: 'We must co-operate with the Turks, tender advice and remove misunderstanding; we must help them to integrate all races and religious communities so that Ottoman unity becomes a reality.'[15]

But despite all Arab assurances the new trend in Turkish policy towards them continued. Not only was decentralisation and recognition of Arabic refused, but the Brotherhood Society which put forward these demands was proscribed. The Arab movement in Istanbul was almost entirely Syrian in inspiration and personnel. It was therefore rash politics that measures little short of active Turkification should have been applied in the administration and the schools in Syria. Litigation and petitions to government departments could be accepted only in Turkish, and this language was made the sole medium of instruction in all state schools above the primary level.

Of the Arab societies formed in Istanbul after the restoration of the constitution only *al-Muntada al-Adabi* was spared by the Turkish authorities. Its members came from all the Arab provinces but there were proportionately more Syrians than others – and these included Muslims and Christians, deputies, civil servants and students. It was tolerated by the authorities partly because it was, at least outwardly, social and literary, and partly because deputies and officials were among its members. But henceforth any Arab organisation with political aims could be formed only outside the Ottoman Empire or underground inside it.

The rebuff administered to Arab hopes of collaboration with the Turks under the Ottoman banner had the immediate effect of driving some influential Arab individuals to extreme demands. To them decentralisation and recognition of Arabic were no longer enough; they now wanted complete equality between the Arabs and Turks as partners in the Empire. This was the aim of *al-Qaḥṭāniyyah*, a secret society composed mainly of Syrian Arab officers in the Ottoman army. It was not destined for survival. Another secret society was *al-Fatah* formed by some half dozen students in Paris whose aim was ultimate Arab independence.

A society calling from a foreign capital for Arab independence need not arouse the same suspicions aroused by an earlier call which also emanated from Paris. In 1905 Najīb 'Azzūri (Azoury), a Syrian Christian who had been an Ottoman civil servant before choosing to live in Paris, published *Le Réveil de la Nation arabe* which explicitly advocated Arab independence of the Turks. But Azoury had been suspected of being in the pay of the French government and his pioneering ideas may not therefore carry the same conviction as those of the students who followed in his footsteps.

But neither the few army officers nor the handful of students in Paris were the unchallenged representatives of general Syrain, still less of Muslim, public opinion. Indeed, more experienced and thoughtful Syrians were still striving for a basis of collaboration with the Turks. This is clear from the formation in 1912 of the Party of Ottoman Administrative Decentralisation with aims indicated by the last two words. Unlike the underground societies, the party operated openly in Cairo and attracted a larger number of members and enjoyed more considerable support in Syria itself and among the Syrians in exile. Rafīq al-'Aẓm and Rashīd Riḍā were two of its prominent members. The first was president and the vice-president was a Christian, Iskandar 'Ammūn.

There were good reasons for lingering Syrian, particularly

Syrian Muslim, sympathy with their Ottoman rulers. Although the Committee of Union and Progress had refused Arab demands; although its Turkish chauvinism was too evident in Syria; although in some Arab Muslim eyes it stood accused of secular and even un-Islamic tendencies; although its reputation was further tarnished by the suspicion of its subservience to the Jews and Freemasons, still the Committee was in charge of the destinies of 'the state of the caliphate'. Many of the scruples about giving it support were soon removed, though only temporarily, by the Italian occupation of Tripolitania in 1911 and the loss of almost all Ottoman territory in Europe to the Balkan League in 1912. To the average Syrian Muslim it was the power and prestige of Islam that was thus diminished.

But the Committee, now under the triumvirate of Enver, Jamal and Talat, learned nothing from these disasters to conciliate the Arab leaders who, notwithstanding the underground and practically ineffectual societies, continued to seek redress by legal means. Beirut was the scene of such an attempt. Both the city and the province of Beirut were the most advanced economically and educationally in Syria if not in the Empire. From the days of Midḥat Pasha, when the chamber of commerce in the city espoused the cause of reform, Beirut had maintained a reputation for taking the initiative.

Early in 1913 a committee representing all communities met, with official sanction, and adopted resolutions which differed little from previous Arab demands in their stress on more say in local government affairs and the recognition of Arabic. The resolutions were enthusiastically supported all over Syria from Aleppo to Palestine. But the Turkish reponse was discouraging, even though at this moment the grand vizier was none other than the 'Arab', Maḥmūd Shawkat Pasha. These matters, the official reply said, were for the elected deputies to settle with other deputies and the Porte in Istanbul. Nevertheless some conciliatory gestures to satisfy minor Arab demands were made, but on the whole the main demands were sidetracked, and further meetings of the Beirut committee were banned by the police.

The next Arab move was in June of the same year when a congress, predominantly Syrian in composition, was held in Paris. The French capital had been the centre for the ventilation of Syrian Arab demands on at least two previous occasions. But the congress was a more formal and representative expression of Arab demands than either the individual Azoury or the secret society of a few students. It is not clear why the congress was not held in a neutral country like Switzerland. It was certainly odd to hold the congress in the capital of the country whose interests in Syria went far beyond cultural matters and railway concession. Some members of the congress had therefore permanently compromised themselves in the eyes of the Committee of Union and Progress.

The Paris congress endorsed the resolutions of the Beirut committee, reiterated the need for decentralisation and the recognition of Arabic both in Syria and in the Ottoman parliament, and added a new demand, probably in deference to the wishes of the more extreme members of the secret societies. This demand, made public for the first time, was for 'a guarantee of the exercise of their political rights by the Arabs through actual participation in the administration of the Empire'.

It seemed for a moment that conciliation with the Turks was near. Through the mediation of the Sharif 'Ali Ḥaidar or 'Abdul-'Azīz Shāwīsh or both a draft agreement on the principles of reform was reached between Talat, representing the Committee of Union and Progress, and 'Abdul-Karīm al-Khalīl, on behalf of the Arab organisations. The agreed headings were endorsed by the Arabs, and accordingly an emissary of the Committee went to Paris and confirmed the agreement with the congress. The president of the congress, 'Abdul-Ḥamīd az-Zahrāwi, went to Istanbul and confirmed the agreement. However, the premature publication of its terms by a foreign news agency deceived the Arabs into the belief that it was finally ratified and they therefore published it themselves. This must have been embarrassing to a government who apparently did not intend to implement the agreement. It was promptly repudiated in the Turkish press.

The agreement went a long way to meet the Arab demands: recognition of Arabic as the medium of instruction in the lower elementary schools and the language of petition to government departments; Turkish civil servants below the rank of governor to know Arabic; devolution of more authority on local government in local affairs; at least three Arabs to be ministers and Arab under-secretaries in the various ministries to be in the same proportion; two members of the senate from every Arab province; at least five

Arabs as governors of provinces; Arabs to be appointed to the state council, appeal courts and the staff of *Shaikh al-Islam*; and finally Arab soldiers to be employed near their own districts, and if sent to distant lands their number to be in proportion to other racial groups in the Empire.[16]

With the failure of the agreement, the vague hopes of an Arab state and an Arab Caliphate, which we have noted in Syria as early as the middle of the nineteenth century, were now revived. An authoritative expression of these hopes is a letter or a message said to have been sent in 1911 by thirty-five Arab deputies to Ḥusain Ibn'Ali, the Sharif of Mecca since 1908, in which they recognised him 'as caliph, alone responsible for upholding the interests of all the Arab lands', and expressed readiness to rise under his leadership in order to shake off the Turkish yoke.

No Arab leader or organisation had worked out in any detail how to achieve independence of the Turks. Without adequate economic and military resources and with little national unity and an unawakened national consciousness, the few leaders of the movement were powerless to act after the failure of their efforts on the constitutional and political levels. They must have considered, at least tentatively as in the message from the deputies to the Sharif, the possibility of revolt. Did they contemplate, at this stage, an alliance with a foreign power, and if so was that power France or Great Britain? There is as yet no evidence of either. But the march of events provided the answer.

Barely a year after the failure of the Talat-Khalīl agreement the First World War broke out. Although Turkey declared her intention to remain neutral she was slowly drawn to the side of Germany. This was not due to a reckless Enver, but to a calculated state policy. Like all Turkish governments before them the Committee of Union and Progress feared first Russian and then French territorial ambitions. After the acquisition of Cyprus and the occupation of Egypt, Great Britain had far less pronounced designs. But such lingering Turkish goodwill was destroyed by Britain's alliance with Russia and France. Rightly or wrongly the Turks calculated that, whatever they did, an allied victory would result in the dismemberment of their empire, while a German victory would leave it intact.

Part Two

THE MAKING OF MODERN SYRIA

8

Syria in the McMahon Correspondence and other British Pledges

I

'THE Ottoman Empire has committed suicide', commented Asquith, the British Prime Minister, when early in November 1914 the Empire finally threw in her lot with Germany in the war. Suicide no doubt it proved to be, but rather a slow one. For the Empire survived long enough to make Syria a major theatre of war and to drive the Syrian and other Arab leaders to the extreme of seeking complete independence. Limiting the discussion, as we must, to Syria, the factors that directly influenced the shaping of its destiny in the next year or two were the wartime Turkish measures, the underground Arab movements, and the policies of the Sharif of Mecca, Great Britain and France.*

One of the immediate consequences of the declaration of war was the unilateral termination of the treaties under which Britain, France and Russia enjoyed capitulatory rights in the Ottoman Empire. Simultaneously the sultan asserted his claim to be the caliph of all Muslims, declared a holy war (*jihād*) against these powers, and called upon Muslim soldiers in their armies to mutiny. Britain had more reason than France and Russia to take the call

* The substance of this chapter and the next two has been built up from masses of heterogeneous British secret documents now open to historians for the first time. Care has been taken to adhere, as far as possible, to the wording of the original texts, and where no note is provided the source is identified by the date and writer and recipient of the document concerned.

seriously, not so much because of distant India and the large number of Muslims in the Indian army, but because of near-by Egypt over which a British protectorate was proclaimed. Across the border in Syria the fourth Turkish army was immediately mobilised with the declared object of freeing Egypt from British occupation. Jamal Pasha, minister of marine, was appointed commander-in-chief with jurisdiction embracing Sinai and Hijaz.

A British blockade of the Syrian coast became immediately effective and brought foreign trade to an almost complete halt. But agriculture was also hit by a conscription introduced at the beginning of the sowing season, on a scale and efficiency hitherto unknown under Turkish rule. Nor did the call on manpower end there, for labour was required for the construction of military roads and railways. The latter represented considerable extensions of the Palestinian section of the Hijaz railway, and the most important of these extensions was the line, with branches, between ʻAffūlah and Beersheba and beyond it in the direction of the Suez Canal.

Other damaging blows to the Syrian economy included the requisitioning of draught animals and the cutting of trees, including fruit trees, by the army. Wood as a fuel had to replace coal, which it was no longer possible to import, especially for running the trains. As a result most of the precious olive groves all over the country disappeared rapidly. Within weeks of the beginning of the war shortage of essential foodstuffs became acute and prices soared to fantastic heights, aggravated by depreciation of the currency. Although some speculated, many an honest merchant was ruined and many hitherto prosperous families were rendered destitute. The country was soon to experience real famine. As if all these misfortunes were not enough, swarms of locusts invaded the country in the spring of 1915 and destroyed the year's crop in the fields and stripped everything green to the bark.

The long-suffering peasants ascribed it all to God's wrath and prayed fervently for His mercy. But the few Syrians capable of political thought and planning saw in the international conflagration an opportunity, and in their country's misfortunes an impetus, to try and secure for it a better future. The Decentralisation Party was based on Cairo and outside Turkish control, but two secret societies were active in Syria itself. With increased experience and membership *al-Fatāh* had now made Damascus its headquarters. Its aims were shared by *al-'Ahd*, a newly formed society of Arab officers in the Turkish army. The two societies soon established contact and drew up a unified programme.

In the process the original Syrian movement for autonomy or independence was gradually transforming itself into a general Arab endeavour for liberation. It was extended first to embrace Iraq, if only because a great many members of *al-'Ahd* came from that country. The joint programme of the two societies may be summed up in a sentence: strive for independence from the Turks, but resist with them foreign domination of any Arab country; or to put it in other words, do not substitute foreign for Turkish domination.

Turkey's entry into the war against Britain made the Arabs in Syria and the adjacent countries an important element in British strategy and policy. British statesmen and soldiers perceived at once the great advantage to their cause of detaching the Arabs from the Turks and encouraging the Arab movement for independence. British moves on these lines began several weeks before the actual rupture with Turkey. On the instructions of Sir Edward Grey, the Foreign Secretary, government departments connected with Arab affairs including the India Office were informed on 1 September that 'directly Turkey joins Germany, His Majesty's Government should at once give every support and encouragement to the Arabs to possess themselves of Arabia and the holy places'.[1]

On the same date Grey informed the ambassadors in Paris and St Petersburg that in the event of Turkey's entry into the war against Britain and her allies the government of India was authorised to make a public announcement that 'no attack will be made by British forces on the holy places in Arabia'. It was desirable, he added, that similar assurances should be given by France and Russia. This was duly accepted by the two powers.

Three days later Sir Louis Mallet, the British ambassador at Constantinople, suggested in a telegram to Grey that if Turkey allied herself with Germany 'one of the most effective weapons would be support and organization of an Arab movement either openly or indirectly'. In Mallet's opinion an attack on the Dardanelles would be 'pulling the chestnuts out of the fire for Russia'. He regarded a British thrust from the Persian Gulf to capture Baghdad preferable. For the success of such a thrust the support of Ibn Sa'ūd and the Shaikh of Kuwait, among others, would be useful.

Three weeks later still, on 24 September, a telegram drafted by the Secretary of State for War, Lord Kitchener, and approved by Grey, was sent to Cairo with a message to ʿAbdullah, the second son of the Sharif of Mecca, asking a blunt question, 'whether he and his father and the Arabs of Hijaz would be with us or against us' in the event of Turkey entering the war on the side of Germany. ʿAbdullah, who had earlier in the year been put off by Kitchener himself in Cairo, returned a guarded but friendly reply. He and his father desired close relations with Great Britain but they required *written* guarantees against Turkish reprisals. 'Stretch out to us a helping hand', the Sharif is reported to have said to the messenger, 'and we will never aid these [Turkish] oppressors'.[2]

Before receiving ʿAbdullah's reply Kitchener returned to the charge. On the last day of October he sent another message with a definite promise and a hint: '. . . If the Arab nation assist England in this war, England will guarantee that no internal [*sic*] intervention takes place in Arabia and will give the Arabs every assistance against external foreign aggression. It may be that an Arab of the true race will assume the caliphate at Mecca and Medina. . . .' And yet neither Kitchener nor the British government as a whole had any settled policy regarding the 'Arab nation' in the peninsula or outside it immediately after Turkey's entry in the war.

On 27 November, Sir John Maxwell, the general officer commanding British troops in Egypt, asked Kitchener about 'the ultimate policy of England regarding Palestine and Syria in connection with the Arab movement'. Kitchener's reply was that as yet no 'distinct line' could be defined. Maxwell had good reasons for asking the question: 'It is necessary [he said] to know what line will be taken, as there is a good deal of nibbling even among [Arab] officers of the Turkish army. But I do not want anything said or done which may afterwards prove to have been a breach of faith.'

2

Not only Maxwell but the British civil authorities in Egypt were then receiving reports of unrest all over Syria, both among the Arab officers in the Turkish army and among the civil population. The reports confirmed that, like the Sharif of Mecca, the Syrian leaders were seeking an opportunity 'to break with the Turks'. According to the same reports there was a prevalent pro-British feeling. In her letter of 5 September, passed by military intelligence to the War Office, Gertrude Bell wrote that 'Syria, especially southern Syria... is exceedingly pro-British... dislike of growing French influence is universal'.

Maxwell himself corroborated this report. In his telegram to Kitchener quoted above he referred to 'considerable pro-English feeling' among the Syrian Muslims and added that 'all except the Maronites are anti-French'. The arrival in Cairo from Damascus of an unnamed dignitary, who had been once a candidate for the office of *Shaikh al-Islam*, was reported in a telegram dispatched on 9 November by Milne Cheetham, acting head of the British Agency. This dignitary is described as one of the leaders of the Arab movement and is quoted as saying that 'the majority of Mohammedans are anxious to come to an understanding with Great Britain and throw off the Turkish yoke, but are deterred from taking action by their fear of France. If given a guarantee that France would not occupy Syria they would side wholeheartedly with Great Britain'.[3]

There seems to be an element of exaggeration in these reports of pro-British sentiments in Syria. But there is also no doubt that a majority of enlightened opinion was for an Arab alliance with Britain and that the small minority of the Maronites desired an arrangement that would place them under French protection. This desire was strengthened by the Turkish unilateral termination of the special régime for Lebanon. The arming of the Maronites against the Turks, on the pattern of their arming against the Egyptians in 1840, was considered even before Turkey entered the war. But it was not proceeded with, on the advice of Sir Louis Mallet.

No doubt the Maronites played a discordant note in Syria. Not only did they remain on the whole aloof from the Arab movement, but they did not share the Muslim and other Christian Arab inclination towards a British alliance. They expected France to occupy Lebanon immediately on the declaration of war. In the expectation of this, some Lebanese Maronites domiciled in Egypt began to raise a force of volunteers, but the British authorities discouraged the move as likely to provoke Turkish reprisal on the Maronites in Lebanon itself.

Nevertheless Maronite emissaries arrived in Greece late in November and secured the agreement of the Greek government to sell them some rifles and ammunition and to ship the weapons to the Lebanese coast, provided a safe-conduct could be given through the British blockade. The Maronites declared they needed the weapons against Turkish 'incursions', but in reality they wanted to be ready for an insurrection to coincide with an assumed French landing. The episode was the subject of exchanges between Athens, London and Paris.

At the Foreign Office in London the scheme was regarded as 'crazy', and if carried out would have led to a massacre of the Maronites. The French government would only agree that a rising was premature but would not discourage it. To the British government on the other hand the scheme was not only premature but dangerous and must not, without active allied support which was not forthcoming anyway, be even tacitly encouraged. If despite the risks the Maronites still wished to proceed the Royal Navy would not oppose nor aid the passage of the arms.[4]

The Maronites did not proceed with the scheme. But the shadow of France began to darken the scene in Lebanon and in the rest of Syria. In deference to France the British authorities had to treat with care reports of pro-British and anti-French feelings among the majority of the Syrians, for already in December 1912 and January 1913 Grey had been forced to assure the French ambassador, in answer to a French press campaign accusing Britain of intrigues to annex Syria, that Britain had no such aspiration. But in the opinion of *The Times* this statement of British *désintéressement* did not mean a formal recognition of a French sphere of interest in Syria or an invitation to France to annex Syria. Indeed, Grey himself confirmed this conclusion in a conversation with the German ambassador. He said that his words to the French ambassador 'did not imply a disturbance of the *status quo*, which it was our object to preserve'.

This was the position on the outbreak of the war. It remained so when British soldiers began in 1914–15 to press for an understanding with the Arabs. But the politicians were still cautious. Consider for example the reception at the Foreign Office of the report that only fear of France stood in the way of an Anglo–Arab alliance. A senior civil servant, George R. Clark, wrote in a minute that France would be difficult to tackle. He referred indirectly to British preoccupation in lower Iraq and their hope of enlisting the support of Ibn Saʿūd and other Arab chiefs in that side of Arabia. If these rose against the Turks, Clark argued, 'the Syrian Arabs will probably be swept in'. The permanent under-secretary, Sir Arthur Nicolson, wrote on the same minute, which was seen and initialled by Grey, as follows: 'We cannot ask for any guarantees from France as to Syria. She regards the province as her own particular heritage. Leave matter alone.'

They did. But not for very long. Ibn Saʿūd did not rise. A British Indian expeditionary force which had captured Basra in November began an advance north in the direction of Baghdad. The threat to Egypt and the Suez Canal, however, remained serious. Preparations for the attack were in progress in southern Syria, while unrest among Arab army officers and the civil population was mounting. The bulk of the Turkish army then in Syria was Arab, three divisions in the province of Sūriyya and two divisions in that of Aleppo. Its officers hoped, if a rumoured British landing near Alexandretta materialised, to seize power in the Arab provinces, including Syria and Iraq. For, if successful, such a landing would have been linked with the Russian front in east Anatolia and would have cut off these provinces from Turkey proper. But to establish Arab administrations in these provinces required prior agreement with at least Britain.

As it happened the British landing was effected not in Syria but at Gallipoli with the object of forcing the Dardanelles and capturing Constantinople itself. To this new front the Turkish high command moved most of the Arab troops from Syria and north Iraq. While this troop movement weakened the Arab capacity to strike, the threat to the capital of the Empire and the seat of the Caliphate gave rise to a further extension of the Arab aims. Not only Syria and Iraq but the Arabian peninsula was now included. A strong element in the Arab movement, whose leaders were predominantly Muslim, thought, not without indirect British encouragement, that the moment was opportune for the restoration of the Caliphate to the Arabs. The long association of this aspiration in the Muslim Arab mind with the Sharif of Mecca turned their eyes in the direction of the then holder of that office, Ḥusain Ibn ʿAli. The first to sound the Sharif on behalf of the nationalists in Syria was a member of the

Damascene family of al-Bakri, old friends of the Sharif. More formal approaches from members of *al-Fatāh* and *al-ʿAhd* came almost simultaneously with the British overtures.

Ḥusain had been restive even before the outbreak of the war. He feared deposition and resented every Turkish attempt to extend central control to Hijaz. Every Turkish troop movement by the Hijaz railway, even in transit to the turbulent Yemen, he regarded as a potential threat to his position. He aspired not merely to maintain his spiritual office but also harboured secret designs of eventually becoming the independent and hereditary ruler of Hijaz and, not without ample encouragement from Arab Muslims, of assuming the office of caliph.

As we have seen the Sharif had already, on his own account, been conspiring against the Turkish rulers. The open rift with them was his reluctance to proclaim the call for holy war in Mecca on the not implausible plea that it would result in a blockade which would starve the people of Hijaz and deprive them of their main source of income – the pilgrims and the donations of provisions from Egypt.

The British government was favourably impressed, and indeed gratified, by Ḥusain's neutrality in the vital issue of the holy war. They sought to strengthen his resolve in oder to diminish the effect of the call for holy war at least on their position in Egypt and to reduce the danger of an invasion under the banner of Arab-Turkish Islam. Kitchener's overtures were intended precisely to do that. They were not unwelcome to Ḥusain, and no less welcome was the approach by the underground Arab movement in Damascus, inviting the Sharif to be its mouthpiece and leader.

The leaders were aware of French ambitions. They knew that in the Maronites France had a small but loyal supporter. They knew also that the majority of the population – Muslims, Druzes and other Christians – feared and detested French pretensions. France was then heavily engaged defending her national territory in Europe and, despite Maronite expectation, could ill-afford to spare troops for involvement in Syria. There was, moreover, no land under French control contiguous with Syria or any Arab country in Asia.

Britain, on the other hand, had long been more involved in Arab affairs in the Near East. Not only did it possess Aden as a colony, not only did it have various treaty relations with chiefs in the Arabian peninsula, not only was it in occupation of Egypt and the

Sudan, but a British Indian army was at that moment fighting its way to Baghdad, the ancient capital of the Caliphate.

Recognising these facts, and realising that without the support of a foreign ally they could not alone shake off Turkish domination, the Arab leaders had to choose between a French or a British alliance. A Russian alliance was hardly a possibility. Russia was even more remote than France, had less naval strength than either France or Britain, and was then reeling under heavy German onslaughts.

The balance was definitely in favour of a British alliance. On the whole the British record in India and Egypt was better, from an Islamic or Arab point of view, than that of France in Algeria, Tunisia and Morocco. There was at least less Arab fear of British than of French territorial ambitions. Finally it was Britain, not France, who showed immediate eagerness to win the Arabs to her side. It is true that the first British approach was only to the Sharif and concerning Hijaz alone. But it was soon translated into an approach to the Arab national movement in Arab Asia.

The story of the negotiations which the Sharif conducted with Great Britain on behalf of the Arab national movement has often been told, but always without reference to the British documents. This is the first account primarily based on these documents. It is restricted to Syria and is designed to show how her political future was decided largely between Great Britain and France.

3

In the early months of the war, Russia began to press the recognition of her old claims to Constantinople and the Straits. The claim was reluctantly conceded by Britain and France. In return France sought and received some Russian recognition of her interest in Syria, but with a reservation about Palestine where Russia had considerable cultural and religious interests.

Once the question of Constantinople had been settled the French ambassador in London approached Sir Edward Grey with the suggestion that Britain and France should define their respective interests in Asiatic Turkey. This was in March 1915. Grey conveyed to the British ambassador in Paris his reply to the French suggestion: while the British government had not yet formulated its territorial desiderata, its mind was made up that 'when Turkey disappeared from Constantinople and the Straits there must, in the interests of Islam, be an independent Moslem political unit somewhere else. Its centre would naturally be the holy places, and it would include Arabia, but we must settle what else should be included.[5]

The dispatch containing this passage was corrected and initialled by Grey himself in red ink. In another passage he said that it was not yet decided whether Mesopotamia should be included 'in this independent Moslem state' or Britain herself would claim it. The five words inside the quotation marks were added in red ink by Grey.

Within the next six weeks or so, Grey had occasion to elaborate these pronouncements to Sir Reginald Wingate, governor-general of the Sudan, and Sir Henry McMahon, High Commissioner in Egypt. He repeated his idea of 'an independent sovereign Moslem state' in the Arabian peninsula, emphasised that it would control the Holy Places and added that it would include more of as yet undefined territories. As to the Caliphate he was definite that it was a matter 'for the Moslems to decide without interference from non-Moslem powers. Should Moslems decide for an Arab caliphate, the decision would naturally therefore be respected by His Majesty's Government.'

Grey went a step further. He authorised Wingate and McMahon to make a public announcement 'at any time or place you think opportune' regarding the Arabian peninsula, the Holy Places and the Caliphate along the lines he indicated to them. Such an announcement was actually made in the form of an unsigned and undated circular. It was widely distributed and reached the Hijaz and, among other Arab leaders, the Sharif of Mecca.

McMahon confirmed that Arab public opinion favoured an Arab Caliphate and that the Sharif would be a popular choice. However, he expressed some reserve concerning the term 'independent sovereign state', since, he said, 'the idea of an Arabian unity under one ruler recognised as sovereign by other Arab chiefs is yet inconceivable to the Arab mind'. But he had no doubt that by position and descent the Sharif was 'the only possible central rallying point for the Arab cause'.

McMahon had thus shown his hand even before the Sharif began the correspondence with him. McMahon had yet to receive confirmation that the Sharif was precisely that central figure and that, when the correspondence started, he had a mandate from the most vocal Arab leaders speaking for the majority of the population in the richest and most advanced of the Arab lands. Unity was the key idea in their scheme. As to the chiefs in the Arabian peninsula their respective positions were to remain virtually unchanged within an Arab confederation or federation under the Sharif as an overlord.

It is clear from the above sequence that London was more liberal than, and far ahead of, the British authorities in Cairo in anticipating the potential of the Arab movement. But the Sharif's natural caution was overcome neither by Kitchener's overtures nor by the announcement made on Grey's instructions. It was the insistent invitation from the leaders of the Arab movement in Syria that made him come out, not merely as a prospective independent ruler of Hijaz, nor as a likely candidate for the Caliphate, but above all as a possible Arab sultan-caliph stepping into the shoes of the Ottoman sultan.

The Sharif was well aware that the movement he was called upon to lead was national, not religious in character, and he accepted this fact without any reserve. The Syrians converted him to their old idea of administrative decentralisation with which they began agitation under the Turks. The liberated Arab lands would form a loose confederation or federation with full allowance for local interests and religious minorities. Thus when in July 1915 he wrote his first letter to McMahon proposing an alliance with Britain in return for recognition of Arab independence, the Sharif spoke of 'the Arab nation'. This is in contrast with the public statement he was to issue about a year later on the proclamation of the revolt. He was then at pains to justify himself to the Muslim world for rising against the legitimate caliph, and had therefore to stress the religious side, the defence of Islam against the godless Committee of Union and Progress.

British recognition of Arab independence was sought within specific limits which embraced the Arabian peninsula (with the exception of Aden), Iraq and Syria (including Lebanon and Palestine). The ensuing correspondence was bedevilled all along by shortcomings on the Arab as well as on the British side. It will soon be apparent that the Arab side lacked diplomatic experience, showed inordinate optimism and gullibility inexcusable in politics and, possibly on account of difficult means of communication, had too many individual 'spokesmen' of the cause.

The British shortcomings were more in individual officials and politicians than in their government. Too often in early Anglo-Arab relations the convictions, prejudices and even ignorance of such individuals were allowed to influence policy with disastrous consequences. Too often amateurishness was allowed to hide behind mysterious phrases and devious language. This was the more regrettable because it was employed in dealing with a people whose national character and speech is notoriously explicit.

The Sharif's first letter fell into the hands of such individuals. It was received under cover of a private note from ʿAbdullah to Ronald Storrs, oriental secretary to McMahon. McMahon had been in Egypt for about six months and all his previous experience was in military and administrative service in India. He was much dependent upon Storrs who had already had some ten years' service in Egypt. Storrs did in fact exercise a great influence in shaping his chief's thought on Arab affairs. His was the responsibility for all translations of the letters exchanged with the Sharif from Arabic into English and vice versa. Storrs's sole helper in this task was an Arabicised Persian who did not prove very creditable later on as an inspector of education under the British administration of Palestine.

Storrs boasts in his memoirs[6] that he was responsible for suggesting the Arabic equivalent of 'protectorate', and goes out of his way to have it printed in Arabic characters – but wrongly. Some of the other Arabic words and phrases which he occasionally reproduces transliterated in Latin characters are not without mistakes. But linguistic proficiency apart, his factual accuracy in reporting was not above reproach. Scarcely had his report on his visit to Arabia in June 1916 been sent to London when McMahon had to telegraph that it was very rough and contained 'many errors'.

Nevertheless he was from the very beginning the first link in the chain of communication between the Arabs and Great Britain. In his minute dated 19 August and marked secret, Storrs states that the Sharif's terms bore an exact resemblance, especially in regard to frontiers, to the views frequently expressed by Rashīd Riḍā, the prominent Syrian Arab leader domiciled in Cairo. And yet Storrs was, like his chief, still in the dark as to the exact origin of the Sharif's proposals. Small wonder that Storrs assumed them to be the Sharif's own and therefore excessive and pretentious, possibly intended as a basis for bargaining. Storrs did not, however, follow even his own guess. Thus instead of negotiations he recommended postponement of any discussion on the question of the frontiers. McMahon had no hesitation in following this line, particularly since he had already committed himself to a fundamental reserve concerning the British government's idea of 'an independent sovereign state', Arab or Muslim.

It is curious that McMahon should have sent to London, to start with, not a full translation of the Sharif's letter but merely a summary with a suggested reply which, as recommended by Storrs, was evasive on the question of the frontiers. London acted on this summary, and the full text arrived later. In addition to the Foreign Office, the departments directly concerned were the War Office and the India Office. Kitchener's interest in the matter had already been noted. The India Office was equally interested because of the treaty relations with Arab chiefs and because of the campaign in lower Iraq. Apart from expressing reserve concerning these two matters, they traced, more accurately than McMahon and Storrs, the origin of the Sharif's terms to the pan-Arab movement. Again more perceptively than McMahon and Storrs, the India Office remarked that a general reply to a specific question might alienate the Sharif. And finally showing more sense of diplomacy than the 'experts on the spot', the India Office suggested that 'Abdullah should be invited to Cairo for negotiations, if only concerning the 'Sharifate'.

A Foreign Office minute dated 25 August on this subject opens with remarks by Clark. 'McMahon and his advisers', he wrote 'are in a better position than any one else to gauge the Sharif's sentiments.' Whether this view is justified or not must be left to the foregoing discussion to suggest. However Clark's logic led him to recommend adhesion to McMahon's draft reply and to suggest 'discussions' rather than 'negotiations', at McMahon's discretion.

The next entry on this minute is by Nicolson who wrote: 'This matter is very urgent... someone should procure the assent of Lord Kitchener and Mr. Chamberlain [India Office] by personal interview. A reply to Sir H. McMahon should go off this afternoon.'

This must have been done at once, for Grey concluded the minute with this order: 'Send the telegram now with Mr. Clark's addition.'

Thus on the question of frontiers McMahon's proposal to return an evasive reply was approved by all concerned. However, McMahon was authorised, if he thought it advisable, to send a 'private message' that the British government was prepared to 'discuss' the matter. And once more a bait was thrown in the Sharif's way. If he was proclaimed caliph by the Muslims the British government 'will welcome the resumption of the caliphate by an Arab of the true race'.

Within hours of receiving Grey's telegram McMahon replied in a secret dispatch No. 94 dated 26 August that he had not availed himself of the permission to suggest discussions to the Sharif. 'The moment', he wrote, 'in my opinion has not arrived when we can safely discuss even a preliminary agreement.' His explanation that it was dangerous for the Sharif to send his son or another representative to Cairo does not make sense, because that was precisely the manner in which contact, by letters and verbal messages, had been established and maintained by the two sides since the beginning of the war. If Cairo was really dangerous, Jiddah might have served as a more convenient and safer meeting place. But it is obvious that McMahon was still for evasion, not for clarification.

The Sharif's prompt reply showed how wrong were the experts in their preliminary assessment of his position. The Caliphate, he wrote, was a side issue; what he wanted was a definite reply on the central question of the frontiers. These were not his demands but those of the Arab people who regarded them as vital for their future. This time it was the Sharif who mentioned Anglo-Arab discussions in his letter, but McMahon ignored the suggestion. And yet while studiously avoiding direct discussions with the Sharif, McMahon and other British officials on his behalf or independently began 'unofficial' discussion with a number of individuals in Cairo, without the Sharif's knowledge and without any attempt to ascertain whether he agreed or disagreed with the tenor of these discussions, their purpose and outcome.

4

These unofficial discussions are known only through British reports which are, like any wartime reports, somewhat one-sided. Their writers were obviously at pains to seek confirmation, not contradiction, of their own point of view, national and personal. Very seldom do we find in them an unfavourable opinion, and if we do it is soon dismissed as proceeding from 'intransigence' or 'fanaticism'. At any rate, written and signed statements from the Arab side are lacking. But before Turkey entered the war, ʿAzīz ʿAli al-Miṣri, one of the founders of *al-ʿAhd*, informed the British authorities in Cairo of his committee's plan to establish an independent Arab state comprising the Arabic-speaking countries roughly south of the line made by the Alexandretta–Mosul–Persia frontiers, and inquired whether Britain would support such a state. After Turkey's entry into the war, ʿAzīz with his Arab associates in the Turkish army hoped to raise a revolt in Iraq.

Grey authorised Cheetham in Cairo to encourage the movement 'in every way possible' and to pay ʿAzīz a sum of money. The money was refused, apparently because, in Cheetham's words, "Azīz and his party showed anxiety as to our ultimate intentions regarding Basra and Baghdad'. ʿAzīz elaborated the position in a conversation with Philip Graves, *The Times* correspondent. 'It is a matter of honour', he said. If Britain proposed to annex these Arab provinces, the Arabs would probably fight with the Turks. If Britain intended to set up an independent Arab state closely allied to herself, then he and his friends would lend their whole-hearted support.

Another record of Arab opinion is contained in an unsigned 'note' on the future of Syria, written in French by Abdullah Sfer Pasha, a Maronite in the service of the Egyptian government, on 19 November 1914, probably at British request. The note is accompanied by a report of Sfer's conversation with Georges Picot, the French consul-general in Beirut who, on the rupture with Turkey, was transferred to the French Agency in Cairo and put in charge of Syrian affairs.

Picot must have given the Maronites in Egypt an impression that a French landing in Syria was a possibility. Hence the scheme of raising volunteers to aid the landing or, at least, to keep the Maronites thinking of France. But Sfer was inclined to the British view that such a move was dangerous to the Christians in Lebanon. On the political future of Syria as a whole, Sfer favoured decentralisation and is generally close enough to the nationalist point of view:

> Les Syriens prient la Grande-Bretagne de les aider à assurer à leur pays un régime basé sur le principe de l'indépendance ou, tout au moins, de l'autonomie. Il ne serait pas juste, en effet, que le Liban ayant toujours joui d'une entière autonomie eût à la perdre en changeant de suzerain; et, d'autre part, le régime dont jouit l'Égypte voisine ne semble pas permettre un autre moins libéral pour la Syrie.[7]

'Azīz's views as recorded by Graves were sent to London under cover of Cheetham's dispatch of 13 December 1914, in which he said that these views 'coincide with those of the Sharif of Mecca and other Arab leaders whose agents are in communication with the Egyptian authorities.'

Cheetham's dispatch was written just before McMahon arrived in Cairo to take office as High Commissioner. In the six months or so before the correspondence with the Sharif started, he had ample opportunity to acquaint himself with the essence of the programme of the Arab national movement as was then formulated – a British alliance that did not prejudice Arab independence. It would seem a great surprise to anyone reading the documents fifty years afterwards how meagre was the information on which McMahon and Storrs based their recommendations to London and how much reliance London placed upon those 'experts on the spot'. Hence it is a singular puzzle why authoritative and written expressions of the Arab demands were disregarded, and policy was based on scraps of evidence or even thoughtless remarks gathered in conversations with individuals.

It is also a mystery how 'independence' could be so whittled down to 'autonomy' or 'tutelage' or 'protectorate' or 'control'. On the very day, 14 July 1915, that the Sharif's first letter to McMahon seeking British recognition of Arab independence was received in Cairo, Sir Mark Sykes, a Member of Parliament then serving with the rank of Lieutenant-colonel as head of an intelligence branch in the War Office concerned with all the Arab countries, revealed a secret British report on the partition of Turkey in Asia. This was the report of an interdepartmental committee under the chairmanship of Sir Maurice de Bunsen, and on which Sykes served as a member. Its report was submitted to the Cabinet on 30 June.[8]

In brief, the report recommended that Britain should acquire Iraq up to Mosul and those parts of Syria south of a line running from the Khābūr-Euphrates to Palmyra, then to Damascus and Acre on the Mediterranean. The rest of Syria was left for France. While speaking of the possible 'annexation' by France of the zone assigned to her, Sykes envisaged in the British zone some Arab government under the 'nominal suzerainty' of the Sharif. (Let us note that this rôle assigned to the Sharif came before his formal approach to Britain seeking recognition of Arab independence.)

Sykes discussed the contents of the report with Maxwell and probably also with McMahon. In addition he discussed their implications with Sultan Ḥusain Kāmil and a few Syrian Arab notables in Cairo. Since we have only Sykes's own testimony of what was said it is important to sound a warning well expressed by two of his admirers in the *Dictionary of National Biography*. Sykes, they wrote, 'had a habit of reading his own thoughts in the minds of others'.

An alternative scheme in the de Bunsen report envisaged, on the fall of Constantinople, the survival of some restricted Ottoman sovereignty in Syria under British and French surveillance. The sultan of Egypt was reported as agreeable to the idea of joining Syria to Egypt, even under British tutelage. Saʿīd Shuqair Pasha, we are told, considered the annexation of any part of Syria by France as 'undesirable from the Syrian point of view, both Moslem and Christian'. If Dr Fāris Nimr is quoted correctly, he agreed, while objecting strongly to the division of Syria and Palestine under any scheme, to place 'Damascus-Palestine' under British 'protection', but objected to the retention of any Turkish power. According to Sykes neither Nimr nor Shuqair 'had the slightest hope of an independent Syria holding together for a day'. (Let us recall that Antonius had represented his father-in-law, Nimr, as one of the authors of the 1880 placards calling for Syrian independence.)

The most consistent and authoritative of Sykes's witnesses was Rashīd Riḍā, but his evidence was 'inconvenient'. Riḍā was for another independent Islamic state, if Constantinople fell – exactly as Grey had stipulated. To Riḍā this state would be 'an independent

Arabia including Syria and Mesopotamia under the Sharif'. He refused to entertain any diminution of the independence of this Arab state. Hence Sykes branded him as a 'fanatic' and added, with obvious irritation, that to men like Riḍā 'force is the only argument they can understand'. If the question of absolute Arab independence was a matter of honour to 'Azīz al-Miṣri it was both honour and religious faith to Riḍā. But Sykes does not report on any conversations with 'Azīz.

What Sykes was trying to get from individual Syrians was acquiescence in a policy he advocated with great persistence: division of control over Syria between Britain and France in anticipation of an agreement between the two powers on such a division. With some native welcome for his idea, Sykes hoped to persuade the French to renounce their claims to southern Syria up to Acre. He even thought they could be persuaded to give up Damascus.

Henceforth indications of British intentions in regard to Syria must be sought not only in the official policy statements emanating from the Foreign Office but also in the views of a few determined individuals such as Sykes. But his was not a lone voice. Others no less influential expressed similar views and championed similar policies. In a note dated 25 August 1915, later sent to Grey, Wingate advocated 'a federation of semi-independent states . . . owing allegiance to a single Arab primate and looking to Great Britain as its patron and protector'.

This probably meant no more than an independent Hijaz under the Sharif as caliph, for outside the Arabian Peninsula Wingate makes provision for 'zones of interest'. The British zone included Iraq and the seaboard of Palestine as far north as Haifa. The interior of Palestine is reserved for 'a special arrangement' in which Russia would participate. The French zone embraced the rest of Syria. In both the British and French zones, the administrations were to be conducted on 'liberal', 'progressive' and 'national' lines.

No doubt McMahon, who had from the beginning shown an aversion to the idea of sovereign Arab independence, found Sykes's and Wingate's ideas agreeable. These ideas were put forward at a time when he had to consider the Sharif's second letter insisting on a definite reply on the frontiers within which Arab independence would be recognised. According to the information then available to him about British and French claims, McMahon might have recommended a direct answer to a direct question on these lines: we can promise to recognise Arab independence only in Hijaz. As to Iraq and Syria our own interests and those of our ally France are involved. Before we can make any promises these interests must first be reconciled with your demands by negotiations among the three sides.

But McMahon was against negotiations. What he did was to seek an Arab opinion, other than that of the Sharif, to confirm a policy roughly along the lines Sykes and Wingate had indicated. By a fortuitous circumstance McMahon encountered at this moment a convenient witness. Lieutenant Muḥammad Sharīf al-Fārūqi, an Arab officer in the Turkish army, deserted to the British lines at the Gallipoli front and was sent to Egypt. He was an Iraqi member of *al-ʿAhd* who had been educated at the military school at Constantinople. He was then twenty-four years old, and obviously had no diplomatic or political experience. There is no evidence that he knew English, and the conversations he had with McMahon and his staff must have been through interpreters from Arabic or Turkish.

The available records contain no signed statement by Fārūqi in any language. What is available is reports of conversations with him and a 'statement' in English embodied in a report by the Director of Military Intelligence, Gilbert Clayton. The report and 'statement' are contradictory on a vital point. In the former Fārūqi is said to have made the extravagant claim that 'he was accredited by the committee [of either *al-ʿAhd* or of its joint committee with *al-Fatāh*] and that through him the reply of England [to the Sharif's offer] may be given'. This was unlikely, considering the presence in Cairo of ʿAzīz al-Mịṣri, senior to Fārūqi in years, military rank and in the hierarchy of *al-ʿAhd*. In the 'statement', Fārūqi is reported to have said more soberly, 'I am not authorised to discuss with you officially our political programme. . . .'

McMahon, who rejected more than once the idea of discussion with the Sharif, the accredited spokesman of the Arab movement, now chose not only to discuss with Fārūqi the vital question of frontiers but also to make what we are told were Fārūqi's views the basis of his recommendations to London. But Fārūqi's evidence as reproduced by McMahon and his assistants is confused and contradictory. He is reported to have marked only Arabia (i.e. Hijaz) for independence, while Iraq and Palestine were to be autonomous under British guidance. Furthermore he recognised French interests in the rest of Syria, but

> . . . a French occupation of Syria would be strenuously resisted by the Mohammedan population. They would, however, no doubt seek England's good offices towards obtaining a settlement of the Syrian question in a manner as favourable as possible to their views and would almost certainly press for the inclusion of Damascus, Aleppo, Hama and Homs in the Arab confederation.

Those familiar with the mental habits of an Arab educated in Turkish schools would immediately suspect that this is a language and a manner of expression entirely foreign to him. His reported dispensation of territory bears too close a resemblance to Sykes's and Wingate's, and is too much at variance with ʿAzīz al-Miṣri's stand on Iraq and Rashīd Riḍā's on Syria and the other Arab lands to carry conviction. According to Clayton, Fārūqi stated that he had sworn on the Koran to uphold Arab independence according to the national programme. How could an army officer, who moreover boasted that he was a descendant of the second caliph, so easily violate his oath and honour? But assuming that the passage quoted in the above paragraph is an approximation of Fārūqi's own ideas, it is a big riddle why McMahon fastened on the illustration and completely disregarded the principle clearly stated in the first sentence.

In his own report of his conversation with Fārūqi, McMahon says that Fārūqi conceded French interests in the 'north west' but emphasised that the Arabs would oppose by force of arms French occupation of the 'districts of Aleppo, Damascus, Hama and Homs'. The word 'district' does not occur in Clayton's report as quoted above, and the mention of the four place-names is not in the same order in Clayton and McMahon. These are not minor discrepancies when taken together with the serious contradictions just pointed out.

Fārūqi's integrity was not above question. In his reported conversations with Clayton and McMahon he sounds more English than the English. He was soon enough employed by the British administration in the Sudan, but when he went to Hijaz he promoted anti-British feeling among the people, and when the Sharif sent him to Cairo as his agent he proved so unsatisfactory that his master wished to replace him by another more agreeable to the British authorities and himself. His later conduct was even less creditable.

And yet Fārūqi is credited by McMahon to be his authority for the phrase in his letter of 24 October 1915 to the Sharif proposing the exclusion of 'portions of Syria lying to the west of the districts of Damascus, Homs, Hama and Aleppo'. It is common knowledge that the interpretation of this phrase has poisoned Anglo–Arab relations ever since.

5

During the first half of 1915 the situation in Syria continued to deteriorate. After the failure of his attack on the Suez Canal, Jamal Pasha gave more attention to the reports on the Arab underground movement, its designs and its contact with the enemy. Army officers whose loyalty was suspect had been moved with their units to Gallipoli, and the remaining forces in Syria were very thinly spread. Jamal feared an enemy landing and feared even more an internal revolt. For if synchronised with an enemy landing, such a revolt would have found him, as he wrote in his memoirs, in a 'perfectly desperate situation', unable to repulse the enemy or suppress the revolt.[9]

The pasha's wrath fell mainly on civilian Muslim notables. Scores were arrested and several of them banished to Anatolia. Prominent men were tried by court martial on various charges including treacherous plans for revolt and treasonable communication with the enemy. None of the Maronites who had actually planned and sought arms for a revolt was apprehended. Eleven Muslim leaders were publicly hanged in a square in Beirut. Among them was 'Abdul-Karīm al-Khalīl. The Syrian cry of anguish reverberated as far as Mecca.

The Germans were quicker than the Turks in realising that repression could not kill the Arab movement. Under German pressure belated Turkish concessions began to be brandished before the Syrians. The German consul in Aleppo took an active part as an intermediary. Reports were spread that the Kaiser had actually persuaded the sultan to grant the Arab demand for autonomy, or to proclaim a dual Turkish–Arab monarchy on the lines of Austria-Hungary.

It was probably as a counterbalance to the Arab national movement that in 1915 Jamal Pasha inaugurated in Jerusalem the Ṣalāḥiyya College (so named after Saladin). The pan-Islamist Shaikh 'Abdul-'Azīz Shāwish was appointed principal and prominent Palestinian and Syrian jurists and men of letters were recruited as lecturers. The college, which taught through the medium of Arabic and Turkish, had a distinct Islamic tone. It continued till 1917 when it was moved to Damascus where it faded away in the last days of Ottoman rule.

British intelligence knew of these German and Turkish attempts to reconcile the Arabs, and the British authorities in Cairo feared that such a reconciliation would present a united Muslim front on the Egyptian border at a moment when British prospects in the whole Near East were rather dark. The Gallipoli expedition failed to achieve its objective; Egypt was still threatened by fresh troop movements in Palestine and the arrival of German equipment and staff officers; the Sanūsi was giving trouble on the western side of Egypt and the borders of the Sudan; the advance in southern Iraq was soon to be halted at Kūt.

To detach the Arabs from the Turks and to thwart the German attempts at mediation was an urgent political and military necessity. The success of such a scheme would weaken the Turkish army, would prevent the revival of the call for holy war and would win the British forces the goodwill of the Arab civil population. On 13 October 1915 Kitchener telegraphed Maxwell: 'The Government are most desirous of dealing with the Arab question in a manner satisfactory to the Arabs. Please telegraph to me the headings of what they want and discuss with McMahon. You must do your best to prevent any alienation of the Arabs' traditional loyalty to England.'

In his reply Maxwell complained that McMahon had not emphasised the presence 'of a large and influential Arab party actually in the Turkish army who are sworn to the cause'. It was necessary and urgent to win them by coming to terms with the Sharif. Maxwell was of the opinion that the time for 'vague generalities' had passed. He concluded his message as follows:

> If their overtures are rejected or a [favourable] reply is delayed any longer the Arab party will go to the enemy . . . which would mean stirring a religious feeling at once and might well result in a genuine *jihād*. On the other hand the active assistance which the Arabs would render in return for our support would be of the greatest value in Arabia, Mesopotamia, Syria and Palestine.

Clayton confirmed that the Turks and Germans had been bidding for Arab support, and added that it was due to Arab hostility to the Turks that the call for *jihād* had so far failed. Should the Arabs side with the Turks against Britain, *jihād* could become 'a very grim reality'. There was little doubt that the Sharif's attitude was that of 'the majority of the Arab peoples'. It was important and urgent to win them by returning a favourable reply to the Sharif. 'To reject the Arab proposals', wrote Clayton, 'or even to seek to evade the issues, will be to throw the Arab party into the arms of the enemy.'

McMahon, too, came to realise the importance and urgency of Arab support. He wrote that they had reached 'the parting of the ways', that they might go against either side in the war, that the Sharif's position had become one of great difficulty and even danger, and that a decision was required without delay. And yet the facts leave no doubt that he himself was responsible not only for the delay, but also for its causes by persistently 'seeking to evade the issues' and of resorting to 'vague generalisation'. He kept the Sharif's second letter of 9 September under consideration till 18 October. On that day he sent a telegraphic summary backed by a personal letter to Grey stressing the urgency of the matter.

Grey and his staff had by then seen all the reports from Cairo. A decision on the vital question of frontiers had to be given in a great hurry, with the result that McMahon was once more allowed discretion to resort to evasion and generalities. It is important to establish how this came about. There is a lengthy minute by Clark dated 19 October with which he submitted a map showing 'the northern frontiers of Arabia as desired by the Sharif of Mecca', marked with red pencil all along the Mediterranean coast and from near Marsina eastward to the Persian frontiers and down to the Gulf. The Arabian peninsula is not shown on this map.

In Clark's opinion, the matter had two aspects: the first military and according to experts very urgent, and the second political and involving British and French interests. He was for an independent

Arab state looking to Britain as its founder, 'with territory rich and wide enough to furnish resources'. He saw no difficulty in reconciling British with Arab interests in Iraq, but in order to win the Arabs to the British side in the war Arab interests and French claims in Syria had to be reconciled. Measures should be taken in order to create the Arab state and 'for this purpose negotiations should start forthwith'. In a short comment, Nicolson agreed, despite the difficulties, to proceed on the lines suggested by Clark. This meant negotiations with both the Arabs and the French.

Grey himself drafted the telegram reply to McMahon in which he incorporated a paragraph put forward by the India Office concerning Iraq. Kitchener's contribution was only an adjective; he suggested the addition of 'warm', which Grey changed into 'cordial', before the word 'assurances'. The first page of Grey's draft is on the notepaper of 10 Downing Street, not that of the Foreign Office. Here is its substance in his words:

> You can give cordial assurances on the lines, and with the reserve about our allies, proposed by you. . . . There is no difficulty in speaking without reserve about Arab Peninsula and holy places. The general reserve you propose is however necessary more especially for the north-western boundaries. . . . But the important thing is to give our assurances that will prevent Arabs from being alienated, and I must leave you discretion in the matter as it is urgent and there is not time to discuss an exact formula. The simplest plan would be to give an assurance of Arab independence saying that we will proceed at once to discuss boundaries if they will send representatives for that purpose, but if something more precise is required you can give it.

But McMahon was still neither for precision nor for official discussion with the Arabs. Once more he neglected to suggest discussion. On this occasion his neglect was tantamount to disobeying instructions rather than exercising discretion. Once more he followed his bent and employed vague language. As regards Syria, he asked the Sharif in the letter dated 24 October to exclude portions 'lying to the west of the districts of Damascus, Homs, Hama and Aleppo' on the ground that they 'cannot be said to be Arab'. He did not say because France was interested in them, since he reserved French interests in a more general phrase that might well cover the whole of Syria and not merely the portions specified.

In a secret dispatch No. 131 dated 26 October addressed to Grey, McMahon explained that he had endeavoured to make the terms of his letter to the Sharif acceptable to the Arabs as well as to leave Britain as free a hand as possible in the future, but he stressed 'the religious importance' of Damascus to the Arabs, though he failed, out of real or feigned ignorance, to say anything about the more important Jerusalem, the third holy city in Islam. He mentioned in his letter to the Sharif only one ally, France, because neither Russia nor Italy had any pronounced 'territorial' claims. On Arab independence and the French claims in Syria as a whole McMahon wrote:

> I have been definite in stating that Great Britain will recognise the principle of Arab independence in purely Arab territory, this being the main point on which agreement depends, but have been equally definite in excluding Marsina, Alexandretta and those portions on the northern coast of Syria which cannot be said to be Arab, and where I understand the French interests have been recognised. I am not aware of the extent of French claims in Syria, nor of how far His Majesty's Government have agreed to recognise them. Hence, while recognising the towns of Damascus, Homs, Hama and Aleppo as being within the circle of Arab countries I have endeavoured to provide for possible French pretensions to these places by a general modification to the effect that His Majesty's Government can only give assurance in regard to those territories in which Great Britain is free to act without detriment to the interests of her ally France.

In plain language and fewer words, and without the use of two different formulae, this means no Arab independence in Syria, even in principle, if France claimed the country. Why McMahon did not say so, and why Grey of all honest men acquiesced in this double-talk is another of the mysteries of the story. The futility of McMahon's use of two formulae was soon exposed when the Sharif, in reply, protested that the portions of Syria McMahon sought to exclude were Arab, there being 'no difference between a Moslem and a Christian Arab'. The first formula was immediately rendered superfluous when its author had to acknowledge in yet another letter the Sharif's contention that the areas in question were Arab, but that France was interested in them.

The Foreign Office had already foreseen the difficulty, but delayed tackling France on Nicolson's instructions. In the great rush on 19–20 October there was obviously no time for consultation.

Before the end of the month, however, discussions with France were definitely sought, but the proposed discussions with the Arabs were forgotten. The British argument with which they planned to confront the French was roughly that the promise to the Sharif was dictated by urgent military necessity in a theatre of war which was the direct responsibility of Britain. While French interest in Syria was not overlooked in the correspondence with the Sharif, it was expected that the French would make moderate claims so as not to frighten the Arabs and rob the British military authorities of the advantage of Arab friendship. British military advantage in the Near East was also to the advantage of France, since no British troops would be withdrawn from France to meet a possible Turkish–German attack on Egypt. With Arab co-operation this necessity would not arise.

But Britain approached the discussion with France with diminished resolve. In his telegram on 6 November informing McMahon of the decision to discuss with France 'the boundaries of an independent Arab state', Grey betrayed, for the first time in the history of this matter, less than his usual grasp of the facts. He obviously succumbed to McMahon's method of regarding the views of individual Arabs expressed orally more authoritative than those of their official spokesman, the Sharif, expressed in writing. Thus Grey wrote: 'I propose to concentrate on getting French consent to inclusion of Damascus, Homs, Hama and Aleppo in Arab boundaries. . . . Our primary and vital object is not to secure a new sphere of British influence, but to get Arabs on our side against the Turks.'

This was amplified and emphasised by Grey in a departmental order over his initials: 'Make it clear that we have told the Arabs we cannot make promises about Syria irrespective of the interests of our allies; that we have no intention of standing in the way of the French there or making claims of our own; that our sole object is to detach Arabs from Turks, and unless this is done Egypt and Sudan may be endangered.'

Two days after this categorical denial of any British territorial interest in Syria, a memorandum dated 15 November on 'Policy in the Middle East' was submitted by Sykes. Like the other British soldiers concerned, he was for detaching the Arabs from the Turks, but he conceded Arab independence only in Hijaz. Over an undefined area in southern Syria and Iraq he recommended the proclamation of 'an internal and external British protectorate' and a similar French protectorate north of the British areas. To put this into effect a landing at Alexandretta was necessary.

About a week later Sykes saw McMahon's correspondence with the Sharif, and in that light submitted revised proposals. He was still for landing a British or an allied force near Alexandretta to which the Arabs could rally. To overcome French susceptibilities, Sykes recommended that, once a British force had cut off the Arab lands from Turkey near Alexandretta, the allies should recognise and protect 'provisional government or governments in the *vilayets* of Beirut, Aleppo, Damascus, Jerusalem and Hijaz and the *Sanjaq* of Dair az-Zur [and] Urfa during the war . . . [and] guarantee the above areas as the minimum of independent Arab territory after the war'.

Under this scheme France was to have exclusive monopoly of economic concessions and supply of advisers in the province of Damascus and the district of Urfa, while Britain, Russia and Italy had similar concessions in the rest of Syria. Iraq was to be administered by Britain on behalf of the Arabs. France should recognise the importance and urgency of forestalling the German attempt at reconciling the Arabs and Turks, and of weakening the Turkish army by Arab defection on the eve of another attempt to advance on Egypt through Palestine. Then notwithstanding Grey, the ultimate authority on foreign policy, Sykes wrote: 'Our task is to get Arabs to concede as much as possible to France and to get Haifa outlet and Palestine included in our sphere of enterprise in the form of concession to us.'

Clark wrote in a Foreign Office minute that Sykes's idea might be put to the French. He doubted whether the India Office would agree concerning Iraq, but 'that can wait for closer discussions with the Arabs'. This minute was initialled by both Nicolson and Grey.

6

The scene was thus set for discussions with the French *and* the Arabs. But while no attempt was made for any discussions with the

Arabs, Anglo-French discussions began in London in November 1915, with Georges Picot as the chief French representative. The military aspect of the Syrian and Arab question was discussed first. A note dated 29 November from the War Office to Clark at the Foreign Office was accompanied by a secret report on the discussions with Picot. According to this report, Picot was 'absolutely uncompromising, and held *no* hopes whatever of France making any offer of independence to the Syrians'. Furthermore, if an expedition to Alexandretta was to be sent, two-thirds of its force must be French.

In the same report the dangers of a united Arab–Turkish front, of a more successful *jihād*, and of the possibility of having to move British troops from France to the Near East, are all suggested arguments for use in discussions with Picot so as to persuade him to be more accommodating. But if despite these arguments the French remained intransigent, the report recommends that Britain should reserve the right to deal with the Syrian question in a manner consonant with the requirements of the security of the British position in Egypt.

But British civil servants could seldom be as firm as that. They were in fact even less successful with Picot than the soldiers. It is clear from the minutes written on 29 November and 1 December by Clark, Nicolson and Grey, partly as comments on Sykes's forecast of possible Turkish 'massacres' of Christians in Syria and the elimination of 'all French holding ground', that the British side was very anxious to convince Picot that France stood to lose as much as, if not more than, Britain by allowing the Arabs to go over to the Turkish–German side, and neglecting to open a front in north Syria.

On the first of December, Clark reported that Picot had remained unimpressed, and that when asked to define the 'French claims' in Syria, he replied that they were 'possession (nominally a protectorate) of the land' from Cilicia along the Taurus eastward to Diyarbak, Mosul and Kirkuk, and from there to Dair az-Zūr on the Euphrates and then along the desert to the Egyptian frontiers. Picot was supported by Ambassador Cambon, who was, in Clark's opinion, more '*intransigeant*' than even Picot.

Nicolson put it to Picot that the Arabs were willing to accept French advisers, to give to France a monopoly of concessions and ample guarantees for French educational and other establishments, all of which might 'develop into a French protectorate'. But Picot remained unmoved; nothing short of French annexation, he maintained, would satisfy France. But he was prepared to recommend to Paris 'to throw Mosul into the Arab pool' if Britain did likewise with Baghdad.

With this provisional offer by Picot began the process of bargaining which led to the division of Syria and Iraq into French and British spheres of influence. The official British stand was still what Grey wrote after reading the minutes by Clark and Nicolson: 'The Arabs will not now be gained by promises without action, and it is hardly worthwhile to pursue the subject. I suppose we must make clear to M. Picot that we have no designs in Syria and can promise nothing about it to anyone [word is illegible] unless the French agree.'

Both of Grey's pronouncements were within days unaccountably disregarded. Another chance of telling the Arabs the stark truth was missed and Britain did soon acquire, through negotiations with France, territorial interests in Syria. It was at this moment that a reply to the Sharif's third letter was formulated. On 10 December a telegram was sent to McMahon informing him that the Alexandretta project was not approved and that there was little hope of obtaining from the French any assurance 'that will really satisfy the Arabs'. But instead of asking him to tell the Sharif this much, he was definitely instructed 'to keep the negotiations with the Sharif in being', to say that as regards Syria 'the interests of others were involved' and that 'a further communication will be sent later'.

McMahon had now to acknowledge that the coastal regions of the provinces of Aleppo and Damascus were Arab and inhabited by Arabs, but since the interests of 'France' were involved the matter required careful consideration and a further communication on the subject would be sent. Nicolson was annoyed that McMahon was explicit in mentioning 'France' to the Sharif instead of 'others'. But no further communication was sent to the Sharif. Instead McMahon sent £20,000 out of the £50,000 he had recommended as subsidy to the Sharif. The Turkish government had cut off their annual donation, and McMahon seems to have calculated that British money, if not assurances, was likely to influence the

Sharif. Once more McMahon's calculation proved mistaken. The Sharif took the money, but insisted in his reply that it was 'impossible to allow any derogation that gives France, or any other power, a span of land in those regions'.

And yet McMahon was not throwing away British money for nothing, as his subordinate Ronald Storrs was more than twenty years later to suggest in his autobiography.[10] Here again Storrs's account is at some material variance not only with the facts, but also with some of the figures contained in documents which must have once passed through his hands.

No doubt McMahon acted on strong military advice. All the evidence available to him confirmed the belief that even 'passive' Arab assistance, to use his own phrase, was valuable in weakening the Turkish army in Iraq and Palestine and thus saving British lives. To the soldiers no less than the politicians that was more valuable than the gold whose expenditure Storrs lamented.

McMahon's stand in this matter was strengthened by Wingate who, speaking from a military point of view, pointed out that the German success in the Balkans, the British check before Baghdad and other military uncertainties in the Near East all tended to reinforce German designs, military and political. At the beginning of December 1915 the Arab question seemed to him 'most critical', and he therefore urged 'further and stronger assurances to the Sharif'.

None was forthcoming, not because of lack of goodwill at the Foreign Office in London but because of France. As a result the Sharif's forthright letters were still evasively or vaguely answered. He was not a head of state and he had not the benefit of a civil service and diplomatic tradition. Direct discussions or negotiations with him were studiously and persistently avoided. Even now when the future of the fairest and richest Arab countries, for which he sought independence, was being decided he was still ignored. But British hands (and tongues) were tied by a recognition, no matter how undefined, of French interests in Syria.

Agreement with France was therefore necessary 'before we can say anything I won't say definite but even plausible to the Sharif'. This was Clark's summing-up in a minute on 11 December. He saw the French taking advantage of the urgency of the Arab question to Britain in order to force recognition of 'preposterous'

French claims in Syria. He was in favour of risking 'the Arab danger' rather than recognising the French claim 'to the whole coast from Egypt to Marsina'. Since the war committee was to consider the Arab and Syria question, Clark suggested it might hear Sykes 'who is not only highly qualified to speak from the point of view of our interests, but who understands the French position in Syria today – and is in a sense sympathetic with it – better probably than anyone'.

Nicolson left it to the committee itself to decide whether to call in Sykes, but Chamberlain suggested reference to the Prime Minister. Asquith agreed to call in Sykes but he also directed that the India Office be represented. These minutes were not seen by Grey, or at least his comments or initials are absent from them. Hence the reference to Asquith.

Picot went to Paris for consultation. There was a lull of ten days without telegrams, minutes and meetings. Then abruptly a one-page typed minute dated 21 December follows the papers discussed above. It is the outcome of a meeting held at the Foreign Office, and attended by Picot, on the subject of 'the future French sphere in the proposed Arab state'. Its terms are as follows:

> French territory, or direct administration [in Anatolia]: southern limit approximately Tarsous – Killis – Birijik – Jezirah; eastward of this to be arranged with Russia.
> Arab state, to include all lands to the south of this line with the following provisions:
> (*a*) Arab state to be divided between England and France into spheres of commercial and administrative interest, the actual line of demarcation to be reserved, but it was agreed that it should pivot on Dair-az-Zūr eastward and westward.
> (*b*) That the Lebanon should, so far as is practicable, retain its present constitution, but that it should comprise Beirut and that the governor should be nominated by the French government.
> (*c*) That the coast as far south as Beirut should be policed and protected by France.
> (*d*) Jerusalem to form an enclave, its boundaries yet to be defined.
>
> The following points were reserved:
> (1) The allocation of the Mosul *vilayet*.
> (2) The position of Haifa and Acre as outlets for Great Britain on the Mediterranean for Mesopotamia.

This very important document was seen and initialled by Nicolson and Chamberlain, but not by Grey or Kitchener. According to its terms nothing of Syria was left for 'the Arab state' except, by implication, the lands east of the river Jordan and the interior districts from Damascus to Aleppo. Thus were drawn the outlines of the so-called Sykes–Picot agreement six months before its birth. It remained for Mark Sykes and Georges Picot to work out the details, more in accordance with the already expressed views of the former than those of the latter. It also remained for the British and French governments to associate Russia in the division of the spoils as finally settled in a tripartite agreement. The Sharif and the Arabs were forgotten.

There are two puzzling questions concerning what took place in the Foreign Office between 10 and 21 December 1915 and Grey's attitude to it. These require further research. The first question concerns Grey's approval of the instruction to McMahon to keep the negotiations with the Sharif in being while knowing that it was hopeless to secure any concession from France satisfactory to the Arabs. The second question is concerning Grey's acquiescence in Sykes's proposal to secure a British 'outlet' on the Syiran coast, despite Grey's own repeated disclaimers that Britain had no territorial designs in Syria.

Sykes was indeed another example of an individual proving himself stronger than the institution he served. He was surely more than an adviser, for in the long run British policy in the Arab land was decided along the lines he advocated and not along those broadly defined by Grey and his professional advisers.*

* This chapter and the next two supersede my paper entitled *The Husain–McMahon Correspondence* submitted in January 1937 to the Royal Commission on Palestine with a map, drawn under my supervision, of the Ottoman administrative divisions of greater Syria in 1914. My paper was published for private circulation, but in 1938 George Antonius published *Arab Awakening* and advanced arguments similar to mine and his book included a map similar to the one I had specially prepared. The Report of the Royal Commission also contained a map almost identical with the one I submitted to them. In the light of much new evidence both my paper and Antonius's account now require drastic revision.

9

Wartime Agreements and Post-War Disagreements – The Arabs, Britain and France

I

THE ambitious plan of an Arab rising in Syria and Hijaz simultaneously had to be abandoned partly because of Turkish action and partly because of British inaction or even opposition. In Syria, where a beginning was seriously contemplated, the plan was frustrated by the movement of Arab troops from Syria to Gallipoli, by the execution of prominent civilian leaders and by the failure of the proposed British landing at Alexandretta to materialise. In the end the revolt began in Hijaz as preferred by Britain. Although the Sharif had accepted British arms and money, it was left to him alone to decide the right moment for a break with Turkey. Accordingly not before the first week in June 1916 did he proclaim the Arab revolt.

On 21 October 1915 Kitchener surmised that 'the Arabs will, I fear, wait until they see which way the war is going to end before they openly decide to break away from Turkey'. On 29 November, Grey wrote that 'nothing will move the Arabs in our favour except military action giving them protection against the Turks'. While it is on record that the Sharif did ask for a British military diversion on the Syrian coast, neither Kitchener nor Grey was proved right. For when the Arabs did revolt, British military prestige in the Near East was very low. Gallipoli had to be evacuated and a British division with its commanding general had to surrender at Kūt in Iraq. Furthermore, Jamal Pasha, with von Kressenstein as chief of staff, had moved his headquarters from Damascus to Jerusalem and begun active preparation for a second attack on the Suez Canal.

The preparations for the attack were accompanied by harsh measures against the civil population. In particular, the 'treason' trial of Arab notables was resumed and purposely prolonged in order to strike terror into the hearts of other potential leaders. Far away in Mecca the Sharif sensed an approaching danger to himself and the cause he led. If he left the initiative in their hands, the Turks had more than enough forces in Hijaz to depose him and scatter his followers.

Enver himself had just inspected the war theatres in the Near East and visited Medina. A force with German staff officers was already in the city, ostensibly on its way to Yemen. It could easily have been employed against the Sharif. Jamal's execution in the spring of 1916 of yet another and larger group of Syrian leaders, including ʿAbdul-Ḥamīd az-Zahrāwi, had greatly incensed the Sharif and contributed to the precipitation of the revolt. From Damascus, Beirut and Jerusalem,* where twenty-three men were publicly hanged, the cry of anguish reverberated once more in Mecca calling upon the lord of the Arabs to avenge Arab blood.

The course of the revolt before its forces captured ʿAqaba and its cause was embraced by a large majority of the people of Syria does not concern us here. But it is important at this juncture to reveal new facts on the British attitude to the scope and purpose of the revolt, and on Faisal's rôle in Syria before his return to Hijaz on the eve of the revolt.

In April 1916 the outlines of the Sykes–Picot agreement were communicated to McMahon, and he and Clayton recommended that its terms should be withheld from the Sharif and all other Arab leaders. To divulge the terms would open a controversy on the Syrian question which was not in the interests of Britain and France. According to McMahon the Sharif was then showing signs 'of taking action' which McMahon hoped 'to confine to Arabia'. The raising of the Syrian question at that moment might have diverted the Sharif's activity 'in an unfavourable direction'. In other words, he might have begun in Syria, instead of Hijaz or possibly in the two countries simultaneously. That would have created difficulties for

* The execution in Jerusalem of the Mufti of Gaza and his son, an officer in the Turkish army, was carried out in 1917, not 1916.

Britain with France when the two powers had just agreed on the partition of Syria.

British fears were well founded. Reports of Russian atrocities against the Muslim population in eastern Anatolia and their capture of Erzurum had greatly pained Faisal and the underground Arab movement in Syria. They feared, moreover, that the Russian advance would soon reach north Syria. Faisal wrote to his father a letter, a copy of which eventually reached McMahon, that with the ʿAnazah beduins he and his friends planned to defend the Syrian Arab homeland, the key to Hijaz.

At this moment Prince Sabah-ud-Din and his party, opposed to Enver and his colleagues, made a peace offer to the allies which included renunciation of Turkish sovereignty over Syria, Iraq and Arabia. Faisal, who remained hopeful of an accommodation with the Turks, was attracted. But neither he nor his friends, still less the allies, could take very seriously an offer from a well-meaning but powerless group. Soon Faisal had to obey his father's summons and to bid farewell to Jamal never to see him again.

But meanwhile Faisal's anxiety about the Russian advance was communicated by the Sharif to McMahon. McMahon expressed appreciation of the Sharif's 'good faith' in a telegram to London on 30 April in which he said: 'In view of dangers of anything that may savour of acquiescence in hostile attitude of Arabs against our allies, I propose urging the Sharif to confine action to Arabia proper and recall Faisal.' McMahon said he trusted the Sharif but not Faisal. He knew, however, that both were against French claims, and therefore 'it would be most unwise to encourage their action in Syria'. To render the Syrian plan impossible of execution, McMahon proposed to withhold the Sharif's subsidy till the revolt began in Hijaz not in Syria.

All of McMahon's recommendations were approved by the Foreign Office in London, and action was taken with regard to Arab anxiety about Russian intentions. After reference to Russia, instructions were sent to McMahon to inform the Sharif that the reported atrocities against the Muslims were perpetrated by Armenian militia not Russian soldiers, and to assure him that the Russian commander-in-chief had no plans of reaching Arab territories 'lying within boundaries indicated in your letter to us in July last'.

Apart from respect for French interests in Syria, Britain was anxious to provide a demonstration to the Muslim world that the Sharif of Mecca, the descendant of the Prophet, was in revolt against the government of the Ottoman sultan-caliph. Furthermore, a revolt in Hijaz was of more immediate military importance to British strategy. There was as yet no plan of a large-scale invasion of Syria through southern Palestine. But any weakening of Turkish preparation for the second attack on the Suez Canal, and any engagement or diversion of Turkish troops elsewhere in the area, was of great importance to British strategy.

According to Jamal Pasha, British military activity east of the canal began only in 1916 after they had concluded the agreement with the Sharif. The revolt which broke out some two months before Jamal's second attack on the canal was thus a blow to the pasha's plans.[1] It may be suggested that this is an exaggeration on the part of a commander who is anxious to account for his failure. But Jamal is substantially borne out on this point by authoritative British accounts.

One such account is by a staff officer, later well known as Field-Marshal Lord Wavell, who served on the Palestine front. He wrote that the value of the Arab revolt to Britain was indeed great: it removed the danger of establishing a German submarine base on the Red Sea; it diverted substantial Turkish reinforcements and supplies from the Palestine front to Hijaz; and its forces protected the right flank of the British army when it began to advance through Palestine.[2] He might have added that it tied down thousands of Turkish troops in Medina and had taken prisoner thousands more in addition to several thousands killed.

Perhaps more important than its military achievement in Hijaz, the Arab revolt gave the Syrians, groaning under Jamal's heavy yoke and powerless to take action themselves, new hope for the future. To the Arab movement in general the revolt provided a rallying point: many Arab officers in the Turkish army began to desert in order to join the Sharif's forces, and prominent civilians outside Turkish jurisdiction were ready with moral and active support. Lingering religious sentiment that had still bound some conservative Muslim Arabs to the Turks was virtually destroyed by Jamal's brutality. To a sizeable majority the Sharif provided a more valid alternative to the Turkish sultan: he was not only a Muslim religious leader but also an Arab nationalist.

2

> 'I am a friend of the British government. What promises I have made . . . I and my sons will, with God's help, keep to the letter. A *sharif* [an honourable gentleman] has one word, and that word he will keep. And I hope that the British government will, according to its past history, keep faith to the letter. . . .'

Thus spoke Ḥusain Ibn 'Ali in October 1916 to two Indian Muslims who visited him in Mecca as pilgrims but reported on the visit as British military intelligence officers. According to their reports the Sharif's forces were deliberately kept short of ammunition. 'I firmly believe', Ḥusain told them, 'that if I get the supplies I ask for I can occupy Syria.'[3]

This contingency was not regarded by the French as impossible. Hence they continued to be suspicious of the British civil and military authorities in Cairo. But according to Wingate, who succeeded McMahon from the beginning of 1917, nothing was done to undermine French interests as provided for in the Sykes–Picot agreement. The French political representatives in Cairo and Jiddah remained unconvinced, and Wingate complained of their meddling with 'Hijaz affairs'. To allay French fears Wingate confirms that the Sharif was kept short even of rifles.[4]

British intelligence was well aware that the Sharif's followers in Syria were increasing. He was at least as well informed about Syrian conditions as was British Intelligence. Syria was on his list of priorities second only to Hijaz. If in the following paragraphs we rely almost exclusively on the latter it is because the Sharif was just as poor a keeper of records as he was a careless diplomatist. Let the fact be clearly stressed that he neglected to convert his understanding with Britain, particularly regarding Syria, into a formal treaty. Like most honourable people of his race at that time he seems to have relied on verbal understanding with a friend even more than on the precise terms of formal covenants. The Sharif's sons shared his trust in Britain. In a conversation with the head of the French mission in Jiddah in February 1917 Faisal stated that 'between Great Britain and the Arabs were unwritten bonds of mutual understanding'.

It is therefore important to note some serious misgivings, ever present from the beginning, in British high quarters about the want of candour with the Sharif. Thus when the outlines of the Sykes–Picot partition plan of Syria were drawn, the Foreign Office consulted the departments concerned. In the replies from the War Office and the Admiralty occurs an identical remark, that Britain and France were in the position of the hunters who divided up the skin of the bear before they had killed it. The War Office, however, added the advice that the Sharif should be informed of 'the approximate limit of the country which we and the French propose to let him rule over'.

But the Sharif had made it clear that he rejected all French claims to any span of territory in Syria. In Syria itself the opinion of the majority, Muslim and Christian, continued to be anti-French. Although he was never for any specific commitment to the Arabs, McMahon advised London to warn Paris of this fact, and showed foresight in remarking that 'in this [Syrian question] lies considerable danger to our future relations with France'.

From the India Office equally clear advice was tendered. The Secretary of State asked whether the British government was not going to convey to the French government the Sharif's categorical rejection of any form of French control in Syria, and added that 'His Majesty's Government may hereafter be under some suspicion of bad faith if, with the information before them, they allow the negotiations to proceed without warning to the other party'.

The advice was not heeded. The skin of the bear was divided in advance among the would-be hunters. The Sharif's terms were simply 'fully understood and taken note of'. But he and the accessible Syrian leaders in Cairo were left in the dark until it was much too late. As to the Syrian leaders who survived Jamal's executions, and the Syrian population as a whole, their hope was pinned, in ignorance of what fate had in store for them, on Britain and the Sharif.

Intelligence reports reaching Cairo bear this out. Apart from their political content, to be noted presently, these reports speak of the misery and hardship which all sections of the population had to endure. Their number was steadily diminished by war casualties, disease and famine. There is, however, no evidence to confirm current assertions that the Jews in Palestine or the Christians in Lebanon were singled out for harsher measures than the Muslim majority. Turkish ruthlessness was in fact indiscriminately applied to Muslim, Christian and Jew alike. Unlike other parts of Syria, Mount Lebanon was spared conscription; men were merely drafted into labour corps and employed locally. Syrian Muslims had to fight in fields as distant as Gallipoli and Sinai.

On the political side three reports deserve special mention. An agent who passed under the name of Muṣṭafa or Maurice according to circumstances was smuggled into Syria through the offshore island of Arwād. He reported the prevalence of a general pro-British and anti-French feeling except among the Maronites. This agent visited Tripoli and Beirut on the coast, and Ḥimṣ, Damascus, Jerusalem and Beersheba in the interiors. Discontent with Turkish rule was widespread, famine and disease were thinning the population, and the Sharif's revolt was popular.

Another report is by a Zionist Jew, 'an inhabitant of Athlit, Mount Carmel', who requested that his name be concealed. He wrote mainly on economic conditions, communications and army formations, and included short notes on senior Turkish and German officers. Although, according to this agent, the Germans respected Muslim customs, their relative comfort was resented by their less fortunate Turkish comrades-in-arms. He gives an interesting detail, a ray of light in a night of utter darkness. Jamal had initiated a scheme for the improvement of the amenities in the major cities under the supervision of a German expert in town-planning. Sanitation was improved, new public gardens laid out, long boulevards opened and mosques constructed. Thus in Jaffa a new boulevard was named after Jamal Pasha by the Governor Ḥasan Bey al-Jābi, who had a new mosque built in the city and named after himself. It is curious that the association of Jamal's name with the boulevard survived, despite the official change to King George V Street after the British occupation.

The third report worthy of note is by the Maronite Émile Eddé, a future president of Lebanon, then a *commissaire* in the French navy. He, too, used the island of Arwād as a stepping-stone to and from the mainland. Picot introduced him to Sykes in Paris in August 1916. In conversation with the latter Eddé, we are told, spoke of a new Christian-Muslim solidarity in Syria, and confirmed that the Sharif's revolt was popular and that 'the Syrians hoped to join in when the opportunity offered'.

Sykes was then compiling and issuing for official use a secret monthly 'Arabian Report', based mostly on official despatches and intelligence reports. In the issue of 2 November 1916 the above reports are supplemented and confirmed. Thus the beduins of Beersheba were 'anxiously awaiting the arrival of the Sharif's troops before rising against the Turks'. So were, according to the same sources, the Druzes in Ḥawrān who like other Syrians saw the moment was opportune 'for complete Arab independence'.[5]

The Beersheba beduins and other Syrians did not wait long. But they welcomed and co-operated with, in lieu of the Sharif's own forces, the troops of his ally, Great Britain. In December 1916, soon after Lloyd George succeeded Asquith as Prime Minister, a secret circular was issued by the Chief of the Imperial General Staff that operations in Sinai might take British troops beyond Rafaḥ, the terminus on the Mediterranean of the international boundary between Egypt and Syria. Because of the political implications of such a development it was deemed necessary to inform France in order to secure her political co-operation, but 'we should do our utmost to avoid the association of any French troops with our own'.

In the end French diplomacy succeeded in foisting upon the Briitsh commander-in-chief a token French contingent and a French political officer who was none other than Picot. An Italian contingent was later added. In the spring of 1917 Wingate was instructed to invite representatives of the Sharif and the Syrian Arab nationalists to accompany the British expeditionary force. Wingate called attention to the difficulty that the Sharif had not yet been informed of the Sykes–Picot agreement. If told he might refuse to send a representative or protest that 'he had not been treated with due candour'. The Foreign Office, now under Arthur James Balfour, evaded the issue. The representatives were to act as liaisons between the army and the civil populations, sign manifestos and approve local arrangements. There was no intention of discussing the political future of Syria with them.

The British advance through Sinia and southern Palestine was relatively easy till von Kressenstein succeeded in building up a defensive line from Gaza to Beersheba, stiffened by companies of German and Austrian machine-gunners. Gaza was shelled by British warships, and the Turkish authorities ordered the evacuation of the bulk of the civil population of the city, in preparation for the coming struggle. In the spring of 1917 the British fought and lost two battles at Gaza. One of the immediate consequences of the defeat was the appointment of a new commander-in-chief, General Sir Edmund Allenby.

3

The Turkish victory at Gaza was no compensation for the simultaneous loss of Baghdad, nor for the failure to crush the Arab revolt and recover Mecca. However, the outbreak of the Russian revolution resulted in the end of fighting on the Caucasus front and the release of large numbers of Turkish troops. Enver, under German inspiration, proposed to use some of these troops for the recovery of Baghdad. Accordingly a new army, optimistically called the *Yıldırım* (Thunderbolt), was formed with headquarters at Aleppo. This army never marched on Baghdad. Instead it was rather belatedly decided to use it on the Palestine front. For a commander it had none other than General von Falkenhayn, former chief of the German general staff on the western front.

It was a delicate task for Enver to impose a German general, no matter how distinguished, upon Jamal. The difficulty was in the end resolved by a division of command which left Jamal with virtually no share in the active direction of the war. Von Falkenhayn was put in command of all the forces in Palestine south of Jerusalem. Under him was von Kressenstein, now in command of an army. The forces in the rest of Syria, including Transjordan down to Hijaz, remained under Jamal. In practice this arrangement meant that all Turkish forces ranged against the British on the Palestine front were under German command.

The 'Thunderbolt' did not prove true to its name. Before von Falkenhayn could bring the bulk of it to the front, Allenby launched at the end of October an offensive on the Gaza–Beersheba line, with superior numbers, arms and supplies. Waterpipes and a railway had been laid by stages as the British forces advanced through Sinai and southern Palestine. When the offensive was launched the pipes and the railway had been brought very close to the actual front.

A break was effected through the Turkish lines at Beersheba which compelled the Turks to evacuate Gaza. Thereafter the British advance to the north was relatively easy. After occupying Jaffa, the bulk of whose civilian population had already been evacuated by the Turks, the British advance northward was halted to the north of the river 'Auja. Then Allenby turned his major assault eastward and up the hills in the direction of Jerusalem, the main objective of the offensive.

The Turkish high command had been requested by the German Emperor not to make Jerusalem a scene of fighting. The Turks, mindful of the sanctity of the third holy city in Islam, agreed. No doubt Allenby was equally anxious to avoid fighting in the Holy City. As soon therefore as the British forces were in the vicinity, the German and Turkish forces evacuated Jerusalem. This was on 8 December; next day the Arab Muslim mayor surrendered it to a British divisional commander. The news was received in London with great jubilation. It was formally announced in the House of Commons by Bonar Law who said that 'General Allenby proposed to enter the city on 11 December, accompanied by the commanders of the French and Italian contingents and the head of the French political mission.'[6]

Despite protests by Indian Muslim residents in London, the British press continued after the battle of Gaza to describe the British advance in Palestine as a 'crusade'. Thus together with Bonar Law's announcement, *The Times* published an editorial which regarded 'the deliverance of Jerusalem' as 'a most memorable event in the history of Christendom'. It pointed out that the presence of French and Italian contingents with the British forces was reminiscent of past French, Italian and English participation in the historic crusades. Towards the end of the article occurs this striking sentence: 'Saladin entered Jerusalem in triumph as General Allenby enters it today'.

To Allenby himself is attributed the boast that 'today ended the Crusades'. If authentic*, these words were less than tactful from a general whose forces contained large numbers of Indian Muslims and whose right flank was protected by Faisal, the son of the Sharif of Mecca. That no respresentative of the Sharif was present at the entry into Jerusalem was due to Clayton's and Wingate's objections.

* What is authentic is Lloyd George's public pronouncement that 'Allenby had fought and won the last and most triumphant of the Crusades' – *The Times*, 7 August 1919.

The Sharif was by then the King of Hijaz to his allies and 'King of the Arab Nation' to his followers. Wingate argued that the presence of the king's representative in Jerusalem might be interpreted as British recognition of his title to the Caliphate, and because of the Sykes–Picot agreement might create political difficulties. Small wonder that the Sharif offered no congratulation on the fall of Jerusalem, a fact which called forth disappointment in London. Wingate ascribed the Sharif's reticence to the Zionist policy of the British government, but it may safely be assumed that the Sharif resented also the 'crusading' colour given to the capture of Jerusalem.

In addition to his own staff, Allenby was accompanied by the commanders of the French and Italian contingents, the French political officer, and the French, Italian and American military attachés. With Allenby at its head the procession entered the city on foot by the Jaffa Gate. The wider gap in the city wall a few paces away from the Gate, which was specially opened for the entry of the German Emperor nineteen years earlier, was deliberately avoided.

From the Citadel steps a brief proclamation, drafted by Curzon and Sykes and approved by the Cabinet in advance, was read 'to the inhabitants of Jerusalem the Blessed and the people dwelling in the vicinity' in Arabic, English, French, Italian, Hebrew, Greek and Russian. It placed the city under martial law and guaranteed the maintenance of the *status quo* in the Holy Places, traditional sites and religious foundations 'according to the existing customs and beliefs' of the adherents of three of the great religions of mankind.[7]

The proclamation was in conformity with a relevant Hague Convention to which Great Britain was a party, and which laid down that in occupied enemy territory the administration should be military and not political and that the military administration should make no attempt to vary or change the institutions of the occupied country before a peace treaty. And yet we are told that Picot chose to challenge Allenby on this very matter. T. E. Lawrence, who entered Jerusalem with Allenby not in the garb of an Arab chief but in the uniform of a British army officer, related that on that same 11 December Picot bluntly told Allenby of his intention to set up 'tomorrow' a civil government in Jerusalem. Flushed with anger Allenby retorted that in the military zone under his control he was the only authority, and that no civil government could be set up unless he certified that the military situation permitted it.[8]

Lawrence's story is almost unbelievable. It may proceed from his well-known anti-French tendencies, or it may proceed from Picot's equally well-known fanaticism in upholding France's claim to *la Syrie intégrale*, or in this case to a share in the administration of the occupied territory which the French government was soon formally to make. But the agreement of which Picot on behalf of France and Sykes on behalf of Britain drew the outlines provided for an 'international' (not a French nor even Anglo-French) administration in Jerusalem, and that only after consultation with the other allies, including the Sharif of Mecca.

4

Allenby's resolve to maintain the religious and political *status quo* remained unshaken until by orders from London the observance of the Hague Convention was relaxed in 1918, first in favour of the Zionists in Palestine and later in favour of France in the Syrian littoral. Until then Allenby refused to allow the official publication in Palestine of the Balfour Declaration of 2 November 1917, in which the British government viewed with favour 'the establishment in Palestine of a national home for the Jewish people' and promised to 'use their best endeavours to facilitate the achievement of that object'. Its text was, however, published in the Cairo newspaper *al-Muqaṭṭam* in the form of a Reuter telegram from London dated 9 November.

Allenby's attitude was probably due to military not political considerations. Palestine was not yet conquered, Turkish and German propaganda was very active and he was naturally anxious to continue to count on the goodwill and co-operation of the Arabs of the country, well over 90 per cent of the population. In the Balfour Declaration their identity was concealed under the phrase 'non-Jewish communities', and nothing was said about their national rights, since the declaration guaranteed for them only 'civil and religious rights'.

Thus were the seeds of an injustice sown in a venture unique in political history and international law. It is unique in that it deliberately and persistently denied political rights to the vast Arab majority, the indigenous inhabitants of Palestine, in order to promote those of a small Jewish minority which was to be created largely from alien immigrants. The ultimate result was never in doubt to the three parties concerned: the Arabs, the Zionists and the British government.

It will be recalled that in 1896 Herzl failed to 'buy' Palestine from Sultan 'Abdul-Ḥamīd. But he returned to the charge in 1901 with different inducements including offers of loans, buying up the bonds of the public debt and naming the sultan as 'the protector' of Jews. Here 'Izzat played his decisive rôle. As the mouthpiece of the sultan he told Herzl that the Jews were welcome to any part of the Empire, *dans une manière dispersée*, provided they become Ottoman subjects and accepted the obligations of Ottoman citizenship. Herzl was prepared to discuss details. But early in 1902 his hopes were dashed. 'Izzat made it clear that Palestine was expressly excluded.[9]

In 1901 regulations were issued limiting the stay of foreign Jews visiting Palestine to three months. The Zionists hoped for better treatment from the Young Turks, reputed to have been infiltrated by Jews, but this hope also was disappointed. Strong objections to Jewish immigration to, and acquisition of land in, Palestine were repeatedly voiced in the chamber of deputies in Istanbul. In Palestine itself a vigorous campaign against Zionist immigration and acquisition of land was conducted by Najīb Naṣṣār, editor of the Haifa newspaper *al-Karmil*, and by 'Īsā al-'Īsā, editor of the Jaffa newspaper *Filasṭīn*. Commenting on the latter's exposition of the Zionist programme, Rashīd Riḍā wrote that if successful the Zionists would leave in Palestine neither Muslim nor Christian and that in Zionist eyes 'the promised land' extended through Syria to the Great River, the Euphrates.[10]

In 1912, when Arab deputies raised the matter again in the Chamber, Talat, then minister of the interior, reaffirmed the government policy of discouraging Zionist activity. And yet Palestine was not completely closed to Jewish immigration. Representations from friendly powers, notably Great Britain and the United States, Turkish inefficiency and Jewish skill in circumventing laws and regulations combined to allow a trickle of Jews to enter Palestine annually up to the outbreak of the war.

By then a nucleus of a community of settlers, immigrants mostly from Russia, Poland and Romania, devoted to the revival of Hebrew and engaged in agriculture, was definitely formed. This community was clearly nationalist and Zionist in aspiration, in sharp contrast to the majority of religious and orthodox Jews already in Syria and Palestine. In the absence of an official census, figures must be quoted with great reserve, especially because different sources cite widely different figures. In 1914 it may be assumed that there was a minimum of ten thousand Jewish nationalist settlers in agricultural colonies in Palestine out of a total Jewish population variously estimated at between sixty and eighty thousand souls, mostly concentrated in the cities of Jerusalem, Hebron, Jaffa, Tiberias and Ṣafad. At the lower estimate this was roughly 8 per cent of the whole population of Palestine estimated at under three-quarters of a million.

The war was more calamitous to the Zionist settlers than to the old-established Jewish minority or the native Arab majority. The settlers were already suspect in the eyes of the Turkish administration. On the eve of the war, the governor of Jaffa, near which some of the new Zionist colonies were established, took exception, *inter alia*, to the settlers' clinging to their foreign nationalites, their neglect to teach Turkish in their communal schools where moreover anti-Turkish sentiment was fostered, and their insistence on leading a separate existence in all aspects of their life with no attempt at blending with their Arab environment.[11]

As most of the non-Ottoman Jews in Palestine were in 1914 of Russian nationality they were given the choice of becoming Ottoman subjects within a specified period or facing deportation. Many chose the first alternative, but some ten thousand, mostly members of prosperous families from the cities, were deported on neutral ships to Egypt. Of those who remained in the country some suspects were, like Muslim and Christian Arab suspects, forced to reside in certain centres in north Syria or in Anatolia. At the end of the war in 1918 the British military administration estimated the total Jewish population at 66,000. Only a minority of these were Zionists and welcomed the Balfour Declaration.

With the history of Zionist efforts before the issue of the Declaration this study is not concerned. One of its immediate results, however, deserves special notice. Soon after the capture of Jerusalem, the Zionists sought and received the approval of the British government for a commission, under Chaim Weizmann, president of the world Zionist organisation, to go to Palestine and act as a liaison between the Jewish community and the British military administration. Wingate and Clayton, who was now Allenby's Chief Political Officer with the military rank of a general, objected to its dispatch, but their objection was overruled and early in March instructions were received from London announcing the impending arrival of the commission. This was the first violation of the Hague Convention, since the commission was a foreign body, with no legal authority to exercise quasi-political control over a section of the population in an occupied enemy territory whose political status was not yet decided by a peace treaty.

Arab hostility to the Zionist ambitions was well known to the British government before and after they issued the Balfour Declaration. In March 1916 Sykes placed it on record that while in Cairo he had been assured by Dr Fāris Nimr and 'Major' Sharīf al-Fārūqi, 'poles asunder on political questions', that 'Arab Christians and Moslems alike would fight to the last man against Jewish domination'. From January 1918 Clayton's weekly reports are seldom without remarks about Arab resentment at 'the preferential treatment' accorded to the Zionists, and Arab Christian and Muslim fears of eventual Jewish government in Palestine.

This feeling became abundantly manifest after the arrival of the Zionist commission which made Jaffa its headquarters. The military governor 'summoned' the *qāḍi* of the city, Shaikh Rāghib ad-Dajāni, together with other notables, to hear an address from Weizmann in which he said that 'Palestine was the goal of the hopes of all Jews . . . their only home where they hope to live always'. In his reply Shaikh Rāghib employed the polite language of an educated Muslim but hinted that the Arabs would recognise only native Jews with whom they always lived in peace. Palestine, he added, had been the subject of controversy and the aim of sundry nations, but he trusted that Great Britain would invite representatives of its Muslim and Christian population to whatever convention would sit to decide its future.

It is a mark of the closed minds of those Englishmen concerned with Palestine after 1917 that when the above was reported to the Foreign Office, a minute was written by Sykes – by then the expert on Arab affairs – which reads in part: 'The governor ought to have taken the precaution of writing out all the speeches himself.' This is another indication of the methods Sykes had been employing since 1915 to produce 'evidence' in support of whatever policy was in vogue. However, his reputation as an 'expert' must in the present case be seriously questioned since he obviously failed to understand that the *qāḍi* of Jaffa would have certainly refused to read a prepared speech. What is still more surprising is Sykes's apparently poor view of the honour of a British army officer. Although he himself was such an officer, his political work seems to have made him forget that a professional soldier was not likely to stoop so low as to cook the evidence.

A notable exception was the military governor of Jerusalem, Ronald Storrs, a civil servant suddenly put in military uniform. He was certainly more accommodating than the governor of Jaffa. Storrs, too, arranged for Weizmann to address a few Muslim and Christian Arab notables. The text of Weizmann's speech is not less than 1500 words, in which he said that he was no stranger to Palestine, that the Jews never relinquished their claim to the country and that they were now returning 'under the wing' of the mightiest power on earth, but they did not intend to take 'the supreme political power into their hands after the war'.

Storrs asserts that he explained the 'purport' of the speech in Arabic. The nature of the explanation depended first upon Storrs's doubtful command of Arabic and next upon his undoubted preparedness to oblige Sykes. He states in no more than sixty odd words, that Kāmil al-Ḥusaini, the Mufti of Jerusalem, 'rejoiced' that Weizmann had 'removed many conceptions' and that he 'looked forward' to co-operation with the Zionists in the future development of Palestine. However, the key to what the Mufti might have said must be sought in his reported quotation of the well-known Muslim guide to the toleration of non-Muslims under a Muslim government: *lahum mā lanā wa ʿalaihim mā ʿalainā* (they will enjoy the same rights and bear the same duties as ourselves).

What the Mufti had apparently gathered from what Storrs chose to tell him was that the Jews sought settlement in a Muslim country under a Muslim government, in alliance with Great Britain. For until then no Muslim or Arab leader in that part of Palestine already occupied by British forces had any doubt that these forces were the allies of the Sharif and that their sole purpose was the defeat of Turkey and the 'liberation' of the Arab lands. The leaflets freely distributed by the British army in Palestine confirmed this belief.[12] It was further confirmed by Allenby's encouragement of recruitment for the Sharif's forces in the Jerusalem district (*sanjaq*) as soon as it was fully in British occupation. He had already ordered the transfer of an 'Arab Legion', formed of officers and men, prisoners of war in British camps, to Faisal's army whose headquarters were then at 'Aqaba. The officers had shown clear resistance to the attempt to place them under foreign orders, British and French.

Let us recall that in the spring of 1918 the secret political arrangements were still as follows: France was the prominent pretender to the Syrian heritage. Under the Sykes–Picot agreement Britain's share, the Haifa enclave, was very small indeed. But with the espousal of Zionist ambitions, Britain became a potential contender for an undefined Palestine. The agreement on an international regime was further weakened by the collapse of Imperial Russia. In another way it was still more weakened by America's entry into the war on the side of the allies. This committed them to some acceptance of President Wilson's principles, chief among which was the self-determination of the liberated peoples. Nevertheless Britain was slowly but surely moving towards denying Palestine to the Arabs, to France, and to an international regime, and claiming it as a British dependency.

One of the earliest British supporters of the Zionist cause was Sykes. From 1915 he had been interested in securing some form of a British protectorate over Palestine for strategic reasons. Zionist colonisation of the country under British protection would conceal purely strategic considerations under humanitarian justification. In 1916 Sykes envisaged that both British and Zionist aims could be achieved under a façade of a Sharifian government. He made some unauthorised reference to the subject in a conversation with Picot when both were in Petrograd. Picot became so excitedly angry that he threatened 'pogroms in Paris'. But Sykes was not deterred. In a telegram dated 14 March 1916 he put forward the proposal to Grey. He referred to a memorandum submitted to the Cabinet in 1915 by Herbert Samuel in which he advocated that, in case of partition of Turkish territory in Asia, Britain should acquire Palestine as a protectorate and encourage Jewish settlement therein. (Asquith disliked the idea and Grey had always disclaimed any territorial ambition in any part of Syria.)

Sykes, who already knew that the Arabs were bitterly opposed to Zionist colonisation, visualised what protest the Sharif would make to the British government: 'You introduced idolatrous Indians in Iraq, French to frenchify the Christian Arabs in Syria, and now decide to flood Palestine with Jews to drive out the Arabs whether Moslems or Christians. Turks and Germans are preferable!'

Since Arab opposition would be so vehement, since France in Palestine was unacceptable to Britain and vice versa, and since Britain was not enthusiastic about an international regime, then Sykes proposed to arrange, in agreement with France and Russia, for the Sharif to appoint one of his sons as sultan of Palestine. The new state would have to give guarantees acceptable to France and Russia concerning the Christian Holy Places, and concerning Jewish colonisation provided the colonists became citizens of the new state.[13]

Grey did not reply to the suggestion of an Arab sultan over Palestine, but he rebuked Sykes for having discussed Jewish colonisation under British auspices with Picot. As to a British protectorate, Grey said that he himself had told Samuel that 'it was quite out of the question'. The significance of this episode lies in the meaning of 'international regime' which one of the two framers of the Sykes–Picot agreement seems to have attached to the term. It seems to have been little more than that devised for Lebanon after 1860. If it could then be arranged under Ottoman Muslim sovereignty, it could now be arranged under Arab Muslim sovereignty.

5

From the beginning Jamal Pasha posed in Syria as a good Muslim and true Ottoman patriot, loyal to the Sultanate and Caliphate. Nothing was then known of his betrayal of religion, state and nation when late in 1915 he opened secret negotiations with Russia seeking to conclude a separate peace with the allies and to secure for himself the hereditary rule over territories which included Syria and Iraq. To achieve his object he was prepared to revolt against the sultan and fight his own comrades.

Russia consulted Britain on the matter. Grey's dispatch of 29 December 1915 to the British ambassador in Petrograd raised no objection to the negotiation provided British commitments to the Arabs and France's claims in Syria were respected.[14] The negotiations came to nothing, but Jamal's duplicity continued. Before as well as after negotiating with Russia he hanged Syrian Arab leaders for alleged offences far less serious than his own. Then, having failed as a general, administrator and traitor, he assumed the rôle of a zealous Muslim once more.

By 1917 the Turkish government and their German allies had realised that it was too late to crush the Arab revolt and that it was advisable from the political and military point of view to make a belated attempt to reconcile the Arabs. At the same time general peace overtures to the allies began to be made both by Turkish liberals in exile and by agents of the government itself. Details of these overtures to the Arabs and the allies were channelled through the British legations in Berne, Madrid and Stockholm. Thus the information that reached Berne between August and October was that Turkey was considering the grant of autonomy to Syria, Iraq and Hijaz and that the German Emperor himself had urged this course.

Some five weeks later the British government let it be known in Berne that they were prepared to offer Turkey continued possession of Constantinople and approval of the end of the Capitulations, but that Armenia, Iraq and Hijaz must be declared independent and that 'genuine and complete autonomy for Syria and Palestine' must be guaranteed.

It was under these circumstances that Jamal Pasha wrote early in November two letters, one addressed to Faisal and the other to his chief of staff, Ja'far Pasha al-'Askari. The British army was then advancing on Jerusalem, and Jamal urged the necessity of restoring Islamic unity and checking the advance. The Bolsheviks had not yet divulged the Sykes–Picot agreement, but enough was already known of its provisions for Jamal to say that the Arabs had been deceived by Britain, who, with her ally France, had aims in Iraq, Syria and Palestine inimical to Arab independence. The Arabs could now attain their national aims through the goodwill of Turkey. He offered amnesty to the rebels and promised safe conduct for Ja'far to Damascus for formal negotiations.

Faisal's position was very delicate. After the capture of ʿAqaba he became practically a 'British' commander under General Allenby. Although he must have realised by then that the Turks stood little chance of defeating the British army in Syria, he was urged by some of his supporters not to ignore the Turkish offers. Even vague disclosures of Anglo-French designs dictated the necessity of exploring rather than rejecting the Turkish overtures.

Already in May 1917 Sykes had held conversations with Faisal and then with King Ḥusain in order to explain, as he put it, 'the principles of the Anglo-French agreement regarding the Arab confederation'. A few days later Sykes with Picot held further conversations with Faisal and Ḥusain, again separately. There is no verbatim record of these conversations, but it is certain that even the existence of an Anglo-French agreement regarding the future of Syria and Iraq was never mentioned. Sykes is neither an independent nor a coherent witness on the attitude of Ḥusain, Faisal and the majority of Syrian Arab leaders in Cairo. And yet if his accounts are read carefully it is safe to assume that even 'the principles' were not acceptable.

Wingate suggested that an approval of a substantial increase in the Sharif's subsidy then under consideration in London might ease the way for Sykes and Picot. London did not agree, and the wrangle between the Treasury, Foreign Office and War Office continued. Meanwhile the Sharif's financial difficulties were mounting. Not only the administration of Hijaz but also the winning of beduin tribes for the cause was affected. More seriously affected perhaps was Faisal's situation at ʿAqaba. His advance to the north in the military as well as in the propaganda sense was somewhat arrested.

But this is not to say that the Sharif's attitude to Sykes and Picot was or would have been influenced by financial considerations. All along he stood for political principles. His acceptance of the very first subsidy at the hand of McMahon was coupled with an uncompromising refusal to grant any position to France. When he faced Sykes and Picot together little change had taken place in his political attitude.

Sykes combined with Picot to extract from Ḥusain some form of recognition of a French position in Syria. Accordingly Picot stated that France intended to take military action on the Syrian littoral similar to the British action in Iraq. Thereupon Sykes asked whether under such circumstances Ḥusain would agree to an arrangement with France similar to that which he had already agreed with Britain concerning Iraq. Sykes asserts that Ḥusain's reply was affirmative. But if so how can it be squared with the following principles which he enunciated in the course of the conversations:

(*a*) Unless he ensured Arab independence posterity would blame him for causing the downfall of the last Muslim power without putting another in its place.
(*b*) He could not agree to any arrangement that would place Muslims under the rule of non-Muslims.
(*c*) The Syrians in general who had entrusted him with their future would accuse him of betrayal were he to agree to place them under foreign rule.
(*d*) He disliked the idea that European advisers in the future Arab states should have 'executive authority'. The acting minister for foreign affairs, Fuād al-Khaṭīb, added that 'that would be the end of Arab independence'.

It was thus under circumstances of uncertainty, doubts and suspicions in Anglo–Arab relations that Jamal's overtures were received. Faisal promptly sent the papers to his father who in turn sent them to the British authorities calling for an explanation of the reported British and French designs on Arab territory. 'Abdullah seconded his father's official letter by a personal appeal to Wingate urging the issue of 'a definite refutation' of Jamal's assertion that Palestine and Iraq were 'reserved' for Britain and Syria for France.

But Jamal's case was greatly strengthened by the coincidental publication in *Izvestia* on 24 November of the full terms of the Sykes–Picot agreement. A few days later they were published in the *Manchester Guardian*. Early in December they reached Jamal. Promptly he read the terms at a public gathering of notables in Beirut. 'Was it for this that the Sharif Ḥusain revolted against the sultan-caliph?' He followed this question by disclosing the fact of his overtures to Faisal.

Wingate submitted that Jamal's propaganda was effective. He was apprehensive lest some influential Syrians round Faisal should persuade him to take Jamal's offer too seriously. He took the precaution of asking Lawrence to watch developments and to discover whether by verbal messages from Faisal more could be learned of the new Turkish policy. But Wingate was more worried about British policy.

'In the present critical state of Arab feeling', he wrote, 'vague or general assurances would not only be ineffectual but harmful.' Accordingly he sought authority to inform the Sharif that Britain was still determined to 'secure' Arab independence and to fulfil promises made through him, that Britain will not 'countenance' any permanent foreign occupation of Palestine, Syria or Iraq after the war, and that these countries will be 'in possession' of their natives.

But London still preferred vague generalities. The draft reply dated 4 February 1918 was approved by Balfour himself who made in the margin this cynical remark: 'I presume this ornate style is pleasing to the Arab mind'. The British government were 'profoundly touched' by the Sharif's 'frankness'. His action was 'typical of that openness and truth which has ever marked the intercourse between H.M.G. and the government of Hijaz'. Then Jamal's statement that Britain and France had designs against Arab territory was dismissed as propaganda. The British government with their allies were 'determined to stand by the Arab peoples in their struggle for the reconstruction of an Arab world in which law shall once again replace Ottoman violence, and unity the artificial rivalries promoted by Turkish officials. H.M.G. reaffirm their former pledges to H. [is] H. [ighness] in regard to the freeing of the Arab peoples.'

Meanwhile Commander D. G. Hogarth was sent in January to convey a message to King Ḥusain. The message has since been labelled with Hogarth's name in the published official version.[15] Part (*b*) of the published message is described as 'the record' of the conversations with Ḥusain. That is not so, since the published version is much shorter than the actual record and is clearly selective. In method of presentation and intent the record is not much different from those Sykes had produced about his 'conversations' with Arab leaders including Ḥusain. They were merely personal reports coloured by wishful thinking and not entirely free from attempts to enhance personal prestige.

Hogarth's report of the conversations is indeed very similar in method and purpose to that of Sykes. Both were belied by Ḥusain's subsequent and *written* expression of views on the very subjects they discussed with him. It must not escape notice that two different methods of approach were adopted by Britain towards the Sharif:

generalities were conveyed in writing but issues of vital political importance by verbal messages of singular vagueness.

Hogarth says he began with chats about topography, natural and social history and even economics in order 'to relieve tension and dispose the King favourably towards less congenial topics'. It is important to note that at the outset Ḥusain remarked that the message was not 'an official document'. Hogarth's notes are not always consistent with the text of the message. What Ḥusain said we have to take on trust. Hence it is very important to observe that the notes mention the 'international control of the Palestine Holy Places'. This is quite different from the 'international administration of Palestine'. Since Hogarth assured Ḥusain that the 'Mosque of Omar' was to remain under exclusive Muslim control he was naturally disposed to agree to an international control over the Holy Places of the Christians and Jews.

But that did not mean abdication of Arab political rights in Palestine. These were indeed reserved in the next assurance. The British government would favour Jewish return to Palestine, but only 'in so far as is compatible with the freedom of the existing population, both economic and political'. It is only in this context that the Sharif's response must be interpreted. In that case 'he welcomed Jews to any Arab country'.

Neither the Hogarth message, however, nor the Balfour message in the 'ornate style' had more than fleeting influence in allaying the Sharif's fears. Neither message said anything about the Sykes–Picot agreement. Nor was the frankness admired by the British government in Ḥusain reciprocated. So within days after Hogarth's departure and the receipt of Balfour's message Ḥusain expressed *in writing* his great anxiety about the future of the Arabs. In a letter dated 3 February 1918 to Wingate he said it would be political bankruptcy if Arab independence was not realised and the Arab revolt vindicated. He was so gloomy that his letter mentioned the two extreme contingencies of abdication or suicide. He cited only one specific cause for anxiety: the reports circulated by Turkish agents 'amongst the Arabs of Palestine that our intention was to put them under Jewish rule and let the Zionists govern them'.[16] Ḥusain's uncertainties were never resolved by his British allies.

6

The first quarter of 1918 witnessed radical changes in the Turkish command in Palestine and Syria. (Aḥmad) Jamal Pasha was recalled; von Falkenhayn did not long survive the disaster that led to the loss of Jerusalem; von Kressenstein had been transferred to the Caucasus. General Liman von Sanders, formerly head of the German military mission, became the commander-in-chief, with headquarters at Nazareth. Under him was (Muḥammad) Jamal Pasha, commonly known as Jamal Pasha the Lesser, with headquarters at 'Amman; Muṣṭafa Kamal Pasha (later Atatürk) at Nābulus and Jawād Pasha at Ṭūl-Karm.

Jamal the Lesser continued his predecessor's overtures to the Arabs, apparently on instructions from Istanbul. For in the summer of 1918 the Turkish government made serious attempts to come to terms with the Syrians. Renewed overtures to Faisal by Jamal Pasha the Lesser formed only one part of these attempts. Another Turkish move was made by the ministry for foreign affairs when it dispatched to Switzerland a Syrian Arab mission composed of 'Ali Riḍā Pasha ar-Rikābi, Riḍā Bey as-Ṣulh, 'Ali Efendi Salām, Fāris Efendi al-Khūri and Professor Jabr Ḍūmit. These emissaries were to discuss with other Syrians in exile a Turkish offer of autonomy on the basis of Arab nationality.

About 5 June peace terms were offered by Muḥammad Jamal to Faisal who acknowledged the offer in a brief and signed letter. About 10 June an unsigned five-point memorandum of Arab terms was sent to Jamal. In the order of their importance these points are: (1) Syrian independence must be of the Austria–Hungary type; (2) all Turkish troops south of 'Amman to be withdrawn; (3) all Arab officers in the Turkish army to be transferred to the Arab army; (4) should it be necessary for the Arabs and the Turks to fight 'against the enemy' together the Arab army must retain its independent command; (5) all stores of supplies and foodstuffs in Syria must be left for the Arab army.

It was Lawrence who, without Faisal's knowledge, obtained a copy of the memorandum from Faisal's secretariat and passed it on to Hogarth who in turn submitted it to the Foreign Office. Hogarth was not certain that the memorandum was Faisal's, but he adds that it could hardly have been sent without his cognisance, and that its terms suggest that it was influenced or dictated by Syrians in Faisal's entourage.

The publication of the terms of the Sykes–Picot agreement increased Arab suspicions of Britain and confirmed their worst fears of France. It provided the Arabs with an excuse to parley with the Turks and encouraged the latter to try and detach the Arabs from the British alliance. At this critical juncture in Anglo–Arab relations a full report of Aḥmad Jamal Pasha's speech at Beirut reached the Sharif. Hitherto military censorship had forbidden its publication in Cairo, and apparently Ḥusain had yet to learn of the hard things the Pasha said about him: that the Sharif had not revolted in order to secure Arab freedom, but to hand over the Arab countries to foreign control for money; that he disrupted Islamic unity for an Arab independence which the provisions of the Sykes–Picot agreement rendered a mirage.

The speech was tendentiously published in *al-Mustaqbal*, a paper issued in Paris by Shukri Ghānim, a Lebanese Christian in close touch with the French government. The paper published all the abuse Jamal had heaped on the Sharif, and stressed only the British share of the Arab countries under the Sykes–Picot agreement. The article administered a severe shock to an already troubled mind. Ḥusain's reaction is described in Wingate's urgent telegram on 16 June:

> He has sent rather a violent telegram to his agent here instructing him to make enquiries about alleged Anglo–French agreement and its scope. You will recall that King has never officially been informed of Sykes–Picot agreement. Agent had asked me urgently to suggest a suitable reply. . . .

Wingate reported that he had advised the agent to tell his master that what the Bolsheviks had disclosed was not a treaty but 'a record of old conversations and provisional understandings'. Jamal, either from ignorance or malice, had distorted the facts and omitted to mention the provision regarding the consent of the native population. Then Wingate asks whether he could say that the agreement was dead.

This permission was not given. While the agreement was no longer in favour, its abrogation or revision required consultation with the French government. But Wingate's 'advice' to Ḥusain's agent was approved. The only addition the Foreign Office could devise was that British policy had been communicated to King Ḥusain in the Balfour message on 4 February. But despite this British prevarication and lack of candour with him, Ḥusain never entertained seriously a reconciliation with the Turks. This cannot be said as definitely of Faisal or at least of the Syrians round him or even of some Syrians in Cairo.

The latter had been subjected to British and, to a lesser degree, French propaganda since the beginning of the war. Martial law imposed limits on their political activities and still more on public expression of opinion. But they tried to overcome some of these difficulties following the publication of the Sykes–Picot agreement and the circulation of rumours of Turkish offers to Faisal. They made formal approaches to the British authorities. One of the results was briefly mentioned on 25 June 1918 by Lord Robert Cecil in answer to a parliamentary question by Lord Winterton. 'A commission of Syrian Arab political representatives', he said, 'visited Palestine early last month and met Moslem and Christian leaders and heads of the various communities in the occupied areas.'

Lord Robert Cecil said nothing about the outcome of the visit. Men like Rafīq al-ʿAẓm, Sulaimān Nāṣīf and Mukhtār as-Ṣulh were not easily side-tracked. A meeting with the Zionist commission arranged by the military authorities tended only to deepen Arab distrust. The three Arab delegates gave the Palestinian Arabs encouragement to offer organised protests against the Zionist policy. Thereafter hardly a report from Clayton omits to refer to Arab apprehension, resentment and protest.

Other evidence of the animation of the Syrian Arabs in Cairo was the submission on 7 May of a memorial, for transmission to the British Foreign Secretary, by Rafīq al-ʿAẓm and six other leaders 'representing the various Arab political societies and of the supporters of the Arab movement'. In measured language, the memorial pointed out the widespread suspicions of British intentions and the reluctance of many Muslim Arabs to completely sever relations with Turkey on account of the uncertainty of their political future. It is unjust, the memorial argues, that British declarations should guarantee the political security of the purely Turkish provinces in

Turkey, Germany's ally, while nothing is said about that of the Arab provinces, despite the fact that the Arabs were Britain's allies.

The Syrian memorialists state that though the Arab revolt began in Hijaz, its corner-stone was laid down in Syria whose secret societies delegated the realisation of their aspirations to the Sharif. Insisting that their organisations represented four-fifths of the different classes of the populations, including the aristocracy, religious leaders, the educated class and tribal chiefs, they discount the value of the committees established in Paris as under French influence and composed of persons unknown in Syria. They ask two specific questions:

> (*a*) Can we assure our people that it is the aim of the British government that the Arabs should enjoy complete independence in Arabia? – which the memorial defines as including, among other lands, Syria. They obviously deemed it unnecessary to add that, to the Arabs, Syria included Lebanon and Palestine.
> (*b*) Is the policy of His Majesty's Government to assist the inhabitants of these countries to attain their complete independence and to form a federation like the United States of America?

The British reply to the seven was delivered to two of them by Hogarth about the middle of June.[17] To begin with one of the two expressed the Arabs' disappointment that in the first place, Britain had not accepted without reservation the territorial limits of independence as proposed by the Sharif and, in the second place, that there was in existence a secret agreement between Britain and France which continued to cause anxiety to the Arabs. In reply Hogarth referred them to the Balfour message of 4 February. And yet the message to the seven is perhaps the clearest British statement of policy on the Arab question.

Britain recognised the 'complete and sovereign independence' of the Arabs in areas that were free and independent before the war as well as in areas liberated from Turkish rule by the Arabs themselves (i.e. certain areas in the Arabian peninsula and Hijaz). It was 'the wish and desire' of the British government that the future government of the Arab countries then occupied by allied forces (i.e. in southern Iraq and Palestine) should be based upon the principle of the consent of the governed, and that the inhabitants of the regions still under Turkish rule (i.e. in north Iraq, Palestine north of Jaffa, Lebanon and the rest of Syria) 'should obtain their freedom and independence'. Asked the meaning of 'the political principles' in the final sentence of the reply, Hogarth 'could not go beyond the words'.

7

The Declaration to the Seven in 1918 cancelled neither the Sykes–Picot agreement of 1916 nor the Balfour Declaration of 1917. But if the principle of 'the consent of the governed' was to be applied the validity of both would be undermined if not completely annulled. That the Syrian Arab leaders were not completely satisfied with the latest British pronouncement is clear from the verbal exchanges with Hogarth and the continuation of the secret parleys with the Turks.

So far as could be discovered the Sharif ʿAbdullah is the only creditable authority who affirms that the negotiations with the Turks led to a definite conclusion just before the final defeat of the Turkish armies in Syria. 'The sultan', he wrote, 'had by an imperial decree proclaimed the recognition of the independence of the Arab countries.'[18] (Confirmation of this unique report would bring into question the legality of British and French action in Palestine, Lebanon, the rest of Syria and Iraq from the summer of 1918 onwards.)

Whatever the nature of the Turkish action it was too late. On 19 September 1918 Allenby opened an offensive on the entire front, once more with superior numbers, arms and supplies. Allenby's plan included an important task assigned to Faisal's forces. They were to cut off the communication junction at Dirʿa three days before the beginning of the offensive. The task was successfully accomplished, thus depriving the Turkish command of the use of the railway south to ʿAmman, west to Haifa and north to Damascus.

All along the front the Turkish positions were overrun, and a general retreat began with the British forces in hot pursuit. Within a week central and north Palestine was occupied, and an advance on Damascus was ordered. The Turks evacuated the city on 30 September. At noon the same day Arab flags were hoisted on the Town Hall while the Turks were still within sight. By the evening Arab and British forces were at the gates of the city. That same night, the Arab Camel Corps, which formed the extreme right flank of the advance, was the first force to enter a city already under an Arab government. Early next morning, Sharif Nāṣir, with Nūri as-Saʿīd and Nūri ash-Shaʿlān and Lawrence in attendance, rode into the city in the name of Faisal and Ḥusain. The Australian Light Horse Brigade, to which had been assigned the task of blocking the roads from Damascus to Beirut and Ḥimṣ, succeeded in the first task, but found it impossible on account of the nature of the terrain in the Barada gorge to execute the second without passing through the city. They did so also on 1 October, followed later on by the formal entry of other British units. The event is well described in the lines by Jamīl az-Zahāwi:

Sunrise removed the curtain of the night,
and revealed the morning of liberation,
When the Arab horsemen came, and the English horsemen
galloping close behind,
When Damascus cried 'God is Great'
and the cry resounded in mount and vale.

The rejoicing in Damascus was marred by a short struggle for power. Faisal's secret committee was forestalled by the Amīr Saʿīd al-Jazā'iri, who claimed to have taken over from the retiring Turkish governor. He at once proclaimed, in the name of King Ḥusain, an Arab civil government with himself at its head, and telegraphed to the mayor of Beirut to do likewise. But Saʿīd was removed in less than twenty-four hours after his assumption of power, and with Nāṣir's approval Shukri Pasha al-Ayyūbi was appointed as acting military governor. The office was actually reserved for ʿAli Riḍā Pasha ar-Rikābi, a general in the Turkish army but in secret league with Faisal's committee. He had been entrusted by von Sanders with the task of 'defending' Damascus against the Arab–British advance. He formally surrendered to a British officer of equal rank and was promptly released to become the military governor of Damascus.

The proclamation of an Arab government in Damascus decided the Turkish governor of Beirut to retire, after handing over officially to the mayor, ʿUmar Bey ad-Dāʿūq, on 1 October. The mayor had already been asked on the previous day by Damascus to proclaim an Arab government which he now promptly did. No British or other allied forces had yet reached near Beirut. The withdrawal of the Turkish army and administration had clearly left a vacuum which the Arab government in Damascus rushed in to fill. The sending of al-Ayyūbi to Beirut was not, in the circumstances, a rash act as pro-French writers represent it. It may have been intended to forestall the French, but, as Faisal was to say to Allenby, it was also to maintain order and in answer to a call from a majority of the Muslim population.

After taking over in Beirut as Arab administrator, al-Ayyūbi proceeded to Baʿabda, the administrative capital of Mount Lebanon, where he reconvened the administrative council and appointed the Maronite Ḥabīb as-Saʿd as governor. Since the war the special status of Lebanon had been terminated and the administrative council suppressed. The Turkish government assumed sole responsibility for the appointment of the governors, and the Arab administration was merely continuing this practice.

On 3 October, Faisal rode into Damascus at the head of a thousand horsemen amid scenes of festive jubilation. To use his own expression, Allenby 'visited' the city on the same day, and held a conference with Faisal, each attended by his staff. It is now necessary to summarise the orders which Allenby had just received. These were given final shape at a conference held at the Foreign Office in London on 30 September with the French ambassador and Picot present. It was agreed that a representative of the French government would act as Allenby's chief political adviser 'in the areas of special French interest' under the Sykes–Picot agreement – the relevant clauses of which were cited. Subject to Allenby's supreme authority the adviser would be permitted to establish in the Syrian littoral provisional administrations, with 'pre-eminence' being given to French troops in this area.

In the Syrian interior the adviser would be the 'sole intermediary on political and administrative questions' between Allenby and the Arab administration, and would, subject to Allenby's approval, supply the 'European advisory staff' as may be required. But the adviser was excluded from military matters or acting as intermediary between Allenby and Faisal, 'the commander of Allied Arab military forces'. Allenby's right, as the supreme authority, to demand the replacement of any advisory, administrative or liaison officers was strictly reserved.

Allenby proceeded tactfully to execute his orders piecemeal. As his telegram of 6 October clearly shows he did not disclose to Faisal the whole Anglo–French plan on their first meeting on 3 October. He informed him, to start with, that Britain and France had recognised 'the belligerent status of the Arab forces fighting in Palestine and Syria as allies'. Then he told him that as commander-in-chief he recognised the Arab administration in the occupied enemy territory east of the river Jordan and northward to Damascus. Finally, and without discussing the political implications, he appointed one British and one French liaison officer with the Arab administration. Nothing was said on this occasion about the occupation of Beirut.

In his reply to speeches of welcome on 3 October Faisal declared that he recognised no distinctions between Arabs on grounds of religion. All those whose language was Arabic (Muslims, Christians and Jews) were equal and entitled to the same rights and subject to the same duties. He was an Arab, one of the people, loyal to the Arabs and eager to revive the Arabic heritage.

When the gist of Faisal's speech was considered at the Foreign Office in London it was described as 'statesmanlike'. On 5 October Balfour sent the following message to King Ḥusain: 'On behalf of myself and my colleagues of the War Cabinet I desire to congratulate Your Lordship [*sic*] on the deliverance of Damascus by the allied forces in co-operation with the army of the noble Amir Faisal and the Syrian Arabs who are fighting for national independence under his leadership.'

On the first Friday after Faisal's entry into Damascus, a prayer was said in the Great Mosque for 'the Commander of the Faithful, Our Lord, the Sultan, the Sharif Ḥusain and his son the Amir Faisal'. This was tantamount to offering Ḥusain the traditional allegiance (*baiʿah*) as caliph. Faisal telegraphed the news to Mecca where Ḥusain had it published in the official newspaper *al-Qiblah*, and replied accepting the allegiance of the Syrians and appointing Faisal as his deputy in Syria.

Faisal translated his own words into actions by calling personally on all the Christian ecclesiastical dignitaries in the city. This gesture was promptly returned when a special service was held in the Greek Orthodox Church at the end of which the patriarch himself offered a prayer for King Ḥusain and his army and for the Syrian Arab mayors. Not to be outdone, Ḥusain sent his 'salutations to all Syrians without distinction between Muslims, Christians or Jews' and urged that justice must be dispensed to all on a basis of strict equality.

However, neither Faisal's nor Ḥusain's statesmanship and tolerance, admired by their English friends and belittled by their French rivals, were enough to ward off the impending political setbacks. Allenby was well aware of the immensity of the difficulties and minced no words in pointing them out to the British government. 'The Arab leaders', he said in a telegram on 7 October, 'have never been officially notified of the terms of the Anglo-French agreement.' Then he goes on to say that the promise contained in the Declaration to the Seven, concerning recognition of Arab independence in areas freed from Turkish control by the action of the Arabs themselves, complicated the situation at Beirut for the commander-in-chief.

Finally he complains that he was not consulted regarding the promise to base the governments in the occupied regions on the consent of the governed. That also complicated matters and made it difficult for him to execute his orders. In another telegram, also on 7 October, he mentioned the proclamation of an Arab government in Beirut and added that the French representative 'will probably appeal to me to install a French military government in place of the Arab administration and will request me to haul down the Arab flag'.

Since the capture of Jerusalem, Allenby's policy had been not to allow the hoisting of any national flags, including the Union Jack, anywhere in the occupied enemy territories. Damascus and the area under Arab administration was an exception, since, to use Allenby's own words, 'when my troops entered the city an Arab government was in being and the Arab flag was flying from the government buildings'. But he was debarred from applying this principle in Beirut and Sidon, and later on in Tripoli and Latakia, where the Arabs took possession and proclaimed allegiance to the Damascus government and hoisted Arab flags before the arrival of British or any other allied forces. This inconsistency with the Declaration to the Seven was the direct result of recognising the special French interest in the northern Syrian littoral to the disregard of the Arabs.

In the interior the French clashed with the Arab administration less than forty-eight hours after Faisal's entry into Damascus. On

5 October the French liaison officer, contrary to the advice of his British colleague, protested to Faisal against the occupation of Beirut by Arab troops. Faisal was advised to ignore this protest since, as stated in Allenby's report to London, the French could approach Faisal on such military questions only through Allenby himself, who as commander-in-chief had the Arab forces under him. Allenby was simply playing for time, not trying to evade executing his orders.

Faisal refused to withdraw the Arab administration from Beirut or agree to the lowering of the Arab flag. He protested that he could not hand over those who declared for and established an Arab administration to foreign control. He remained unconvinced after an assurance that no other flag would fly in place of the Arab flag. He insisted on an assurance from the commander-in-chief himself, endorsed by the British and French governments, that French control would be a purely military arrangement and without prejudice to a political settlement.

Allenby sought authority to give the required assurance, and by his orders a French military governor was installed and the Arab flag was hauled down. The appointment of two liaison officers, one British and one Arab, made no difference. Nor did the strongly worded protest lodged with the commander-in-chief by Muslim and some Christian notables. In Sidon the change-over was attended by violent resistance which had to be quelled by force. In Latakia, where Allenby first recognised an Arab governor, the change was effected by British troops taking over in the first instance.

As Allenby's chief political officer, Clayton reported that Faisal was 'much upset . . . and tendered his resignation [as a military commander under Allenby]'. But five days later Allenby arrived in Damascus and gave Faisal the assurance he had asked for, duly approved by the Foreign Office. In Allenby's words, Faisal was further assured that the allies were 'in honour bound' to reach a settlement 'in accordance with the wishes of the peoples concerned'.[19]

8

Clayton's assessment of the Beirut episode is illuminating. In his opinion nothing short of a declaration from the British and French governments in the sense of Allenby's assurances could relieve tension in the Arab camp and restore confidence in Faisal's leadership which had been seriously challenged. Faisal himself was still not convinced that the professed military arrangements were without political significance, nor that the French would not use their administrative powers to further their own interests to the prejudice of those of the Arabs. He regarded himself 'as a guardian who had pledged his honour to secure the freedom and independence of the Arab people of Syria'.

Such a declaration had in fact been under consideration since the beginning of July 1918 if not earlier. It was first intended as one from Britain to King Ḥusain. Its aim was to mitigate the 'unsettling effect' of the Sykes–Picot agreement on the Arabs, to conciliate 'democratic forces' within the allied camp which regarded it as an imperialist instrument and in particular to bring its provisions in line with President Wilson's principles. After several consultations between Sykes and Picot it was decided to issue the proposed declaration in the name of the British and French governments. Two draft formulae were submitted, the one concerned with the principle of 'the consent of the governed' and the other with 'a period of tutelage', also with the consent of the governed, before self-government or independence.

Balfour himself referred the matter to the Eastern Committee under Lord Curzon. In August Hogarth submitted another draft formula which expressly excluded Palestine and lower Iraq. Lord Robert Cecil revised it drastically and suppressed the reference to Palestine and lower Iraq. Allenby's victory in Syria heightened Anglo–French diplomatic exchanges which culminated in the conference on 30 September in the Foreign Office in London where it was agreed to issue a declaration or declarations in order to emphasise, among other matters, that there would be no annexation of territory, that the establishment of an Arab state or states would be upheld, that the government or governments would be under native rulers, and that 'Europeans' would be merely assistants and advisers.

France continued to raise objections to the British draft which specified Iraq and Syria. A French diplomatic trap was laid, and the usually wary English fell into it. The French ambassador suggested that the proposed declaration should be of general application and that there was no need for the specific mention of only Syria and Iraq. Lord Robert Cecil, Balfour's right-hand man, rejected the French suggestion, put in different forms three times between 19 and 22 October, because it 'would be difficult to square with our declared policy in [*sic*] Palestine'. The French now knew what they had suspected all along: Britain coveted Palestine for herself under the cover of Zionism.

This was the first official revelation that, even before securing the agreement of France and other powers, Britain intended to seek sole control over Palestine, to deny the Arab majority of its population both self-determination and self-government, and to disregard, in their case alone, the principle of the consent of the governed – all in order to facilitate the establishment of a Jewish national home. Whether a bargain was struck at this stage for France to have a free hand in Lebanon and Britain in Palestine must remain for the present a mere conjecture. For when the Anglo–French Declaration was issued it mentioned, as Britain desired, only Iraq and Syria, although the Declaration was officially circulated in Palestine as in the other territories. Clayton reported that the majority of the people in Palestine took it for granted that the Declaration applied to them. Military governors who had themselves distributed the copies were unable to enlighten the dubious. Clayton sought clarification and the Foreign Office told him on 4 December 1918 that Palestine was excluded, but this was for his 'private information'. Thus Britain intended to exclude Palestine but deliberately concealed her intention and acted as if it was not excluded. Apparently she relied on her military occupation to do what she pleased with a conquered territory.

The text of the Declaration was shown to President Wilson who, exactly like Faisal, feared that 'force of circumstances' could create 'spheres of influence' for the two great powers. He preferred small and neutral nations as advisers. Meanwhile the policy of concealment was not abandoned or even varied. It was left to Allenby to tidy up the mess for the politicians. The responsibility had already been shifted from their shoulders to those of this soldier whose diplomacy was, under very awkward circumstances, manifestly more honest than theirs. As stated above, and contrary to current accounts, he did not face Faisal with the whole of the unpleasant truth on their first meeting. He took special care to reveal as little of it as was necessary at a given moment. It is doubtful whether he ever revealed the whole of the Anglo–French design to Faisal or any other Arab leader. Like the politicians he too sought a talisman in the superficially soothing words of the Anglo–French Declaration, finally issued on 8 November.

Meanwhile Allenby had by the last week in October set up three military administrations, each under a chief administrator directly responsible to him. These were: (*a*) Occupied Enemy Territory (South), under a British army officer and comprising the Turkish divisions of Jerusalem, Nābulus and Acre (Palestine); (*b*) Occupied Enemy Territory (North), under a French army officer and comprising Mount Lebanon, the city of Beirut and the Turkish divisions on the littoral up to Alexandretta; (*c*) Occupied Enemy Territory (East) under Rikābi Pasha and comprising all the Turkish divisions from Ma'ān and Aleppo.

Allenby's instructions to the chief administrators are noteworthy. They were reminded that the administration was a military and provisional one, without prejudice to future settlement, and therefore they were not to indulge in 'any political propaganda or to take part in any political questions'. Their administration was to be according to the law and usages of war, and the Turkish system of government and existing machinery and personnel were to be utilised.

Under the guise of military convenience the dismemberment of Syria was now an accomplished fact. King Ḥusain was so unhappy about those 'arrangements in Palestine, Syria and the neighbouring countries' that he mentioned again the extreme contingencies of abdication or suicide. Wingate's assurances, with Allenby's blessings, were of no avail. Ḥusain could not, for example, conceive of a country prospering with its access to the coast entirely under foreign control. 'As for the Islamic world' he was certain that he had now failed to vindicate the revolt and this amounted to political suicide.

Faisal's position in Syria was anomalous. He was still the commander of the Northern Arabian Armies, but not yet legally the head of a state. He had appointed Rikābi as military governor of all Syria, but under his instructions Allenby could recognise the appointment only for the interior. This was probably the extent of Allenby's recognition of Faisal as the 'supreme authority in Syria in all Arab matters whether administrative or military'. Faisal was, however, surrounded by nationalists from the three zones. Their aim was the realisation of the programme of Syrian unity and independence. There was no general desire to tie Syria to Hijaz except in a loose confederation with the mere acknowledgment of the nominal overlordship of Ḥusain. The Damascus administration under Faisal planned for a decentralised independent state within geographical Syria comprising Lebanon and Palestine as well as the interior.

The fiction that the military zones had no political significance did not convince them. They remained as suspicious of France as ever. The new suspicion of Britain and her intentions regarding Palestine began to be expressed in formal protests in Jerusalem and elsewhere. The rigorous military censorship and ban on public meetings and demonstrations did not prevent a united Palestinian Arab front, Christian and Muslim, recording a series of protests and staging demonstrations. This was the only means of expressing their wishes. While the Zionists had direct access to the military administration through the Zionist commission the Arabs had none, not even through army liaison officers.

Palestine was a major problem for Faisal second only to the problem of French pretensions. He trusted he could settle matters with Britain but not with France. As soon as the approximate limits of the zones became known Faisal was incensed to discover that the French zone extended deep into the interior and included areas which had already declared for, and had in fact established, Arab administrations, such as Ḥāṣbayya, Rāshayya and Ba'labakk. Faisal's communications to the north had to be through the last town. 'Let the people decide', under the supervision of an allied commission, telegraphed Faisal to Allenby, making it clear that this time he would resign. Allenby gave way and ordered the French administrator not to extend his control to these districts.

While Allenby was tackling these military and political matters, the pursuit of the retreating Turkish forces was continued inland beyond Damascus and along the coast north of Beirut. The advance from Damascus was preceded by an Arab force under Nāṣir. The remnants of the Turkish forces were rallied by Muṣṭafā Kamāl Pasha for a last stand near Aleppo, but soon the attempt to defend the city was abandoned. After some hand-to-hand fighting in the streets, Nāṣir occupied the city on 25 October. Five days later

Turkey signed an armistice with the allies, and hostilities ceased on the last day of the month. The military operations were at an end, but the political struggle was only beginning. On the very day the Anglo-French Declaration was published the British government, acting on very strong recommendation from Allenby, invited King Ḥusain to send a deputy to represent him at the allied and peace conferences in Europe and placed a warship at his disposal for speedy transport. Ḥusain accepted the invitation and appointed Faisal as his representative.

9

The dismemberment of greater Syria was accomplished by devious but effective means under the mask of temporary military administrations. To all intents and purposes each of the military administrations in the three zones did its best to determine and shape the future political control of its zone: British in Palestine, French in the rest of the Syrian littoral and Arab in the interior. In the process professedly temporary positions were consolidated for permanence.

Some reconstruction began even before the end of the war. In the extreme south, Palestine suffered greater damage than the rest of Syria, because it was the scene of prolonged military operations. As a result agriculture, the mainstay of the life of the country, was crippled and most of the orange groves and many orchards between Gaza and Jaffa were destroyed. This material loss was aggravated by the evacuation of the civil population for which both the Turkish and the British military authorities were responsible. The former ordered the evacuation of the bulk of the population of Gaza and Jaffa, the latter ordered the evacuation of several villages along the front line just north of Jaffa.

After the occupation of Jerusalem, the British military authorities repaired and extended the railways and roads, largely to serve army requirements, but the improved system of communication was also used to bring supplies from Egypt for general consumption. Gradually the population of evacuated cities and villages returned to their dilapidated or half-demolished houses, and the farmers began to work their fields and restore life to their orchards and groves. If the damage done to agriculture could slowly and partially be repaired, there was still no foreign and hardly any domestic trade. The shortage of manpower, whether as a result of military service, war casualties, disease or poverty was very serious indeed.

The British army spent a great deal of money in the country and created some demand for labour. Their project of draining the marshes near the ʿAuja river was, for example, intended primarily to protect the army against malaria, but it also provided employment to destitute villages and beduins in the neighbourhood. In January 1918 Allenby reported that revenue had already been levied under the Turkish laws, and that a beginning had been made in restoring the health and educational services, and in reconstructing the municipalities. For the whole of Palestine the revenue in 1918–19 was estimated at £661,813 of which £126,866 was assigned for general administration, £50,861 for health, £15,331 for education and £14,393 for grants and loans to municipalities. (According to Allenby the Turks had spent £28,000 per annum on education in the *sanjaq* of Jerusalem alone.) The total amount spent on relief was £331,905 which came from, among other organisations, the (British) Syria and Palestine Relief Fund, the American Red Cross and the Zionists. But while the first two organisations extended their help to all sections of the population, help from the last source was confined to the Jews.

The British and American relief work was extended to the Syrian littoral, especially Lebanon, supplementing the work of Catholic missionary and other bodies. To start with, the French military administration itself had relatively little to do with relief except as overseers. The administration received its financial support from Allenby, not from France. At first this administration lacked even the staff with which to administer the territory. The French government had taken all possible precautions to get the French political position recognised, but apparently had made no preparation to assume actual control. This proved to be beyond the capacity of the small French detachment in Allenby's army. On 31 October its commander telegraphed to Paris that he could play no prominent part because of shortage of cadres, lack of administrative personnel and inadequate material.[20]

In the interior conditions had throughout the war been relatively better than in Palestine or in Lebanon. Apart from the drain on manpower and resources, little material damage was suffered. The agricultural economy was strained but escaped major disruption. Certain districts like Ḥawrān even profited from the war by marketing their grain at inflated prices. Trade never came to a complete standstill as it did on the littoral. There was open access to Arabia and Egypt through desert routes which the belligerents could not control, and an illicit trade was conducted by smugglers who sold to peripatetic merchants rice, coffee, sugar, cloth and other articles which ultimately found their way to the market of Damascus and elsewhere.

There was little need for any major relief work or repair of war damage. Apart from the political uncertainty, the difficulties were mainly administrative and financial. Civil and military personnel hitherto employed by the Turks formed the backbone of the Arab administration, reinforced by a large number of young and inexperienced army officers and revolutionaries. In Palestine the native element was employed in subordinate positions supervised by British senior officers, and a similar system prevailed in Lebanon. In the Damascus administration the supervision was in Arab hands – in reality in the hands of ex-Turkish officials from Rikābi downwards. These men could not change their habits overnight. Even the change of the official language from Turkish to Arabic was not easy, and special courses in letter-writing had to be given to civil servants.

The financial difficulty was more serious since it limited the freedom of political action. As Allenby's chief Political Officer wrote, the Turks had collected the year's taxes, and Faisal's administration could not be carried out without the continuance of the British subsidy, then estimated at £150,000 a month. France saw the political implications of Faisal's dependence on British money and at once proposed to give Faisal's administration a loan. The proposal was strongly resisted by the British government who had not yet made up its mind as to giving France a free hand in Syria with the exception of Palestine. From the War Office the Director of Military Intelligence wrote that 'it would be a mistake to allow the French to obtain prematurely any financial hold on the Arab government'. The attitude of the Foreign Office was summed up by Lord Robert Cecil who wrote in an undated minute early in November that 'it would be a grave disadvantage to the Arab government if it got into the entrails of French financiers. This may be intimated privately to the Treasury.' The intimation was effective: Faisal was saved from French financiers but placed at the mercy of British politicians.

Apart from immediate lack of revenue there was another economic disadvantage which Faisal had to tolerate right from the beginning. Under the Sykes–Picot agreement, as under Allenby's military administration, the Arab zone had no outlet to the sea. But for Allenby's strong objection the French would at once have made Beirut a naval base, even before the allied blockade was formally lifted. Allenby insisted that Beirut was essential for the supply of the armies in Syria. In fact he continued to insist on retaining complete control of traffic by sea and land and the movement of all persons to or from the three military zones.

The French challenged his authority more than once. Barely ten days after his installation in Beirut as Allenby's subordinate, the French military governor refused, pending consultation with the French government, to publish Allenby's order on the replacement of Turkish paper currency by Egyptian. Allenby allowed no delay and reminded his French subordinate that he was responsible to the commander-in-chief alone who permitted him no communication with any government. The French ambassador was called to the Foreign Office and gently told that they backed Allenby but that if the French government had any special wishes they were prepared to make them known to Allenby.

The second challenge was more serious. Disregarding the ban on political propaganda, the French liaison officer in Damascus made it known to the Druzes of Ḥawrān that France, not Britain, was to have the paramount position in the Arab zone and that it was in their interest to send a delegation to the French authorities in Beirut. In response to Faisal's protest Allenby summoned both the French liaison officer in Damascus and the acting French political adviser in Beirut. What he told them is not recorded but may well be imagined. The encounter took place only three days before the issue of the Anglo–French Declaration.

The third and most serious challenge came from Picot himself who was officially Allenby's chief political adviser. In December he secretly arranged, with permits signed by himself as *Haut commissaire de la république française en Syrie*, a title Allenby never recognised, for a delegation of five members of the Lebanese administrative council to proceed to France and Europe with authority, which they did not possess under the Lebanon statute, to ask for a Lebanon separate from Syria and with larger territory under French protection. The delegation was stopped at Port Said pending instructions from London. The instructions were a triumph for Picot but damaging to British prestige and reputation: for political reasons let this delegation proceed but prevent any other.

A quick protest came from some of the Druzes in Lebanon. The Talḥūqs wrote that the delegation did not represent the views of the majority which regarded Lebanon as part of Syria and its separation from it as detrimental to its political and economic interests. Apart from its repercussions in Egypt where there was a strong desire to send a delegation, protests from all over Syria and Palestine were officially submitted, all making substantially the same point: it was unjust to bar more representative groups from proceeding to the Peace Conference. According to Clayton there was a great deal of bitterness in the protests since the prohibition came so soon after the pronouncements about self-determination. His conclusion deserves to be quoted in full especially seeing that as a forecast they remained valid for the next three decades: 'There appears to be no immediate risk of a serious outbreak, but the ratification and attempted execution of the Sykes–Picot [agreement] in addition to the Zionist programme would undoubtedly necessitate the retention of an effective army of occupation for many years to come.'[21]

10

From the Peace Conference to the Fall of Damascus

I

KING ḤUSAIN had, according to Wingate, continued to express grave anxiety about the future of Syria even after the issue of the Anglo–French declaration. He proposed to proceed to London himself in order to negotiate with the British government. That was surely a belated move. It came at a time when the British government viewed Ḥusain in a different light. With the end of the war in the defeat of Turkey, Ḥusain was less useful and there was less desire on the British side for immediate discussion of the Syrian question than during the war. For one thing, Britain began seriously to covet Palestine and was preparing to buy off French agreement by conceding the rest of Syria to exclusive French influence. For another, Britain was in military occupation of the whole territory, and was determined to devise a settlement at leisure.

The Peace Conference was, of course, a convenient excuse for delay and disclaiming responsibility. But meanwhile neither Ḥusain nor Faisal nor even the native population themselves were allowed to take any precipitate action such as a declaration of independence. The military authorities controlled the press, telegraph, travel and the holding of public meetings, and in the circumstances expression of public opinion was restricted and on occasion manipulated.

Ḥusain was now more than ever powerless to act without British support, and he could not gain that support without surrendering vital Arab interests to the French and the British. But in view of Allenby's insistence that the assurances he had given to Faisal with the approval of the British government should be honoured, it was considered desirable to invite Ḥusain to send a representative to the Peace Conference. Such an invitation, in Wingate's words, 'might go to mitigate his disappointment at the details of the final settlement'. Accordingly on 8 November a message from the Foreign Office, disguised as a personal note by Lawrence, was sent to Ḥusain suggesting that he should inform the allied governments of his intention to send a representative, and adding that 'I hope you will send Faisal'.

The British government was anxious to represent the move as Ḥusain's initiative so as to avoid argument with France. Ḥusain accepted the invitation, even though, according to Wingate, he was then 'uncertain how far Faisal was prepared to execute his policy and . . . not a little suspicious of Colonel Lawrence's influence with his son'.

On receiving Ḥusain's acceptance, the Foreign Office informed France that Allenby had reported that Ḥusain intended to send a representative, and the British government took the opportunity to suggest to him to send Faisal, 'who had been up to now in close touch with both the British and French authorities in Syria and Palestine'.

Although Britain, and later on also France, recognised Faisal as the representative of the Kingdom of Hijaz, the king himself refused, after four different formulae had been submitted to him by the British agent, to send Faisal except as 'the representative of the Arab government'. To Ḥusain this government embraced his own in Hijaz, the one established in his name in Damascus and also potentially any government to be set up in Iraq.

The French protested that there was no prior consultation. They pointed out that Faisal may have been the envoy of the recognised King of Hijaz, but not of an unrecognised Arab kingdom or government elsewhere. In particular, they contested Faisal's right to speak in the name of the Arab population of Syria, but agreed to give him an opportunity of asking for the constitution of a state, controlled by France and Britain, in the zones under their respective administrations in Syria. The British government retorted, less precisely and rather compromisingly, that they regarded Faisal 'as the representative of our co-belligerent and ally King Ḥusain, sent to be present in Paris during the discussions of the Peace Conference in order to voice and look after his father's interests'.

Faisal's passage through France was marked by a mixture of French pique and politeness. They made their guest wait too long before he was received by President Poincaré. But they referred to him as 'His Royal Highness' and to his father as 'His Majesty', an embarrassment to the English who had hitherto, in agreement with the French, addressed Ḥusain as His Lordship (*ṣāḥib as-siyādah*), King (*malik*) of Hijaz. The matter was referred to King George V, who recognised 'the necessity' of following the French example. Accordingly on 10 December His Royal Highness Prince Faisal was welcomed in London.

There is no need to dwell on the ceremonial receptions. Faisal was received at Buckingham Palace by King George V who conferred upon his guest the chain of the Royal Victorian Order. Later on Faisal was entertained by the Lord Mayor at the Mansion House. More important, however, were his discussions with ministers. Faisal's immediate problem was French claims in Syria. For the rest he was just as confident as his father that the Arabs could come to an amicable arrangement with Britain in Iraq and Palestine. In this he was ultimately disappointed.

On 11 December, the second day after his arrival in London, Faisal called on Balfour, with Lawrence acting as interpreter. A record of the conversation, drafted and corrected by Balfour himself, was sent to the King, the Cabinet, the British ambassador in Paris and the High Commissioner in Cairo. Balfour does not say whether Faisal discussed with him the future British policy regarding Syria, Palestine and Iraq. He merely states that Faisal was 'as violently anti-French as he was undisguisedly pro-British', that he complained of Allenby's action at Beirut where the Arab flag had to be lowered, and that he said that if the French showed 'aggressive designs' he would attack them at once. He knew he could not resist the might of France but he and his followers would rather perish in the struggle than submit to foreign domination.

Speaking in general, without confining himself to the French question, Faisal stressed that foreign control would be 'intolerable' to the Arabs. If they had to submit to it at all they would rather endure bad government by the Turks. In his own hand Balfour altered the last phrase to read as it does in the final text 'Moslem Government'. Faisal is more likely to have used the former in the concrete rather than the latter in the abstract.

Balfour records himself as saying only one thing – that Faisal was 'in error as to the true character of French designs', and that was based surprisingly not on his diplomatic knowledge of the facts but on a report, published as if purposely on 11 December in *The Times*, reproducing an earlier report in *Matin* of a reply by Clemenceau to the Syrian Central Committee of Shukri Ghānim, in which he referred to the arrangements respecting Syria as of a *caractère absolument transitoire*, and that they would be reviewed by the Peace Conference. Furthermore, France was determined to secure *l'évolution de la Syrie vers une civilisation pacifique*.

This is of course too vague a proof of French designs, and Balfour knew it. No doubt Balfour knew then more than he wished to disclose, even of French designs. Clemenceau had been in London only a week before Faisal's arrival, and while in London struck a bargain with Lloyd George. The two prime ministers agreed in principle to revise the allocation of spheres under the Sykes–Picot agreement: France to renounce claims to Mosul and Palestine in favour of Britain, in return for British recognition of exclusive French influence in the rest of Syria. This fresh Anglo–French redistribution of the spoils on the eve of Faisal's visit rendered his mission hopeless before it began.

From the moment he arrived in Europe Faisal had to depend entirely on Lawrence, not only as an interpreter, Ḥusain's suspicions notwithstanding. Ḥusain and Faisal could expect wholehearted support from Lawrence only in their resistance to French claims, and on this subject he was more embarrassing than helpful. For the rest Lawrence's views were very close to official British policy. While he advocated an Arab state or states in Syria and Iraq, he was also for a British Palestine and concessions to Zionism.

In February 1918 Clayton had written to Sykes that he had urged Lawrence to impress upon Faisal 'the necessity of an entente with the Jews'. If Lawrence did then try he must have failed, for when the British military authorities arranged for Weizmann to visit Faisal at his camp near ʿAqaba, Faisal made it clear that he was a soldier and that policy on Palestine was made by his father at Mecca. Despite propaganda reports to the contrary, Faisal promised nothing and Weizmann returned empty-handed.

Six months later, when Faisal came to London, pressure was

brought to bear on him. Lloyd George had just secured Palestine from Clemenceau, and it was thought that the British Zionist policy needed only to be clinched with Faisal, without any reference to the Palestine Arabs. Barely twenty-four hours after Faisal's arrival in London Weizmann was thrust on him, and Lawrence acted as interpreter – whether of Faisal's policy or of that of the British government is now open to grave doubt.

We have only Weizmann's version of the conversation. The record reads like a Zionist propaganda handbill, but making allowance for its partisan nature there emerges from it as credible one main point: that both Faisal and Weizmann, for different reasons, were against the provisions of the Sykes–Picot agreement and the French claims in Syria–Palestine. Furthermore, Faisal appears to have been tempted by Weizmann's reference to American Zionists using their influence with the United States government to oppose the Sykes–Picot agreement.

Faisal was still counting on British assistance to rid Syria of French claims. If he agreed in principle to a British trusteeship over Palestine, an agreement which the British politicians and the Zionists sought, he presupposed the extension of the agreement to the rest of Syria which Faisal was eager to save from partition under the Sykes–Picot agreement. That this was in fact his principal aim is clear from the fact that as soon as he discovered that Britain was interested in a trusteeship over Palestine only, he protested that this was tantamount to a partition of Syria and refused to recognise it. His attitude to the Zionists changed accordingly. Whatever they claim he agreed to privately, he publicly made it clear how much of the Zionist programme he was prepared to tolerate in a Palestine which formed part of an Arab federation.

Lawrence's influence with Faisal over the Palestine question and Zionism has hitherto remained obscure. Fresh evidence tends to indicate that Lawrence was very close indeed to the pro-Zionists among the British politicians. There is reason to doubt whether he did always faithfully interpret Faisal's Arabic. Indeed, some of the records of conversations, letters and telegrams attributed to Faisal betray signs that they were written directly in English and not translated from Arabic originals. By phraseology and tone, if not also by content, they breathe a spirit more akin to Whitehall and Oxford than to Damascus and Mecca. Circumstantial evidence tends to confirm the view that on Palestine Lawrence was Balfour's agent. It was Balfour himself who resisted strong representations from the Foreign Office and confirmed Lawrence as an adviser to the British delegation at the Peace Conference. Has this fact any relation to Lawrence's dark reference to his readiness to 'join in the conspiracy'?[1]

There is, moreover, conclusive evidence that Lawrence did assume on Faisal's behalf, and probably without his authority, some executive powers which Faisal was not likely to delegate. Thus in the first week of January 1919 an important telegram for Faisal from Zaid, Faisal's brother and deputy in Damascus, was received at the Foreign Office via the British military authorities, as all such telegrams had to be sent in this way. It expressed anxiety at the lack of news on the progress of negotiations in London, and asked for an urgent reply 'to tranquillize public opinion'. A reply sent through the same channels purports to be from Faisal, but was written in English in Lawrence's hand and submitted to the Foreign Office 'for despatch if approved. T. E. L.' It runs as follows: 'It is impossible for me to send you news of the negotiations which are proceeding, or to say what I think might ruin my case. In my opinion things are going well. I leave for Paris tomorrow, and hope to send you certain news in ten days time.'

At the same time another telegram was received from Sharif Nāṣir, the military commander in Aleppo, addressed to Faisal asking a similar question. The reply also in Lawrence's hand reads as follows: 'I am engaged in discussing the future of our country with our allies, and can only tell you now that things are going well. . . .' Still another telegram was sent to King Ḥusain shortly after Faisal's departure, also written by Lawrence. It says nothing about Syria, Palestine and Iraq, but assures Ḥusain regarding a dispute with Ibn Saʿūd.[2]

Taken together these telegrams show Lawrence in a new light. As Faisal's interpreter at all the interviews in London he knew very well that Faisal had completely failed, not only to execute his father's policy but to safeguard the minimum of independence for Damascus. According to a record of Faisal's conversations with Edwin Montagu, Secretary of State for India, at which Lawrence acted as interpreter, Faisal allegedly refrained from saying a word about Iraq and voluntarily left Palestine for British discretion. But he complained of the weakness of the British government and expressed disappointment that he could not modify their view that the Sykes–Picot agreement was still valid. If all this was true why then deceive Zāid about negotiations, Naṣir about discussions and distract Ḥusain's attention from the main issues in Syria and Palestine which worried him more, at this time, than Ibn Saʿūd?

2

Lawrence's hitherto unknown conversion to the idea of an Anglo–Zionist arrangement for Palestine must have been accomplished despite reports of fierce Palestine Arab opposition. As Balfour's freelance adviser on Arab affairs, Lawrence had access to Foreign Office papers and some were definitely referred to him for comments. Accordingly he was not ignorant of the repeated Palestine Arab appeals and protests, first to the British government and later also to the Peace Conference and President Wilson. But Lawrence appears to have been converted to Sykes's assumption that in order to save Damascus Faisal must sacrifice Palestine, an assumption which rests on no basis of the facts of British policy.

On 6 January 1919 Sykes was in Aleppo, and the following is the text of a gratuitous telegram he sent to Weizmann via Ormsby-Gore at the Foreign Office. Speaking of the growth of anti-Zionist agitation in Syria the telegram adds: 'I have seen the Arab Committee and impressed upon them that such a policy would be absolute ruin to their case, and told them that if such policy continued I would withdraw help . . . and have no more to do with [the Arab] movement.'

Sykes was careful to instruct Gore to paraphrase the telegram and then destroy the original, but the above copy survived in the Foreign Office files. Lawrence took no such precautions when he sent a telegram from Paris in the name of Faisal to Zaid as follows: '. . . Anti-Zionist articles in your Damascus papers. . . . Please explain privately to ʿAli Riḍā [ar-Rikābi] that the Zionist Committee is helping us very much here in Paris, and that I am most anxious to retain their goodwill. Do your best to control the press on this point.'

These attempts to silence protests against the British government's Zionist policy, coupled by determined efforts, in which Lawrence played a prominent part, to seek Faisal's sanction of that policy are difficult to understand. Both moves are irreconcilable with the British attitude to Faisal's credentials. They asked him to be armed with authorisation to speak in the name of the Syrians in the zone under his administration, but prevented him from seeking such authorisation from the people of Lebanon and Palestine. Furthermore, the British government was well aware that Ḥusain's instructions were for Faisal to ask for Arab independence in all Arab territories and that he was given no authority to sign away Palestine or any other part of the Arab homeland. Nor was the British government ignorant of the formal request submitted by the Palestine Arabs, Muslims and Christians, to the Peace Conference asking for their own representatives to appear before the international body. This request was not granted, but that of the Zionists, themselves not natives of Palestine, was.

Here it is necessary to clarify the so-called Faisal–Weizmann agreement of January 1919. The Zionists were then in desperate need for some Arab recognition on the eve of the presentation of their case to the Peace Conference. All that Weizmann could then report to the Foreign Office on the outcome of his interview with Faisal were generalities of no consequence. He made no mention of an 'agreement'. That there was none is corroborated by other facts. During his second visit to London in the autumn of 1919 Faisal made a declaration published in the *Jewish Chronicle* on 3 October that Palestine was an inseparable part of Syria, that he would guarantee to the Jews equal rights with the Arabs and autonomy in their religious and educational affairs, and that he would approve of controlled immigration to a Palestine forming a district in an Arab Empire. But, he said, 'the Arabs would fight to the last ditch' against the separation of Palestine from Syria or its subjugation to non-Arab control.

The Zionists were much dismayed by this clear declaration, but Weizmann produced neither an 'agreement' with Faisal, nor himself pleaded with the Foreign Office for intervention. Instead Herbert Samuel was sent with a copy of a letter Faisal was alleged to have written to the American Zionist, Felix Frankfurter, the previous March (repudiated by Faisal when the Zionists used it at the Shaw inquiry in 1929). The Foreign Office recognised that Faisal's declaration would complicate and embarrass their Zionist policy, but neither Hardinge nor Curzon would agree to say a word to Faisal. A member of their staff had already established the fact that Weizmann's agreement with Faisal was 'in the nature of a general understanding [i.e. to combat the Sykes–Picot agreement] and not a written document'.[3]

The basis of the story of an agreement is a draft in English (of which no Arabic version was ever made) submitted by Weizmann to Faisal through Lawrence. The latter supplied Faisal with some verbal explanation of its contents, but Faisal was very careful not to fall into the trap. He wrote a protective note in Arabic which reads:

> If the Arabs attain their independence as we demanded in our memorandum dated 4 January 1919 addressed to the British Foreign Office I shall approve of the articles contained in this [document]. If the slightest change or adjustment is made [in meeting the demands], I shall not be bound by a single word in this contract (*muqāwalah*) which will be null & void and of no account and no validity, and I shall not be answerable in any way.

Lawrence gave Weizmann on a slip of paper a clearly rough and, by the omission of 'Arab independence', misleading translation, with some words crossed out, which reads: 'If the Arabs are established as I have asked in my manifesto addressed to the British Secretary of State for Foreign Affairs I will carry out what is written in this agreement. If changes are made I am not answerable for failing to carry out this agreement.'

In either case what Faisal was prepared to do was on the lines of his public declarations, subject to Palestine being part of his Syrian dominion. But Weizmann saw the propaganda value even of a rejected document. In his own hand he added to Lawrence's translation the words 'of January 4', after the word 'manifesto' and kept the slip for future use. The draft itself, but without Faisal's Arabic note or Lawrence's rough translation thereof, was passed to David Hunter Miller, a member of the technical staff of the American delegation to the Peace Conference, as an 'official' document, and Miller included it in his well-known collection.[4] Even a wary writer like Antonius fell into the trap and took the document at its face value.

However, neither Weizmann nor any other Zionist made any reference to the 'agreement' in the evidence before the Shaw Commission in 1929, when only the Frankfurter letter was produced with the result mentioned above. In 1936, when both Faisal and Lawrence were dead, and while the Arabs of Palestine were in revolt against British rule and the Zionist policy, Weizmann published the 'agreement' in *The Times* and *The Palestine Post*, with a facsimile of Lawrence's rough translation, but not of Faisal's Arabic.[5]

That was not the end of Lawrence's part in Faisal's affairs. It was by Balfour's own arrangement that Lawrence was attached to the British delegation at the Peace Conference as 'one of the advisers on special subjects'. He had no official standing with Faisal's delegation, and yet he continued to exert an influence, complicating Faisal's already complicated relations with the French and committing him more deeply to depend upon the British. Before leaving London it was clear that Faisal's dependence on Britain was useless. He was told that Britain was still bound by the Sykes–Picot agreement, the terms of which with a map were given to him for the first time. Henceforth any support Britain might give him would stop short of a conflict with France on his account. His best course was, according to British assessment, to come to terms with France.

Small wonder that Faisal began to pin vague hopes on American support. But despite Wilson's personal inclination to uphold the principle of self-determination, and despite active lobbying by Howard Bliss, President of the Syrian Protestant College in Beirut, Faisal's cause was as doomed in Paris as it had been in London. His exchanges with the English and his memoranda and personal plea to the Peace Conference were some form of dialogue with the deaf. Syrian affairs had either been already settled or were being settled between two great powers. Faisal's appeal to 'the conscience of mankind', his insistence on the independence and unity of the Arab provinces freed from Turkish rule, his conciliatory language and moderation in his references to Palestine and Lebanon, were all of no avail. His failure was not so much due, as it has often been stated, to the claims of the Lebanese and the Zionists, whose legitimate aspirations might have been reconciled within a decentralised Syrian state, as to the old ambitions of France and the new claims of Britain which could be met only in the partition of Syria.

Faisal's exchanges with Clemenceau were in reality between one abandoned by his only ally and another given the trump card by that same ally. Although his case was morally and legally very strong, Faisal spoke from a position of physical weakness. Clemenceau had little or no moral case, but he was legally covered by the 1916 agreement with Britain which both sides held as still valid. It is not true that Clemenceau or any French politician treated Faisal except with the usual French courtesy, much as they regarded him as inconvenient for their cause. The French government conferred upon him the *croix de guerre avec palme*, and Clemenceau ordered his *chef du cabinet militaire*, General Mordacq, to decorate Faisal with it. (The current story that it was General Gouraud who performed this function is not correct.) However, Faisal signed no agreement with Clemenceau and made no verbal promise on this occasion to accept a French mandate. He had reason to expect a better prospect at the hands of an international inquiry.

The most tangible result of Faisal's prolonged stay in Paris was an acceptance of the idea of an interallied commission with the function of ascertaining on the spot the wishes of the inhabitants of Syria regarding their political future. The idea did not, however, originate in Paris. It had been, in one form or another, one of the standard demands since 1917. It was first formally made to the Peace Conference in January 1919 when Michel Lotfallah, on behalf of the Syria Union Party, requested the dispatch of 'an American or interallied commission to supervise a plebiscite of the Syrian people'.[6]

In the meantime the system was being devised under which the principle of trusteeship or mandate was agreed in theory. From the beginning it had been assumed by the great powers that this principle would apply to, among other territories, the Syrian provinces. But the same great powers whose territorial or other ambitions in Syria had been thwarted by their unwilling acceptance of the principle of self-determination now sought to achieve their ends, short of annexation of territory, by offering or imposing themselves either as trustees or mandatories.

In an attempt to maintain the integrity of Syria and rid it of exaggerated French ambitions, Faisal tried in vain to interest Britain in assuming the trusteeship over a Syria that would include Palestine but possibly exclude Mount Lebanon in favour of France.

Britain had already disinterested herself in assuming any such function except in Palestine. This British striving to secure a mandate for Palestine alone and the hankering of the Maronites in Lebanon after French protection made a French mandate over Syria, less Palestine, inevitable, irrespective of the wishes of the majority of the population.

The international commission of inquiry was expected to discover, among other matters, what trustee or trustees were acceptable to the Syrians. Since the wishes of the people in Palestine, Lebanon and the rest of Syria were already well known to the parties likely to lose by the inquiry, the commission was sabotaged before it embarked on its duties. France, who knew that except in the Maronite district in Lebanon and among the scattered Catholic communities elsewhere she was not wanted, refused to take part until British troops were replaced by French troops. Britain, who had fundamental reservations about the application of the principle of self-determination to Palestine, declared that it was in the circumstances 'inexpedient' to take part. Italy made no move, and the American section of the commission was left to conduct the inquiry alone.

The British withdrawal was partly to placate France, but largely to protect the Zionist programme. Balfour had been officially against the application of the principle of self-determination to Palestine since the draft of the Anglo-French Declaration was under consideration in 1918. On 19 February 1919 he wrote to Lloyd George that 'in the case of Palestine we deliberately and rightly decline to accept the principle of self-determination'. Accordingly on 22 March he objected to the inclusion of Palestine in the sphere of the interallied inquiry, but, as he says, failed to convince Wilson and Lloyd George.

Balfour, however, put on record his objections in a memorandum dated 23 March. Since, he wrote, the commissioners were required by their terms of reference to advise on the establishment of 'national governments and administrations deriving their authority from the initiative and free choice of the native population', they were bound to find that the Arabs would wish an Arab national government, and that the commissioners' report would contain a statement to the effect that 'the present inhabitants of Palestine, who in a large majority are Arab, do not desire to see the administration of the country so conducted as to encourage the relative increase of the Jewish population and influence'. In that case, Balfour continues, the task of a future mandatory, whether Britain or America, in promoting Zionism would be 'greatly embarrassed' and the difficulty of carrying out that policy 'much increased'. Britain and America, he concluded, have publicly declared their adhesion to a Zionist policy, and this policy could not be abandoned 'without giving a shock to Jewish opinion throughout the world'.

3

'We cannot accept to be divided like cattle!' Thus Faisal telegraphed to Allenby at the end of May, in view of persistent reports that the interallied commission was not coming and that a French army was on its way to Syria to replace British forces. If these reports were true, Faisal said, it would amount to deciding the fate of the country without consulting its inhabitants. Faisal had already in the middle of May mentioned to Allenby that a general national assembly was being called and that it might declare the independence of the whole of Syria. Allenby warned Faisal of the dangers of such a declaration in defiance of the Peace Conference where the matter was still *sub judice*.

Allenby, however, knew of other dangers and on 30 May warned both the War Office in London and Balfour in Paris that the situation was 'extremely grave', that the Arabs might be forced by circumstances to fight both the French and the British and that should this happen the position of the British army in Syria and Palestine would be 'seriously endangered'. British (and Zionist) intelligence reports warned Allenby that the Arabs of Palestine were secretly arming under the inspiration and guidance of Arab army officers from Damascus. Likewise British (and French) intelligence reports warned all concerned of a growing belligerent spirit in Damascus, and of a plan by the chief of staff of the Arab army, Yāsīn Pasha al-Hāshimi, for an immediate attack on the small French forces before reinforcements could outweigh the military balance in their favour.

Once more Allenby warned Faisal of the dangers of any action that would 'bring you in conflict with my troops'. The term 'my troops' still meant both the British and the French forces in Syria. Whether he was bluffing or in earnest, Faisal was restrained. A soothing message was sent on 2 June, with Balfour's authority, to Cairo. It explained why the French and British sections of the commission had not been sent and added that the American section would arrive 'almost immediately', and authorised the publication on its arrival of an assurance that 'the British Government will give fullest weight to their advice'. On the same date Balfour himself sent a confidential telegram to Clayton instructing him to inform Faisal that Britain was 'determined not to take a mandate for Syria'.

This was in answer to an inquiry by Faisal, who had just heard from the Hijaz delegation in Paris that the mandate was inevitable. It was then too late for Faisal to alter the trend of the campaign he had been conducting in preparation for the commission. But he made independence the ruling principle of any mandate he and his people might accept.[7]

On 10 June the American commission landed at Jaffa amid great Arab anxiety and perplexity. Faisal was on that day in Aleppo, and from there telegraphed to Allenby enquiring whether it was true that 'the commission was only a show and that the fate of the country had been already decided'. Allenby's reply was milder and more reserved than the declaration made with the authority of Balfour. The commission, said Allenby, would advise the supreme council as to the wishes of the people. Britain was unwilling to accept a mandate for Syria but 'will give fullest weight to the advice of the commission in the council'.

British disclaimers of any interest in a mandate for Syria studiously avoided any mention of Palestine, over which Britain was secretly seeking a mandate, and in the process making the partition of Syria inevitable. On 26 June Balfour urged Lloyd George not to wait for a peace treaty with Turkey before deciding on the mandates for Syria and Iraq. He recommended that the Arab provinces should be detached forthwith from Turkey and placed under mandate: British in Iraq, French in Syria and American or British in Palestine. It was only a matter of time before this was substantially adopted as British policy.

That policy, and its French counterpart, placed Faisal finally under the complete influence of the nationalists. Henceforth he was the mouthpiece of the Syrian congress, his own creation, and appeared before the American commission as such. Within a Syrian union he was for conciliating minorities and establishing equality between all citizens irrespective of religious faith. He would respect the special status of Lebanon with the guarantee of the powers. Elsewhere a system of administrative decentralisation would be followed, taking into account local or regional interests. He told the commission that he personally had been prepared to accept a limited and controlled Zionist programme in Palestine, but extreme Zionist pretensions had so frightened the people that they had now decided to reject the programme in its entirety.

The resolutions of the Syrian congress were first communicated to the commission and by 4 August reached Balfour in Paris and Curzon in London. The congress members representing the three regions were either elected according to the regulations of Ottoman parliamentary elections or, where this was not allowed by British or French military authorities, were given written authority from the notables of their localities. Except perhaps for Mount Lebanon, either the same representatives or others of the same views would have probably been returned under any other system. The congress asked for the complete independence of geographical Syria as a constitutional monarchy with safeguards for the rights and status of minorities, and declared its intention to elect Faisal as king of a united Syria. Should the Peace Conference, however, disregard this desire and decide to apply the system of mandate its application must not infringe independence and must be restricted to technical and financial matters and its duration must not exceed twenty years. As mandatory, the congress named first the United States as the most disinterested power. Great Britain was the second choice provided she would maintain Syrian territorial unity. France was definitely rejected. So also was the Zionist claim to Palestine, but native Jews were guaranteed equal rights with the Arabs. Both the Sykes–Picot agreement and the Balfour Declaration were condemned as contrary to the rights of native Syrians.

The salient conclusions of the commission reached Curzon through the acting chief political officer on 6 August, summarised under four heads: (*a*) general desire for Syrian unity, (*b*) France will not be accepted 'peaceably as a mandatory' in the Syrian interior, (*c*) the Zionist programme can be carried out only against the wishes of the Arabs 'by force', (*d*) Syrian desire for 'Anglo-Saxon' assistance to uphold independence deserves encouragement. These conclusions were no surprise to the Foreign Office. 'They confirm', wrote a high official in a minute, 'all we heard from our own people on the spot.' Curzon concluded the minute majestically: 'Daniel come to judgement!'

As soon as the commission left Syria dark rumours began to circulate once more. The Syrian congress became restive and there were elements clamouring for an immediate declaration of independence. Faisal's position became increasingly difficult. He wanted to proceed to Europe at once. France was against it, and the British authorities did not wish to challenge France on this matter. They made Lawrence advise Faisal to delay. Still perplexed, Faisal instructed the Hijaz delegation in Paris on 17 August to ask the Peace Conference not to decide the Syrian question before his own appearance in person.

On the same day Faisal sent a letter and a memorandum to Lloyd George through Allenby in which he asked whether Britain was giving 'the fullest weight' to the finding and advice of the American commission. In particular he protested against Britain's desire to take a mandate for Palestine alone, contrary to the wishes of the people and involving 'a division of the Arab countries and a return to the unjust agreement of 1916'. Faisal gave notice that as he could not acquiesce in a division of Arab territory he must now identify himself openly with the sentiment of the people and be ready 'to shed the last drop of his blood with them'.

Before receiving a reply Faisal sent a telegram to Allenby, quoting press reports that Britain and France had actually divided up the Arab countries, and asking for a denial or confirmation of these reports. King Ḥusain and 'Abdullah each sent a similar inquiry to Cairo. Allenby evaded the question by saying he was going to England and would find out the answers there. However, Cheetham was authorised to reply to Mecca that the matter was still pending at the Peace Conference.

No doubt it was, but neither Allenby nor Cheetham was empowered to give straight answers to straight questions. The mystery, if it was any longer a mystery, was with Lloyd George himself who had assumed responsibility for the Syrian question. On 9 September he began talks with Allenby at Deauville when Faisal's letter was handed to the Prime Minister. As soon as the nature of the British decision was known to Allenby he advised that it was of 'the first importance' that it should be conveyed by the Prime Minister to Faisal in person. Accordingly on 10 September Lloyd George sent an urgent invitation to Faisal who arrived in London on the 18th.

On the very day he received Lloyd George's invitation Faisal told de Laforcade, Picot's deputy, that he would insist on the unity of Syria 'from Gaza to Taurus'. Two days later Cheetham passed to London a telegram from Ḥusain to Faisal asking him to beware of the partition of the Arab countries and reminding him of the fate of the petty Muslim states in Spain after the break-up of the empire of 'Abdur-Raḥmān III in the eleventh century.

4

A mounting French press campaign, backed by diplomatic pressure, embarrassed Anglo–French relations in 1919. The main complaint was that the French presence in Syria was still insignificant compared with the British, and that some local British officers were acting contrary to French interests. Colour was lent to these accusations by Allenby's restriction of the size of French forces to the actual needs of administration in the littoral and to token units near Damascus and Aleppo. The Arab representations to the American commission were distinctly anti-French; so were the resolutions of the Syrian congress. Both added fuel to the flames of French fury.

Allenby formally denied that any of his officers acted improperly, and went out of his way to show his goodwill to French claims. He warned Rikābi, in the presence of Picot, against the consequences of Arab reluctance to co-operate with a French colonel appointed by Allenby as financial adviser. Rikābi's point of view reflects the different meanings attached to the post by the Arabs and the French (and for that matter the English). Rikābi said he had asked Allenby for an 'adviser', not a 'controller'. Allenby's denial and the demonstration with Rikābi, both designed to impress the French of his impartiality, had no influence on the French press campaign.

Balfour was very sympathetic to the French point of view. On

22 May he addressed a memorandum to Lloyd George urging the withdrawal of British troops from Syria with the exception of Palestine. He argued that such a withdrawal would not be a 'betrayal' of the Arabs, since France had promised 'in the most explicit terms' to apply the principle of self-determination in Syria. Faisal should be told so, with a recitation of the Anglo-French Declaration of 8 November 1918. (Nowhere is Balfour's cynicism so naked as in this statement which disregards Britain's obligation under that same declaration to apply the principle of self-determination to another part of Syria, namely Palestine.)

Lloyd George preferred to bide his time, but Balfour returned to the charge with a more detailed, and not less cynical, memorandum dated 11 August. In it he expressed concern at the strained Anglo-French relations and went on to insist on the imperative necessity of satisfying the French at the expense of the Arabs in Syria. This second memorandum has recently received an undeserved commendation in a book by a professor at the American University of Beirut. Its author gave Balfour credit which the Foreign Office staff at the time withheld from their chief, as well as criticising him in harsh terms.

A minute by George Kidston, the head of the Middle East section, described the memorandum as admirable in indicating broad lines of policy, but its author was taken to task for not realising the difficulties of its application in details. As regards Syria, Balfour's 'sole aim' was to resolve the difficulties with the French but he 'ignored entirely the much graver problem' of resolving those with the Arabs. Furthermore, Balfour wished Palestine to go to the Zionists 'irrespective of the wishes of the great bulk of the population'. That in satisfying either the French or the Zionists the result 'will entail bloodshed and military repression never seems to have occurred to him'. This minute was seen both by Hardinge and Curzon.

But civil servants seldom make policy. In two weeks' time Lloyd George himself decided to follow the Balfour line. Excuses were easy to find. A peace treaty with Turkey was taking a longer time than anticipated and garrisoning Syria was costing the British taxpayer enormous amounts. Accordingly an *aide-mémoire* was prepared for the Prime Minister at Deauville in which he proposed to replace British by French troops in Syria provided 'regard will be had to the engagements and declarations of the British and French governments not only as between themselves but as between them and the Arabs'. As from 1 November British troops in Syria were to be withdrawn to occupy only Palestine 'defined in accordance with its ancient boundaries: from Dan to Beersheba'. The new distribution of 'garrisoning' responsibilities was 'a purely temporary and provisional arrangement . . . without prejudice to the final settlement of mandates and boundaries'. The document made the revealing error of drawing the boundary between the zones of Arab and French occupation along 'the Sykes–Picot line' and said so.

These proposals were spontaneously made by Lloyd George to Clemenceau who accepted the part concerning the replacement of troops but not the proviso. That took place on 13 September. Five days later Faisal arrived in London, and began talks with Lloyd George the following day. Lloyd George had kept the Foreign Office in the dark till the substance of his new agreement with Clemenceau was published by Reuter on the very day of Faisal's arrival. Only then did he communicate the *aide-mémoire* simultaneously to the Foreign Office, Faisal and Cairo. All were told that the Peace Conference had already 'taken note' of the document.

As in 1918 so in 1919 Faisal came to London to find that Lloyd George had destroyed his chances of any success by an agreement with Clemenceau, concerning Palestine then and Syria as a whole now. The Anglo-Arab exchanges that followed were therefore conducted in an atmosphere of unreality, doomed to failure and bound to deepen the gulf that began to separate the Arabs from Britain. But it must be recognised that Faisal's punishment at the hands of the British government was 'more in policy than in malice'. And policy is dictated by national interests and seldom pays permanent regard to friends.

Nevertheless Faisal's discussions and exchange of letters with Lloyd George and Curzon, who on 24 October succeeded Balfour as Foreign Secretary, deserve a separate treatment if only because they deal with the McMahon correspondence, the British declaration to the seven Arab leaders, Wingate's reply, approved by the Foreign Office, to Ḥusain's inquiry on the occasion of Jamal Pasha's disclosure of the Sykes–Picot agreement, and the Anglo-French declaration. Basing himself on these official communications, Faisal asked: 'Has the consent of the people been obtained for the proposed occupation?' He asked the question in his letter of 21 September to Lloyd George, and in his letter of 11 October complained that the question 'remained unanswered'. There was still no answer.

Faisal might have met with more success had he invoked these commitments in 1918 when the situation was still relatively fluid. In the autumn of 1919 British and French interests in Syria had been more or less settled between the two powers. By then if British politicians had to make a choice they were more likely to avoid offending the French at the expense of the Arabs than the other way round. And that was precisely the course they followed, and they found little difficulty in producing *ex post facto* justifications for their action. Thus they argued that Britain had obligations to both the Arabs and the French and these obligations were complementary not contradictory, even the Sykes–Picot agreement which, according to the new explanation, was not communicated to the Sharif because it was 'in complete conformity' with the British undertaking to him.

With that argument the British promise of Arab independence, even in a part of Syria, was practically set aside. Its meaning was foreign tutelage, on the ground of a newly discovered Arab unfitness for independence. 'There is no authority of weight', wrote Curzon to Faisal on 9 October, 'who believes that the people of Syria can stand alone at the present time.'[8] This means that they needed guidance and advice provided by an advanced nation as a trustee. There were three possible powers who might act in that capacity. The first, Great Britain, had declared to the Peace Conference and to Faisal himself as early as March 1919 that she would not accept the responsibility in Syria, without, however, indicating that she was secretly planning to be the trustee for Palestine.

The second likely power was the United States. But the possibility of American acceptance of this responsibility was ruled out after Wilson's illness and return to Washington. There remained the old claimant, France, whose military forces were to take over in three weeks' time. Faisal was urged by his British allies to discuss the new 'military' dispensation with the French, which implied the acceptance of a French trusteeship or mandate. It mattered little whether the implication, which was meant in all seriousness by both Britain and France, contradicted the professed 'provisional' nature of the replacement of troops. And Curzon's note quoted above did not omit to give Faisal some friendly advice that his hint of military resistance to the proposed arrangement would not serve the Arab cause.

With his formal protests Faisal made counter-proposals. He questioned the wisdom of causing certain disturbances of the peace for the sake of replacing a provisional occupation by another provisional occupation. When in 1918 Arab troops and administration were withdrawn from the coastal region he was assured by Allenby that, irrespective of the national character of the occupation forces, the whole country was to remain under his unified control till its fate was decided by the Peace Conference. If the *status quo* could not be maintained till then Faisal was prepared to assume responsibility for public security and French as well as British troops should be withdrawn from the interior and the coastal regions. Otherwise the Peace Conference should appoint a committee of Arab, British and French representatives under the chairmanship of an American to study the problem and report urgently.

Lloyd George rejected these proposals, and accepted the last in a modified form. British troops would be withdrawn, Britain would not take a mandate over Syria and, owing to Wilson's illness, the Peace Conference would be unlikely to be ready to discuss Syria 'for months'. The committee proposed by Faisal should concern itself only with the problems of withdrawal and replacement of troops. But even this was not acceptable to Clemenceau who wrote acrimoniously to Lloyd George insisting that it was a matter for France alone to come to an arrangement with Faisal without British interference or American participation.

Faisal's protest that the British desire to seek a mandate for Palestine alone meant the partition of Syria came too late. He was outmanœuvred by his British allies. If any part of their policy lacked candour with and justice to the Arabs it was that concerned with Palestine. It always had something of questionable morality to hide. Until the Anglo–French agreement about replacement of troops, Britain had no valid title to the territory of Palestine other than conquest. For even under the Sykes–Picot agreement its future administration was to be decided in consultation with the Sharif of Mecca. This was entirely ignored by Lloyd George and Clemenceau in December 1918.

Again, the promise to the Zionists was limited by the promise to the Arabs contained in the Hogarth message that the 'political and economic freedom' of the Palestine Arabs was safeguarded. This freedom was publicly confirmed by Britain and France in their joint declaration on 8 November 1918. Although this declaration was proclaimed in Palestine, and a report by the military governor of Jerusalem confirms that the eight copies he had received were displayed in the most prominent places in the city, the British government had secretly never intended its application in Palestine.

Nor did the agreement between Lloyd George and Clemenceau give the British government a valid right, in anticipation of a decision by the Peace Conference, to impose herself as mandatory contrary to the wishes of the native population. Without going into the question of whether Palestine was included in the McMahon pledge of 24 October 1915, which question we reserve for a separate study, Britain was in honour bound to respect, in Curzon's phrase, every 'authority of weight', British and American, which reiterated that a British mandate committed to Zionism could only be maintained by force. If the British government handed Faisal, as he bitterly complained, 'tied feet and hands' to the French, they passed a sentence of death on the Palestine Arabs and contrived to prolong the agony of its execution for three decades.

Faisal's appeal 'in the name of humanity' to the Supreme Council was, in the absence of Wilson, like that of the plaintiff in the Arabic proverb whose oppressor was none other than the judge. The two powers, he said, considered only their own interests, and in the process destroyed the unity of Syria. Their action was not only a threat to the peace of the country but was also likely to have religious repercussions in Syria and the Muslim world.[9]

Next Faisal had to struggle with Clemenceau. The first round of negotiations reached a deadlock; for Clemenceau wanted to discuss only military questions and Faisal political. Robert de Caix, who managed the campaign for French claims in Syria, had a hand in the negotiations, and he told a member of the British delegation to the Peace Conference that France aimed at a mandate for Syria 'very like a protectorate'. Another French source in close touch with the British delegation reported that in a second round of talks with Clemenceau, Faisal reached an agreement, the two main points of which were: (*a*) Faisal would be proclaimed King of a Syria that would include the coastal area but not Lebanon, Tripoli and Alexandretta, and Clemenceau would use his good offices to get Palestine included; (*b*) French advisers to the Arab government would be servants of the Syrian state not of France; (*c*) French troops would not occupy the Biqāʿ (Coele-Syria). Faisal did not sign, but took the draft with him to consult the Syrians. He arrived in Beirut on 14 January 1920. As a clear evidence of the British withdrawal there was already installed in Beirut a new French High Commissioner and commander-in-chief in the person of General Henri Gouraud.

5

It is now necessary to cast a glance at the domestic situation in Syria during the year or so after the armistice. Conditions remained unsettled in the three military zones of the country, largely because of political uncertainty. The Arab zone, to take the largest part of the three first, was apart from this uncertainty handicapped by financial and administrative disadvantages. Lack of access to the sea deprived it of income from customs and made it more dependent upon a foreign subsidy. In the year under review revenue was estimated at £1,340,582 and expenditure at £2,275,906. Fighting shy of foreign control, the administration profited little from the services of a British financial expert and nothing from a French. It preferred to invite Saīʿd Shuqair Pasha, a Lebanese who had had experience under the British administration in the Sudan, to put its finances in order.

On the whole the Arab administration may be described as a continuation of the Turkish, conducted through the medium of Arabic and inspired by Arab national sentiment. By his prestige Faisal was its acknowledged head. But his past experience was military, not political or administrative, and he was obliged by political necessity to be absent in Europe on two occasions for nearly six months. His brother and deputy Zaid was even less experienced, and had to depend upon the nationalists, both military and civil. The executive head of the administration was Rikābi, the military governor, assisted by non-political directors of departments whom Allenby insisted on regarding as advisers. The arrival of the

American commission and the meeting of the Syrian congress had the effect of creating a council of ministers in all but name. From August the directors became responsible, in addition to routine administration, for political decisions, under the general guidance of Faisal or his deputy. Three of the six directors who formed the council were Christians: Iskandar 'Ammūn for Justice, Sa'īd Shuqair for Finance and Jubrā'il Ḥaddād for Public Security.

At the beginning, Allenby's supreme control checked excessive political activity. But with the emergence of the Syrian congress as the virtual constituent assembly this control became gradually less effective, and political parties began to assert their existence. Foremost among these were two: *al-Istiqlāl al-'Arab* (Arab Independence) successor of *al-Fatāh*, and *al-Ittiḥād as Sūri* (Syrian Union), both with adherents in the three zones and among Syrians outside the country. The army was much under the influence of politically-minded officers, including the chief of staff, General Yāsīn Pasha al-Hāshimi. In the summer of 1919 the congress, the parties, the army and the country as a whole were restive and impatient of the delay of a settlement.

Just before he was called by Lloyd George to Europe, Faisal himself told British political officers that in the face of rumours of partition and foreign occupation there was a popular demand for a general mobilisation. The news of the impending replacement of British by French troops forced the hands of the Arab administration, and in the absence of Faisal's stabilising influence an order was in fact issued for the conscription of 12,000 men. Allenby demanded the withdrawal of the order and de Laforcade the internment of Yāsīn and the dismissal of Rikābi. Allenby had anticipated these reactions when he expressed anxiety that the Arabs might in desperation be forced to fight both the French and the British.

The gravity of the situation was heightened by rumours of a secret agreement between Faisal and Muṣṭafā Kamāl for a united Islamic resistance to 'infidel' control of either Arab or Turkish territory. A copy of such an alleged agreement was actually communicated to the British delegation in Paris. In his discussions with Lloyd George, Faisal himself spoke of the danger of his national movement being forced to assume a religious character. The call for a new *jihād* was openly published in the Damascus press and in a proclamation on behalf of Muṣṭafā Kamāl in Aleppo. Apart from the latter's challenge to the allies in Anatolia, Egypt was then in revolt and Iraq restless on the brink of another defiance to British rule. Allenby took action: Yāsīn was interned, ammunition was withheld from the Arab army and the payment of the British subsidy to the administration suspended. Furthermore, on learning from intercepted and deciphered telegrams from Faisal, Zaid and Ḥusain that the latter was about to send financial assistance to Damascus, Allenby extracted a written guarantee that no part of the British subsidy to Hijaz would go to Damascus. By these measures combined, the clamour of the nationalists was rendered empty talk and resistance to the French (or the British) was thus effectively killed. The French won their battle against Faisal, not at Maisalūn, but in London and Cairo.

In the coastal zone where the new French forces were to be landed, the French military administration under Allenby's supreme authority had from the beginning no easy passage except perhaps on Mount Lebanon. To the north and south and particularly on the border with the eastern zone, the French encountered frequent trouble and even fighting, and not all of it could be fairly ascribed to instigation from Damascus. Much of it was in fact rooted in old Muslim antipathy to the French and part of it was the result of the bitterness created in 1918 when Arab administration was by Allenby's orders 'temporarily' replaced by French.

Under the new dispensation the French military administrator assumed direct powers and controls, through French officers, in most districts except Mount Lebanon where, as under the Turks, native district officers were appointed. Except in small centres, however, these native officers invariably had French 'advisers' whose 'advice' must be accepted. In practice therefore there was, to start with, less native element in the administration of Lebanon than under the Turks before the war. At any rate this native element was drawn mostly from the Catholics, a minority in the entire zone. This Catholic minority was given relatively more power than any other religious or national group, Muslim, Druze, and other Christian. The Muslims in particular were suspected of anti-French tendencies and were accordingly distrusted.

The French military administration itself, rather more than the mere wishes of the Maronites, decided the future course of sectarian politics in Lebanon. A minority was given preferential treatment at the expense of most of the other minorities put together in an enlarged Lebanon. All responsible Arab nationalists, from Ḥusain and Faisal down to the members of the Syrian congress, made ample allowance in their schemes for the special status of Lebanon and the Maronites in it. But the Maronites, when they came to power, always refused to co-operate, and made no reciprocal allowance for the status of the Muslims in Beirut and the coast, or for that matter for the status of other Christian minorities.

Another and smaller minority was steadily given a privileged position at the expense of the overwhelming majority in the southern zone. For British policy went to greater extremes in support of the Zionists in Palestine than the French in support of the Maronites in Lebanon. Allenby's promise to maintain the *status quo* till the Peace Conference decided the political future of the country was set aside by repeated political decisions in London. The military administration of the country was more British than that of Lebanon was French. All senior executive officers were British including nine Jews, at least two of whom were prominent Zionists, one the public prosecutor and in charge of the courts, and the other a district governor. No Arab, from Palestine or elsewhere, held any of the executive posts. The few who were employed in an advisory capacity were largely non-Palestinians who came with the British army from Egypt and the Sudan.

From the beginning the Palestine Arabs took every opportunity of impressing upon the British government that the Zionist policy was a violation of the rights of the Arab majority and could be carried out only by force. This was confirmed by all British authorities: Wingate, Allenby, Clayton and their staff. But the Zionists had the means, which the Arabs completely lacked, of influencing British politicians in London. Weizmann had easy and personal access to Balfour and his staff, and he inundated them all with lengthy letters and memoranda on every aspect of the Zionist aspirations. As already pointed out, the Zionist commission under Weizmann went to Palestine in anticipation of Britain becoming the mandatory power, to 'supervise' the preparations for the execution of the Balfour Declaration. To use their own term they planned to face the Arabs with a number of *faits accomplis* that would render reconsideration by any British government impossible.

Weizmann wrote to Balfour from Palestine on 30 May 1918 that 'the Arabs who are superficially clever and quick-witted worshipped one thing only – power'. With the British army in occupation it was therefore safe to do anything. Weizmann made many far-reaching demands including the transfer of some 250,000 acres of state domain to the Zionists, and 'the handing over of the Wailing Wall to the Jews'.[10] The second demand involved dispossessing the Muslims of a property which was a religious foundation (*waqf*). The Wailing Wall formed a part of the boundary of al-Ḥaram ash-Sharīf area in Jerusalem, the third holy place in Islam. It was precisely from this spot that widespread Arab-Jewish riots were triggered off in 1929.

A month after the armistice Weizmann made still more demands, accompanied with exaggerated, and often imaginary, accusations against British officers who were not in his estimate completely and openly Zionists. The case of Storrs is the most glaring example of the Zionist refusal to be satisfied with a discreet supporter. In a secret report Storrs wrote he was a convinced Zionist, and by his actions gave ample evidence of it. He covered up Weizmann's extremism by producing, with little respect for truth, a garbled gist of his speech in Jerusalem. He allowed a Zionist demonstration, and disallowed an Arab counter-demonstration, on the first anniversary of the Balfour Declaration and himself delivered a friendly speech at the Zionist ceremony. He badgered the Mufti of Jerusalem on several occasions to transfer the property adjoining the Wailing Wall to the Jews and was ordered to desist when Muslim anger created anxiety in the Foreign Office.

Storrs had, however, compromised himself in Weizmann's eyes because he attended an Arab school ceremony where a map inscribed *La Palestine arabe* was displayed and some speakers cheered: '*Vive la nation arabe! vive la Palestine arabe!*', and Storrs failed to protest at these 'unmistakably anti-Jewish sentiments'. Henceforth Weizmann missed no opportunity in his correspondence with the Foreign Office to attack Storrs, to object to his promotion and even to demand his removal.

Small wonder if Storrs lost his initial enthusiasm for the Zionist cause, and adopted Clayton's method of reporting the facts of Arab reaction to Zionism without softening twists. Thus Storrs's comments on the resolutions of the first Palestine Arab congress, which met in Jerusalem from 27 January to 10 February 1919, sound pro-British first and foremost and are less coloured by a Zionist bias. He correctly stated that the congress met as a direct result of the Anglo-French declaration. He enclosed a British intelligence report and a summary of the resolutions. His only regret was that Britain who had been popular in 1917 was now definitely unpopular.

According to the English translations provided to Storrs, the congress passed several resolutions, the most significant of which was the demand for an independent Palestine government, in federal connection with the rest of Syria, and the rejection of the Zionist pretensions but with an offer of equal rights to native Jews. The independent government of Palestine would accept British assistance only if free from the commitment to the Zionists. But for the Zionist policy of the British government, Storrs wrote, the Palestine Arabs would have asked for autonomy under British protection. These and other resolutions were telegraphed to the Peace Conference. Their reception at the Foreign Office was gloomy: the minutes ascribed British unpopularity to the Zionist policy, and regarded the resolutions as a triumph for the pan-Arabs and the Sharif.

British popularity began to decline not only in Palestine but in Syria as a whole, first on account of Zionism and later because of Lloyd George's capitulation to France. The decline continued till unpopularity was transformed into hostility and hatred. In Syria and Iraq the Arab reproach began to be heard literally in Shakespeare's phrase: 'Your words and performances are no kin together'. For contrary to the proclaimed principles of consent of the governed and self-determination, Iraq was ruled on colonial lines and Syria was partitioned with France, and a large slice thereof was promised to foreign Zionists.

Concurrently with this outraged national feeling, religious feelings began to stir the conscience of some Arab Muslims who could not be indifferent to the humiliations Britain and her allies were inflicting on Turkey. Rashīd Riḍā expressed a general feeling when he wrote a memorandum to Lloyd George in which he said that it seemed to the Muslims that Britain and her allies reserved 'justice and liberty' for Christians and Jews, and that their denial to the Muslims proceeded from '[European] Christian fanaticism against Islam for which Britain and France were responsible'.

The European Christians had in the end to give way before Muṣṭafā Kamāl who commanded a national army on a national territory mostly inaccessible to his enemies. No comparable circumstances favoured the Arabs in Syria. In the north Lloyd George's decision was, despite Faisal's protests, put into force, so that by the end of 1919 the Arab administration was left to face the build-up of French might on the coast. By then too Palestine's fate was sealed. London, the local administration and the Zionists acted on the certain assumption that Britain would be the mandatory power.

No attention was paid to the wishes of the Arabs, 90 per cent of the population. The series of *faits accomplis* was continued. Zionist pressure secured the appointment in September 1919 of a self-styled Zionist as chief political officer in place of Clayton, and immigration began with the arrival of 'technicians'. So much had the Foreign Office come under Zionist influence that Weizmann could obtain an order for Allenby to withdraw a scheme of loans to farmers on the ground, detailed in seven pages, that it was 'the most serious menace to the realisation of the Jewish national home'. But Allenby stuck to his guns. The measure, intended for the benefit of all farmers, Arabs and Jews, was a Turkish practice which the British military administration was bound by international law to maintain.

Nor was this all. A directive, first suggested by Herbert Samuel and issued with Balfour's authority, told the military administration that the mandate would probably be conceded to Britain and that any form of its terms would embody the Balfour Declaration. The Arabs must be warned against 'agitation' and that, in Samuel's phrase, which reappeared in the directive, the future of Palestine was a *chose jugée*. The directive was not, however, intended to convert the Arabs but the neutral British administrators. The new chief political officer himself reported that it was inexpedient to divulge its terms to the Arabs.

6

The scene was thus set for more open confrontations between Arab national aspirations and foreign designs and ambitions, with the

Zionists protected by British bayonets in Palestine, and with the undisguised might of France in the rest of Syria. The redistribution of garrisoning duties between Britain and France was not a temporary military measure; it was nothing less than a prejudgement of the fate of Syria as a whole, and a preparation for regularising the division of the country into a British mandated territory and a French mandated territory.

Faisal returned to a Syria seething with discontent, not only against Britain and France but also against reports of his policy. Zaid had with great difficulty been able to avert open revolution when demonstrations were actually staged in Damascus against him and his absent brother. King Ḥusain himself telegraphed to Faisal repudiating in advance any action he might be compelled to take which was inconsistent with the independence and unity of the Arab lands. Faisal's embarrassment was great when he saw the text of his father's telegram published in the press.

This was the state of public opinion Faisal had to contend with. He himself was known to have inclined to an accommodation with France but he quickly perceived he could follow this line only at the risk of his leadership. Delegations came to see him in Damascus from all over the three zones with reports of widespread discontent. All made a similar demand in Faisal's own words: 'independence is taken not given'.

According to the British liaison officer in Damascus, Faisal's position after his return became increasingly difficult, he was 'rapidly losing power' and control of affairs was passing into the hands of the 'extremists'. It was under these circumstances that he asked for a British declaration of policy regarding Palestine and Iraq. Both Allenby and Milner (then in Cairo on a mission) recommended the issue of such a declaration. Without waiting for a reply, Faisal desired this message to be conveyed to the Foreign Office: 'Any decision incompatible with Arab aspirations concerning Syria, Palestine or Mesopotamia taken without Faisal's presence will not be acknowledged by the Arabs and will cause great difficulties in the future. . . .'

The 'extremists' who were said to have gained ascendancy over Faisal were actually the members of the Syrian congress. It was not a perfect assembly, but it is correct to say that it reflected fairly accurately the wishes of the majority of the Syrians in the three zones with the possible exception of Mount Lebanon. As already mentioned its members were elected or selected according to the system of Ottoman parliamentary and municipal elections. Several members were in fact ex-deputies of the pre-war Ottoman chamber. When the British, and more actively the French, opposed the holding of open elections in their zones, members were provided, according to custom, with written authorisation by local notables, themselves acknowledged as representatives of the people. It is therefore safe to assume that under any other system almost the same members would have been returned, or at least members with identical or similar views. This assumption is borne out by recalling the names of the men who led the opposition to the French and British mandates in Syria and Palestine.

On 7 March a telegram from Allenby informed London of 'great demonstrations' throughout Syria and Palestine and that Faisal was forced to convoke the congress in Damascus on the previous day, and that it intended to declare independence and elect him king. He could refuse only at the risk of being disowned which, in Allenby's judgement, would have resulted in the opening of immediate hostilities against the British and the French. Faisal was anxious to know what attitude the British government would adopt. It was too late to wait for a reply. On Sunday 7 March the congress session continued well into the night. Next day its resolutions and declaration of independence were read from the balcony of the Town Hall, and Rikābi was asked to form a government.

Allenby's preliminary news was considered by British and French representatives at the Peace Conference then assembled in London for a discussion of the terms of a peace treaty with Turkey. They agreed on a joint message which Curzon telegraphed to Allenby a few hours after the Syrian congress had actually declared independence. The telegram stated that it had always been intended to consult Faisal before 'any final decision' by the Peace Conference which he was now invited to attend 'with as little delay as possible'. The British and French governments, however, hoped the congress would take no step that would prejudice a settlement by the Conference. They wished to impress upon Faisal that 'neither government desired a conflict, [but that] the future of Syria may be seriously compromised if any irresponsible action is taken by the congress that would place the case of the Syrian people in opposition to the friendly and liberal intentions to which the British and French governments have given repeated expression.'[11]

The preamble to the congress resolutions recapitulates the stages of Arab struggle for political freedom from the Turks, Arab participation in the war on the side of Britain and her allies, and the British and other allied promises and declarations. It goes on to express the Syrian Arab desire, after one-and-a-half years of waiting under foreign occupation and military administrations, to achieve their aspiration of independence. The declaration itself consists of: (1) the independence of geographical Syria including Palestine, with safeguards for minorities, and the rejection of the Zionist claim to a national home; (2) the election of Faisal as a constitutional king of Syria; (3) the application of the principle of administrative decentralisation including safeguards for a special régime in Lebanon as it was constituted before the war.

The Syrian congress itself had nothing to do with the declaration of the independence of Iraq. Its members merely demanded (*naṭlub*) the independence of Iraq so that it could with Syria form an economic and political union. The congress which actually declared the independence of Iraq and elected 'Abdullah its king was composed entirely of Iraq representatives who according to *The Times* numbered twenty-nine, only nine of whom were soldiers and the rest lawyers, writers and merchants. They, too, had authorisation from notables and tribal chiefs to take the decision they had taken.

Because of the British position in Palestine and Iraq, where no native administrations comparable to the one in Damascus had been set up, the immediate British reaction to the Damascus declaration was more violent than the French. However, on 13 March the two governments agreed on informing Faisal that they regarded the proceedings of the 'self-constituted' congress as null and void, that the future of Syria, Palestine and Iraq must be 'determined by the allied powers acting in concert' and that Faisal should return to Europe and 'place his case before the Peace Conference'.

On the same day Curzon spoke hard words to the French ambassador. The crisis had arisen because France had rejected British advice and insisted on establishing for herself a position in an area where she was hated not loved. Since then matters had become worse by Gouraud's disregard of British warnings against the occupation of al-Biqāʿ, an occupation which infuriated the Syrians and led to a chain of serious incidents. 'Thus', concluded Curzon, 'the future of France and Great Britain in those parts of the world was imperilled because of the way in which the French government, in pursuance of traditional or historical aspirations, had insisted on forcing themselves into an area where the French were not welcomed by the inhabitants. . . .'

Curzon might have applied his own logic to the British position in Palestine. Here the British government was warned not by French but by British authorities, from Allenby down to the most junior intelligence officer, that the Zionist policy could be imposed on Palestine only by force, and the vast majority of the population did not 'welcome' a British mandate because of that policy. Small wonder that the Palestine Arabs lost no time in endorsing the Damascus declaration. A huge demonstration carried the written endorsement to the British military governor in Jerusalem as well as to the American, French and Italian consuls.

In Beirut the declaration was celebrated, despite the French ban, with fireworks, and the mention of 'our sovereign King Faisal' in the prayers in the mosques. Throughout Syria and Palestine there were similar marks of celebration. The British were wise enough not to interfere in what Muslims said in prayer at their mosques in Palestine, but the French did interfere to prevent the mention of Faisal's name in the mosques in Beirut and elsewhere.

It must be stated that not all Syrians wanted Faisal as their king. The Maronites were on the whole hostile. The French saw to it that the Lebanese administrative council registered a protest followed later on by a declaration of independence which, however, the French kept in cold storage. In addition there were sections of the Druze community who stood aloof and showed little or no enthusiasm for Syrian independence. Otherwise Allenby's assessment that the resolutions of the Syrian congress represented the views of 'the vast majority' was correct.

While thus quietly correcting Curzon's view of the Syrian congress, Allenby sent in the next week or two several telegrams, with the tenor of which Milner concurred. Allenby warned of the certainty that Britain and France would have to fight the Arabs in order to maintain their positions, and called attention to the danger of creating a general anti-European and anti-Christian feeling among the Arabs, and to the possibility that Faisal might be thrown into the arms of Muṣṭafā Kamāl. Allenby then urged the recognition of Faisal's sovereignty over Syria and Palestine and the right of Iraq to form with the first two territories a confederation, provided the special claims of France in the first and those of Britain in the second and third territories were acknowledged. Allenby believed Faisal would accept this arrangement, which would allow the present administrations to continue undisturbed and would also 'simplify the Zionist problem'. Without recognition, Faisal was not likely to attend the Peace Conference.

Curzon and Lloyd George together framed a reply to Allenby. The former Viceroy of India was, like his permanent Under-secretary of State Hardinge, also a former Viceroy, very sensitive about Iraq. Hence the sharp and categorical reply concerning this country: Faisal had no claims. (But was he not the representative of Ḥusain who undoubtedly had?) Nevertheless Faisal could be recognised 'as the representative of the Arab peoples of Syria and Palestine', provided he came to the Peace Conference with the corresponding recognition of 'the special positions' of France in Syria and Lebanon and of Britain in Palestine including in this case 'the obligation to provide a national home for the Zionists'.

More in touch with political realities on the spot than Curzon and his staff in London, Allenby doubted whether Faisal would attend the Peace Conference unless assured that the peace treaty with Turkey would provide for the unity of Syria and Palestine under one 'suzerainty'. This time Allenby 'emphasised', not merely mentioned, the danger of refusing to recognise the declaration by the Syrian congress as expressing 'the will of the majority'. Furthermore, Faisal should be allowed to send a plenipotentiary, since his absence would put the extremists in control.

According to Curzon, Britain and France were by the end of March agreed in principle on the recognition of Faisal as king of Syria under British and French mandates, each power making separate arrangements with him for her own interests and those of her protégés, notably the Zionists and the Lebanese respectively. All this required personal discussion before validation by the Peace Conference. Curzon was content to deal with a plenipotentiary, but the French insisted on Faisal's personal appearance. They had more to settle with him and reserved the right to be consulted on whatever arrangement Britain might make with Faisal regarding Palestine. The next meeting of the Peace Conference was scheduled to take place at San Remo later in April.

A combination of factors bedevilled the proposed settlement. France was not in a hurry and insisted on Faisal's formal acceptance of her rôle as mandatory for Syria and Lebanon. Britain was animated by similar considerations as to Palestine (if not also Iraq). The British inclination to the proposed settlement was further undermined by Zionist pressure on the one hand and Palestine Arab opposition on the other. Under these circumstances Faisal's reluctance to go to Europe, even without prior recognition or sufficient Anglo–French assurance, seems in retrospect to have weakened the Arab cause. The Zionists made a strong objection to the inclusion of Palestine in the Syrian state. They had been agitating for 'frontiers' that went far beyond Lloyd George's 'from Dan to Beersheba'. They wanted all the territory west of the Hijaz railway and all the headwaters of the river Jordan almost to the outskirts of Damascus. These extreme demands were insisted upon by, among others, Herbert Samuel, who under a smooth exterior was the most effective opponent of Faisal's sovereignty over Palestine.

Samuel had been grooming himself with the blessing of his Zionist colleagues for the rôle of British high commissioner long before the mandate was assigned to Britain. He went to Palestine in order to study 'the administrative and economic' problems that had to be tackled on the assignment of the mandate to Britain and the expected establishment of a civil administration. While engaged in this task in Palestine, Samuel sent a secret telegram to the Foreign Office objecting to the proposed arrangement with Faisal as incompatible with 'complete British control' and as tending, moreover, 'to take life out of the Zionist movement'. From a British politician who was also an ardent Zionist this is understandable. But the assertion contained in the same telegram that neither Faisal nor his supporters expected the unity of Palestine with Syria is a gross misrepresentation of the facts.

7

The Peace Conference met at San Remo in Faisal's absence. By a decision of the Supreme Council the mandate for Syria was given to France and that for Iraq to Britain. It was decided to include in the peace treaty with Turkey an article on the recognition of the independence of Syria and Iraq. As to Palestine, the peace treaty was to include nothing about its independence but merely to entrust its administration to a mandatory whose duties were defined, in the words of Curzon's telegram of 26 April, 'by a verbatim repetition of Mr Balfour's declaration of November 1917'. The mandatory was not named, but by an independent decision of the Supreme Council Britain was 'declared' the mandatory power over Palestine. The frontiers between these territories were to be decided later on, but 'Syria' in the above arrangement included Lebanon.

San Remo set at nought the resolutions of the Syrian congress and sealed Faisal's fate as king of a united Syria. And yet according to Curzon he could still appear at the next meeting of the Peace Conference in Paris and 'state his case'. France was still prepared to recognise him as king of Syria provided he accepted her mandate. Britain was ready to follow suit, but no longer as regards Palestine. Curzon's justification is neither fair to Faisal nor in accordance with the established facts: according to Curzon Faisal had 'known' of the British intention enshrined in the Balfour Declaration and had 'acquiesced' in it. From Curzon's words it appears that the British and French politicians were more anxious to obtain Faisal's validation of the mandates than they were to meet the demands which he had already stated and which hardly needed restatement. Curzon himself made it clear that Faisal was required to work out with France the terms of the mandate; with Britain not even that, merely the frontiers between Syria and Palestine.

In conveying the San Remo decisions to Faisal yet another concealment was adopted as regards Palestine. It was this time Allenby who resorted to it, but with the approval of the Foreign Office. Allenby omitted all reference to the separation of Palestine from Syria, Faisal's sovereignty over it and the demarcation of frontiers because, he explained, 'any such suggestions would, I feel sure, finally defeat the object which His Majesty's government have in view, and would decide Faisal to refuse to attend in Paris. He had always insisted on the indivisibility of Syria and Palestine as a cardinal point in his policy.'

The Arab leaders were thunderstruck. The news from San Remo was particularly stunning for those in Palestine. Even Lebanon was alarmed at the lack of any specific mention. The Hijaz delegation lodged a formal protest with the Peace Conference and later also with the League of Nations: that the mandates were allotted contrary to the rights of the people to self-determination. The separation of Palestine from Syria was not only in opposition to the wishes of the population but also in complete disregard of the unity of the two parts of the country in race, language, tradition and economy. The Arabs revolted against the Turks, their brethren in religion, and fought against them on the side of the allies for independence, not to exchange one foreign ruler for another. The San Remo decision, together with the refusal to recognise the Arab government in Damascus, was a defeat for the moderate Arab elements who desired co-operation with Britain and France.

Faisal saw through the stratagem of concealment. He said he had 'no right' to discuss the mandate, implying no doubt that the Syrian congress had rejected France on its own account and Britain on account of its Zionist policy. But while noting the recognition of the independence of Iraq and Syria, he complained of the ambiguity about Palestine which 'can in no way be separated from Syria'. He challenged Curzon's assertion of his, Faisal's, acquiescence as a misunderstanding. 'All that I have admitted', he said, 'is to safeguard rights of Jews in that country as much as rights of the indigenous Arab inhabitants.' He called attention to the determined Palestine Arab opposition to the Jewish national home. He affirmed the Arab view that Palestine was included in the Arab territories promised independence in the McMahon pledge. He trusted that this British promise to his father regarding Palestine would not be superseded by that to the Zionists. He said his father was entitled, even under the Sykes–Picot agreement, to a say in the future of Palestine. (He did not, surprisingly, refer to the Hogarth message guaranteeing the political and economic freedom of the Arabs of Palestine.) He was ready to go to the Peace Conference on one condition: 'If only I receive a positive declaration to my agitated people stating that the Conference does in no way allow Palestine to be separated from Syria. By such means alone I believe we can come to a solution which would safeguard interests of all concerned. In the meantime I am urgently in need of an answer.'

A parallel communication regarding the San Remo decisions was conveyed to Faisal by Millerand who had in the meantime succeeded Clemenceau. In his reply Faisal was evasive about the mandate but was ready to negotiate the form of 'assistance' Syria might require from France. He took the occasion to protest against the disregard, in the French message, of the 'unity and indivisibility' of Syria. On this point, Faisal said, the French message caused unrest in the country second only to the reference in the British message to a Jewish national home in Palestine.

Faisal's evasion must have irritated the French. But he was no longer free, even if willing, to accept the French mandate without authority from the Syrian congress. Nor would the congress agree to his journey to Europe without recognition of his kingship by the powers. The moderate elements had indeed lost ground all over Syria since San Remo. Rikābi's ministry had to give way to one under Hāshim Bey al-Atāsi. In the French zone, even among the Christians including some influential Maronites, there were loud complaints of direct French control. There were still louder complaints in Palestine at equally direct British control and the preferential treatment accorded to the Zionists.

Violent explosions were now not unexpected. Apart from raids and counter-raids between the French and Arab zones, with deterioration in public security and its bad consequences in stagnant trade and disturbed farming, the French had to quell large-scale revolts, notably among the Nuṣairiyyah in the north and the Matāwilah in the south. Against the latter a military expedition, composed of three colonial infantry battalions and one squadron of *chasseurs d'Afrique* supported by artillery, was sent in the last week of May. In addition to those killed in the fighting, thirty-six persons were condemned to death, ten were banished, and several others had their homes demolished and property confiscated. The chief centre town, Bint Jubail, was virtually destroyed, and thousands all over Jabal 'Āmil were rendered homeless.

In the week following the French expedition, Faisal addressed two messages to Lloyd George. In the first he invited the Prime Minister 'in the name of humanity' to mediate. He informed him that he had explained to Gouraud that such measures would hamper his, Faisal's, efforts to establish peace and order and would render his absence from Syria unwise. In the second message he protested against the French arming of the Christians, and said this would result in religious fanaticism and would defeat his own efforts to weld together Christian and Muslim in a national unity. Once more Faisal said these developments made it very difficult for him to proceed to Europe. On 26 May he had already written a letter to Lloyd George expressing his intention to proceed to Europe, 'but the absence of any reply to my last letter to Lord Allenby concerning the fate of Palestine, coupled with the disturbed state of the western zone . . . give me much cause for anxiety'.

Faisal's anxiety was thus concerning the whole of the Syrian littoral, whether under the French in the north or under the British in the south. But while the independence of the north was acknowledged in principle at San Remo, it was completely denied to Palestine in the south. Not only was the Balfour Declaration incorporated in the San Remo decision, but the national and racial character of the vast Arab majority was once more concealed beneath the meaningless expression 'non-Jewish communities'. This majority was accorded only 'civil and religious rights'. The British promise of safeguarding its 'political and economic' rights was completely forgotten.

To the Palestine Arabs, therefore, the San Remo decision was a national calamity and an injustice, greater even than the Balfour Declaration. Two-and-a-half years of pleading and protest did nothing to mitigate the misfortune. The Damascus declaration of independence and the Anglo-French refusal to recognise it heightened the tension, and the first signs of violence in Palestine began to appear. Whatever attitude Faisal might have adopted to the harassment of the French he had never countenanced hostile action against the British. And yet hostile incidents began to take place. Some were in the nature of raids by marauders, but others were unmistakably harassment operations inspired by politicians, if not also soldiers, from Damascus. A few examples for March and April must suffice. Two attacks on the Zionist colony of Metullah in the Ḥūlah area resulted in its destruction and the killing of six colonists. Two other attacks on British garrisons in Samakh and Baisān resulted in the wounding of a British officer and the shooting down of an R.A.F. plane. There is no official record of the Arab casualties in any of these attacks.

The most serious eruption by the Palestine Arabs themselves, however, occurred in Jerusalem on Sunday 4 April and the following few days. It was the first of a series that darkened the history of Palestine for three decades. It happened during Christian Holy Week and the Muslim Nabi Mūsā festival. This festival is a religious–national celebration said to have been first instituted by Saladin to coincide with the Christian Easter. In a lunar calendar the festival sometimes coincided also with the Jewish Passover. Since Turkish times it had attracted large crowds from the neighbouring villages as well as special contingents from Hebron and Nābulus who came with banners and marched singing patriotic songs.

As the Hebron procession reached the Jaffa Gate on 4 April, on its way to the Ḥaram, it was addressed from the balcony of the Arab Club by the mayor, Mūsā Kāẓim Pasha al-Ḥusaini, 'Ārif al-'Ārif and al-Ḥāj Amīn al-Ḥusaini. The latter displayed a large portrait of Faisal and called for cheers for 'our King'. The applause was repeated to the refrain of '*Faiṣal yā sulṭān!*', punctuated by cries of 'down with Zionism'. Soon afterwards when the procession was inside the Jaffa Gate the riot began – a court of inquiry could not establish how.

So serious was the outbreak that the Yorkshire Regiment had to be called from church service to restore order. The civil police, both Arab and Jewish, proved unreliable and the entire force was disarmed and confined to barracks. As a result of the riots, and the military action to suppress them, five Jews and four Muslim Arabs were killed, eighteen Jews, one Muslim and three Christian Arabs were seriously wounded.

At the time of the riots there was in Palestine one British soldier for every twenty-four Arab inhabitants, and yet the outbreak could not be prevented. The report of the court of inquiry was not published, but one of its conclusions was reproduced in an official paper. This conclusion was that the underlying cause of Arab unrest and their resort to violence was 'a disappointment at the non-fulfilment' of British wartime promises.[12]

The news of the riot reached the British delegation to the Peace Conference then meeting at San Remo. In London the Foreign Office considered with the War Office, even before the allocation of the mandate to Britain, the desirability of detaching Palestine from Allenby's military and political control and the appointment of a civil governor with administrative experience. But it must not appear that the change was on account of the riots or a reflection on the military administration. The name of Lord Meston, who had distinguished himself in administrative and financial capacities in India and acquired a high reputation for conciliation, was mentioned as a possible candidate.

Reconciliation of the Palestine Arabs to the Zionist policy of the British government was not, however, entrusted to a neutral but to a Zionist, who had already pronounced the future of Palestine as *chose jugée*. Lloyd George himself offered the post of High Commissioner to Herbert Samuel on the very day that the mandate for Palestine was given to Britain by the Supreme Council. It was certainly not by chance that Samuel, who had just returned from Palestine, could manage to be in San Remo, where not only Lloyd George and Balfour but also Weizmann and Sokolov were present on that fateful day.

Curzon was also there, but since he succeeded Balfour as foreign secretary he seemed to have abandoned his reserve and scepticism regarding the Zionist policy of the government. He was now, contrary to all the views he held and already quoted above, reconciled to that policy. So were all members of the Foreign Office concerned with Palestine. Kidston, who had spoken against Balfour's Arab policy, had vanished from the Palestine scene. Is it too fanciful to suggest that before stepping down Balfour came to an understanding with his successor on this matter? Curzon was very ambitious and aspired to the highest office – was it not conducive to his purpose to please the two architects of the Zionist policy of the government, Lloyd George and Balfour?

As a mark of the change in Curzon's attitude he began to resist Faisal's representations on Palestine. Faisal had immediately deplored the Jerusalem riots and stated, in a telegram to Allenby, that his policy had always been to promote 'concord' between the Arabs and native Jews in Palestine. But the Zionist plan of ultimately 'establishing Jewish government' had caused great unrest not only in Palestine itself but all over Syria. Almost simultaneously Sokolov called at the Foreign Office to say that the Zionist Organisation 'wanted Faisal to have no more to do with Palestine'. No doubt the Arab cheers for 'our King' in Jerusalem were a contributory factor, but the Zionist demand was received with approval.

Nevertheless Faisal continued to make representations on Palestine. Even before Samuel's appointment was officially announced, Faisal lodged a formal protest, not because Samuel was a Jew but because he was 'a Zionist whose ideal is to found a Jewish state upon the ruins of a large part of Syria'. Curzon's reply betrayed an unconvinced convert. After mentioning Samuel's undoubted administrative ability and experience he argued that as a Zionist who had authority with the Zionists, 'coupled with his well-known sympathy for the Arabs' he could be depended upon to hold the scales even. Curzon trusted that Faisal and the Arabs would find in Samuel 'a sincere friend'.

Samuel's own actions and words quoted earlier, and his attitude to the Palestine Arab national aspiration to be presently mentioned, are a truer index of his loyalties than Curzon's homily. Needless to say Faisal's protest was ineffective; so was also Allenby's warning that Samuel's appointment would cause disorders. The appointment was confirmed and Samuel was knighted. On 30 June he arrived in Palestine and on the next day a civil administration was established. Samuel's arrival was marked by extraordinary military precautions. Seven Arabs accused of a conspiracy to assassinate him were arrested and detained. Furthermore the fact that Samuel was appointed commander-in-chief in addition to his appointment as High Commissioner was deliberately suppressed, even in the message he brought with him to the people of Palestine from King George V.

The message was skilfully and widely advertised before the day of its public delivery, and an expectation of a conciliatory policy was encouraged, thus furnishing an inducement for notables to accept the invitation to hear it. But all those who attended were greatly disappointed when they discovered that the central point in the royal message was that measures would immediately be taken for the establishment of a Jewish national home. The Arabs, now called 'the general population' in the message, were merely assured that these measures would not affect their 'civil and religious rights'. The sense of deep disappointment was dramatically represented by the Jaffa notables who in answer to enquiries said, 'We have just returned from the funeral of the Holy Land!'

But they themselves were very much alive. They and the representatives of other centres all over the country sent identical telegrams to Samuel: 'With all due respect to His Britannic Majesty and to your person we protest against the San Remo decision and your appointment'. The political struggle was resumed, and preparations began for holding the third Palestine Arab congress. It was somewhat delayed by the shock of the occupation of Damascus by the French and Faisal's disappearance. For some time the Palestine Arab leaders were stunned by the calamity, but they soon rallied and the congress was held in Haifa in the middle of December 1920.

Its main demand was for 'a native Palestine government responsible to an elected legislative assembly' in conformity with British contemplated action in Iraq and Transjordan. The resolutions proceeded to express dissatisfaction with Samuel's administration as 'contrary to the wishes and rights of the people'. Copies of the resolutions, signed by the president of the congress, Mūsā Kāzem Pasha al-Ḥusaini, former mayor of Jerusalem, were sent by telegram to the League of Nations and the British Prime Minister and by letter to all governments with diplomatic representatives in Palestine (Samuel was furnished with a copy).

Samuel had already shown his bias in the first report to Curzon on 12 July, in which he said that the King's message had 'reassured' the Arabs and that only the 'extremists' were dissatisfied. He and Wyndham Deedes, his chief secretary, went to absurd lengths in enlarging on these assertions. According to Deedes the delegates to the Haifa congress 'represented hardly anyone but themselves and they themselves were not worthy of representation'. According to Samuel the degree of support the delegates had had was 'far from indicating anything in the nature of a national movement'.

And yet Samuel could not ignore the movement. He knew that the draft mandate had yet to be ratified and that in the meantime the League of Nations could vary its terms and consequently limit the application of the Balfour Declaration. He knew that the Treaty of Sèvres with Turkey had to be reconsidered by the allies. He knew further that there was a vigorous press campaign in Britain stressing the possibility that the British taxpayer might be saddled with a permanent burden in establishing a Jewish national home for the Jews. The Palestine Arab leaders were equally alive to these considerations and renewed their efforts to persuade the British government to reconsider the Arab case 'in the name of justice and humanity'. To counteract the Arabs, Samuel took it upon himself, without prior reference to London, to issue an official communiqué which is unique in the realms of politics by its finality: 'There has been, *and will not be*, any change in the policy of His Majesty's Government'.

Indicative of this strange preclusion of any reconsideration is the attitude of all those who were now in charge of the Palestine problem at the Foreign Office: Sir John Tilley, Hubert Young and Eric Forbes Adams. A minute by Forbes Adams dated 19 January 1921 disposed of the resolutions of the Haifa congress, and no one objected. He wrote: 'I don't think we need take any notice of this, even to the extent of sending an acknowledgement.'

At this juncture the oversight of the affairs of Palestine was passing from the Foreign Office to the Colonial Office. When in March the Secretary of State for the Colonies, Mr Winston Churchill, paid a visit to Jerusalem he received an Arab deputation headed by Kāzim Pasha. Churchill had already seen the request for a native representative government made by the Haifa congress. All he could say, with Samuel at his elbow, was that the British government was determined to keep both parts of the Balfour Declaration: Jewish national home with civil and religious safeguards for the Arabs. In a word, for the execution of the Balfour Declaration the Arabs must be deprived of political rights. The deadlock was complete and remained so during the entire mandatory period.

8

The change from military to civil administration in Palestine was relatively easy because of two and a half years of British occupation. The presence of a large garrison ruled out the possibility of any organised armed resistance either to the military or civil administration. Resistance had to be confined to the political field, but even here political activity was not free before the Anglo-French declaration, and some restriction remained in force down to the arrival of the American commission and even after its departure.

The French had a more difficult task in Syria. They had first to build up their military strength in the littoral, and they had to reckon with an established Arab administration, with its own army in the interior. After San Remo they became increasingly convinced that the mandate could be imposed on Faisal's government only by military occupation. This French attitude is indicated by the laconic remark made by Millerand to Samuel in the last week of June: '*Je me chargerai de Faisal, moi!*'

It was more ominously revealed in Syria itself. Alarmed by massed French troops at Zahlah and near Aleppo, Faisal decided, instead of sending a delegation, to go to Europe himself. He became still more alarmed when the French informed him that the invitation was no longer open and that the question of Syria had been 'settled'. At Faisal's request the British liaison officer in Damascus went to Alexandria to report to Allenby that Faisal feared an imminent French attack. On 10 July Allenby telegraphed this news to Curzon and also a message from Faisal to Lloyd George, seeking an assurance that in Faisal's absence no change would take place 'in the military situation at frontiers'.

No such assurance was forthcoming; nor would the British undertake, in defiance of the French, the arrangements for Faisal's journey. The French knew they could now deal with Faisal alone. Not only had he not recognised the French mandate over the Syrian interior, but he had taken an active interest in the affairs of the littoral. He insisted on his right to be consulted, and actually protested against French repression in Jabal 'Āmil. He was in fact a rallying point for forces opposed to France in all Syria, including even Lebanon, where in the midst of the crisis a challenge was flung in the face of Gouraud.

A proposal had been for months under consideration by the Lebanese administrative council to send a delegation to Europe and to defray the cost from a loan to be repaid either by the Lebanese authorities or by contributions from the Lebanese in America. An appeal for contributions had in fact been published, and the loan was obtained from 'Ārif Na'māni, a wealthy Muslim merchant in Beirut. Members of the council must have been as displeased with French direct rule as many other Lebanese. A majority of the twelve members of the council passed a resolution insisting on 'the complete independence and neutrality of Mount Lebanon' within frontiers to be agreed upon with the government of Damascus, with which good relations were an imperative necessity in order 'to avoid chaos and bloodshed' and to safeguard economic interests. To achieve the last object the council resolved to seek the appointment of a joint commission. The preamble to the resolution refers to the 'difficulties arising from ambitious politicians and fame-hungry generals'.

The French authorities arrested the members while on their way to Damascus where it was planned for them to join a Syrian delegation to Europe. They were subsequently tried for 'high treason', intrigues and acceptance of bribery from Faisal's agents. Only one of the twelve members was acquitted. The others were sentenced to various terms of imprisonment, banishment, fines and loss of civil rights. (It will be recalled that the very first delegation sent by the Lebanese council went under Picot's auspices and at the expense of the French government.)

The resolutions of the Lebanese administrative council do not represent a mere 'incident'. Dissatisfaction with French direct rule was widespread, even among the Maronites. Indeed, one of the members of the council who voted for the resolutions was the brother of the Maronite patriarch. The episode had, however, little influence on the new French attitude to Faisal which had already been formed. On 29 June the British ambassador in Paris reported a hardening in this attitude. Since he refused to come to the Peace Conference to 'regularise' his position, the French government was no longer bound to recognise him or have him imposed upon them by the British government. Further communication with him would be from the French government alone, 'if they thought fit to communicate with him further'.

Nūri as-Saʿīd, who was in Beirut to arrange for Faisal's travel to Europe, came back on 11 July with a verbal version of an ultimatum which, Gouraud told him, was ready to be sent to Faisal. Faisal immediately suggested an inter-allied committee for arbitration. His government informed the diplomatic corps and the Syrian congress of the concentration of French troops 'to the west and north' and of the verbal report of Gouraud's demands. The government also suggested arbitration, affirmed its readiness to negotiate and insisted on its desire for peace. Gouraud's ultimatum came on 14 July in the form of 'a note' addressed to His Royal Highness the Amir Faisal 'in the name of the French Government'.

After a long introduction listing complaints, Gouraud's note made five demands to be accepted or rejected as a whole within four days: (1) unconditional acceptance of the French mandate, (2) acceptance of the French Syrian paper money based on the franc, (3) abolition of conscription and reduction of army effectives to the numbers on 1 December 1919, (4) French military occupation of the railway and the stations from Riyāq to Aleppo (the first, and Jisr Shāghūr, on the way to the second, having already been occupied), (5) punishment of persons implicated in hostile acts against the French.

Gouraud had ample means to enforce, and Faisal practically none to resist, these demands. Gone were the days in the autumn of 1918 when he could threaten the 2000-strong French force on the coast. Gone also were the days of the autumn of 1919 when Yāsīn's threat of exploiting the British withdrawal by dislodging the still small French force could be taken seriously. By the summer of 1920 the French military strength had become so formidable that the same Yāsīn, now back from internment and once more chief of staff, had to recognise the stark truth. His army was very short of ammunition and petrol and there was no prospect of replenishment. It could face the French in battle for a few hours without any hope of winning. Its active strength, exclusive of new recruits still under training, was about 5000. Gouraud had under his command in Syria alone, and exclusive of his forces in Cilicia, over 80,000. His army was, moreover, better trained and equipped. It had tanks, heavy guns and aeroplanes which the Arab army entirely lacked.

There is no written evidence in the British documents that Faisal's acceptance of the ultimatum was with British advice. However, neither the delay in Gouraud's receipt of official acceptance of the ultimatum nor the circumstances of the extension of its time limit were significant or had any real decisive influence on the course of events. What was both significant and decisive was the presentation of new demands which constituted a second ultimatum with a much shorter time limit.[13] Perhaps the most difficult of the demands was the acceptance of a French mission in Damascus both to supervise the execution of the terms of the ultimatum and to work out details for the operation of the mandate. Careful examination of all the demands leaves no doubt that the French had decided on direct rule without Faisal. His acceptance of the original ultimatum was a realistic bow to the inevitable. But it was misunderstood by the zealots among his followers and exploited by a 'fame-hungry' French general.

Faisal's order for demobilisation of the new units of the army and the withdrawal of troops from forward positions facing the French, together with the news that far from effecting a reciprocal withdrawal the French had continued the advance in the direction of Damascus, caused a widespread riot in the city, and hostile crowds marched towards Faisal's residence and had to be fired upon with consequent loss of life. The Syrian congress which refused to ratify the government's acceptance of the ultimatum was dissolved by Faisal's order. He had thus given clear evidence of his desire to come to terms with Gouraud, even against the resistance of his people. He assured the general that the acceptance of the terms of the original ultimatum would be honoured and was in fact being honoured. But the acceptance of the new demands would lead to civil war. That was enough for Gouraud. He invented a pretext that a company of 'Sharifian' cavalry had attacked his army, and ordered the march on Damascus.

Whether the decision to resist was taken with or without Faisal's consent is not clear. But it was a matter of honour for army officers and a mark of blind fury on the part of civilians. On 24 July, remnants of the Arab army under Yūsuf al-ʿAẓmah, the minister of war, together with a motley crowd of armed civilian volunteers, stood in the way of the French advance at Maisalūn. The French backed their crushing superiority in numbers by the use of tanks, heavy guns and aeroplanes. Yet the engagement lasted longer and French casualties were heavier than expected. The Arab casualties were much heavier, including the minister of war himself who fell leading a company of his men in a desperate attack.

In Gibbon's phrase, shades of night were closing in about Damascus. Next morning the French entered it without opposition. (They had entered Aleppo on 23 July.) What prompted the move is not exactly clear, but Faisal told Allenby later on that he left Damascus, with al-Atāsi and other ministers, for al-Kiswah on the Hijaz railway to the south in order to spare the city 'the horrors of street fighting'. However, he left behind Nūri as-Saʿīd to negotiate with the French. To further the negotiations Faisal appointed ʿAlā' ud-Dīn ad-Durūbi, known to be acceptable to the French, as prime minister. But it soon became clear that Faisal himself was not acceptable. For hardly had he returned to Damascus, an old warrior without armour, a Samson shorn of his hair, when he was formally informed of 'une décision du gouvernement français' asking him to leave on 28 July. He protested that France had no right to deprive him of the authority and title given to him by the Arab Syrian people, and described the French entry into Damascus as a violation of the principles of the League of Nations and contrary to international morality.

He had, however, no option but to leave. A special train took him with Zaid and a small entourage to Dir'ā where he stopped to consider what course to follow. But the French, fearful of his influence in Ḥawrān, threatened to bomb the city from the air if he remained in it. In any case the British authorities discouraged his idea of entrenching himself in Transjordan, the southern part of his kingdom. They assured him that the French had no intention of extending their control so far south, and hinted at the possibility of his candidature for the throne of Iraq. They eased his passage to Haifa on the way to Europe and further negotiations with the British government.

Under the Sykes–Picot agreement Transjordan was in the British sphere of influence. Before the expiry of Gouraud's ultimatum, King Ḥusain telegraphed to Lloyd George that he was sending 'Ali or 'Abdullah to Syria 'to share with their brothers their fate'. He did send 'Abdullah with the Sharif 'Ali Ibn Ḥusain, but it was some time before their presence in Transjordan presented a problem both to the French and the British. Meanwhile Samuel tried to exploit the situation in order to extend the frontiers of Palestine to the east across the Jordan as had already been urged by the Zionists and indeed as had strongly been recommended by Samuel himself. He recommended a British military occupation of the country and even wrote that the country did not desire an Arab ruler. If Faisal's presence in Dir'ā or Transjordan was feared by Gouraud, his presence in Transjordan and even his temporary sojourn at Haifa proved embarrassing to Samuel. Deputations from all over Palestine went daily to Haifa to pay homage to 'our King'. Samuel was probably right that Faisal's presence east (or west) of the Jordan would have created unrest 'dangerous both to the French and ourselves'. It was Allenby who suggested that Samuel and not himself should extend a courtesy welcome to Faisal. In ignorance of the policy of the British government, Allenby had no advice to offer to Faisal. In any case he himself was proceeding to England on 4 August.

Samuel was eager, for British, Zionist and French considerations, to speed up Faisal's departure. Some twenty-four hours before Faisal was scheduled to leave Haifa by special train, Samuel wrote to him on 16 August that at the request of local chiefs in Transjordan it was proposed to appoint British officers to help them 'organise their own government'. Faisal replied on the same day, and the letter was handed personally to Samuel at Lydda station. He said the Sykes–Picot line left Ḥawrān in the British zone – was it now intended to give up that district to the French? He had no objection to the presence of British officers 'in my absence', but he did not know the meaning of 'organise their own government'. The status of Transjordan must remain exactly as it was before the French occupation of Damascus.

Faisal's downfall had both eased and complicated matters for the British and the French. By the summer of 1920 they had placed themselves in opposition, to a varying degree, to Arab national aspirations, both in the south and in the north. It was therefore unfortunate that the League of Nations, next to the Peace Conference, paid scant heed to the first Arab appeals, and consequently became associated in the Arab mind with partiality to the two great powers, sanctioning or condoning what was in Arab eyes French injustice in the north and British injustice in the south. The protest of the Hijaz delegation against the San Remo decisions submitted to the Peace Conference and the League of Nations was merely noted. King Ḥusain's appeal to the Council of the League to intervene in Syria was referred to France, since in the absence of a peace treaty with Turkey it was 'beyond the council's province' to intervene where in international law the war still continued and the League's mandate was not yet legally in force. (The drafter of this reply was Balfour, who next to Lloyd George was the chief architect of the policy that led to disaster after disaster in Syria and Palestine during the next three decades.)

Until the mandate came into force, Britain and France ruled by force, without the consent of the governed. In the sure anticipation of legalising their positions each of the two powers began, after Faisal's downfall, to tidy the affairs of its sphere. On 5 August it was made known through *Le Réveil* that Gouraud intended to extend the area of Mount Lebanon. On 1 September he proclaimed an independent Grand Liban, embracing not only the old Ottoman district but also the city of Beirut and the districts of Tyre, Tripoli, al-Biqāʿ and Baalbek.

This territorial aggrandisement of Lebanon was at the expense of Syria. It did not, however, remove the obvious facts of direct French rule. Thus the first governor of independent Lebanon was Commander Albert Trabaud, a French naval officer, whereas powerful sections of public opinion favoured the appointment of a native governor. Even the administrative council which was elected and enjoyed a measure of autonomy under the Turks was placed now under direct French control. The old recalcitrant council was dissolved, and a new one composed of sixteen members was appointed, not elected. The members were invited to elect their own chairman, but under French pressure Dāwūd ʿAmmūn and not the more senior Ḥabīb Pasha as-Saʿd was chosen. Thereupon the latter, who must have annoyed the French not only by his former association with Faisal's short-lived administration but also by his public demand for a native governor, resigned only to be given a banquet in his honour in Beirut.

If Lebanon, the darling of France, was administered on colonial lines and with direct French control, conquered Syria was not expected to fare better. In fact it fared worse, for here the French knew that the majority of the people had nothing but hatred for France in their hearts. Hence the nationalist ideal of unity and independence was nullified by the French, who created division and imposed French control. Religious, even sectarian, and regional interests were promoted at the expense of the national. The Syrian territory under French mandate was in a few months divided into: (1) Grand Liban, (2) the state of Damascus, (3) the government of Aleppo, (4) the autonomous Alaouite (Nuṣairiyyah) district, and (5) the autonomous Mountain of the Druzes. Within the third division, Alexandretta enjoyed a special regime bordering on autonomy. In every centre of a state there was a *délégué*, a representative of, and with functions analogous to, the High Commissioner. In every department of the administration there was a *conseiller* who controlled more than advised the officials. French officials were in evidence in every department, even the municipalities and Muslim religious foundations.

We have seen that even more direct British rule had been established in Palestine west of the river Jordan. Direct rule it also remained under the civil administration. In Transjordan, however, native autonomy was conceded largely as a continuation of the Faisal regime. ʿAbdullah arrived at Maʿān as 'commander of the forces of the Syrian national insurgents', and was greeted with great enthusiasm by Arab nationalists and considerable apprehension by both the French and the British. In December 1920 he issued a proclamation 'to the Syrian brethren'. A printer's proof copy was seized by Samuel's officers in Haifa. The corrections which the photostatic copy in my possession shows belie Samuel's statement that the Haifa press refused to print the proclamation in which ʿAbdullah declared his aim to be 'the expulsion of the aggressor' and the restoration of the Syrian national rights. Another proclamation was circulated by Sharif ʿAli to individual notables in ʿAjlūn district.

The French ambassador in London was instructed to ask whether Britain could not 'suppress' the movement. By then Faisal was in London negotiating with the Foreign Office. The British were still anxious to placate France. Accordingly they exploited the situation and asked Faisal to use his good offices. It is a mark of his realism that he complied and telegraphed to his father that 'hostile action' might hamper the negotiations in London. Ḥusain undertook to restrain ʿAbdullah, but the latter, despite his professed friendship to the British, was bound to heed the wishes of the men who answered his call, officers in Faisal's army and civil servants in his government, tribal chiefs and other enthusiasts. Great emotion was generated by the arrival at ʿAmmān of three Muslim women from Damascus who offered to serve as nurses in ʿAbdullah's army. They addressed recruits and called for revenge against the French. Indeed, Aḥmad Muraiwid sent a message to Samuel that Arab friendship to the British in Transjordan was contingent upon British non-interference with the coming operations against the French. Samuel ignored the warning when he informed the French in advance of an impending Arab attack on the railway line north of Dirʿā.

At the end of January, Samuel reported that a large-scale Arab attack on the French from Transjordan was imminent, and suggested that the only way to prevent it was British military occupation. Curzon refused to entertain the suggestion. He was soon to

III The Post-war Dismemberment

hand the ball to Churchill on the transfer of the oversight of Palestine and Transjordan from the Foreign Office to the Colonial Office. In a minute dated 25 February 1921 Curzon outlined a 'political' solution of the whole Arab question in greater Syria and Iraq. This last country Britain was now ready to make an Arab principality. If the French were wise they would do the same in Syria, but the British were not going to fight them over it. As to Palestine, Curzon himself thought the Zionist policy was 'a mistake' but it was the policy of the cabinet, now ratified at San Remo. In Transjordan, Britain was ready to establish an Arab state under an Arab prince provided he did not involve the British in trouble with the French and did not 'squabble with Palestine'.

On 2 March 'Abdullah arrived in 'Ammān. Two weeks later Churchill held a conference in Cairo to work out Curzon's outline policy in detail. Among his staff was Lawrence who advised against inviting 'Abdullah to Cairo and suggested that he should see Churchill in Jerusalem. Accordingly on 27 March 'Abdullah and Churchill came to an agreement as laid down by Curzon, with the exception that no stipulation was made against 'Abdullah's interest in Palestine. According to Samuel, the agreement was for a period of six months and covered two main heads: (1) 'Abdullah was 'to carry on the government of Trans-Jordan' with the assistance of a few British representatives, 'under the direction' of the high commissioner for Palestine; (2) 'Abdullah promised to exert his influence to maintain order and public security, and he was 'very definitely given to understand that there must be no attacks on the French'.[14]

By this arrangement a further fragmentation of geographical Syria was accomplished. The southern part of Faisal's kingdom became a new state under British mandate. The Sykes–Picot line now formed a final *de facto* boundary between two areas, the one mandated to Britain and the other to France. The juridical validation of the division in international law had to wait for the signing of a peace treaty with Turkey and the approval by the League of Nations of the final terms of the mandates.

Up to this point the history of all these territories has been treated as that of one country. However, by military and political action, both national and international, Lebanon, Palestine and Transjordan had gradually, between 1917 and 1921, emerged as separate political entities. Henceforth their history must be treated as that of individual states, and our concern must from now on be confined to the history of the remaining territory that became known in common usage as Syria.

11

'A Sacred Trust of Civilisation' – The French Mandate

I

THE theory of the mandates system, as distinct from its application by Britain and France, has an important element of benevolent and disinterested idealism in it. Its ultimate objective was to lead underdeveloped and dependent nations to a higher level of civilisation and political independence. To the two powers who undertook its practical application in greater Syria, however, the system was a necessary concession to a world conscience aroused against the usual practice of annexation and colonial expansion after victorious wars.

Article 22 of the Covenant of the League of Nations laid down that the well-being and development of the inhabitants of territories not yet able to stand alone by themselves under the strenuous conditions of the modern world was 'a sacred trust of civilisation', and that advanced nations were to be charged with the task of executors of the trust on behalf of the League. Paragraph 4 of this article refers, without naming them, to the Arab provinces of the Ottoman Empire: their inhabitants had reached a stage of development when they could be provisionally recognised as independent nations 'subject to the rendering of administrative advice and assistance by a mandatory until such time as they are able to stand alone'. Their wishes were to be 'a principal consideration' in the selection of a trustee or mandatory. Once in charge of the trust or mandate, a mandatory was required to render an annual report on his management of the trust, and the report was to be scrutinised on behalf of the League Council by a permanent mandates commission created for the purpose.

Thus a mandatory was regarded as an agent of civilisation appointed by the League of Nations for a specific purpose. In practice, however, France was selected as mandatory for Syria, contrary to the wishes of its inhabitants, by the Supreme Council of the allied powers, and the League of Nations had nothing to do with it. The contract with the League was a *fait accompli* before it was entered into and it was through the contrivance of France that the mandate was conferred upon her. Furthermore, the mandatory itself drafted the terms of the mandate, which were formally approved by the Council later on. These circumstances forecast the disparity between theory and practice.

While the Covenant dwells only on the interests of the mandated peoples, the terms of the mandate add those of the mandatory and invest him with wide powers which could be and indeed were abused. This was inevitable in view of the already known ambitions of Britain and France in the Syrian territories and consequently the weakness of their moral fitness to act as trustees. For with the exception of Mount Lebanon the wishes of the inhabitants were not taken into consideration either by Britain in Iraq and Palestine or by France in Syria. As a result, the introduction of mandatory regimes was accompanied by violence: riots in Palestine, revolt in Iraq and war in Syria – and these continued during the entire period of the mandate in Palestine and Syria.

Nor did the two mandatory powers, already in military occupation of the territories concerned, adhere to international law by maintaining the *status quo* pending a peace treaty with Turkey or at least the formal approval of the terms of the mandate by the League Council. As a matter of fact the mandate for Syria (and Lebanon) was not approved till 24 July 1922 and did not become effective till fourteen months later, following the signing of the Treaty of Lausanne by which Turkish sovereignty over the territories was extinguished. This treaty did not come into force till 6 August 1924.

Meanwhile the French High Commissioner was empowered by the French President, as the mandatory, to govern by decree. But at the same time martial law which had been proclaimed by Allenby in 1918 was allowed to continue in force till 1925 and in restricted districts for some time afterwards. Not only Gouraud but also his successor General Maxime Weygand made rather excessive use of government by decree, particularly in the matter of creating or suppressing new states within Syria. By 1925 this policy culminated in preserving four distinct units: Greater Lebanon, the Nuṣairi (henceforth Alaouite in conformity with French usage) and Druze governments, and the government of Aleppo–Damascus labelled Syria.

The French justified their action as a response to demands for *local* self-government. In the eyes of the Syrian nationalists, however, it was nothing less than *divide et impera*. A sincere mandatory gave a lead to and was not led by undeveloped people under his charge. The example of Britain in Iraq was a glaring contrast. What would have happened had the British encouraged sectarian, racial and regional ambition to develop? Iraq would have been fragmented to an even greater extent than Syria was. But the French had maintained – and they had no choice but to maintain – a customs and currency unit of the whole mandated territory in Syria and Lebanon.

In the first years of the mandate the French treated the Syrian interior much as a conquered territory. After its occupation, Damascus was singled out for harsh treatment. A fine of two hundred thousand gold dinars was imposed on the government as reparations, and the inhabitants were required to surrender fifty thousand rifles. Lesser fines were imposed on Ḥawrān and the Druze areas, but little headway was made in disarming their inhabitants. The remnant of the Syrian army was converted into a police force. Military courts sentenced to death scores of notables, mostly in their absence, including prominent members of the Syrian congress. A number of other notables were interned or forced to reside outside their localities. Some were imprisoned on the offshore island of Arwād while others were sent to French colonies overseas. A rigorous press censorship was introduced, and some newspapers were bought with subsidies. Cash gifts and annuities were given to a number of influential persons of all communities.

But despite these and other measures the condition of the country remained for some time disturbed and public security far from satisfactory. The first serious shock to the French was the attack on an armoured train in which a Franco-Syrian party was travelling on official business. The train was attacked in Ḥawrān and members of the party, including the prime minister ad-Durūbi, were killed. From Dirʿa to Aleppo, and from Latakia and Beirut to the interior, rail and road communications were frequently cut off by raids, blowing up of bridges, derailment and looting of trains and ambushing of military convoys.

There were organised risings in Aleppo district by Ibrāhīm Bey Hanānu, in the Alaouite district by Shaikh Ṣāliḥ al-'Ali and in Jabal 'Āmil by Kāmil Bey al-As'ad. Punitive expeditions were invariably engaged in pitched battles. Thus against Maḥmūd al-Fā'ūr and Aḥmad Muraiwid, operating near the borders with Palestine and Transjordan, were sent four companies of infantry with field artillery and aeroplanes. As a result of the engagement forty French casualties were admitted to hospital. From January 1919 to April 1920 the French lost in Syria 150 officers and 3432 men killed, in addition to a total of 2400 wounded. According to a report by the British military attaché in the Paris embassy the total cost of maintaining the French army of the Levant in 1922 amounted, in round figures, to 383 million francs.

Matters were made worse for the French by marauding attacks from the Turkish side of the frontiers. So great was the strain on the French military resources that according to a report by the British General Headquarters in Cairo based on reliable French sources, withdrawal to Lebanon was actually contemplated.[1] Gouraud had, however, scored a success in securing the submission of al-Fā'ūr who was promptly pardoned. It was while returning from a visit to al-Fā'ūr that Gouraud was ambushed in June 1921. He himself escaped unhurt but his aide-de-camp was killed and the Syrian prime minister, Ḥaqqi Bey al-'Aẓm, wounded. Gouraud had, of course, been unnecessarily provocative on his first visit to Damascus after its occupation. He is reported to have said in a speech at the tomb of Saladin: '*Ma présence ici consacre la victoire de la croix sur le croissant!*'[2]

2

All these events occurred before the League of Nations took official cognisance of them. The annual reports of the mandatory power to the League are naturally one-sided, and are better read together with the minutes of the Permanent Mandates Commission in which their examination is portrayed. It is noteworthy that the commission took an early opportunity to state that hostility to 'French influence' and indeed to 'the mandatory system itself' had never been relaxed. Nor were the Syrians reconciled to it on account of the manner in which it was applied. They were in fact both aggrieved and disillusioned for political, administrative, economic and cultural reasons.

The political grievances were due to the fact that the mandate was imposed by force of arms and hence all its consequences were suspect. This major difficulty remained unresolved and the wounds of 1920 unhealed down to the end. It weakened the inherent liberal intentions of the mandates system. The mandatory power was not regarded as a benevolent trustee but as an enemy in disguise who had certain interests of his own to serve. The French, for their part, distrusted the Syrian nationalists and during the first formative years ran the country without them or through puppets. They maintained French governors in all the states save in Aleppo–Damascus, and French advisers and inspectors and other officials left very little to Syrian initiative.

A movement towards elective councils gave no satisfaction, even in Lebanon. From this stronghold of French influence a petition signed by two hundred citizens was sent to Paris complaining of maladministration, corruption and rigged elections. The truth is that in all the 'Levant States' including Lebanon, an all-pervasive French control continued to operate in the administrative and legislative spheres, either openly or behind a thin native façade. Thus the first head of state in Syria after the introduction of local and central elective councils was the Francophil Ṣubḥi Bey Barakāt, more Turk than Arab in speech and antecedents. Small wonder that the appointment was unpopular among the nationalists.

Nor did the mandatory regime bring early improvement in the economic situation. On the contrary, its measures caused widespread discontent: increased taxation, rise in prices, stagnation in trade and unemployment in the cities. The tying of the Syrian currency to the franc was, of course, intended to facilitate trade with France, but it had disastrous consequences for the Syrian creditors, especially when the franc lost much of its purchasing power in the foreign markets. The Permanent Mandates Commission administered an ill-disguised censure of the measure. It saw in it a move prejudicial to Syria's financial independence which must necessarily be part of her political independence, the ultimate aim of the mandate.

Financially Syria had so far been more of a liability than an asset to France. Not only had the French treasury to bear the enormous cost of an army of occupation but also to bear the entire cost of the High Commission with its elaborate administrative machinery. In addition, France was saddled with the task of receiving and settling thousands of Armenian refugees who through French policy had to leave Cilicia. Furthermore, French prestige demanded a greater expenditure on the cultural and charitable institutions already in Syria and the establishment of some new institutions, chief among which was the *Institut Français* in Damascus for oriental studies.

Yet there is good evidence that right from the beginning a combine of French bankers and capitalists, acting through the director of the *compagnie maritime du Maroc*, had concerted plans through their various industrial, commercial and financial organisations for exploiting Syria's resources and promoting French trade there. For this purpose Gouraud's reports on economic affairs were sent both to the ministry for foreign affairs and to the director of this combine. The British Foreign Office who received this information from the consul in Damascus referred it to the embassy in Paris. Secret inquiries by their agents confirmed the accuracy of the report in every detail. However, the plans for large-scale French economic penetration were, for a variety of reasons, never executed.

In the general cultural sphere, the operation of the mandate created tensions at different levels. On the human level the Syrians resented first that as an agency of their 'civilising' mission the French employed Senegalese troops who were at a much lower stage of development than the Syrians, and whose behaviour created a variety of scandals. The Syrians resented next the conduct of inexperienced French officials who were no better educated than the native notables to whom they were empowered to give orders. The arrogance and tactlessness of such officials heightened the tension, and the free use of the term *sales syriens* deepened resentment. To conservative elements the insulting term was doubly humiliating coming as it did from those who almost from the beginning of their rule fouled the atmosphere of at least Beirut with *demi-mondaine artistes* and licensed prostitution.

Nor were high French officials always above reproach. Syrians, and indeed also Lebanese, had often to complain of corruption and high-handed methods, and to compare the French official with the Turkish to the disadvantage of the former. Perhaps the worst case was that of Colonel Couse, liaison officer with Faisal's government and *délégué* after the occupation. He was, according to a report by the British consul, removed from office for peculation. Such lapses on the part of agents of civilisation, no matter how isolated, greatly undermine its claim for adoption by an allegedly less civilised society.

So much by way of illustration of the general causes of Syrian cultural revulsion. There were other and still deeper causes. The strongest exception was taken to the deliberate French policy of imposing their culture and language. They forced state *primary* schools, in addition to secondary and higher schools, to teach French. They gave the curriculum a strong French bias. They made French an official language in the courts. The Syrians feared that the French were trying to do in Syria what they had been doing in Algeria since 1830: to frenchify an essentially Arab Muslim society. They had no warrant to do so even under the terms of mandate.

To say all this is not to deny that there were redeeming features in the operation of the mandate. These will be noted where relevant at different stages. The earliest and most obvious achievement of the French was the construction of roads and the repair of the railways, both for military purposes to start with but ultimately beneficial to the country. It is necessary to recall that the railways and much of the public utilities such as water and electric supply already were or came under French concessionary companies.

In the administration the French introduced their elaborate and on the whole expensive bureaucracy. But it was efficient especially in financial matters. The state budgets were carefully controlled so that almost always they showed a surplus. Whether this was desirable in a country crying for social and economic development we shall consider in due course. But some attention was paid to public amenities, village schools and agricultural credit banks, particularly in the Alaouite and Druze areas where direct French control was anxious to show the blessing of its civilising mission.

These areas, with Lebanon, were marked for some form of *permanent* mandate.

However, persistent claims by the French and their advocates for the credit of having effected marked improvements in Arab education in the Aleppo–Damascus state are greatly exaggerated. These claims take no account of the fact that the French inherited a working state system, a legacy from the Turks through the Faisal administration. The French controlled the extension of this system and made every effort to have it conducted on French lines. They suppressed a military school established in Damascus by the Turks and enlarged by Faisal. They also suppressed a private Muslim school in the city which was under Faisal's patronage, possibly because it had a nationalistic programme.

Private schools, Muslim, native Christian, and foreign Christian missionary, were allowed to continue under the provision of the Ottoman education laws, confirmed by an *arrêté* of 31 August 1921. Carefully selected schools from among these various private establishments began to receive grants-in-aid either from state funds, or from the budget of the French High Commission. An indication of the type of institutions thus favoured may be seen in the May 1922 issue of the *Bulletin officiel* which includes three decrees assigning grants to the *Collège Grec-Catholique de St Sauveur*, *École Arménienne catholique mixte*, and *École des Alaouites à Damas*.

Higher Arab education was, as a part of the state system, subject to the control of a French 'adviser'. It will be recalled that apart from two training colleges, the one in Damascus and the other in Aleppo, the Turks had established a school of medicine in Damascus. This was revived during the Faisal administration and a new school of law was established. The two schools of medicine and law (with 141 and 111 students respectively in 1924) formed the nucleus of the later Syrian university. In addition the Arab Academy, established during the Faisal administration, became a semi-official body devoted to studies for the advancement of Arabic learning.

3

No sooner had the country been outwardly pacified under Weygand than it was plunged into a bloody and prolonged revolt. For the

Druze insurrection of 1925 soon assumed the character of a general Syrian rebellion against French rule. It had a small beginning in the resentment at the brusque manner with which the third French High Commissioner, General Maurice Sarrail, treated the Druze chiefs who asked him to honour an agreement with de Caix concerning the government of their territory. In July 1925 Sulṭān al-Aṭrash raised the banner of revolt by seizing Ṣalkhad, the second largest town in the area, and virtually annihilated a French column sent to recover it. A much larger force was then sent under General Michaud only to meet a similar fate. These spectacular successes brought to the Druze mountains discontented nationalists, old friends and associates of Faisal, chief among whom was Nasīb Bey al-Bakri with other members of this well-known Damascene family and Dr ʿAbdur-Raḥmān Shahbandar, the foreign minister in Faisal's last government, now president of the newly formed People's Party (*Ḥizb ash-Shaʿb*). Under his influence a national government was proclaimed, and Sulṭān al-Aṭrash called for all Syrians to join the cause of liberating the whole country, 'sea-coast and interior', from foreign occupation.[3]

Another French attempt, this time under General Gamelin, to crush the revolt made no permanent headway. Emboldened by success the rebels extended their operations to al-Ghūṭah, the rich oasis encircling Damascus, and penetrated the city itself. The French garrison withdrew to the citadel leaving tanks to patrol the main streets. Sarrail happened then to return to the city from a tour of inspection, and ordered the bombardment of the city from the citadel and the use of tanks and aeroplanes. This operation continued for three days. Estimates of casualties vary considerably, but there was no disguising the widespread destruction in the bazaar and residential quarters and the serious damage to the Sināniyya mosque and the ʿAẓm Palace. The immediate effect was an exodus of refugees who filled every road leading out of the city. Economic life, in addition, received a shattering blow from which it took years to recover.

Sarrail's deed shocked the whole world, and as a result of protests in France itself he was recalled in a matter of days. But far from suppressing the revolt, Sarrail's barbarity caused it to spread still further, particularly to the Nabak district and south Lebanon. At one time the rebels threatened Beirut, the seat of the High Commission. The extension of the revolt to wide areas of the country caused havoc with the economy. Not only were trade and industry paralysed, but the agriculture of the affected areas suffered much damage. French punitive measures on the countryside made matters worse. For security reasons they cut down fruit-trees in the Ghūṭah, imposed collective fines and took hostages. The visitation of the troops impaired and in certain cases destroyed village life.

The arrival of a civilian high commissioner in the person of the senator and journalist Henri de Jouvenel raised some expectation of peace. He began with Lebanon where in May 1926 he had the Lebanese Republic proclaimed with a native president, Charles Dabbās. De Jouvenel made it known that as soon as the interior returned to normal a similar policy would be applied. But meanwhile Aḥmad Nāmi Bey, a Francophil Circassian with a more Turkish than Arab background, was appointed as provisional head of the Syrian state. Nothing was changed in the Alaouite or the Druze areas, the latter still in a state of siege.

By the first article of the mandate France was required to frame 'in agreement with the native authorities' an organic law within a period of three years of the coming into force of the mandate. Only in Lebanon was this stipulation honoured. But de Jouvenel conducted protracted and in the end fruitless negotiations with the nationalists, the rebels and certain independent individuals.

Simultaneously another attempt was made to crush the revolt, particularly after the arrival of troop reinforcements. The attempt met with little success, and once more French fury fell on the city of Damascus, a haven for rebels driven out from other fronts. The French again bombarded the city with more savagery than on the first occasion and resorted to the inhuman step of cutting off the water supply of the Maidān quarter containing nearly a quarter of the population. The quarter itself was virtually destroyed by artillery and aircraft bombing and over a thousand of its inhabitants were killed. Thus a civilian high commissioner proved no less savage than a soldier. Indeed, de Jouvenel, who sanctioned the bombardment, dismissed members of the Syrian government and banished them, together with others, to Arwād because they were suspected of sympathy with the rebels.

France was tardy and too brief in reporting on the Syrian revolt to the League of Nations. When at long last further reports were submitted at the express request of the Permanent Mandates Commission, and de Jouvenel appeared before the Commission to answer questions, he robbed the members of much thunder by declaring that France hoped to achieve peace in the territory by negotiating a Franco-Syrian treaty modelled on the Anglo-Iraqi treaty of 1922. That treaty was the immediate outcome of the Iraqi revolt and the British desire to make some amends to Faisal.

Thus it took France nearly ten years from the Sykes–Picot negotiations to realise the force of Syrian–Arab nationalism and to recognise the necessity of working with rather than against it. Since those negotiations France had tacitly agreed to seek a position in Syria analogous to that of Britain in Iraq. Britain had already set the pace, but France was still reluctant to follow the British example. There has always been a lingering French regret that the original ambition of annexing Syria or at least declaring a protectorate over it had been frustrated first by British policy and then by the mandate system. The French were always sensitive to the repercussions of developments in Syria on their position in the Arab countries in North Africa.

The fifth high commissioner, Henri Ponsot, was a professional diplomatist with experience in the Levant section of the ministry for foreign affairs in Paris. Like the civil servant he was, Ponsot was not in a hurry to give effect to his predecessor's declaration in the name of the French government. He took a preliminary step in February 1928 when a person more or less acceptable to the nationalists was appointed head of state in Nāmi's place. He was Shaikh Tāj'ud-Dīn al-Ḥasani whose task was to hold elections for a chamber of deputies. The elected chamber met in June under the presidency of Hāshim Bey al-Atāsi, who was also president of the strongest single political party in the assembly, composed of the so-called 'extremists' and better known as the National Bloc (*al-Kutlah al-Waṭaniyya*) in which the Christian as well as the Muslim nationalists were represented.

After two months the chamber produced a draft constitution, article 2 of which is a mere echo of the resolution by the Syrian Congress in 1920. It declared that 'the Syrian territories detached from the Ottoman Empire constitute an indivisible political unity; the divisions which have taken place between the end of the war and the present time leave this unity unaffected.'

Thus neither the detachment of Palestine nor the territorial aggrandisement of Lebanon, still less the fragment states of the Alaouites and the Druzes, was recognised. Not unexpectedly Ponsot objected to this article and to five others. He suggested their separation (*disjonction*) from the draft and the abbreviation of article 2 to read that 'Syria constitutes an indivisible political unity'. The suggestion was refused, and Ponsot replied first by adjourning and then by proroguing the chamber *sine die*.

4

The deadlock continued till May 1930 when Ponsot, who had in the meantime been to Paris for consultation, promulgated the constitution, adding a rider which practically invalidated the objectionable articles and substituting his own version for article 2. At the same time he dissolved the chamber. Simultaneously he promulgated organic laws or statutes for the governments of the Alaouites, the Druzes and Alexandretta, as well as regulations for a machinery of the administration, under French control, of the common interests of all these units in the mandated territory. All the documents were sent to Paris for submission to the League of Nations.

Shortly afterwards Ponsot himself appeared before the Permanent Mandates Commission in Geneva. He argued that the *local* autonomy of the Alaouites and Druzes was in accordance with the terms of the mandate and the wishes of the people concerned. As for Alexandretta it was 'neither a state nor a government, but a Syrian province enjoying certain privileges, the existence of which can in no way be considered as prejudicial to the unity of Syria'. That was the word of France on Alexandretta which was to be belied by her deed only six years later. On the general Syrian question, Ponsot made another pronouncement:

> The mandatory power has always kept in view the obligation prescribed in article 22 of the Covenant to guide these territories gradually towards complete independence as soon as their populations are in a position to stand alone. That is the absolute rule which guides our actions. I think no one has ever doubted our intentions concerning Syria and the Lebanon.[4]

France's intentions were indeed very much doubted in the two countries concerned, particularly in Syria. Ponsot's own actions provided justifications for doubt. Thus the Syrian constitution as supplemented and amended by him cannot be said to have been framed, as required by the terms of the mandate, 'in agreement with the native authorities'. It is clear that at the end of the first decade of the French mandate there was little evidence of a genuine desire on the part of the French to rejoin the Syrian fragments they had created, still less to entertain the possibility of the reattachment to Syria of districts annexed to Lebanon in 1920. Nor was there much evidence of relaxing French control over the administration, finance and judiciary, to name only three key services.

Meanwhile rebellion began to fade away in 1926 and the state of siege was gradually lifted. But the damage done to the Syrian economy during the past few years was now aggravated by a world economic depression which hit Syria the harder because of the connection its currency had with the franc. However, a political settlement could not be postponed indefinitely. Late in 1931, Ponsot took steps to give effect to the constitution he had promulgated. He decided to end the provisional government and to hold elections for a chamber of deputies, so that a constitutional government would emerge and negotiate a treaty with France. The elected chamber met for the first time in June 1932 with the nationalist 'extremists' outnumbered three to one by collaborationist 'moderates'. Muḥammad 'Ali Bey al-'Ābid became president of what was now the Syrian Republic, and the veteran Ḥaqqi Bey al-'Aẓm was asked to form a government.

Soon afterwards Ponsot began tardily negotiating or scheming a treaty with this government. Before the negotiations were concluded Ponsot told the Permanent Mandates Commission that France was contemplating the development 'in the near future' of a treaty zone and a mandated zone. The former was to be restricted to the Syrian Republic in the Aleppo and Damascus provinces. The latter embraced the rest of the mandated territory: Lebanon, and the Alaouite and Druze areas. But even under the terms of the mandate there were only two territories, potentially independent sovereign states: Syria and Lebanon. In international law the territory that was not recognised as Lebanon was Syria, including the Alaouite and Druze areas and Alexandretta.

Ponsot had thus prejudiced in advance the chances of co-operation with the nationalists. They reacted swiftly: their two members in the government resigned and all their deputies boycotted the session of the chamber which approved the government policy of accepting Ponsot's proposals. At this juncture he fell ill and Comte Damien de Martel, a former ambassador, was appointed as successor. De Martel's arrival coincided with outbreaks of violence in Damascus followed by the resignation of a 'moderate' minister. Nevertheless the government empowered the prime minister to sign the treaty as presented by the French, and this was done on 16 November 1933.

Professedly modelled on the Anglo-Iraqi treaty of 1930, it was inferior to it in that the French retained too much control and Syrian unity was ignored and even Syria's sovereignty was left in some doubt. However, it provided for the progressive transfer of certain responsibilities to the Syrian government and, after a preparatory period of four years, for France to use her good offices to secure the admission of Syria to the membership of the League of Nations. France was ready, after the ratification of the treaty, to bring the administration of religious foundations and judicial appeals in the Alaouite and Druze areas under the authority of the Syrian state. Since even a 'moderate' government regarded these areas as parts of her territory, the French were ready to examine a possible modification in the autonomous status of the two areas immediately Syria's request for admission to the League was presented.

The treaty was denounced on many counts, chief among which was the forfeiture of unity and the sanctioning of French military occupation of the whole country. When it was presented to the chamber a storm of protest broke out, and a general strike accompanied by disorders was declared in Damascus. De Martel realised that the treaty stood no chance of acceptance, and he suspended the chamber indefinitely, asked the president to withdraw the treaty from the cognisance of the chamber and empowered him to rule by decree. The treaty was dead and once more Franco-Syrian relations reached a deadlock.

Nothing of special significance happened till 1935 when the National Bloc, influenced no doubt by world events and developments in Egypt and Iraq, began to assert itself as the militant opposition to French inaction. A police raid on the Bloc's offices in

Aleppo and Damascus and the deportation of two of its leaders were the signal for widespread and prolonged disturbances which forced de Martel to reopen parleys not only with a new Syrian government but also with the nationalists. As a result a Syrian delegation was invited to Paris for the purpose of negotiating a new treaty.

The negotiations lasted some six months and half-way an *impasse* was reached. But then as a result of a French general election a new left-wing government under Léon Blum came to power. With this government the Syrian delegation signed on 9 September a treaty, almost identical with the Anglo-Iraqi treaty of 1930. Like its model, the Syrian treaty was also to lead, three years after ratification, to membership of the League of Nations. The question of the Alaouite and Druze areas was solved by the French promise to transfer the prerogatives of sovereignty over these two areas to the Syrian government and to institute in each area special administrative and financial régimes similar to that already in force in autonomous Alexandretta, itself an integral part of the Syrian Republic.

At the general elections for a new chamber the National Bloc won an overwhelming victory. Accordingly Hāshim Bey al-Atāsi became president, and Jamīl Mardam Bey prime minister. The treaty was unanimously approved by the chamber in December 1936. Meanwhile Lebanon desired to come to a similar arrangement with France and a parallel treaty was rapidly negotiated and signed before the end of the year. The conclusion of these two treaties required some agreement between Syria and Lebanon regarding the 'common interests' until now under complete French control.

5

Following the announcement of the terms of the Franco-Syrian treaty, Turkey raised the question of the provincial district of Alexandretta, claiming for it virtual independence on a parity with Syria and Lebanon. France and Kamalist Turkey had come to an agreement in 1921 concerning a special administrative regime for this Syrian district within the French mandated area. Neither side had any reservation about its character as an integral part of Syria.

However, the agreement provided for the Turkish population (87,000 out of 220,000 according to French estimate) full enjoyment of facilities to develop their own culture and 'an official status' for the Turkish language.

Late in 1936 the Turkish demands were much more drastic. After inconclusive diplomatic exchanges, France and Turkey agreed to submit the dispute to the Council of the League of Nations. In January 1937 a settlement was reached distinctly in favour of Turkey. Its essence was to constitute the district of Alexandretta as a separate political entity with full internal independence under a statute and a fundamental law of its own. Its connection with Syria was restricted to customs and monetary matters, and its foreign affairs which were to be conducted by Syria after independence.

In the summer of 1938 when elections for an assembly were to be held under the new dispensation, France was more occupied with the larger problems of Germany and central Europe, and gave way to Turkish pressure on a number of vital matters including the co-operation of Turkish troops for the maintenance of order during the elections. By this and similar means the Turkish minority won 22 out of the 40 seats. When the assembly met for the first time it elected a Turk for a speaker, another Turk for head of the state, renamed the territory the Republic of Hatay, and appointed an all-Turkish cabinet.

Not content with these victories, the Turkish government exploited the strained world situation to an even greater extent and pressed for the annexation of Hatay. Britain and France were very eager to secure if not a Turkish alliance at least Turkish neutrality in a European conflict that seemed inevitable. It is said that Britain, who had given Turkey a big credit loan for rearmament, persuaded France to sacrifice Alexandretta as a price for gaining Turkish goodwill. France capitulated by signing an agreement in June 1939, ceding the territory to the Turkish Republic.[5] This was clearly a grave violation of article 4 of the mandate which stipulated that the mandatory was required to see that 'no part of the territory of Syria and Lebanon is ceded or leased or in any way placed under the control of a foreign power'.

It was a clear betrayal of trust by France, and a shattering blow to the prestige of the Syrian nationalists who had negotiated the 1936 treaty of friendship with her. Even the main prize which this treaty gave to the Syrian nationalists was now taken away. They were justly proud of having secured the reunification of the Alaouite and Druze areas with Syria under a decentralised arrangement. But the reunification was soon questioned by separatist elements allegedly encouraged by local French officials.

The truth is that the sudden coming to power was not always skilfully managed by the National Bloc, more out of inexperience than bad intentions. A similar problem arose in the Jazīrah province which now expressed a desire for autonomy. Remote on the upper Euphrates, extensive in territory and mixed in population (Arabs and Kurds, Muslims and Christians, recently augmented by Assyrian refugees from Iraq), the territory had been very difficult to administer since Turkish times. Dair az-Zūr special district, now part of this province, had been formed by the Turks in order to tame and civilise the beduins. This element of the population, hardly changed in the meantime, added to the complexity of the administration of the province.

Nor was this the last of the National Bloc's trials. It came to power as a result of the successful conclusion of a treaty of friendship with France. Now that the treaty, still unratified, had failed its first crucial tests, the chronic mistrust of France was revived and the supremacy of the Bloc began to be challenged. Following a general amnesty many prominent nationalists in exile, including the redoubtable Shahbandar, returned to Syria. He publicly criticised the terms of the treaty itself and ridiculed its lack of ratification by France. He gathered round him a good number of supporters and formed an opposition party which significantly included, in addition to some two dozen deputies, important representatives of the three separatist areas: the Alaouites, Druzes and Jazīrah.

Within the Bloc itself dissension developed. The long delay in France's ratification of the treaty and Mardam's readiness to amend it and, in an exchange of letters, to defer to further French wishes particularly in respect of minorities and French schools, revived the old uncompromising spirit. Shukri Bey al-Quwwatli resigned from the government, and was soon surrounded by others of similar persuasion, both from his own party and from other parties. They voiced dissatisfaction with the changed political atmosphere and insisted that the two basic national aims of unity and complete independence were not negotiable.

Another disappointment was the failure of a Syro–Lebanese conference to agree on the future administration of the 'common interests' with the result that their control remained exclusively in French hands. In 1937 the total receipts of the common interests amounted to over nine and a half million Syrian pounds, most of it realised from customs.[6] It was apportioned between Syria and Lebanon by the French authorities. Next to direct taxation Syria's largest revenue was from customs.

The Syrian economy had hardly recovered from the great losses and dislocation during the rebellion when it was plunged, in the early thirties, into a period of depression lasting five years. Most of the time Syria had an adverse trade balance, not only with France but also with Britain and other countries. For 1935 the value of imports from France was over four and a quarter million Syrian pounds while Syrian exports to France were valued at one million and a third. For the same years the imports from and exports to the United Kingdom were three million and 385,000 Syrian pounds respectively.

And yet there were various factors which contributed to economic development: good inland communications, enlargement of the port facilities at Beirut, increase in land under cultivation by the application of irrigation schemes, and more security in land tenure through the initiation in different areas of a cadastral survey. These were achievements to the credit of the mandatory authorities who were hindered, however, from making more advance in the social and economic fields by their preoccupation most of the time with military and political problems. Hence the total benefits look in perspective more symbolic than spectacular.

Thus agriculture, the main occupation of the rural population, was left by the French where they had found it: traditional methods extracted from the soil substantially the same products. Village life was hardly touched by development except perhaps in opening some village schools. No large-scale drainage was undertaken, either as land reclamation or as a measure against malaria. The cities by contrast were definitely improved at least by the introduction or improvement of public utilities and transport. This goes to show that the mandatory authorities paid more attention to urban than to rural areas.

There were two beneficial projects worthy of note, incidental to the mandatory regime but developed within its jurisdiction. The first was the construction by the Iraq Petroleum Company of a pipeline from Kirkuk to Tripoli across Syria. It brought no oil royalties as yet but it was nevertheless useful because of the demand it created for labour. The second was the opening of the Nairn motor transport service across the desert between Damascus and Baghdad.

The above review would be incomplete without further reference to the subject of education in the years preceding the outbreak of the war. (There was hardly any advance in this or any other social service during the war.) Before citing facts and figures to show that on the whole the French contribution was inadequate, it is fair to mention two French activities which deserve unqualified praise. The first was the *Service des antiquités*, which formed a department in the High Commission, and whose efforts were evident in the museums in the major cities and in the care bestowed on the preservation and maintenance of public monuments. The second was the *Institut Français* in Damascus which concerned itself with academic research, as testified by the production of monographs and papers by the distinguished orientalists who worked under its aegis.

French achievements in Syrian education cannot boast of such distinction. In the reports of the mandatory power to the League of Nations, schools are classified in three categories: state, native private, and foreign. On schools in the first category the French set their impress in the curriculum, the teaching of French and public examinations. Over those belonging to the Uniate churches in the second category, the French influence was extended through grants-in-aid and public examinations. In this category only the Muslim schools and some Greek orthodox schools which received no grants and offered no pupils for French examinations, escaped. French influence predominated over two types of schools in the third category: those directly supported by the High Commission and those conducted by Catholic missions, French or French-speaking. American, British and other foreign schools remained independent, and had to conform to the French system only in the matter of examinations and in the interests of their pupils.

French supervision of state schools has been very severely criticised, on national and educational grounds, as seeking illegally to frenchify the product. But even in quantity the French achievement is open to criticism. Only a fraction of the total of school-age children was actually at school, not for lack of desire, for there were never enough school places for those who applied for admission, as will be mentioned below.

Only the French themselves can estimate the success of their own schools and whether they realised the objects for which they were opened. In 1938 there were 71 of them in Syria (excluding the Alaouite and Druze districts) with 11,493 pupils almost equally divided into boys and girls. In the same year there were 152 Syrian students in French institutions in France, and 330 in the schools of medicine and law in Damascus. It is not clear why the French failed to keep alive an agricultural school at Salamiyyah.

The following table gives a picture of the state schools in 1938: derived from the last official report to the League of Nations:

	Number of Schools		*Number of Pupils*	
	Boys	*Girls*	*Boys*	*Girls*
Primary	370	80	38,870	15,483
Secondary (including teacher training)	9	3	2,764	460
Technical	4	1	587	347
High	4	1	330	26
	387	85	42,551	16,316
	472		58,867	

In the same year, 1938, the state budget showed a surplus of over three-quarters of a million Syrian pounds. Why was it not spent on providing at least places for applicants at schools? The French advisers, educational and financial, appear to have been more concerned with statistical neatness and oblivious of the 'civilising mission'. How inadequate was this French achievement may further be illustrated by a comparison with the British achievement in Palestine, itself declared inadequate even by official British experts. In 1938 there were in Palestine 402 state schools with 49,400 pupils, including 11,555 girls. Considering the disparity between the two countries in size and population, the British achievement, despite its inadequacy, was distinctly better than the French. A leading Arab educationist states that after assuming power the National Bloc produced a plan for educational expansion, but the execution of the plan was frustrated by political difficulties arising from France's failure to ratify the treaty of friendship.[7]

6

The political difficulties alluded to will presently be mentioned more specifically. Together with other internal and external problems they produced considerable unrest which tried the capacity of the National Bloc to the utmost. Their coming to power coincided with the outbreak of the Palestine Arab revolt in 1936. From the beginning the Palestine Arab struggle against the British Zionist policy was regarded by Syrian nationalists as part of the movement towards the emancipation of the whole of Syria. Accordingly Syrian volunteers took an active part in the Palestine revolt; indeed one of the leaders of the revolt was a Syrian army officer. Exiled Palestinians led the resistance from Syria and supplied it with arms and money. In Blūdān in Syria a pan-Arab conference was held in support of Palestine in which prominent members of the Bloc participated.

While still in power the Bloc witnessed helplessly the influx of Armenians from Alexandretta on its cession to Turkey. In 1921 many more Armenian refugees came from Cilicia after its evacuation by France in favour of Kamalist Turkey. In 1933 thousands of Assyrian refugees came from Iraq. These considerable racial and religious augmentations of the complex Syrian population complicated the social atmosphere and caused tensions. While the initial cost of receiving the refugees was borne by the French High Commission, the new arrivals had ultimately to be an additional burden on the Syrian economy and their assimilation, if effected at all, was not without strain.

The severest strain on Syrian life remained, however, political, centred at this stage on the single question of French failure to ratify the treaty. That France had second thoughts was apparent almost immediately the treaty was initialled. The reasons for this change are rather complex, reduceable to the fact that France had to consider her own interests in a rapidly changing international atmosphere. She had to take note that some of Italy's ambitions pointed in the direction of territories under French protection in North Africa. She had to take more serious note of the German position in central Europe and the economic penetration of the Balkans which extended to Turkey.

These were some of the portents which made France reluctant to weaken her entrenched position on the shores of the eastern Mediterranean. It was easy to find pretexts to prolong the term of direct French control in Syria: the inexperience of the national government; concern for the future welfare of the minorities; and consideration for the wishes of the separatists. Furthermore, France herself wanted more guarantees for the continuance and development of her cultural institutions and economic interests. As stated above, Mardam twice made concessions on all these matters, and certain others including defence, in negotiations with the French ministry for foreign affairs. The only *quid pro quo* he obtained was to fix 30 September 1939 as the end of the transition period.

France remained hesitant and the Syrian nationalists lost patience. Mardam could no longer carry all the National Bloc with him and his agreements with the French were never presented to the chamber. The concessions he had made were unacceptable to, among others, Shahbandar and Quwwatli and their respective supporters. To the chamber and the government, however, the treaty as negotiated in 1936 had become like a charter of liberty which they were determined to defend. Frustrated by prolonged French inaction, the chamber took the matter into its own hands and on the last day of 1938 adopted a unanimous resolution. While it affirmed a desire for friendship with France, the resolution upheld the treaty as negotiated, repudiated any amendments to its terms, and empowered the government, in the interests of the unity and independence of the country, to assume full powers at once.

This amounted to another declaration of Syrian independence. And there to take the challenge was the new High Commissioner, Gabriel Puaux, who arrived only a few days after the adoption of the resolution. His first public utterance confirmed the fears of the nationalists that the treaty had been scrapped. France, he declared, had 'a mission' in Syria and her presence in the country was in the best interests of its inhabitants. Although this might have been a hint of the danger of a general war, the national government waited for about a month before taking action. Receiving no assurance whatever about the treaty, and noting that the High Commissioner still ruled by decree even on vital matters which were now its sole responsibility, the Syrian government formally notified the High Commission in February that they intended to act in accordance with the instructions of the chamber and to assume the functions hitherto performed by the mandatory authorities. The government refused the high commissioner's demand to withdraw this notice, and he compelled their resignation.

It was impossible to form a stable government amid continued unrest, strikes and disturbances. The High Commissioner assumed responsibility for internal order: he had a number of prominent nationalists arrested, imposed strict press censorship and used French troops to quell disturbances. With the authority of the French government he made an official announcement that the international situation required a new agreement with Syria *on the basis of* the 1936 treaty and the amendments negotiated by Mardam. The Syrian chamber replied by adopting another unanimous resolution towards the end of May, affirming its conviction that the 1936 treaty without any amendment formed the only basis of an agreement with France.

Under these circumstances none of the nationalists of any party was ready to form a government. Matters became worse when Puaux re-established by decrees the autonomy of the Alaouites and Druzes and by another decree placed the Jazīrah province under direct French control. President Atāsi resigned the same day that these decrees were published. Thereupon Puaux suspended the Syrian constitution, dissolved the chamber and appointed civil servants as directors, each in charge of a government department under the High Commissioner's supervision.

The end of the 1936 treaty was complete. Two months later the Second World War broke out.

7

The outbreak of the war in 1939 may be taken as marking the practical end of the social benefits, such as they were, of the French mandate. The remaining years of its life, culminating in the final liquidation of French political influence, were more than ever occupied with military and political affairs. It is therefore appropriate at this junction to take a closer look at the French 'civilising mission'. But to do so judiciously it is essential to adopt a sceptical attitude both to the French annual reports submitted to the League of Nations and to the Arab petitions that occasionally reached the League. It is far safer to rely on the observations made on these reports and petitions by the independent members of the Permanent Mandates Commission. But we must be on our guard since their independence was tempered by restraint in criticising a great power and tact in questioning its accredited representative.

It is not intended, nor is it necessary, to cover the whole ground. Suffice it for our purpose to supplement our previous discussion with allusions to a few specific questions as illustrative of the manner in which the French prepared the Syrians, as required by the mandate, to stand alone. Let us take the question of education first. On this subject the Norwegian member, a lady of high qualifications and mature experience, asked pertinent questions and made most revealing remarks. In 1930, after ten years of French supervision, she noted that male illiteracy was 66 per cent and female 80 per cent. Though de Caix could give no figures, the demand for admission to schools was far in excess of the available accommodation. Only 39 per cent of the boys and 17 per cent of the girls of school age were actually at school. With the natural increase in population there was little prospect of improvement and a danger that the rate of illiteracy would increase rather than decrease.

The Norwegian member's questions forced de Caix to admit that the adoption of the French system in admission to state schools amounted to discrimination against those who did not follow it. She took the specific case of the school of medicine in Damascus where only a *bachelier* stood a chance of admission. According to de Caix, French lecturers with no knowledge of Arabic were appointed in the school and this was one of the practical reasons for requiring knowledge of French from students seeking admission. He said that the appointment of French teachers was in order to raise standards and on account of the paucity of texts in Arabic. He said nothing about the overriding policy of spreading French influence in every department.

Turning to another subject, we find that in 1934 de Caix was questioned by a Spanish member concerning the French tendency to favour officials rather than elective municipal councils, since 40 out of the 99 councils were presided over by officials. He was also asked whether the French controlled the administration of the Muslim *awqāf*. De Caix was evasive: the appointment of officials at the municipalities was not a policy but to increase efficiency, and the French High Commissioner had a delegate at the *awqāf* council. Similar evasive answers were given to equally important questions. Thus to use the euphemistic terms of the French reports, 'press supervision' was alleged to have been under native control, and 'supervised residence' was not a penalty but an administrative precaution. However, on this last question de Caix was not allowed to get away with it. Count de Penha Garcia retorted that 'a measure depriving a citizen of his liberty was only admissible in virtue of a law governing its application or of a police order; otherwise, it became quite arbitrary.'

So far as could be discovered the handing over of the administration of the Hijaz railway – virtually a Muslim *waqf* – to a French concessionary company went unchallenged. But searching questions were asked concerning agriculture, industry, trade and emigration. Members referred to the shaky agricultural banks, to the fall in prices, to the dying silk industry, to the fact that in 1933, for example, the imports from France ranked first while Syrian exports to France dropped to fifth place, and in general to 'the marked disproportion' between imports and exports resulting in an unfavourable trade balance. De Caix's answers were seldom as revealing as the questions themselves. On the subject of emigration, however, he admitted that in one year during the period of depression, over ten thousand left Syria and Lebanon and never returned.

All these departments of Syrian life were within the competence of the French mandatory authorities to shape and develop in the interests of the native population. The evidence is overwhelming that they failed to score the degree of success they and their advocates claim. An effort has been made above to cite hitherto little-known or little-used facts and figures to enable the reader to judge for himself.

But this review of the scene on the eve of the war would be incomplete without some reference to the rise of certain ideological elements in political life. These elements were mainly communist and fascist. From the beginning of the national struggle for independence all Syrian and Arab political parties shared a common element generally based upon the ideas of European nationalism, democracy and liberalism. Hence the post-war disillusionment was the greater because it was, to the Arab mind, caused by the failure of two great powers, Britain and France, to apply democratic and liberal principles. Stripped of its details, the dialogue between Arab nationalists and British and French politicians really revolved round one single question: why the most advanced democracies failed to live up to their principles in their dealings with the people of Syria?

This disillusionment with the practice of British and French mandatory administrations was only one of the factors that made possible the reception in the 1930s of communist and fascist ideas. From the 1920s individual native communists, some with training in Russia, had been trying to form trade unions and ferment labour unrest. They sought to achieve these and other ends by personal contact and the distribution of clandestine leaflets. But they were not yet taken too seriously by the public or the police. Under the management of Khālid Bakdāsh, however, the movement achieved cohesion and driving force. A Kurd by race, Syrian by domicile, he was among the few Syrian communists to receive Russian training. By 1936 his group was regarded as an unrecognised party and merited a mention in the French annual report to the League of Nations.[8] By then it had become a communist practice to participate in strikes declared in protest against the devaluation of the currency and to support the Franco-Syrian treaty and the demand for Syrian unity.

Thus the Syrian communists identified themselves with the main principles of the ruling National Bloc. They criticised the Franco-Lebanese treaty as infringing Syrian unity, and later condemned as imperialism the surrender of the Syrian territory of Alexandretta to Turkey and direct French control in the Jazīrah province. They refrained from directly challenging the rich landlords. This accommodating attitude secured for the communist party a tacit official recognition with the right to publish a newspaper of its own. But soon after the outbreak of the war the party and the paper were suppressed by the French authorities.

There was never a fascist party in Syria, but in 1932 the Syrian Nationalist Party (*al-Hizb as-Sūri al-Qaumi*) was established with a touch of fascism in its make-up especially as regards the leadership. It was founded by Anṭūn Sa'ādah, a Lebanese Christian, as a secret organisation among young people. It preached a doctrine that all the inhabitants of geographical Syria, including Lebanon and Palestine, constituted a nation which was neither Arab nor Muslim nor Christian nor even a combination of the three. This doctrine was naturally regarded by the established political leaders as subversive in Lebanon and unpatriotic in the rest of Syria. The Lebanese authorities in particular took stern measures, including the trial and imprisonment of Saʿādah and some of his followers. But internal development made the government relent. In 1937 they granted the party licence to publish its doctrine. Like the communists, this party too made vigorous protests against the gradual surrender of Alexandretta to Turkey.

Having consolidated the party in Syria, the leader decided in 1938 to seek support, probably financial, among the Arabs in South America where he had lived for many years before. On his way he visited both Rome and Berlin. That was enough to compromise the party in the eyes of the French authorities, who soon after the outbreak of the war proscribed it and arrested its leaders and many of its members.

8

Many Syrians who had experienced the rigours of Turkish martial law during the First World War had the misfortune to witness the inauguration of similar French measures at the beginning of the Second. The proclamation of a state of emergency was felt at different levels. To the masses it held the fearful prospect of a repetition of the shortages, privation and misery which had been their lot only a quarter of a century earlier. To the politicians it sounded a stern warning to keep quiet for the duration and backed the warning by the arrest and internment of several political suspects. To the mercantile community it portended curtailed trade at a time when the economy of the country was in a depressed state. With the Syrian constitution already suspended, the French High Commissioner now sought to tighten his grip on the whole mandated territory by suspending the Lebanese constitution.

After taking such precautions to safeguard internal security, France sought to safeguard the external. The eastern Mediterranean was safely under British and French naval surveillance. The land frontiers of the French mandated territories were safe under British allies. The only possible danger was the northern frontier with Turkey. Accordingly Britain and France rapidly negotiated and signed on 19 October 1939 a treaty of mutual assistance with Turkey. It guaranteed Anglo-French assistance to Turkey in the event of her resisting aggression by another European power, and the mutual assistance of the three powers in the event of aggression by a European power in the Mediterranean area. The provisions of the treaty were equally binding as bilateral obligations between Turkey and each of Britain and France. A protocol expressly absolved Turkey of any obligation to be involved in a war with Russia.

Anglo-French command of the sea and the control of a large land-mass embracing Egypt, Iraq and the mandated territories in Syria and Palestine rendered the fears of immediate shortages of essentials rather unfounded. Agricultural production was hardly affected, a certain amount of foreign trade was still possible and internal trade in local products remained normal. In wartime, however, profiteers and hoarders somehow prosper, despite official control of supplies and prices. The mandatory authorities who had given a rest to politics seem also to have given themselves a rest from showing imagination in the economic and social fields. They were on the whole content to enjoy the comparative peace which paradoxically was brought about by the war. But this fair weather did not last long. In the spring of 1940 the storm broke with the German offensive in Europe.

Weygand's recall from Syria to command the French armies on the western front was too late to avert disaster. Just as the way of the German army to Paris was open, Italy declared war on France and Britain. The fall of Paris was followed by an armistice signed by the veteran Marshal Philippe Pétain, who at the head of the new French government took Vichy as their seat. The armistice was challenged by a hitherto little-known officer, General Charles de Gaulle, and the challenge was converted, through the assistance of the British government, into the beginning of the Free French movement.

Italy's entry into the war, together with the fall of France, altered the naval and military balance in the Mediterranean against Britain. There was considerable British anxiety lest the French fleet should be surrendered to Germany or lest Italian and German forces should occupy Syria and Lebanon. A British declaration made it clear that such occupation would be opposed. Almost simultaneously the French fleet at Oran was attacked by a British naval squadron, ostensibly to prevent its possible surrender to Germany. Thereupon France broke off diplomatic relations with Britain.

These developments in Anglo-French relations had a profound influence in Syria. The frontiers with the British mandated territories were virtually closed. The Iraq Petroleum Company was ordered to stop piping oil to and across Syria. A blockade of the Syrian coast was instituted. Except for Turkey the French mandated territories were now cut off from their neighbours. The result was a shortage of essentials, a sharp rise in food prices and further depreciation of the paper currency.

An Italian armistice commission arrived in Beirut about a month after the terms were signed. They were soon followed by various German agents and officials who concerned themselves mainly with propaganda, playing on Arab hopes and fears regarding, among other questions, Palestine and Alexandretta. The French defeat and Arab experience of British and French policies since 1918 rendered German propaganda successful with a segment of Arab nationalists. But the British could still depend on such old friends as the Amir ʿAbdullah and Nūri Pasha as-Saʿīd. The former, in alliance with and through Shahbandar, soon revived his brother Faisal's scheme of a Syrian state within its natural frontiers. The latter followed some time later with a scheme of Arab unity of which more will be said in due course. But Shahbandar who acted first was removed by assassination which, though his assassins were found guilty and hanged, remained somewhat of a mystery.

Before the end of 1940 Puaux was recalled and was eventually succeeded by General Henri Dentz. His assumption of office coincided with a worsening of the economic situation and loud protests by the unemployed and hungry. Despite an official ban, demonstrations were held with the slogan 'We want bread!' Other essentials were both in short supply and beyond the means of the masses. Under these circumstances the politicians could no longer be restrained. Shukri al-Quwwatli in particular played a prominent part in the agitation and the negotiations with the authorities that followed.

A general strike was proclaimed in Damascus and the French sent out troops in tanks and armoured cars to disperse demonstrators. But the strike, accompanied by some rioting, spread to other cities, with fatal casualties among the population and the security forces. Dentz could not come to an agreement with the nationalists who demanded the immediate recognition of Syria's independence and the formation of a national government. He arranged, however, for the unpopular council of directors to resign and appointed a hitherto non-political figure, Khālid al-ʿAẓm, as *chef du gouvernement*, an office combining that of president and prime minister. None of the members of the National Bloc joined this government. (A similar change was introduced in Lebanon.)

Such partial restoration of native participation in the government made little difference to the economic situation which continued to deteriorate in the early months of 1941. Nor was the political situation any better. The Syrian nationalists became more and more exasperated by a defeated France who insisted on her right to control the destiny of their country. They regarded any legal claim France may have had to do so lapsed on her withdrawal from the League of Nations in April 1941.

But in addition to their exasperation with France the Syrian nationalists nursed an old grievance against Britain for what they regarded as an unjust policy in Palestine. These feelings were shared, perhaps in an exaggerated degree, by Iraqi nationalists, who had in addition their own grievances against the British. That Arab leaders in all these countries could obtain no concessions from either Britain or France was at once frustrating and opening possibilities for German propaganda. Still more possibilities were opened by the success of German arms in the Balkans, Greece, Crete and North Africa. Some of the antecedents of the Rashīd ʿĀli *coup d'état* in Iraq and the war with Britain must be sought in cumulative Arab disappointment.

The events in Iraq served to dissuade the British government, and in particular Churchill, from underrating the danger of alienating the Arab nationalists. British representatives in the Middle East had warned the government against this tendency and insisted on the necessity of conciliating the Arabs. Although Churchill did not heed these warnings, and continued to ignore them in the case of

Palestine, he was now willing to let soothing words be authoritatively spoken on the eve of his government's decision to occupy the French mandated territories of Syria and Lebanon in co-operation with de Gaulle. The Foreign Secretary, Anthony Eden, expressed not only 'sympathy with Syrian aspirations for independence' but also for the larger aim of Arab unity. He began by stating that Britain 'had a long tradition of friendship with the Arabs', and concluded by his government's pledge to give 'full support to any scheme [of Arab unity] that commands general approval'.[9]

Eden's statement was well received. Its timing, soon after the end of Rashīd 'Āli's regime and before the invasion of Syria and Lebanon, was masterly, and no doubt calculated to win the goodwill of at least the Syrians. The pretext for the invasion was the use of Syrian airfields by German aircraft lending assistance to Iraq. Its real cause was, however, long-term strategy: to forestall any German occupation that would imperil the British military position in the Middle East. Accordingly on 8 June 1941, and in the words of the British communiqué, 'Free French troops, with the support of Imperial forces' entered the territory. But the numerical strength and the general importance of the forces involved were the reverse of what these words would suggest.

The Free French and the British government had agreed on political pronouncements to be made on the day of the invasion. On behalf of the former, General Georges Catroux said in a proclamation to the inhabitants of Syria and Lebanon: '*Je viens mettre fin au régime du mandat et vous proclame libres et indépendants.*' Henceforth, the proclamation continues, they were sovereign and independent peoples with full liberty to form separate states or to unite in a single state. Relations with Free France would be regulated by a treaty to be negotiated between native representatives and Catroux himself. He ended by calling attention to the economic advantages of lifting the blockade, resumption of trade and establishing relations with the sterling area. This proclamation was backed by a statement issued in Cairo in the name of the British government who 'supported and associated themselves with the assurance of independence' and promised the lifting of the blockade and facilities for trade and relations with the sterling area.

Both the French and British pronouncements called upon the inhabitants of Syria and Lebanon to rally to the allied cause. This was an important factor in their calculations. Another of their calculations, however, went wrong. Dentz offered not token but very stiff and prolonged resistance, and withstood the attack for more than a month. But finally the last High Commissioner in Syria of the French Republic sought and received honourable terms of surrender which were signed on Bastille Day. De Gaulle appointed Catroux, the commander-in-chief of the Free French forces in the Levant, as his delegate-general and plenipotentiary in Syria and Lebanon.

9

The French have always used the term 'independence' in relation to Syria in a sense different from its usual meaning. In this the Free French proved to be very much like their predecessors. Only two weeks after Catroux's announcement of Syrian independence and the end of the mandate, de Gaulle stipulated that the independence and sovereignty of the Levant states was to be established by new treaties negotiated, on the basis of the 1936 treaties, guaranteeing 'the rights and interests' of France. Until then the mandate was to remain in force and Catroux to assume the functions of high commissioner under his new title.

De Gaulle was suspicious of his British allies lest they had designs to supplant France in Syria and Lebanon. On this subject he received authoritative assurance that Britain had no such designs. But it was British policy to see Syria and Lebanon realise their independence, not only because of the British endorsement of Catroux's proclamation but also as part of a desire to conciliate Arab national leaders.

Syria was now garrisoned largely by the British Ninth Army and the small Free French force. Both formed a part of the British operational command based on Cairo. The British army in Syria did not directly concern itself with political affairs or the civil administration. These were the province of the Free French who had to comb their ranks for suitable replacement for those Frenchmen who chose to be repatriated. Despite this division of functions there was considerable friction and ill-feeling between the two allies, largely owing to French suspicion and hypersensitiveness. A British liaison officer, General Sir Edward Spears, later the first

British minister to Syria and Lebanon, was the particular object of much French grumbling.[10]

As ordered by de Gaulle, Catroux stepped into the shoes of Dentz. Nothing was changed except the names. While in Syria, a few days before the armistice with Dentz, de Gaulle made unsuccessful attempts to secure the collaboration of the National Bloc on the basis of the 1936 treaty as amended by Mardam. Catroux's more patient negotiations with Hāshim Bey al-Atāsi afterwards were also fruitless. Rather than recall the chamber or hold new elections, Catroux had recourse to the strategy of his predecessors: he scorned the 'intransigents' and sought the 'moderates'.

An old friend and collaborator with the French, twice prime minister in such an emergency before, was now recalled to assume the office of president. He was Shaikh Tāj'ud Dīn al-Ḥasani. Ḥasan al-Ḥakīm was appointed prime minister. This French-appointed, not Syrian-elected, government was the witness on 28 September 1941 of Catroux once more declaring the independence and sovereignty of Syria. (Following similar appointments a similar declaration of Lebanese independence and sovereignty was made on 26 November.)

On this occasion, however, Catroux laid down so many conditions that independence and sovereignty were robbed of most of their meaning. 'A final settlement' with France had to be reached in the form of a treaty. Although the Alaouite and Druze areas were reunited with Syria as after the 1936 treaty, nothing was said about the possibility of union between Syria and Lebanon. Catroux would merely use his good offices to facilitate 'economic collaboration' between two separate states.

The worst stipulations were described as dictated by wartime necessity. They included allied (or French) control of the armed forces, the police and gendarmerie, communications, and all the public services and economic resources of the country. Add to this certain departments which had been under the direct control of the High Commissioner, and now reverted to his successor, and hardly anything remained within the competence of independent and sovereign Syria. Of these important departments to remain under French control mention may be made here of *intérêts communs*, which included customs, of *troupes spéciales*, locally recruited from small minority groups and forming part of the

French army, of *sûreté générale*, the security forces for keeping internal order, and of *contrôle bedouin* – to say nothing of French schools and cultural institutions.

Whether real or fictitious, Syrian and Lebanese independence was promptly recognised by Britain, and Spears was appointed minister to the two states. However, their most powerful neighbour Turkey withheld recognition, as did the most important power, the United States, both on technical grounds; the former did not recognise de Gaulle, and the latter still had diplomatic relations with the French government at Vichy. The only fully independent Arab state, Saudi Arabia, recognised Syria but not Lebanon. Egypt recognised the independence of Syria but not its French-appointed government. Iraq decided to postpone recognition until constitutional governments were set up.

The caution of these Arab governments and the aloofness of the Syrian political leaders was not without justification. The Free French proved very dilatory in establishing constitutional governments, and made themselves unpopular by the incompetence of their officials, particularly in dealing with the economic situation. Lebanese as well as Syrians, Christians and Muslims, were equally disillusioned. The Syrian nationals saw the writing on the wall when de Gaulle and his team returned to the old theme of France's 'civilising mission' in Syria.

To the Syrian people – indeed to any people – civilisation takes second place after bread. Whatever political pretensions the French had, they were dependent upon the British for financial support and the supply of arms, and later on America also. Before the war the various departments of the French High Commission spent the equivalent of two to three million pounds sterling in Syria and Lebanon on services directly under its control. This money came from France, and the Free French now had to do without this source. Syria and Lebanon were somewhat compensated for diminished French spending by admission to the sterling area and to the general economic unit under British military control. The two countries were soon embraced by the economic planning of the Anglo-American Middle East Supply Centre in Cairo. Furthermore the British army created considerable opportunities for remunerative employment by undertaking public works, the most important of which was the Haifa–Tripoli railway.

The most serious economic problem remained the same: the necessity for a regular supply at stable prices of essential foodstuffs, especially wheat or flour. The measures taken by Anglo-French collaboration with local authorities were not on the whole successful, partly through the malpractices of profiteers and partly through lack of confidence in paper currency and the French administration in general. Not for the first time did the dissatisfaction of the masses reinforce the determination of the politicians. But if the latter could be controlled by exclusion from office and other restrictions, nothing, not even force, could prevent the masses from staging, as they often did, 'bread riots'.

Political inaction by the Free French lasted for some eighteen months. It was deplored by their British allies and resented by the Syrians and Lebanese. Political instability tended to aggravate economic instability and to arrest social progress. Little constructive work can be recorded to the credit of the shackled and unpopular government. Even the business of local government was paralysed. The military uncertainties in North Africa had, no doubt, some influence on Free French political action or inaction in Syria, but essentially the problem was still the old French reluctance to concede the reality of Syrian independence.

De Gaulle was now installed with the *comité français de la libération nationale* in Algiers. Catroux was by his side much of the time until his final transfer from Syria. To manage French affairs in Syria and Lebanon there was a former ambassador, Jean Helleu, first acting for and later successor to Catroux. Early in 1943 Helleu was authorised by de Gaulle to announce the intention of restoring the suspended constitutions of Syria and Lebanon and of forming provisional governments for the purpose of holding elections for chambers of deputies.

The Syrian chamber met in August and elected Shukri al-Quwwatli president of the Syrian Republic, and he appointed Saʿdullah al-Jābiri prime minister. (The Lebanese chamber met in September and elected Bishāra al-Khūri president and he appointed Riyāḍ as-Ṣulḥ prime minister.) Egypt, Iraq and Saudi Arabia now recognised without any reservation both Lebanon and Syria. The accession of these two new members strengthened the Arab states in their tentative striving towards some form of unity. As stated above, Arab political leaders had since the outbreak of the war made unsuccessful approaches to the British and French with a view to securing concessions regarding Palestine, Syria and Lebanon. It was also pointed out that the failure of these moves made some Arab leaders amenable to German overtures, and contributed in no small measure to Rashīd 'Āli's *coup d'état* in Iraq.

With a changed military and political atmosphere, however, Nūri Pasha as-Sa'īd, then prime minister of Iraq, put forward concrete proposals to the British government in 1943 for a Syrian union with safeguards, under international guarantees, for the Christians in Lebanon and the Jews in Palestine and the special status of Jerusalem. A united Syria under these proposals could form with Iraq a nucleus of a larger Arab unity to which other Arab states would adhere. The greater Syria scheme did not succeed, but the second part of Nūri's proposals resulted ultimately in the formation of the League of Arab States.

10

Scarcely had the two national governments been installed than they showed their determination to exercise the prerogatives of sovereignty. They wished, for example, to amend their constitutions so as to purge them of the traces of mandatory restrictions, to assume control of their sources of income including the customs, and to incorporate the *troupes spéciales*, whose rankers were Syrian or Lebanese citizens, into national forces. To these and other demands de Gaulle's answer was, in substance, that the mandate was still in force and would continue to be until terminated by the League of Nations or its successor, that the transfer of power must be achieved gradually in agreement with the French, and that the transfer of some of these powers must be within the framework of treaties with France, if not after their conclusion.

In abstract theory, de Gaulle could maintain that the mandate remained in force until terminated by the League of Nations in agreement with the mandatory power. But the mandatory power, the legitimate French government in metropolitan France, had withdrawn from the League in April 1941. It is therefore very difficult to see the basis of de Gaulle's claim to rights derived from the authority of the League when his movement neither had relations with the League nor was recognised as the government of France.

On this as on many occasions in the past, the French were using a language unintelligible to the Syrians and not conducive to reaching an understanding with them. A conflict was unavoidable, and it was with Lebanon, the traditional friend of France, that it began. The Lebanese government initiated legislation designed to annul all provisions in the constitution inconsistent with independence and sovereignty, including reference to the mandate, mandatory power, the League of Nations and the French language. Despite French warnings which amounted to threats the legislation was passed, received the presidential approval and was duly gazetted.

Two days later, in the early hours of 11 November 1943, French marines and Senegalese troops, acting on the orders of Helleu, raided the private homes of the president, the prime minister and most members of the cabinet and arrested them. An hour later Helleu published decrees suspending the Lebanese constitution, dissolving the chamber and declaring the legislation in question null and void. This caused a great storm in Lebanon which involved the use of troops and loss of life. A wave of strong condemnation swept over Syria and all the Arab states. What doomed the French, however, was American disapproval and vigorous British action.

Lebanon like Syria was within the jurisdiction of the British commander-in-chief for the Middle East, and military necessity dictated that tranquillity in these countries and their neighbourhood was essential in wartime. Besides, Britain had underwritten the Free French proclamation of the independence of Lebanon and was in honour bound not to let it be flouted in this violent and arbitrary manner. Accordingly the Free French were bluntly asked to recall Helleu and to release and restore the prisoners. When the French showed some reluctance to comply, the British government delivered what amounted to an ultimatum. The commander-in-chief had been authorised to declare martial law in Lebanon, and 'if the President of the Republic and the Lebanese ministers have not been released at 10 a.m. on 22 November, they will be set free by the British troops.'[11]

The prisoners were released, Helleu recalled, and the French position irretrievably lost. Helleu's successor, General Beynet, and his staff appeared to have been chastened, at least temporarily. Thus without the slightest French protest the Syrian chamber passed legislation similar to that passed by the Lebanese chamber. This did not hinder arrangements made then, in the course of 1944, to begin and continue the transfer of power from the French to the two new states. The French made, however, some significant reservations concerning the French schools and the *troupes spéciales*. They desired to safeguard the future of the schools by treaty, and to hand over the troops within its framework.

The conclusion of treaties with Syria and Lebanon was indeed foreshadowed in Catroux's proclamation of their independence in 1941. But much had happened since then. For one thing, Helleu's action alienated Syrian public opinion and damaged beyond repair the chances of friendly accommodation. For another the independence of the two states was recognised in 1944 by the two major powers, the United States and the Soviet Union, and both powers made it clear that they did not favour any special position in the two states for any power. That alone doomed the French chances of persuading Syria and Lebanon to conclude treaties safeguarding special French interests.

Besides, the wisdom of a tie with France was no longer apparent, not even to Lebanon. The recovery of Occupied France and the assumption of power by a provisional government under de Gaulle in Paris made no difference. The Lebanese and Syrian prime ministers each separately declared that his country had no intention of concluding treaties with any power before a general peace conference was held. Beneath this attitude there was a real anxiety, born of past experience, that treaties could not be negotiated freely while the two countries were still occupied by French troops.

Another crisis was thus in the making from the beginning of 1945. While the presence of British troops in Syria and Lebanon was accepted by Syrian and Lebanese politicians as a temporary wartime measure with no political design behind it, the presence of French troops was feared precisely because of political designs. The lesson of November 1943 was only the most recent illustration of how ruthlessly the French forces could be used to coerce a national government. But the immediate cause of the quarrel, this time with Syria, was not the large question of the military occupation of the territory; it actually began in the cultural sphere, a very sensitive subject to the French.

Late in December 1944 the Syrian chamber passed an education law with a clause which though educationally sound was considered offensive by the French. The clause stipulated that 'no foreign language will be taught in primary schools'.[12] This was an indirect way of saying that the teaching of French to Arab children between the ages of six and eleven, as had been the practice during the mandatory period, was abolished.

The incident must have confirmed de Gaulle and his associates in the demand for a recognition of France's 'right' to pre-eminence in Syria and Lebanon. This included safeguards by treaty of French cultural institutions and the French right to maintain military bases in the two countries. It is clear from the pronouncements and demands of the two sides that they were irreconcilable. Their reiteration publicly served only to increase the estrangement and heighten tension. Matters came to a head when French proposals for treaties were presented almost simultaneously with the disembarkation from a cruiser in Beirut harbour of Senegalese troops, whether as reinforcements or replacements was really of no importance.

Everything in the French proposals was already known. France wished to conclude treaties that would safeguard her cultural, economic and strategic interests. The first two might have been negotiable, but the third was difficult to negotiate: it concerned military, air and naval bases; it sought to perpetuate a fearful military occupation. Only after the conclusion of such agreements, the French proposals stated, could the *troupes spéciales* be transferred from French to native command. The implication was that in default of agreements French forces would continue in occupation.

Syria and Lebanon rejected the proposals. They refused to negotiate under the duress of French military demonstration. Further disembarkation of troops led to strikes, riots and clashes with the French. There were serious disturbances and clashes in Beirut, Tripoli, Damascus, Aleppo and elsewhere. The French used armoured cars, machine guns and aeroplanes to suppress the disorders. Aleppo and Ḥama suffered severe damage and considerable civilian casualties. But the worst fate was reserved for Damascus which for the third time since 1925 was subjected for three days to prolonged shelling by field-guns and bombing from the air. Among the public buildings destroyed or damaged was the Syrian chamber of deputies. About 80 gendarmes and 400 civilians were killed and nearly 500 wounded. It was virtually a war between the armed forces of Free France and the civilian population of Syria.

All British appeals, including one from Churchill to de Gaulle to avert the clashes before they occurred, were of no avail. Later attempts to arrange a cease-fire were apparently frustrated. The Syrian president and government appealed to the British government to intervene. As in 1943 so in 1945, it was a British interest to maintain tranquillity in Syria, Lebanon and the neighbouring countries. These countries were on the lines of communication to the Far East where the war with Japan was still raging. Accordingly de Gaulle was informed that the British commander-in-chief in the Middle East was ordered to restore order in Syria.

On 1 June the local British commander was authorised to issue the following order to the French commander in Damascus, with the warning that force would be used, if necessary, to secure their complete execution. All French troops and armoured units to be withdrawn to barracks outside the city and all machine-gun posts to be removed. No French soldier to be allowed out in the streets of the city. The French barracks to be placed under British guards. Should the French troops thus confined to barracks open fire the barracks would be bombarded. (Nothing was said about French civilians, but these were also escorted out of the city.) Similar if less rigorous measures were taken in other centres.

Any hope of salvaging the French position was now vain. Both embittered and hostile, Syria and Lebanon were strengthened in their resolve to resist French claims by developments in the international and Arab fields. After completing certain formalities the two states were invited to the San Francisco Conference which inaugurated the formation of the United Nations. Membership of this organisation was soon to give the two states an international forum to clinch their argument against the French. Then a week after the bombardment of Damascus the Council of the Arab League adopted resolutions confirming Syria and Lebanon in their refusal to give any special position to France and endorsing their demand for the evacuation of French forces.

Basing themselves on the Arab League resolutions, Syria and Lebanon declared a common policy which reaffirmed their determination to refuse any special position to any power, to insist on evacuation of French troops and to proceed with the dismissal of French officials in their service. (Syria had, in consequence of the fighting with French forces, ordered the closure of all the French schools. They were later allowed to open only on a basis of equality with other foreign or native private schools, subject to the Syrian law.)

At last de Gaulle made a symbolic bow to the inevitable. Exactly two months after the end of the war in Europe he offered this same fact as his reason for beginning to hand over the *troupes spéciales*. French forces had already begun a withdrawal from the Syrian interior to the Mediterranean littoral but these forces lingered much longer than any pretext convincing to the Syrians and Lebanese could explain. De Gaulle had not yet given up all hope of bargaining, nor exhausted all dilatory tactics. He ignored the excitement and the repeated incidents between his troops and the civil population and as late as 31 December 1945 sent a few hundred 'replacements' which again disembarked at Beirut to the accompaniment of strikes, protests and further disturbances.

The Syrian and Lebanese governments took the case to the United Nations, and secured a public French promise to evacuate the two countries at the earliest possible date. An Anglo-French military arrangement was rapidly made for a phased and simultaneous withdrawal of British and French forces, since the Syrians and Lebanese were anxious for British troops not to go before the French. By mid-April, Syria was completely evacuated, and the 17th of the month is celebrated as a national holiday. Lebanon was evacuated by the end of August except for some technicians who left about Christmas. Lebanon reckoned 31 December as a national holiday marking the completion of the evacuation of foreign troops.

Beynet's exit had already been quietly and unceremoniously arranged in sharp contrast to Gouraud's pompous arrival in 1919. France's 'civilising mission' and the League's 'sacred trust of civilisation' both passed into history.

12

The Burden of Independence

I

At no time did the Syrian nationalists work out in detail what to do after securing complete independence. Now that it was a reality and the French were safely out, the burden of independence fell heavily on the shoulders of the Syrian political leaders. They faltered often enough and made mistakes, but on the whole the net result in the economic and social fields has been creditable.

To begin with, the government of independent Syria had to make considerable economies in the administrative machinery. There was, for example, no need any longer for the elaborate apparatus of translation into French and the duplication of work it involved. The whole bureaucracy was overstaffed, and after dispensing with the services of French officials the Syrian authorities found it necessary to effect some retrenchment of native officials. Much of the money thus saved was diverted to the social services. Special attention was paid to education which showed spectacular expansion, at least in quantity. Thus new admissoins to state primary schools had risen within three years to more than double the corresponding numbers for the years before independence. Expenditure on national education was second only to that on national defence in the state budget.

In external affairs the most immediate questions were the settlement with Lebanon of the common interests and with France of future monetary policy and liquidation of French assets. In their approach to economic matters Syria and Lebanon showed a divergence in sharp contrast to their united front in the political struggle to wrest independence from France. The two countries failed after independence, as they failed once under the mandate, to come to a working arrangement concerning the common interests, particularly the customs. Syria pressed for a common tariff policy for the protection of native industry and agricultural produce, while Lebanon was bent on building her economy on a policy of *laissez-faire*.

The divergence led ultimately to the termination in 1950 of the customs union between the two countries which had been maintained throughout the mandatory period. Then, at the end of the joint negotiations with France concerning future monetary policy, Lebanon signed the agreement but Syria decided against it. As a result Syria withdrew from the franc bloc and established independent exchange controls, and thus the currency unit in which Syria and Lebanon had joined since 1920 came to an end.

The disruption of the customs and currency union emphasised Lebanon's separate entity. The so-called 'national pact' had already ensured for it internal peace and external security: agreement with the Lebanese Muslim leaders, alignment with Syria in the struggle against France, and adhesion to the Arab League pact had secured both Syrian and general Arab recognition of Lebanese independence within the frontiers imposed by Gouraud in 1920. While this was a political triumph for all concerned, it was also a triumph for the separatists in Lebanon. Henceforth Syria could not claim the return of the annexed districts, and the disruption of the economic union made the possibility of political union less likely than ever before.

Such a union was now a mere aspiration in the programmes of some political parties, such as for example the Syrian Nationalist Party, or a utopian dream in the Amir 'Abdullah's schemes. His revival of the idea of Greater Syria after the war encountered formidable obstacles: Lebanese insistence on complete independence, insufficient support for 'Abdullah among the Arabs of Palestine added to Zionist intractability, republican leaders in Syria who did not favour a monarchy, and finally inter-state Arab jealousies.

But it was not solely 'Abdullah's personal ambition which brought the question of Greater Syria to the fore once more. It was the great anxiety about the political future of Palestine in the face of Zionist public demand, with strong backing in the United States, for a Jewish 'commonwealth'. In 1919 Faisal proposed to solve the Zionist question by the arrangement for an autonomous Jewish district in a united Syrian state. 'Abdullah did no more than revive this outstanding Arab aspiration for Syrian unity, with safeguards to minorities.[1]

And yet, domestic Arab difficulties apart, British policy was on the whole not favourable to the scheme, particularly in regard to Palestine whose problem the British government now sought to solve by other means. Yielding to immense pressure at home and from the United States, the British government decided that they would not impose any policy by force – the very thing they had done since 1918 when they imposed the Zionist policy in the face of mounting Arab resistance. The meaning of the new British policy was clear: they would not enforce their own policy as laid down in the 1939 White Paper because the Jewish minority opposed it.

When the problem of Palestine was referred by Britain to the United Nations the usual procedure of investigation by a committee was adopted. On the basis of the committee's report the General Assembly adopted on 29 November 1947 a resolution partitioning Palestine for the setting up of an Arab and a Jewish state.

This is not the place to go into details, and a minimum of facts must suffice. The United Nations resolution was rejected by the Arabs of Palestine and by the Arab states, who all decided to oppose its execution. On the other hand the Jews accepted it, but the British government refused to enforce it and announced its intention to terminate the mandate and withdraw British forces and administration by the middle of May 1948.

Meanwhile the Palestine Arab rejection of partition was expressed in violent demonstrations and widespread disorders. The situation soon deteriorated into an Arab-Jewish civil war. While Britain was still in control, the Arab states could do nothing other than encourage popular movements to send arms and volunteers surreptitiously. Throughout the winter of 1947–8 it seemed as if the Arabs were succeeding in frustrating the practical application of partition. But in the spring the well-trained and armed underground Jewish military and terrorist organisations resorted to methods calculated not merely to fight Arab irregular forces but to strike terror into the hearts of the civil population. A number of exposed Arab villages close to Jewish settlements were attacked, houses demolished by dynamite and young men lined up and shot. The worst was the case of Dair Yāsīn where old men, women and children were massacred in cold blood. These outrages caused a general panic and a mass retreat of the Arab population to safer areas. In this way a number of towns and villages and considerable territory allocated to the Arabs by the United Nations were occupied by Jewish forces while the British army and administration were still in the country.

When the Arab regular armies intervened on 15 May it was too late. On the previous night the state of Israel was proclaimed and recognised within an hour by the United States. By then the Arab community in Palestine had suffered grievous losses, and its morale was undermined. The hope it pinned on the Arab armies soon proved vain. Not only did these armies fail to recover lost ground, but in the long run failed to hold all the Arab territory that was not in Jewish occupation.

This colossal failure had a profound reaction in all the Arab states, but was quicker to appear in Syria. Violent political strikes and demonstrations, in which students took part, resulted in clashes with the police and loss of life. The political unrest was exacerbated by an economic slump and labour strikes, particularly in Aleppo where as everywhere a shortage of petrol handicapped transport and modern industrial plants. In the background was the army whose senior officers felt very strongly that they had been let down by the politicians. In December, with mounting criticism of his administration, Mardam submitted the resignation of the government.

Martial law had to be declared, and the chief of staff, Colonel Ḥusni az-Zaʿīm, assumed the task of restoring order. Schools were closed, the press was subjected to military censorship and public meetings controlled. Meanwhile unsuccessful attempts were made by one politician after another to form a government until after two weeks of suspense Khālid al-ʿAẓm managed to do so. In his statement to the chamber the prime minister sought to mollify public opinion by his insistence on the imperative necessity of liberating Palestine and rejecting all schemes of partition.

Despite warnings that the army must be kept away from politics, the new government allowed martial law to remain in force and tried to cultivate Zaʿīm. But two matters bedevilled relations and increased tension between politicians and soldiers. The first was the trial by a special tribunal of an army officer, a nephew of

Mardam, on a charge of negligence which resulted in sending arms bought for the army in Europe on board a ship that was to call at Haifa. The second was the proposal, in a budget designed to cut public spending, to reduce the allowances of army officers, to begin some demobilisation and to postpone new conscription. Senior army officers regarded the trial as an attempt by the politicians to shift the blame to the army, and the budget proposal as another attempt to diminish the army's stature.

No Syrian government could ignore dissatisfaction in its army for long. The ʿAẓm government lacked the courage to ignore even rabble-rousers. Its policy was more influenced by agitators than by its independent judgement. Even the chamber was swayed by agitators, both inside and outside its walls. Thus when early in 1949 the government was about to sign a monetary agreement with France and another with an American oil company for the construction of a pipeline from Saudi Arabia through Syria to Sidon on the Mediterranean in Lebanon, fierce opposition in the chamber and student demonstrations prevented it from doing either. Syrian aversion to a continued link with the franc bloc is understandable, but by the rules of ordinary economics the rejection of $21,000 per annum in transit dues and protection fees is difficult to explain except on emotional political grounds: America had sponsored the partition of Palestine and given immediate recognition of Israel.

It was quite clear by the spring of 1949 that there was a deadlock in the operation of democratic parliamentary government in Syria. The only power in the land that still possessed freedom of action was the army. Zaʿīm had been suffered by the politicians, including the president and the prime minister, to make political representations. The warning that such tolerance might cause developments on the Iraqi model went unheeded.

2

On 30 March 1949 Zaʿīm staged a smooth and bloodless *coup d'état*. The president and the prime minister were placed under arrest, and later on the chamber was dissolved and political parties banned.

After forcing the resignation of the president and prime minister, Zaʿīm made himself head of state and finally, through a referendum in which he was the sole candidate, president. Several measures were introduced by decree including a civil code modelled on the one operative in Egypt, abolition of family *waqf*, introduction of income tax on personal income and commercial and industrial profits, and extension of voting rights to women with sufficient educational qualifications.

Some of these and other measures were popular and survived their author. But Zaʿīm's politics were rather opportunist. His first inclination towards union with Iraq was soon reversed, when both Saudi Arabia and Egypt did not favour it. Before long the new regime was recognised by all the Arab states, and also by Britain, France and the United States. However, its days were numbered.

Zaʿīm's shifty politics, his tendency to exhibitionism and extravagance and the assumption of too much personal power alienated an important element of his comrades in the army. Professedly to rectify Zaʿīm's errors, Colonel Sāmi Ḥinnāwi staged another *coup* on 14 August. Both Zaʿīm and his prime minister were summarily tried by a court martial and shot. A military junta under Ḥinnāwi disclaimed any intention of meddling in civil affairs. Accordingly the veteran former president Hāshim Bey al-Atāsi was asked to head a provisional government which was to hold elections for a constituent assembly that would draft a new constitution. (The constitution produced under Zaʿīm, like that of 1930, was tacitly set aside.)

When the new assembly met in December it elected Atāsi president. The question of the day was, however, Arab unity. Apart from idealism, Syria's shaky political existence needed some prop in the form of a greater Syrian unity or a federal union with Iraq. But the same internal and external forces that opposed such a scheme were still operative. Besides, neither the politicians nor the soldiers, who were hovering not so far in the background, were unanimous on what course to follow. The frequent change of government was a symptom of this indecision and instability.

Inconclusive wrangles in the assembly and outside it on the twin subjects of unity and the provisions of the new constitution were ostensibly the excuse for Colonel Adīb Shishakli to carry out the third *coup* within nine months. On 19 December he had Ḥinnāwi arrested and later allowed to leave the country. In a proclamation, Shishakli stated that the army considered it their duty 'to safeguard the security of the country against the intrigues of Ḥinnāwi, [As'ad] Talas [who was under-secretary for foreign affairs] and some politicians, with foreign elements'.

The last two words conceal a reference to Britain who was suspected of promoting through Nūri as-Sa'īd and others the union with Iraq or Jordan or both. Shishakli was not the only Syrian to fear the extension of British influence from these two countries to Syria through such a union. Others in high places pointed out that Iraq and Jordan enjoyed less independence than Syria. In joining the one or the other, or both, Syria was bound to end with some loss of her independence. Needless to say the proposed union was at least shelved if not completely abandoned.

A loan of $6 million from Saudi Arabia may have been the price. With the freedom of agitators curtailed by the army the agreement with the American oil company was signed. The loan and the agreement gave a timely supplement to the national income.

Meanwhile the passage of the new constitution in the assembly was proving stormy. Leaving aside the change of government, formation and reformation of political parties and the squabbles of factions as of little or no permanent significance, we turn to consider the drafting of the constitution which raised questions of permanent historical interest and deserve to be noted here. Working under the chairmanship of Dr Nāẓim al-Qudsi, the drafting committee examined fifteen Asian and European constitutions while engaged in its task. The draft they produced erred on the side of precision and going into great details.

Liberalism, democracy and social justice are writ large in the constitution. Its preamble stresses the freedom of the individual and his right to justice and liberation from poverty, disease and ignorance. These and many other sentiments are spelled out in several articles that amount to a bill of rights, which include, *inter alia*, habeas corpus, inviolability of the home, freedom of opinion, guaranteed employment, and free education as a birthright.

Arab unity was not forgotten. Syria, declares its constitution, 'is a part of the Arab nation'. But the article in the draft constitution which aroused the greatest controversy was the stipulation that

Islam was the state religion. Here it is necessary to recall the stages, covered in the previous chapters, of the transformation of an Ottoman Islamic state into national successor states, largely secular, of which Syria was one. The process was much advanced by the need for Christian-Muslim solidarity in a national struggle against foreign rule. In Syria under the mandate religion, even sectarianism, was stressed by the French more than, or at the expense of, nationalism. After the removal of French control the secularists exploited the necessity for national solidarity and pressed their claims on the majority, and almost always succeeded in having their way. The same method was adopted with similar results when the Syrian draft constitution was debated.

Against the naming of Islam as the state religion were ranged the 'godless' socialists (including the Syrian Nationalist Party, the Arab Socialist Party and the Arab Renaissance), the Communists, the leaders of the Christian religious communities and some influential individuals. Among the latter perhaps the most important was Fāris al-Khūri who stood for an adaptation of the popular nationalist slogan that religion was a matter for the individual with his God, while the state was for all citizens of all religions.

Those who held the opposite view showed little organised effort. Anxious no doubt to continue to conciliate the Christian minorities, the other and larger parties, composed mainly of Muslim notables, inclined to a tolerant approach, so much so that Qudsi of the People's Party abstained when the issue was voted on by his drafting committee. There was one important exception. The Muslim Brethren were openly and very strongly for the stipulation. Not only did they stage demonstrations in favour of it, but their leader and deputy in the chamber, Muṣṭafā as-Sibāʿi, warned his colleagues of the danger both to Islam and Arab nationalism of secularism which he equated with atheism and materialism. He was wholeheartedly supported by the *ulema* whose Friday sermons became so inflammatory that the government had to arrest some of them at the Umayyad Mosque.

In the end a compromise formula was agreed. It was a revival of the phrase used in the 1930 constitution that the religion of the president of the republic was Islam. The compromise was, however, more comprehensive than this, as the preamble and article 3 show. While Islamic law was declared as 'the main source' of legislation, the rights of all the religious communities were reaffirmed. Finally, since Islam was the religion of the majority of the citizens of the republic, due respect would be paid to it and its ideals.

On 5 September 1950 the new constitution was adopted by the assembly which immediately converted itself into the new chamber. President Atāsi reappointed Qudsi as prime minister, and to all appearances constitutional civil government had been restored. But despite protestations to the contrary the soldiers did not leave politics to the politicians. Colonel Fawzi Silu, an associate of Shishakli, had to be the minister of defence in every government, and Shishakli exercised powerful influence over the government and the chamber.

Three weeks after the adoption of a constitution with high-sounding phrases about personal liberties, a deputy was arrested by the military police on a charge of being an agent of King ʿAbdullah of Jordan engaged in compromising the integrity of Syria. Soon afterwards other political arrests for alleged political conspiracies took place. The subsequent trials were on the whole a discredit to army intelligence, and tended to undermine the prestige of government and chamber. Objections to army interference in civil affairs and politics were silenced with the standard and intimidating phrases of the demagogues. In March 1951 Qudsi's government resigned.

The formation of four ephemeral cabinets, the last not surviving twenty-four hours, revealed the real seat of power. No prime minister could take office without consulting Shishakli and accepting his permanent nominee for the ministry of defence. In the circumstance there was a desire among the politicians to restore the portfolio of defence to a civilian minister. Deputies were anxious that the gendarmerie should revert to the control of the ministry of the interior and not continue under the army. Accordingly when at last President Atasi could persuade Maʿrūf ad-Dawālībi to form a government the prime minister-elect took the portfolio of defence himself and declared his intention to introduce legislation debarring the army from interference in civil or political affairs.

3

At once Shishakli removed his mask. Within twelve hours he struck his blow. On 29 November 1951 he carried out his second *coup*, the army's fourth since March 1949. The new prime minister and the prominent members of his cabinet were arrested and the 'noble Syrian people' were told that the army had taken over. Dawālībi refused to resign as a condition for his release, but President Atāsi himself resigned, whether as a result of pressure or in protest is not clear. Thereupon Shishakli as chief of staff and president of the supreme military council resumed the powers of the executive and promptly dissolved the chamber.

Four days later Silu was invested by a military proclamation with the powers of head of state and prime minister, and the business of routine government was entrusted to under-secretaries or civil servants, with army officers placed in key positions. The supreme court, the only body which could challenge the legality of the regime, was dissolved and its functions transferred to the ministry of justice. The major political parties were banned and eventually also the two socialist parties that had maintained some alliance with the army. A rigorous press censorship was imposed. Teachers, students and members of literary and sports clubs were forbidden to engage in political activities, and the Syrian University was purged of professors who refused to sign an undertaking to this effect.

Partly to mitigate their assault on constitutional government and partly out of conviction, the new regime resumed what had been initiated under Zaʿīm: social and economic reform by decree. The regime issued a statement after its first three months in office and a second statement after another three months setting out the achievements. Both statements were signed by Silu as head of state and prime minister, and addressed to the Syrian people.[2] Making allowance for their apologetic nature and their depreciation of previous regimes there remains some substance that deserves attention.

The two statements use the phrase 'social justice' and 'raising the standard of living of the common people'. Among the steps taken towards these goals were the following: initiation of a programme of building new schools, hospitals and roads; beginning of drainage and irrigation works on the Khābūr project and a survey by a Dutch company of the Ghāb project for similar works; distribution through an agricultural bank of imported seeds, tractors and motor pumps; the introduction of more direct taxation and the raising of the rate of income tax for higher income; allocation of nearly 20 per cent of the ordinary budget to education and the insistence on raising the standards in secondary schools by the compulsory teaching of English and French.

Among other and later measures to the credit of the military regime were the following: allocation to smallholders of state domain by setting an upper limit to the amount of such land any established landlord could hold; advance of credit to peasants and small industrialists by an agricultural and an industrial bank; the establishment of a central bank on the recommendation of Hjalmar Schacht; introduction of tariffs for the protection of the industries of Aleppo and Damascus; encouragement of cotton growing; and the initiation of a scheme for converting Latakia into a modern harbour capable of receiving ocean liners.

Meanwhile Shishakli was consolidating his position. First he assumed the office of deputy prime minister. Then he organised the Arab Liberation Front, the only political party allowed by the regime to function. The committee of civil servants commissioned under his supervision to draft a new constitution completed its task in May 1953. The product retained much of the 1950 constitution but greatly increased the powers of the president at the expense of the chamber. He was to be elected not by the chamber but directly by the electorate. The ministers were to be responsible not to the chamber but to the president. The former president Atāsi was one of those influential people who condemned this constitution.

Shishakli was the only candidate for the presidency and he was returned with an overwhelming majority. Silu retired from public life and left Syria for Saudi Arabia. Shishakli's next move was to produce a parliament that supported his regime. A new electoral law, drawn up under his direction, prepared for elections in October. A belated lifting of the ban on political parties was ignored and the more influential parties boycotted the elections. Shishakli's party won an overwhelming victory.

It looked as if the regime was now firmly in the saddle. But politicians were not idle; they plotted in secret and took care to promote discontent and to publish seditious leaflets. In January 1954 signs of the coming explosion began to appear. There were prolonged and violent student strikes. There was a very serious incident in the Druze mountains. A nephew of Sulṭān Pasha al-Aṭrash was jailed on suspicion of promoting sedition, and an attempt to free him resulted in a pitched battle and the dispatch of a punitive expedition.

Shishakli's reactions were those of a frightened dictator. He proclaimed martial law, and suspecting a plot between the politicians, the Druzes and King ʿAbdullah, ordered the arrest of prominent men including a former prime minister and a former speaker of the chamber; even Hāshim Bey al-Atāsi was placed under house arrest. But Shishakli's end was near. On 25 February an army coup in Aleppo, which soon spread to the rest of the country, sent him twenty-four hours later to the refuge of the Saudi Legation in Beirut and finally to Riyadh.

After a short period of critical confusion it was agreed to restore both President Atāsi and the 1950 constitution, but to hold early elections for a new chamber. Two problems faced the restoration government: how to keep the army out of politics, and how to associate all political elements in the business of government. The gendarmerie was transferred to the control of the ministry of the interior without a hitch. But there remained in the army discontented cliques as a danger to any Syrian government. It was even harder to establish a balance between the political parties or to persuade them to co-operate in a coalition government.

The political parties were indeed legion, and this is a convenient moment to mention some of the most influential. The National Bloc never recovered from its reverse in Palestine, and Zaʿīm's coup proved a shattering blow. Two nationalist parties were constituted from its wreckage and largely from its old members, the Nationalists proper and the People's (Shaʿb) Party. The number of those who called themselves Independent was large enough to constitute another party. The two pre-war ultra parties regained their vitality after a period of comparative inactivity. The Communist Party resumed its policy of support for national liberation while in the process propagating its own ideology. However, it suffered a great setback when the Soviet Union voted for the

United Nations partition of Palestine and later recognised Israel. The Syrian Nationalist Party resorted to violence in Lebanon, and their leader sought asylum with Zaʿīm but was later handed over to the Lebanese authorities who executed him after a trial. This party had now added the appellation 'socialist' to its name.

Since 1941 two other socialist parties had come into existence. One was the Syrian Arab Socialist Party (Akram Hawrāni) and the Arab Renaissance (Baʿth) Party (Michelʿ Aflaq and Ṣalāh'ud-Dīn Baiṭār). After Shishakli lifted the ban on parties the two amalgamated as the Arab Socialist Baʿth Party. Its ideology is secular pan-Arab nationalism with a socialist philosophy and revolutionary undertones.

Embracing an almost opposite ideology was an association that acted as a political party – the Muslim Brethren, an extension of the mother organisation in Egypt. The Brethren stressed Islam before regional or general Arab nationalism and maintained that the latter was meaningless without the former. They too had revolutionary tendencies.

The Democratic Bloc, led by 'the leftist millionaire' Khālid al-ʿAẓm, flirted both with the Baʿth and the Communists and commanded considerable support among the Independents who constituted the 'floating' electorate.

When elections for a new chamber were held in September 1954, they were by all accounts completely free and the results may therefore be taken as an indication of party strength. They reflect in fact a significant shift, from the old guard to the new revolutionaries. To be sure the old guard, the conservatives, with the independents still held the majority of the 142 seats, but the Baʿth won twenty-two seats, the Syrian Nationalist Party two seats and the Communists one seat. The Muslim Brethren did not contest the elections as a party, but supported individuals who were members of their association or were in sympathy with its ideas. At least two prominent deputies were elected in this manner: Muṣṭafā as-Sibāʿi, the Brethren's leader, and Maʿrūf ad-Dawālībi, the former prime minister ousted by Shishakli.

The presidency of the republic was not in question, since it was agreed that Atāsi should continue till the end of his term in 1955, as if Shishakli's *coup* had never taken place. But a government, even a coalition, was difficult to form. After unsuccessful trials by old hands a compromise was found in the appointment of Fāris al-Khūri as prime minister. Khūri's government, like its immediate predecessors and successors, was short-lived. These cabinets were so ephemeral that it would not be enlightening to dwell on their instability and inefficiency.[3]

4

On the surface the problems that faced Syria (and the neighbouring Arab countries) in the few years before the Suez crisis in 1956 were, apart from preoccupation with the future of Palestine and the menace of Israel's existence, domestic politics and the execution of certain social and economic development measures. In reality, however, even purely domestic affairs depended to a degree on the policies and interests of the major powers in the Middle East as a whole. To begin with, the tripartite declaration of 1950 made by Britain, France and the United States concerning the maintenance of armistice lines and a balance of armament between the Arab states and Israel antagonised the Arab world almost as much as did the partition of Palestine.

Thus when in the following year Egypt was invited to join these powers and Turkey in a Middle East defence organisation the invitation was rejected. To Egypt and the other Arab states, defence meant against Israel; to these powers it meant against Russia. Besides, Egypt was against the whole idea while her territory was, and would have continued to be, occupied by British troops under another label. She became even less likely to join a western defence pact after the revolution of 1952 which eventually placed Jamāl 'Abdu'n-Nāṣir (Nasser) in power, at the head of a socialist and pan-Arab neutralist regime. The regime was ready enough to come to an agreement with Britain for the evacuation of British troops, but not for any defence alliance as envisaged before.

The United States, however, was actively promoting such an alliance. Ever since America replaced Britain in helping Greece to prevent a communist take-over, and ever since American active support helped the creation of Israel, American involvement in the Middle East had become an accomplished fact. Containment of communism was the aim of American policy. If the Arabs refused to play others must be found. Promises of American aid brought Turkey and Pakistan together in 1954 in a defence pact. Other countries forming links between the two were invited to join. Iraq was persuaded to adhere to the pact in the following year, because Britain agreed to do so and to free Iraq from some outdated restrictoins under the Anglo–Iraq treaty. This was the origin of the Baghdad Pact, and the cause of a rift in the Arab camp. It had immense influence on the course of Syrian politics. Syria followed Egypt in rejecting the idea of joining a western defence alliance, and each declared their intention of strengthening the existing Collective Security Pact signed under the auspices of the Arab League.

From the beginning of 1955 Syria turned generally more and more in the direction of Egypt. A defence pact was signed with Egypt and Saudi Arabia that foreshadowed an Arab federation open to all states without foreign commitments – a clear thrust at Iraq. The military aspect of the pact strained Syria's relations with Turkey who was reported to have moved troops close to the frontiers with Syria. This must have been a form of blackmail, or an encouragement to a segment of Syrian opinion that favoured adhesion to the Baghdad Pact. For Turkey knew well enough, even before Syria's formal assurance, that the Arab pact was designed with Israel not Turkey in mind.

The Syrian opinion that favoured an alliance with the West against communism was represented mainly by the Syrian Nationalist Party and a few influential individuals like Ḥasan al-Ḥakīm. The Ba'th Party took exactly the opposite view. The two views were brought to the fore by the murder in April of Colonel 'Adnān al-Māliki, deputy chief of the general staff. At the trial the prosecution sought to establish that the accused, mostly members of the Syrian Nationalist Party and sympathisers, had conspired with agents of the United States with a view to overthrowing the Syrian government and installing another amenable to American influence.

The protracted trial had the effect of alienating Syria from America and her allies, and of preparing the way for a swing towards friendship with Russia. It had the further effect of eliminating the Syrian Nationalist Party from Syrian politics. Not only was it dissolved and its assets confiscated, but its members and associates in the civil service and army were dismissed. Eight of the accused were sentenced to death, five *in absentia*, and eighteen to various terms of imprisonment. Only two of those condemned to death were actually shot; the third's sentence was commuted to life imprisonment.

The suppression of the Syrian Nationalist Party was in a sense a triumph for the communists. But the growth in Syria of a tendency to cultivate friendship with Russia must not be mistaken, as it was in the middle of the 1950s, as an acceptance of communism. It was partly a protest against continued Western support for Israel and denial of justice to the Arabs of Palestine, particularly the refugees, and partly as a desire to secure arms and loans without political conditions.

Positive moves towards the Soviet bloc were made from 1954. In that year Russia and a number of her satellites participated in the International Fair at Damascus, and a Soviet cultural centre was opened in the city. This was followed by the visit to Russia of a Syrian parliamentary delegation. In 1955 a trade agreement was signed under which Russia supplied machinery and chemicals and bought agricultural products. In the following year a cultural agreement was signed for the exchange of teachers and the introduction of the teaching of Russian in some Syrian institutions. A Syrian military mission visited Russia also in the same year. Later still an arms deal was negotiated with Czechoslovakia, and a Czech firm subsequently won a contract to build a government-owned refinery at Ḥimṣ. In addition a barter trade agreement was concluded with Poland.

At the same time Syria was turning away from the United States and her allies. The Johnson Plan for the apportionment of the waters of the Jordan river with Israel was rejected by Syria, probably because it was so much favoured by the United States government. American technical assistance, commonly known as Point Four, was also rejected. Syria even rejected a loan of $25 million offered by the International Bank of Reconstruction and Development to finance development projects recommended by a team of experts sent by the Bank at the request of the Syrian government.[4] It was represented by agitators as 'American imperialism', possibly because the Bank was in Washington.

Such was the general political atmosphere in Syria when in August 1955 the presidential elections were held amid an economic slump. There were two candidates: Khālid al-'Aẓm, then minister for foreign affairs, and the former president Shukri al-Quwwatli who had lived in Alexandria since 1949 and returned soon after Shishakli's downfall. 'Aẓm, a rich landowner and leader of the newly formed Democratic Bloc, counted on the support of some twenty-eight deputies and an unknown number of supporters from minority parties including the Ba'th and the Communists. Quwwatli had followers among all the old guard politicians and his chances remained precarious till the People's Party decided to support him. He was elected after a second ballot.

Quwwatli lost none of his old capacity to sound the clarion call of unity. In a message to the chamber and to the public he called for a national government and a united political front including all the parties. He specifically mentioned the danger of Israel's territorial expansion at the expense of the Arabs and warned the Syrians to be prepared. The call did not go unheeded. What came out of it was a national charter to serve as a guide to future governments in internal and external affairs. All the parties, including the Communists, subscribed to it.

There was hardly anything new in the national charter; it laid down general principles which no party or politician could not endorse. Under foreign affairs, Syria's determination to remain neutral between the West and the East, to refuse to join any foreign military alliance and to continue to struggle with other Arab states against Zionist imperialism, was categorically reaffirmed. Under domestic affairs, special stress was laid on strengthening the army and civil defence, raising by public subscription additional funds for the armed forces (which realised over four million dollars) and proceeding with social and economic development schemes designed to increase the national wealth, raise the standard of living and promote 'social justice'.

Here it might be asked how such schemes of social and economic development could be executed without foreign technical aid and capital, for while these were refused from western sources they were not sought to any great extent from the Soviet bloc. At this stage there was no more than a trend in that direction, largely for the supply of arms. Syria still preferred to proceed with her plans using her own resources. Her economy was of course based on private enterprise in which the state exercised little control, though increasing guidance. Thus the reclamation and irrigation schemes were financed from public funds, but entrepreneurs and not the state cultivated the reclaimed land.

And yet Syria earned an increasing amount of foreign money without any political risks, money which was directly or indirectly used for development in that it increased the treasury receipts. The source of this money was the oil companies whose pipelines from Iraq and Saudi Arabia passed through Syrian territory to the Mediterranean ports. Transit dues and fees for protection and other services were paid in accordance with agreements between the companies and the Syrian government. These agreements were frequently revised, always to Syria's advantage. Thus in 1955–6 the Iraq Petroleum Company paid £6·5 million in transit dues, and an agreed lump sum of £8·8 million on the ratification of the agreement.

Without major foreign aid, however, Syrian achievements during the first decade after independence are impressive indeed, despite and sometimes as a result of military *coups*. Let us take a few examples to illustrate the spectacular growth in agriculture (with the reminder that Syria's economy was largely agricultural and only one-tenth of its national income was derived from industry). The area of cultivated land had been doubled since 1938, cotton production had risen to eight times its pre-war level and grain production had doubled in the years 1943–53.[5] New machinery was introduced only on a small scale, and the growth in production was due to reclamation and irrigation works which opened virgin soil in the Jazīrah province and elsewhere for development. Similarly the machinery introduced in industry was not on any large scale, and the small growth here was the result of an increase in local demand for locally produced articles. A certain amount of textiles and grain was exported every year, but most of the industrial and agricultural products were consumed locally by an increasing population with demands for clothing, food and housing.

Despite economic growth traditional methods die hard. The ox-drawn plough was perhaps more in evidence than the tractor, and the old handloom was still competing with the modern textile mill. But increased sophistication in the population and judicious application of capital by investors necessitated the adaptation of the skills of the old generation of artisans to new methods and machinery in the production, among several other new commodities, of sugar, cigarettes, cement and glass. The process ultimately led to the training of a new generation of skilled artisans and labourers in these and other industries.

5

Quwwatli's second presidency proved even more turbulent than the first. Once more it was the Palestine question which set off a chain of actions and reactions that upset the whole Middle East. Early in 1955 Israel launched a surprise military attack on Egyptian positions in the Gaza area, which revealed to Nāṣir the insufficiency of his weapons even for defence. Refused supplies by the West, he turned to the Soviet bloc and concluded a deal with Czechoslovakia for the supply of arms.

Nāṣir's move encouraged those in Syria who had been advocating a similar move since 1951. But neither Egypt nor Syria had any definite intention of dealing only with the Soviet bloc to the exclusion of others. Hence Egypt's project of building the High Dam was planned on this assumption. Loans had been negotiated with the International Bank, Britain, the United States and the Soviet Union. The withdrawal of the American promise of a loan, immediately followed by the withdrawal of a similar British promise, provoked the nationalisation of the Suez Canal Company.

The rest of the story that culminated in the concerted Israeli and Anglo–French attacks on Egypt does not directly belong to the history of Syria. Nevertheless it had profound repercussions on Syrian politics and history. Some time before the crisis Syria declared her intention of negotiating union with Egypt. A few days before the tripartite attack on Egypt a joint military command of Egypt, Syria and Jordan was set up. That neither of the two allies went to Egypt's help was at the express orders, twice repeated, of the Egyptian commander-in-chief who saw the futility of involving Syria and Jordan. For in the face of the Anglo–French intervention Egypt could lend neither Syria nor Jordan any military assistance.[6]

Junior Syrian officers, without orders from the government, did, however, try to hamper oil supplies to Britain and France at great cost to Syria and Lebanon and at greater cost to Iraq. Several pumping stations of the pipeline of the Iraq Petroleum Company were blown up immediately after the Anglo–French attack was launched. Permission to repair the line and allow the flow of oil was given only after British, French and Israeli forces had evacuated Arab territory. A fortuitous result of the tripartite attack was the personal intervention of President Quwwatli with the Soviet government. He had been on a state visit when the attack was made, and his presence in Moscow may have accounted for the vehemence of the Soviet threats to Britain and France. But Quwwatli returned with more tangible promises of Russian technical and economic aid and supply of arms.

One of the strange episodes in Syrian history during the Suez crisis was the trial of some forty politicians, including deputies, army officers and members of the dissolved Syrian Nationalist Party, on a charge of conspiring with Iraq, Britain and France to take advantage of the confusion and overthrow the Syrian government and to call in the Iraqi troops then stationed in Jordan since the beginning of the crisis. The accused were tried early in 1957 by a military court, since martial law declared on account of the crisis was still in force. Heavy sentences were passed. Among those condemned to death was ʿAdnān al-Atāsi, a deputy and son of the former president. It was only the pressure of Arab public opinion, particularly outside Syria, that saved his neck. He was among those whose sentence was commuted to life imprisonment.

Since many of the accused were prominent politicians of the old school, the trial administered another blow to their diminishing prestige. Although still numerically important they pulled less weight than minority parties or groups with better organisation and tactics. Both the Baʿth and the Communists stood to gain from the discredit of the old politicians. For somewhat different reasons both parties were against the traditional oligarchs and for national liberation and greater unity among the Arab peoples. The two parties maintained an uneasy alliance with each other as well as with the independent Democratic Bloc led by the 'red millionaire', Khālid al-ʿAẓm.

The accession of the radicals to power is reflected in Ṣabri al-ʿAsali's second cabinet formed on 31 December 1956. The ministries of foreign affairs and national economy were given to the Baʿth, while Khālid joined as minister of state, later of defence. The three ministers exercised a much greater control over policy and public affairs than their representation in the chamber warranted. But the Baʿth had a special appeal to the younger intelligentsia and counted a number of army officers among its sympathisers. Khālid now stood as the champion of an orientation towards Russia. That such a left-wing minority could exercise so much influence was largely because of the weakness of the right-wing majority.

This trend in Syrian politics continued until the discovery of yet other foreign conspiracies increased an anti-western feeling in the country. In July 1957 it was officially announced that a spy ring centred in the British Embassy which had been interested in information about communist influence in Syria had now turned its attention to spying on the army. In August another official announcement accused the United States of plotting to overthrow the Syrian government and replace it by another more agreeable to American policy. Accordingly three members of the Embassy, including the military attaché, were asked to leave the country. The United States replied by giving the Syrian ambassador his passport and asking the American ambassador then on leave not to return to his post.

Once more the left exploited the situation and succeeded in installing members or sympathisers in key positions in the civil and diplomatic services and in the police and army. These successes were so greatly exaggerated that American statesmen, ever sensitive about real or imaginary communist influence, believed that Syria had turned communist and that a communist take-over was imminent. Neither contingency was, however, possible. Of the two left-wing parties the Communists had the least chance of forming a government by constitutional or other means. The other party, the Baʿth, was Arab nationalist with a socialist, not communist, philosophy. These facts must have been known to the Americans who were really anxious about the growth of Soviet influence through the supply of arms and economic aid in an area which had been a western preserve. In the very month the above mentioned American conspiracy to overthrow the Syrian government was uncovered, Khālid al-ʿAẓm, by then deputy prime minister with supervision of defence, finance and development, returned from Moscow with promises of further economic aid and arms.

It was in this atmosphere that the so-called Eisenhower doctrine had been developing since Suez.[7] After the final eclipse of British and French influence in the Middle East there was, according to American reasoning, a power vacuum which communism might fill if not forestalled by America. Accordingly Eisenhower offered to help, with money, arms and if necessary armed forces, those states that feared 'armed aggression from any nation controlled by international communism'. It was refused by Syria, the most dangerous spot in American reckoning. Once more America was reminded that to the Arabs the menace was Israel, America's protégé, not communism.

Like the invitations to join western defence alliances the present American offer was regarded as interference in Arab affairs. This feeling was crudely and undiplomatically expressed by a press comment that a vacuum existed not in the Middle East but in Eisenhower's head. Such popularity as he had gained for his opposition to the tripartite attack against Egypt was almost entirely abolished by the suspicion, symbolised in the story of the August 1957 plot to overthrow the Syrian government, that America was seeking to impose her own 'new imperialism' in place of the old British and French imperialism.

But unlike the attempts of 1951 and 1954–5 the present American initiative was more successful, perhaps because of the subtlety of its indirect application. American aid was accepted by Saudi Arabia, Jordan and Lebanon, and that constituted the second rift on the score of defence in the Arab camp since Iraq joined the Baghdad Pact. The result was to increase the feeling of insecurity and isolation in Syria. She was now completely encircled: by the enemy in Israel, by a potentially hostile Turkey, and by two sister Arab states consorting with potential enemies according to Syrian assessment. This left only Egypt towards which Syria had been moving since 1955. The movement was now greatly accelerated by events.

Syria was subjected to indirect but mounting American pressure. There was fear of either Turkey or Israel being used as a stick to beat the Syrian government. Thus following a visit by an American under-secretary of state to Ankara, Baghdad, Beirut and Amman, Turkish troops were either concentrated or purposely held manoeuvres near the Syrian border. Syria immediately lodged a complaint with the United Nations against Turkey and the United States. Simultaneously the Syrian and Egyptian armies were placed under a joint command, and a token Egyptian force was landed at Latakia. While two Soviet warships arrived at the port, Khrushchev issued a violent warning to Turkey. For their part the United States declared that they would help Turkey, their NATO ally.

In reality, however, neither of the two great powers wanted the Syrian affair to develop into a major war. Behind the scenes, at the United Nations and elsewhere, the parties to the conflict smoothed over their differences and by December the crisis was past. Turkish troops had either been withdrawn or had completed their manoeuvres and America and Syria agreed to resume diplomatic relations. America must have perceived the predictable course of Arab politics in the face of external danger. Although Syria was suspected of designs to annex Jordan, and that suspicion strained its relations with Jordan and Iraq and even Saudi Arabia, these and other Arab states declared their unanimous support of Syria against possible aggression (in this case Turkish with American backing).

But Syria's movement towards closer relations with Egypt was more evident than any other in the Arab camp. External dangers and internal political instability made it imperative. Egypt's support during the Turkish–American crisis provided an object lesson. Before the crisis was resolved an Egyptian parliamentary delegation visited Syria in November and was invited to attend a session of the Syrian chamber, when a joint resolution was taken urging the two governments to open negotiations for a federal union. Thereafter the Baʿth party was the principal promoter of the union, despite the hesitation of the Egyptian government and President Nāṣir himself. The success of the move was due largely to the efforts of the Baʿth party. That a minority party could carry the majority with it was due to its espousal of a popular national cause which no other political group could oppose and survive. Arab unity had been the aim of the national movement since its inception in Syria itself. It was frustrated by the imperialism of Britain and France. Now that imperialism had gone there was a splendid opportunity to join Syria to Egypt and lay the corner-stone of Arab unity by opening the way to other Arab states to join.

So much has been said about the Baʿth tactical aims of out-manoeuvring other rival Syrian parties, and even more about an exaggerated communist danger, that the fundamentally idealistic character of the move has been blurred. There was an essential affinity between the Baʿth's philosophy and Nāṣir's socialism. But when it came to discussing terms Nāṣir knew that the Baʿth did not represent Syria. Accordingly other political and military leaders were drawn in, including ultimately President Quwwatli and his prime minister. The delegation that hurried to Cairo met a sympathetic but reluctant Nāṣir. He certainly needed much persuasion.

When in the end Nāṣir was persuaded he laid down certain conditions suggested to him by the Baʿth and accepted by other Syrian leaders. The two countries must unite, not federate; the union must be approved by the Syrian and Egyptian people through a plebiscite; the army must not interfere in politics; and all political parties must be dissolved to give place to the National Union as in Egypt. On 5 February 1958 Quwwatli announced the impending union with Egypt and nominated Nāṣir for the presidency. Four days later he called upon Lebanon to join, with guarantees of its special status, and invited other Arab states to consider moves in that direction.

The union with Nāṣir's presidency was approved by an overwhelming majority, and was formally proclaimed on 22 February. Quwwatli stepped down and retired with the honour of being declared the first citizen of the United Arab Republic. Under the new dispensation Syria became the north region and Egypt the south region of the union. Each region had its local executive council and ministers, but the union cabinet sat in Cairo, the capital. The first union cabinet was composed of fifteen Syrians and twenty Egyptians. There were four vice-presidents, two of whom were Syrians, the last prime minister and a prominent Baʿth leader. A national assembly of 400 members, one-fourth from Syria, was envisaged pending the election of a national union in Syria from whose members representatives to the National Assembly would be selected.

6

To judge by the first outburst of public enthusiasm the union with Egypt was immensely popular in Syria. Nāṣir was received in Damascus as a national hero, and there were great expectations that the union was the first step towards the United Arab States. There is ample evidence that similar enthusiasm for the union and expectations for the future prevailed among nationalists outside Syria.

Nevertheless the formation of the United Arab Republic was a challenge to the old regimes in a number of Arab states, particularly those tinged with western connections or sympathies. Their rulers knew that Quwwatli's appeal fired the imagination of many nationalists among their subjects. They were aware of the emotional appeal of Arab unity to the politically conscious even among the masses. They were accordingly the first to react, but not as suggested by Quwwatli. If the move towards the Syro-Egyptian union by the autocratic Imam of Yemen is disregarded as of no immediate significance, the action taken by the Hashemite kings of Iraq and Jordan is very striking. Their best answer to the challenge was to form a federation of their two kingdoms which, however, failed to arouse much enthusiasm in the Arab world.

Given the choice the large majority of Muslims in Lebanon would certainly have opted for union with Syria. But Lebanon as a whole, already shaken by internal strife and divided over the issue of American aid, was from May 1958 the scene of a domestic insurrection which the United Arab Republic was accused of fomenting by 'massive intervention'. The United Nations observers found nothing to justify the accusation, which appears to have been made as a smoke-screen to hide a desire to invite American intervention. Such intervention had already been contemplated, and its necessity became apparent in July following a revolution in Iraq which overthrew the monarchy. American marines were immediately landed at Beirut at the request of the Lebanese president, 'for the protection of American lives and for the encouragement of Lebanon to defend its sovereignty and integrity'. Almost simultaneously a British parachute brigade was landed at ʻAmman in response to a request from King Ḥusain who feared that his throne might not survive another shaking such as it had suffered the previous April.

American and British intervention not only angered the United Arab Republic but was resented at the United Nations. The Soviet Union condemned it in strong terms. In the end it was the statesmanship of Dag Hammarskjöld, not any agreement among the major powers concerned, that resolved the crisis. He suggested, and the Arab states agreed unanimously to reaffirm, the principle of non-interference in one another's internal affairs embodied in the Arab League Pact. Once this was done the machinery of the United Nation was used to get the United States and Britain to agree to withdraw their troops, and Lebanon to withdraw her complaint. By the beginning of November the crisis was resolved on these lines.

There is no evidence that Syria or Egypt had planned to absorb by force either Lebanon or Jordan, but there is little doubt that the outcome of the revolution in Iraq was a disappointment to pan-Arabists. Instead of promoting the cause of Arab unity by bringing his country closer to Syria and Egypt, the revolutionary ruler of Iraq, 'Abdul Karīm Qāsim, proved to be a separatist with a leaning towards communist elements. His feud with Nāṣir on that account is irrelevant to our subject, but more will be said about another attempt to bring in Iraq after the disappearance of Qāsim.

The United Arab Republic, however, survived the upheavals of the summer and autumn of 1958 by the removal of the potential danger of the presence of foreign troops close to her borders in Lebanon and Jordan. The return of peace was particularly welcome in the Syrian region where certain economic disadvantages had followed, but did not result from, the union with Egypt. The first year of the union was one of severe drought which continued for three years and, aggravated by locust invasions, resulted in a considerable reduction in agricultural production. Export trade was none too sound. Before the Suez crisis the greatest volume of exports was to Britain and France, who between them accounted for one-third of the total. The crisis had greatly reduced that trade, and contributed moreover to a new economic policy.

Contact with the Soviet bloc marked the beginning of this new policy, generally associated with Khālid al-'Aẓm. On his return from a visit to Moscow in 1957 he announced that he had concluded an agreement for marketing Syrian grain and cotton and that Russia had promised development loans, without political conditions and at a rate of interest more favourable than that of the International Bank. These loans were intended for financing power stations and irrigation works at the Euphrates, Orontes, Yarmūk and other Syrian water resources, a railway from Latakia to the Jazīrah province, various roads and bridges, chemical works for fertilisers and assembly plants for tractors.

The loans were about £S535·5 million at 2½ per cent interest.

Repayment, either in Syrian products or in freely convertible currency, was spread over twelve years. The above total was covered by twelve separate agreements each related to specific projects. Syria had the option of obtaining the required equipment and technical assistance for any of the projects from other countries if she could get more favourable terms than the Russians offered. Nearly a quarter of the expenditure envisaged under a ten-year development plan came from the Russian loan. In the fiscal year 1958–9 it was £S15·8 million out of a total of £S80·8 million; in 1959–60 it was £S43·4 million out of a total of £S161·1 million.[8]

Nothing in these plans was changed after the union with Egypt. The union government gave these plans its blessing. Indeed this government sought to accelerate the development by measures of its own which were designed to bring the Syrian economy into step with that of Egypt. Six months after the inauguration of the union two agrarian reform laws were passed. The first concerned agricultural labour and tenancy. Among other provisions it fixed minimum wages and maximum working hours, provided for the security of tenants and ensured for them fair shares of the crop. The second provided for the expropriation against compensation of land above certain limits and the distribution of the surplus land thus acquired to landless farmers, including beduins, at low prices payable over a period of forty years plus 1½ per cent interest per annum.

At the same time the constitutional change was slowly taking shape. The first step was the creation of the National Union which was to perform the functions of the old political parties. The Baʿth made every effort to delay its creation, hoping to gain control. In this they were disappointed, for when elections in the Syrian region were held in July 1959 they secured small representation, or roughly one in every forty. The Baʿth leaders had already been disappointed that, contrary to expectations, Nāṣir did not take the Baʿth members of his government as philosophers and guides. They now anticipated that they would pull even less weight in the forthcoming National Assembly.

The Baʿth grumbling about the 'domineering' Egyptians was rooted not in ideological differences but in a failure to exert more influence and power. It dawned upon them, as if for the first time since they had eagerly sought the union, that neither they nor the

Syrians as a whole could have more than a minority voice. Full realisation of this fact made them succumb to the chronic Syrian malady: habitual hostility to any government they cannot manipulate.

If union was the Baʿth's aim then the wider Arab national interest, not those of a political party, should have been the ruling principle of their conduct. For in such a common cause idealism, like love, 'suffereth long' and does not distinguish between a majority and a minority. The Baʿth surely helped to create the U.A.R. and as surely contributed to wreck it. In December 1959 the four Baʿth members of the government tendered their collective resignations, having failed in a rather conspiratorial manner to persuade some Egyptian members to do the same. There is no evidence that they discussed their complaints, of whatever nature, in the cabinet or with the president. Nor did they publish any intelligible explanation.

Henceforth Nāṣir depended on Colonel ʿAbdul-Ḥamīd Sarrāj, regional minister of the interior in Damascus, who before the union had been in charge of military intelligence and wielded great influence. But Syria has never been easy to govern throughout its recent history. It experienced Egyptian rule in the nineteenth century when Ibrāhīm Pasha found the Syrians very difficult. It is not known whether Nāṣir drew any lessons from the experience of his predecessor. But he tried to be conciliatory by posting the Egyptian first vice-president to Damascus with this end in view. And when finally the National Assembly was inaugurated in Cairo in 1960, over half the Syrian members had been members of the last chamber of deputies – thus old notables were not passed over in favour of new elements, but the Baʿth remained a minority group.

The Syrian executive council was encouraged to implement the agrarian reforms. These were first applied in 116 villages and £S5 million was allocated for loans to aid the settlement of new tenants on the land. Afforestation was undertaken near Damascus, Ḥama and Latakia. A Yugoslav firm was awarded a contract to build a new port at Ṭarsūs. A new dam on the Orontes was actually completed. Nāṣir himself inaugurated a railway to link Latakia with Aleppo. Trade between the two regions was liberalised, with the balance in favour of Syria, the value of whose exports to Egypt was in 1959 some £S68 million, and imports from Egypt £S41 million.

Further measures were adopted to bring the Syrian economy into step with that of Egypt. In the spring of 1961 the Syrian banks, except the Central Bank which was the state bank, were nationalised. The nationalisation decree stipulated that all banks must be joint-stock companies, each with a minimum capital of £S3 million. At least 35 per cent of the capital must be owned by the state. In July major industrial and commercial concerns were nationalised.

While the agrarian reforms were popular among the peasants and labourers, they constituted an assault on the privileges of the rich landlords who had hitherto formed the core of the political leaders. The nationalisation laws affected in another way the rich landlords who had employed capital in industry, commerce and banking, as they affected the comparatively new entrepreneurs who amassed fortunes specially during and after the Second World War. But the agrarian reforms and the nationalisation laws were undoubtedly designed to effect more equitable distribution of the national wealth and to realise a measure of much invoked 'social justice'.

Abstract justice was invoked by some Syrian elements when they claimed that their just interests, which some of them tended to equate with those of Syria, had not been respected in the union. These elements included the conservative rich who lost position and some fortune under the union, the opportunists who infiltrated the National Union, some ministers who rightly or wrongly complained of lack of influence on policy, a few members of parliament whose oratory found no scope in Cairo, and some small merchants and shopkeepers who were irritated by new procedures and restrictions. There is no evidence that the Ba'th resorted to active subversion after the resignations.

But none of these elements, alone or in combination with some or all of the others, could wreck the union. It was in the end the usual Syrian method: a wing of the army in alliance with conservative politicians and with the encouragement of two neighbouring states staged the familiar *coup* on 28 September 1961. Syrian soldiers, like Syrian politicians, complained of too much subordination to Egyptians, even though they knew in advance that they would be under Egyptian command. They also complained that their pay had to be reduced to the lower Egyptian level. Added to these complaints was the constant factor of the chronic itch in the Syrian army to interfere in order to right grievances, real or imaginary.

Although the union and Nāṣir personally had a large following in the country and in the army itself, he decided not to oppose the *coup* by force in order to avoid shedding Arab blood. But the indecent haste with which Jordan and Turkey recognised the leaders of the *coup* provided circumstantial evidence of their complicity. Nāṣir broke off diplomatic relations with both states.

7

The Arabic equivalent of secession (*infiṣāl*) with its derivations immediately acquired a bad connotation in the modern Arabic political vocabulary. The secessionists who proclaimed the Syrian Arab Republic after the disruption of the union with Egypt had therefore a difficult task to justify their action, particularly in the face of Nāṣir's decision to retain the name United Arab Republic as a challenge and an aspiration. Hence the prime minister of the new Syrian regime hastened, ten days after assuming office, to put forward to other Arab governments a plan for a federation. The regime's position was, however, greatly strengthened when the secession was publicly approved by the former prime ministers and the two leading Baʿth members who had previously resigned from the union government. Nevertheless the secession cost the Baʿth a considerable loss of members through protest resignations.

One of the first acts of the new regime was to amend the electoral law. By the middle of November a new constitution was formed declaring the Syrian Arab Republic as an independent sovereign state and 'part of the greater Arab homeland'. A plebiscite on the constitution and a general election were held simultaneously. Nāṣir's open supporters boycotted both, but the electorate approved the constitution and returned an overwhelmingly conservative chamber. Nāẓim al-Qudsi, of the People's Party, was elected president of the republic.

His party and their associates of landlords and rich merchants were the enemies of nationalisation and disliked the agrarian reforms. They were now in power, and early in 1962 the nationalisation laws were repealed and replaced by much milder government control over large concerns. The agrarian reform laws could not be repealed without causing social unrest, and hence they were enfeebled by amendments. From Cairo the voice of Nāṣir thundered that the Syrian regime did not represent the wishes of the Syrian people, and 'capitalists and monopolists' could not be trusted as guardians of social reform.

Without Nāṣir's recognition the Syrian government was as isolated as when four years earlier their predecessors threw themselves into his arms. Once more the old itch seized the army. On 28 March 1962 the president of the republic, the prime minister and prominent members of the chamber were arrested. In the army's estimate they had failed to work for Arab unity and abused their office. Demonstrations in the principal towns demanded reunion with Egypt, and senior army officers held secret conversations with Nāṣir. Apparently he refused to intervene because of lack of absolute unanimity in the army. He had been elected president by a vast majority and was not prepared to come back through minority groups.

After a period of two weeks' suspense and confusion, the army restored Qudsi with a more 'progressive' prime minister but the chamber remained dissolved. At the same time the chief of staff announced that the army desired 'a sound Arab unity with the liberated Arab states headed by Egypt'. A bargain with Qudsi seems to have been struck, for immediately on his release the largest business combine was renationalised, and the agrarian reform laws re-enacted with the minimum of amendments. A little later forty mechanised or semi-mechanised flour mills were nationalised.

Mercifully political upheavals interfered little with the execution of development plans or the agrarian reforms. Thus in the summer of 1962, land acquired under the agrarian reform laws was distributed to landless tenants in five villages in Ḥimṣ province, and to similar tenants in twenty-three villages in Aleppo province. In the same summer the dam on the Orontes was inaugurated.

It is noteworthy that the great landowner Khālid al-'Aẓm, who became prime minister in September, declared that his government would uphold the principle of 'social justice' and proceed with the agrarian reforms. It would also work towards Arab unity and restitution of the Arabs of Palestine and maintain neutral policy in international relations. But the secessionist regime as a whole was a dismal failure. None of the four successive governments lasted more than four months. Quarrels between the politicians and factions in the army rendered stable government impossible. The country was steadily heading towards another upheaval.

Such an upheaval, however, took place in Iraq first. On 8 February 1963 an army *coup* put an end to Qāsim's regime and brought to power a branch of the Baʿth party. The head of state was the chairman of the National Revolutionary Council, General ʿAbdu's-Salām ʿĀrif. As a friend and admirer of Nāṣir, he headed a delegation to Cairo and attended the celebration of Arab Unity Day on 22 February, the anniversary of the formation of the union between Egypt and Syria.

Two weeks later on 8 March the army took over in Syria and set up a National Revolutionary Council under the chairmanship of General Luai al-Atāsi which invited the Baʿth leader, Ṣalāh Baiṭār, to form a government of military and civilian ministers. One of the first actions of the new government was to issue a statement in which they declared that their aim was to lead Syria back to reunion with Egypt, this time in company with Iraq. At the same time General Atāsi declared that the army had been purged of secessionists. A little later the Revolutionary Council placed civilian secessionists, including former ministers, under restrictions.[9]

Baiṭār had lived to regret and withdraw his public approval of the secession. He now thought he was in a stronger position to negotiate with Nāṣir. It is true that the Baʿth had in 1961 been split into its two original components, and that it had been further weakened by the withdrawal of those who disapproved of the secession, but its Iraqi allies compensated in a way for the losses. The truth is that the Baʿth needed Nāṣir's prestige, but he had not forgotten the 'crime' of their collective resignation. He now made it clear that he would reunite with Syria but not with the Baʿth. Nor would he negotiate with Syria through Iraq.

Accordingly it was a delegation of a coalition Syrian government that joined an Iraqi delegation in talks with Nāṣir in March-April 1963. A record of the talks was officially published in Cairo in some 600 small-type pages, abounding in Egyptian and Syrian colloquial Arabic and with occasional sparkles of humour.[10] The accuracy of the record was challenged by the Baʿth after they had fallen out with Nāṣir but, despite their claim that they had 'complete minutes of the talks', they did not publish an alternative account nor did they produce convincing evidence that the Cairo record is not a substantial representation of the actual exchanges.

If the record shows the Syrian Baʿth leaders as vague, incoherent and tongue-tied it is largely because they were supplicants and had much to answer for to a Nāṣir who was naturally anxious, before committing himself to another venture, to hold an inquest on the failure of the first union, to review the conduct of the Baʿth while it lasted, and to discover their motives in seeking another and wider one.

In the end an agreement was reached on 17 April 1963, virtually on Nāṣir's terms:[11] it was for a presidential system embracing the three 'regions' in a tripartite federal union. On the constitution and president of the federal union a referendum was to be held not later than five months after the agreement. The constitutional establishment of the federal state was to begin on the date of the announcement of the results of the referendum. A transition period of twenty months was to follow for adjustment. (Syria had then, according to an official bulletin, a population of 5,307,753.)

Scarcely had the Cairo agreement been signed when discord reappeared both in the Syrian army and government. While the Baʿth glorified Nāṣir they were at loggerheads with his supporters in Syria. A purge of some of these in senior positions in the army led to the resignation of three non-Baʿth ministers in the coalition. Despite official pronouncements the Baʿth leaders themselves were not really decided what attitude to take towards the proposed union. The confusion of thought and action was reflected in Baiṭār's contradictory measures. He had some politicians and army officers arrested and charged with causing the 'crime' of secession in 1961, and he renationalised the denationalised banks which Nāṣir had nationalised. And yet his minister of the interior, General Amīn al-Ḥāfiẓ, suppressed with a severity reminiscent of General Sarrail an uprising of Nāṣir's sympathisers in Aleppo and Damascus. On 18 July he used planes, tanks and artillery to suppress the uprising in Damascus staged by civilians and some army officers. Twenty men, including eight soldiers one of whom was a colonel, were executed on the spot by a firing squad.

Four days later Nāṣir declared the agreement of 17 April was with the Syrian people, not with the Baʿth. He could not deal with a secessionist government that did not represent the Syrian people, nor with its leaders who showed no respect for humanity and moral law.

The rift between the Baʿth and Nāṣir was once more public. It was reflected immediately in a shift of power inside the Revolutionary Council. General Atāsi was replaced by General Ḥāfiẓ, the 'butcher' of 18 July who had before the end of the month become chairman of the Revolutionary Council, commander-in-chief, deputy prime minister and minister of defence in addition to being minister of the interior. In a cabinet reshuffle the latter post was a few days later given to Dr Nur'ud-Dīn al-Atāsi. In November a new cabinet was formed with Ḥāfiẓ as prime minister. As chairman of the Revolutionary Council he was also head of state. Baiṭār was now given not a cabinet post, but the decorative title of deputy chairman of the council.

Unity remained the official aim, and public declarations confirmed it in very strong terms. Thus on 28 September, the anniversary of Syria's secession from the union with Egypt, the Revolutionary Council declared that the day was 'the most tragic in our recent history'. Rejected by Nāṣir, the Syrian Baʿth leaders turned to their comrades in Iraq with a view to establishing a bilateral union. The utmost they could settle was a 'military union', and even this was soon to end in failure.

The Baʿth in Iraq proved even less united and efficient than their Syrian brethren. In November 1963 ʿĀrif took over complete control as president, and appointed a cabinet which quickly lost its Baʿth complexion. He strengthened the ties with Egypt at the expense of loosening those with Syria, and this unfortunate country found itself once more completely isolated and without friends. In addition to the quarrel with Egypt she had now picked another with Iraq. Her relations with Jordan were strained and there were incidents on her borders with Lebanon. She still had an unfriendly Turkey to the north and the enemy in Israel to the south-west.

At the end of 1963, while still talking of Arab unity, Syria was engaged in an inter-Arab propaganda war that served only to increase disunity. But in January 1964 one of those surprises in Arab politics took place. The Arab League, at Nāṣir's suggestion, called a summit conference of heads of states to consider what measures could be taken to prevent or counteract Israel's project of diverting the Jordan waters. Syria as represented by Amīn al-Ḥāfiẓ advocated military action, while other heads of state, including Nāṣir, felt that the Arabs were not yet ready for such an adventure.[12] Accordingly they decided to divert the waters of the tributaries Ḥāṣbāni, Bānyās and Yarmūk, rising in Lebanon, Syria and Jordan respectively, and to set up a joint military command as a defensive measure against a possible Israeli attempt to interfere.

The diversion scheme prepared by a committee of experts envisaged two stages: a long-term one which included the construction of dams and power stations and would take some eight to ten years to complete, and a short-term one which provided for irrigation canals and reservoirs and would take two years to execute. A special board, with an executive committee in each of the three countries concerned, was appointed under the chairmanship of the secretary-general of the Arab League who was to report progress to the next summit conference.

Until this was held at Alexandria in September 1964 the trend of Syrian politics was unmistakable. More and more power was concentrated in the hands of Ḥāfiẓ and less and less in those of Baiṭār. Although both, as well as the majority of the ministers, belonged to the Ba'th, and the leadership of the Revolutionary Council was professedly collective, there was in practice little distinction between Ḥāfiẓ and his military predecessors. According to a sympathetic observer, Syria had been delivered into the hands of 'a military dictatorship'.[13]

8

One of the redeeming features of a rather sombre political atmosphere was an unimpeded economic and social development. The vagaries of Ba'th politics were thus relieved by progress in agricultural and industrial production and even some improvement in the balance of trade. A ten-year development plan, which aimed at doubling the national income by 1970, began to pay dividends in the expansion of the social services.

There was a remarkable achievement in the field of education: for the first time in Syria's history places were provided at primary schools for *all* children born between the last quarter of 1956 and the end of 1957, immediately on reaching the statutory age of admission. Secondary education was so reorganised that its abstract content had been radically modified. About 26 per cent of the total pupils were in 1962–3 following various technical courses. In the same year five million Syrian pounds were allocated for the development of the university of Damascus and another five million for the expansion of the newer university of Aleppo.[14]

The budget of the development plan had been apportioned between public and private sectors. From 1964 the former was given more prominence because of a more vigorous 'application of socialist principles'. The shares of the two sectors for that year were, in round figures, £S316 million and £S197 million respectively. Of the former sum nearly 32 per cent came from foreign, largely Soviet aid. Allocations for the various projects, from the Euphrates dam and hydroelectric station to agricultural and industrial development schemes, public buildings, roads, railways, education, health and public utilities, are detailed in an official report with a wealth of statistics.[15]

There was now a separate ministry of agrarian reform through whose agencies land continued to be acquired and allocated to landless farmers who were immediately encouraged to form co-operatives. Furthermore, the Baʿth followed and extended Nāṣir's policy of nationalisation. This embraced among other industrial concerns weaving and spinning companies, firms that dealt with the processing and distribution of foodstuffs or the imports or manufacture of pharmaceutical and building material. The profits of the nationalised concerns were shared with the workers who also benefited, in certain areas, from a state housing scheme.

Apart from party members the Baʿth popularity was to be found among those peasants and workers who were the beneficiaries of these schemes. But it cannot be denied that the core of what remained an essentially conservative society evinced little sympathy for the regime. Indeed, there were powerful elements, religious, conservative and even liberal, who were definitely hostile. It was a gross simplification for the Baʿth to brand all these elements as reactionaries and feudalists. There were honest thinkers among them, who were disturbed by the Baʿth's domestic policy and its futile foreign policy.

Nor can it be denied that along with political upheavals and economic development there was a silent social revolution which, in different measures and at different levels, pervaded all strata of society. In the superficialities of dress, food, furniture and housing, urban society was virtually westernised. Even rural society did not remain unaffected through easier means of communication and visual and aural aids such as cinema, radio and the pictorial press. For both urban and rural areas the spread of education was hastening the process of change and affecting the ideological basis of society.

The revolution – political, economic and social – which Syria had been going through since independence had, despite official protestations to the contrary, presented a challenge to Islamic values. By the time the Baʿth came to power conservative Muslim opinion began to be disturbed, not so much by socialism which is not irreconcilable with Islam, as by an uncompromising secularism which drove religion out of public life.

It was not 'reaction' nor 'feudalism' nor 'fanaticism' but honest belief that voiced vigorous protests in 1964. The movement began in April at Ḥama when the *imams* denounced the 'godless' Baʿth from the pulpits of the mosques. This was followed by student demonstrations and strikes in the city. From a mosque minaret the muezzin proclaimed 'God is great! Either Islam or the Baʿth'. On the pretext that shots were fired on the security forces from the minaret this edifice was shelled and its fall caused the death of sixty-five members of the congregation. Public anger was so great that a state of emergency had to be proclaimed.

The spread of the movement to Aleppo was just averted by the personal intervention of Nur'ud-Dīn al-Atāsi, the minister of the interior. He hurried to Aleppo and met merchants, trade unionists and other citizens, and explained that the flare-up at Ḥama was not between believers in God and atheists. 'We are', he declared 'believers in God and are faithful to the homeland.' However, Damascus itself was the scene of the next protest later in the same month. An *imam* of one of the city's mosques denounced the Baʿth regime as the persecutors of his class, enemies of individual freedom and shedders of innocent blood.[16]

These protests were accompanied by public demands for the end of the state of emergency and the return to parliamentary government. Some Syrian opposition groups outside the country published the view that the Baʿth had betrayed its own principles and turned 'regionist and fascist'. It may not therefore be an accident that on 24 April an interim constitution was published.[17] It describes the 'Syrian region' as a popular, democratic and socialist republic, and its inhabitants as a part of the Arab nation and believers in Arab unity.

As in former constitutions the religion of the head of state was Islam, and Islamic law was 'a major source of legislation'. But one of the novelties of this constitution is the stress on public ownership of the means of production. The former parliamentary system was tacitly scrapped: legislative powers were vested in the National Revolutionary Council, and executive powers in a presidential council and the cabinet. The judiciary remained independent, though military courts could monopolise much of its function. (The title of president of the republic was abolished by decree and the chairman of the Revolutionary Council assumed the position of head of state.)

This constitution did not diminish, indeed it exposed, the basic weakness of the Baʿth's title to govern the country. They came to power though a military *coup*, and their title had never been tested by a general election. In the practice of domestic government and in relations with other Arab states, the Baʿth cannot boast of major success. The party stood for 'unity, freedom and socialism'. Their contribution to Arab unity, despite public utterances, was a dismal failure, and in their conduct of government they paid scant respect to the freedom of the individual citizen or that of opposition groups. There remains to their credit a good measure of success in socialism, if tarnished by much bloodshed.

The brutality and sacrilege exhibited by the government at Ḥama did not check and appeared to have sharpened the opposition. The smouldering fire of opposition remained until there was a flare-up on 22 January 1965 in Damascus. In the Friday sermons in the city mosques the *imams* called upon the people to oppose the government 'in defence of religion and freedom'. Several *imams*, including a professor of Islamic jurisprudence at Damascus University, were arrested and sent for trial before an extraordinary military tribunal.

The government described the arrested persons as 'reactionaries and capitalists' bent on disturbing the peace in their opposition to nationalisation measures. The tribunal sentenced five of them to death, and the government confiscated sixty-nine shops whose owners refused an order to reopen when a protest strike was observed. The presidential council assumed by decree the power to appoint and dismiss *imams*, a power hitherto vested in the council for religious foundations.

In accordance with the familiar conduct of military regimes, the more opposition Syria's rulers met the more powers they assumed. Thus by decree they prolonged the life of the interim constitution to the end of July 1967. The ruling party itself was at the same time undergoing change. In May 1965 ʿAflaq retired as secretary-general and Dr Munīf Bazzāz was elected to succeed him. There were signs of differences among the members of the Revolutionary Council and the cabinet, which came to the surface later in the year. In September the strong man of the council gave up one of his top posts. Amīn al-Ḥāfiẓ resigned, or had to resign, as prime minister and was succeeded by Dr Yūsuf Zuʿain. In December Nur'ud-Dīn al-Atāsi, vice-chairman of the presidential council, with two other members resigned. Almost simultaneously Zuʿain submitted the resignation of his government, and was succeeded early in January 1966 by Ṣalāḥ Baiṭār.

The climax was reached on 23 February when, as a result of an army *coup*, Ḥāfiẓ and other senior members of the presidential council and cabinet were arrested. Two days later Atāsi emerged as the new chairman of the presidential council and soon Zuʿain returned as his prime minister. This *coup* was unique in the long series in that it was engineered by one wing of the ruling Baʿth party against another. It destroyed such unity as the party had presented in Syria and resulted in the dissolution of its old organisation and the ousting of its old leaders. Their successors in power were more doctrinaire socialists and militant nationalists.

They maintained a precarious hold on the reins of government, not without fear of deposition by the same means that had brought them to power. Like all their predecessors, if not to an even greater extent, the new regime pursued a belligerent policy on the Palestine question. As heirs of the early Syrian nationalists they regarded Palestine as the southern part of Syria. But they lacked the military strength to face Israel alone and refused to accept Nāṣir's assessment that the neighbouring Arab states were not yet ready for a showdown. Hence the encouragement of Palestine Arab commando raids on Israel from bases inside Syria. The routes of infiltration usually ran through Syria and Jordan.

Israel's repeated reply to these raids was carefully prepared surprise military attacks on villages inside Arab territory. No Arab army ever replied to these attacks in kind, not even when in July 1966 Israel used planes over Syrian territory for the first time. The Arab weakness had been publicly proclaimed when the scheme for the diversion of the waters of the Jordan tributaries was first whittled down by the second summit conference and then virtually shelved by the third. The frustration of Arab public opinion was well described by the question posed by the organ of the Baʿth party itself: 'Why do we only talk while our enemy acts?'

But the new Syrian government did more than talk on the home front. In August the second five-year development plan was approved with a budget of £S4955 million. Its aim was, according to Atāsi's declaration at the opening of the International Fair at Damascus, 'to guide Syria scientifically towards a developing socialist society . . .'. Later in the year Zuʿain declared that the second stage of the development plan was in full swing and that nationalisation had 'eliminated' capitalism. Before the end of the year an agreement was signed with Russia for the construction of the first stage of the Euphrates dam, and another with Czechoslovakia for the expansion of the Ḥimṣ refinery.

Nationalisation had its difficulties, however. In a community long accustomed to free enterprise, the more vigorous prosecution of nationalisation tended to create panic among the entrepreneurs, and this led to a flight of capital, particularly to Lebanon. But despite inevitable strains and stresses the socialist measures, now nearly a decade old, began to impress upon increasing numbers among the masses that they were at last enjoying a fair share of the national wealth.

9

To consolidate the economic and social benefits of the development plans Syria needed internal stability and absence of external complications. Both were denied her. In September 1966 an attempt by the old Baʿth leaders to regain power was foiled. The army officers and others who planned the *coup* fled to Jordan and were given political asylum. Although strictly in accordance with Arab tradition, Jordan's action was condemned by the Syrian government. Syria's major external problem, however, was Israel whose leaders began from the spring of 1966 to utter threats to 'teach a lesson' to those of her neighbours from whose territory Palestine Arab commandos, notably *al-Fataḥ*, launched their raids. Public threats by Israel were a new development. But they served only to draw counter-threats from the Syrian leaders, who declared their intention 'not to hinder the efforts of the Palestine Arabs to regain their homeland'.

The demilitarised zone between Syria and Israel remained one of the danger spots, and exchange of fire across the demarcation lines was frequent. Such an exchange was followed in July by an air battle. Syria's rulers were the prisoners of their own public statements of policy. They could not repudiate them and maintain themselves in power. On the other hand they realised that they could not gain their objective through their own military strength. They turned to Cairo and in November signed a joint defence pact with Nāṣir. It had two serious weaknesses: it did not cover 'limited' conflicts, and gave Egypt no air base on Syrian territory.

Nevertheless it has been surmised that this pact, fortified by Soviet warnings to Israel, diverted the next major Israeli surprise attack from Syria to Sammuʿ village in Jordan. This attack was condemned by the Security Council as an unwarranted aggression. Jordan had in fact managed, at the expense of her reputation in the Arab world and among the commando organisations, to keep peace along the armistice lines for nearly ten years.

Sammuʿ may therefore be regarded as a turning-point in the escalation towards war. The attack was intended as a lesson to the Arabs in general, and it was immaterial whether the chosen target was in Syria or Jordan. It revealed a tougher policy supported by still tougher military action. Both were backed by skilful propaganda that represented the destruction of Arab villages as defensive measures. But to all intents and purposes the lesson was lost on both Jordan and Syria. In Jordan the monarchy survived the test with the greatest difficulty, but Ḥusain continued his refusal to form a national guard or co-operate with the Palestine Liberation Army. His relations with Syria remained bad, and with Egypt not much better.

The Syrian leaders learned even less from the Sammuʿ attack. They continued to breathe fire, but refused Nāṣir's offer to provide them with adequate air cover against surprise attacks on the Sammuʿ pattern. They seem to have assumed that their conflict with Israel would remain 'limited' to verbal war and occasional border incidents. Indeed, in the first two months of 1967 they were more occupied with the dispute with the Iraq Petroleum Company than with military strategy. Early in March 1967 agreement was reached whereby Syria obtained an extra £5 million on the 1955 agreement which doubled the total income from this source.[18]

A month later, on 7 April, a false sense of security was severely exposed when following one of those 'limited' conflicts a major air battle was fought and Israeli planes appeared over Damascus. If Ḥusain survived with great difficulty the humiliation of Sammuʿ, the Baʿth leaders survived the implications of the air battle with surprising ease. They knew they could not invoke the pact with Egypt, nor blame Nāṣir for not coming to their aid from his distant air bases.

The Baʿth government survived a second no less serious crisis, this time on the internal front. In the first week of May a magazine issued under army auspices carried an article which was an open attack on belief in God and religion. There was an immediate and violent wave of Muslim protest and a general strike was observed in Damascus, on the assumption that the government intended their party doctrines as a substitute for religion. However, the government denied any previous knowledge of the intention to publish such an article and accused the United States Central Intelligence Agency of inspiring it. The author of the article and the editor of the magazine were jailed, but so also were those shaikhs who led the protest movement.

In the application of socialism, and indeed of all government measures, the Egyptian revolution sought and on the whole succeeded in enlisting the support of the religious leaders. The Syrian Baʿth never succeeded in conciliating, still less in co-operating with, such leaders. Even before they came to power, Muslim opinion regarded the Baʿth party with suspicion if not hostility. The affair of the army magazine might have had more serious repercussions had not the country been immediately faced with a grave crisis with Israel.

Once more threats were uttered and their nature was such that the next Israeli action would not be confined to a 'limited' conflict. Hitherto Israel's surprise attacks were in the nature of hit-and-run raids, though increasing in strength as time went on. Now the threat was to topple the government in Damascus. How could this be done without an outright invasion?

The chain of actions and reactions that culminated in the Israeli attack on 5 June 1967 requires longer perspective for study. The outbreak of the war is, however, the terminal point in this history of modern Syria. It evokes in the writer's mind reflections which are perhaps not fashionable these days. He ventures to hint at one of them: Syria had often in history marched under the banner of Islam to victory and glory; it had yet to prove that it could do so under the banner of Arab nationalism.

Notes

CHAPTER I

1. *Correspondance de Napoléon Ier* (Paris, 1858–70) xxx, 6, cited in J. C. Herold, *Bonaparte in Egypt* (London, 1963) 263.
2. C.-F. Volney, *Travels Through Syria and Egypt in the Years 1783, 1784 and 1785* (London, 1787) ii, 329.
3. Volney, *Travels*, ii, 140, 168, 181, 251.
4. The stations and their amenities are listed in J. L. Burckhardt, *Travels in Syria and the Holy Land* (London, 1822) 656–61.
5. Ḥaidar Aḥmad Shīhāb, *Tārīkh Aḥmad Bāshā al-Jazzār*, ed. A. Chibli and I.-A. Khalifé (Beirut, 1955) 125–8.
6. 'Abdur-Raḥmān al-Jabarti, *'Ajā'ib al-Āthār fi at-Tarājim wa al-Akhbār* (Cairo, A.H. 1297) iii, 47.
7. The figures in this section are from Herold, ch. ix.

CHAPTER 2

1. Ḥāfiẓ Wahbah, *Jazīrat al-'Arab fi al-Qarn al-'Ishrīn* (Cairo, A.H. 1354/1935) 252.
2. Mīkhā'īl Mishāqa, *Al-Jawāb 'alā Iqtirāḥ al-Aḥbāb*, selections edited by A. J. Rustum and S. Abū Shaqra (Beirut, 1955) 33–4.
3. Cited by 'Abdul-Qādir al-Maghribi, *Majallat al-Majma' al-'Ilmi al-'Arabi* (Damascus, 1929) ix, 648 f.
4. Burckhardt, *Travels*, 188; see also 169, 194.
5. Ḥaidar Shihāb, *Tārīkh Aḥmad Bāshā al-Jazzār*, 184.
6. Ṭannūs Shidyāq, *Akhbār al-A'yān fi Jabal Lubnān* (Beirut, 1859) 490.
7. [Archbishop] Yūsuf ad-Dibs, *Tārīkh Sūriyya* (Beirut, 1903) iv, pt 8, 645–6.
8. Rev. As'ad Manṣūr, *Tārīkh an-Nāṣirah* (Cairo, 1924) 66.

CHAPTER 3

1. As reported by the English consul on 20 June 1811 and quoted by H. Dodwell, *The Founder of Modern Egypt* (Cambridge, 1931) 107.

2. As reported by the French consul on 1 May 1825 in a letter published in A. Rabbath, *Documents inédits pour servir á l'histoire du christianisme en orient* (Paris, 1910) ii, 118.
3. A. J. Rustum, *A Calendar of the State Papers from the Royal Archives of Egypt Relating to the Affairs of Syria* (Beirut, 1940) i, 129, 135, 147–8.
4. Rustum, *Calendar*, ii, 18.
5. Paul Carali (ed.), *Ḥurūb Ibrāhīm Bāshā al-Miṣrī fi Sūriyya wa al-Anāḍūl* (Cairo, 1927) 29.
6. See the two circulars in A. J. Rustum, *Material for a Corpus of Arabic Documents Relating to the History of Syria under Mehemet Ali Pasha*, i (Beirut, 1930) 87–9; ii (Beirut, 1931) 31–2.
7. Qusṭanṭīn al-Bāshā (ed.), *Mudhakkirāt Tārīkhiyyah* (Ḥarīṣa, Lebanon, n.d.) 90.
8. Rustum, *Documents*, iii–iv, 231. Cf. Al-Bāshā (ed.), *Mudhakkirāt*, 150–1. An Arabic demonstrative pronoun 'this' is missing from Rustum and is responsible for the erroneous impression that the document was in Muḥammad 'Ali's words, whereas its terms leave no doubt that it was in Bashīr's.
9. Rustum, *Calendar*, iii, 201.
10. Rustum, *Documents*, iii–iv, 73–5.
11. Mishāqa, *al-Jawāb*, 131.
12. Rustum, *Calendar*, iv, 231.
13. Mishāqa, *al-Jawāb*, 132–6.
14. Mīkhā'il ad-Dimashqi, *Tārīkh Hawādith ash-Shām wa-Lubnān*, ed. L. Ma'lūf (Beirut, 1913) 106.

CHAPTER 4

1. Rustum, *Calendar*, iv, 264.
2. Al-Bāshā (ed.), *Mudhakkirāt*, 245, 247.
3. Public Record Office (London) F.O. 78/444 (Turkey): Dispatch dated 17 September 1841 from Young to Ponsonby.
4. F.O. 78/447: Dispatch No. 9 dated 20 May 1841 from N. W. Werry to Lord Palmerston. Cf. dispatch No. 33 dated 20 November 1841 from R. Wood to Lord Aberdeen.
5. F.O. 78/621, pt. 1: Dispatch No. 3 dated 1 February 1845 from Moore to Aberdeen.
6. United States, *National Archives* (Washington) Record Group 59, vol. ii: Dispatch dated 1 September from Consul J. Hosford Smith (Beirut) to Secretary of State Daniel Webster.
7. *Hadiqat al-Akhbar*, 28 August 1858.
8. *Archives du Ministère des Affaires étrangères* (Paris) Turquie, vol. 249: Dispatch dated 12 February 1827 from Chevalier Regnaut, consul at Sidon, to Baron de Damas, Secretary of State at the Ministry for Foreign Affairs.
9. F.O. 78/961: Memorandum dated 28 March 1853.

10. F.O. 78/670: Letter dated 16 May 1846 from Hugh Rose to Vice-Admiral Sir William Parker (on leaving Syrian waters).
11. F.O. 78/962: Dispatch dated 29 June 1853 from Finn to Clarendon.
12. *The Missionary Herald*, li (1855) No. 1, p. 1.
13. F.O. 78/1221: Dispatch dated 8 April 1856 from Kayat to Clarendon.
14. A. H. Finn, *Palestine Peasantry* (London, 1923) 17.

CHAPTER 5

1. F.O. 78/1389: Dispatch dated 9 March 1858 from Consul J. Skene to Clarendon.
2. F.O. 78/1519: Dispatch dated 24 May 1860 to Lord John Russell and dispatch dated 30 May 1860 to Sir Henry Bulwer, from Consul N. Moore.
3. *The Missionary Herald*, lvi (1860) 241, 243, a communication from Henry H. Jessup.
4. F.O. 78/1519: Dispatch dated 9 May 1860 from Consul Moore to Ambassador Sir Henry Bulwer.
5. United States *National Archives* (Washington) Record Group 84, vol. i. Report dated 26 July 1860.
6. *The Druzes and the Maronites under the Turkish Rule from 1840–1860*, (London, 1862) 115–19.
7. Muḥammad Kurd 'Ali, *Khiṭaṭ ash-Shām*, iii (Damascus, A.H. 1343/1925) 81, 85, 86.
8. London Jews Society, *The Jewish Record* (1864) 286; (1868) 61.
9. Kāmil al-Ghazzi, *Nahr adh-Dhahab fi Tārīkh Ḥalab* (Aleppo, 1923–6) iii, 388–401.
10. American Board of Commissioners for Foreign Missions, *Annual Report* (1868) 55.
11. F.O. 78/1670: Dispatches dated 10 July and 27 October 1862 from E. Rogers to Sir Henry Bulwer.
12. F.O. 78/2194: Dispatch dated 7 December 1871 from Skene to Sir Henry Elliot.
13. *Khiṭaṭ ash-Shām*, iv, 71.
14. For details see A. L. Tibawi, 'The American Missionaries in Beirut and Buṭrus al-Bustāni' in *St. Antony's Papers, Middle Eastern Affairs*, no. 3 (1963) 170 f.

CHAPTER 6

1. See *The Times*, 25 February 1878, p. 5 under 'The Peace Negotiations'.
2. F.O. 78/2768. See the printed minutes marked 'Cabinet' and 'most confidential' dated 23 May 1878.
3. F.O. 226/195, a file containing nothing but the two reports, in clean drafts but unsigned, the first dated 26 March and the second 10 April 1878.

4. The facts are culled from Layard's very lengthy and confidential report, F.O. 78/2960 no. 99 dated 20 October 1879, to the Marquis of Salisbury.
5. Ali Haydar Midhat, *The Life of Midhat Pasha* (London, 1903) 32.
6. See the correspondence in *The Life of Midhat Pasha*, 77–94.
7. F.O. 78/1389, dispatch No. 20 dated 31 July 1858 from J. Skene to P. Alison.
8. *The Arab Awakening* (London, 1938) 54–5.
9. F.O. 78/3131, dispatch No. 2 'confidential' dated 19 May 1880 from Moore to Secretary of State with copy to ambassador.
10. F.O. 78/3091, dispatch No. 226 'confidential' dated 9 August 1880 from George Goschen to Granville.
11. F.O. 195/1306, 1369: dispatches dated 3 July 1880 from Dickson and 3 August from Jago to Ambassador George Goschen, and dispatches dated 3, 14 and 17 January from Dickson to chargé d'affaires.
12. Muḥammad Rashīd Riḍā, *Tārīkh al-Ustādh al-Imām* (Cairo, A.H. 1350/1931) ii, 523–32.
13. Full details in my article 'Russian Cultural Penetration of Syria-Palestine in the Nineteenth Century' in *The Royal Central Asian Journal*, liii (1966) pts 2 and 3.
14. M. Lowenthal (editor and translator), *The Diaries of Theodor Herzl* (London, 1958) 152.
15. F.O. 78/3911, dispatch No. 15 (commercial) dated 4 November 1886 from V. C. Eyres to the Earl of Iddlesleigh.
16. S. Tolkowsky, *The Gateway of Palestine* (London, 1924) 183–4.
17. Muḥammad Kurd 'Ali, *Khiṭaṭ*, iv, 80.

CHAPTER 7

1. C.M.S. *Proceedings* (1883–4) 61.
2. F.O. 78/4172, dispatch dated 21 March 1887 from Consul Dickson to Ambassador White.
3. *The Foreign Missionary*, xlv (1886) 291, a communication from Henry H. Jessup.
4. *Al-Manār*, xii (1909–10) 313.
5. *Archives du Ministère des Affaires étrangères*, Turquie (Beyrouth), vol. xxv (1881): A report dated 25 November addressed to Gambetta.
6. The facts and figures on the Syrian railways are derived from 'Abdul-Wahhāb al-Māliki's chaper in *Khiṭaṭ ash-Shām*, v, 176 f.
7. The Emperor's itinerary for the next twenty days is based on the reports of *The Times*' special correspondent.
8. The reference here is to the third edition printed at the Adabiyya Press in Beirut in 1900 which is clearly marked that the first edition was licensed in 1879.
9. The two letters are discussed more fully in A. L. Tibawi, *American Interests in Syria 1800–1901* (Oxford, 1966) 286–7.

10. See the catalogues of the American and Catholic press, Beirut, for 1884 and the following years.
11. *Index*, vol. viii (1887–8) communications Nos. 12 and 129 from W. Bird and J. S. Dennis respectively.
12. M. K. 'Ali, *Al-Mudhakkirāt* (Damascus, 1367/1948) i, 36. (The author cites an obviously wrong date for the event.)
13. L. Cheikho, *La Littérature arabe au XIXe siècle* (Beirut, 1910) ii, 162, where numerous other samples in classical Arabic are preserved.
14. *Al-Manār*, xii (1909–10) 956–9.
15. Anīs al-Maqdisi, *al-Ittijāhāt al-Adabiyya fi al-'Ālam al-'Arabi al-Ḥadīth* (Beirut, 3rd ed., 1963) 119–20.
16. For the Arabic and Turkish text see *al-Manār* xvi (1931) 638–40; a somewhat different account of the negotiations and the agreement is given by Jamāl Pasha, *Memories of a Turkish Statesman 1913–1919* (London, 1922) 57 f.

CHAPTER 8

1. Note from Sir Eyre Crowe to India Office in F.O. 371/2139.
2. Telegrams from Kitchener to Cheetham on 24 September and from Cheetham on 31 October. F.O. 371/2139.
3. Telegrams and letters cited are from F.O. 371/2141.
4. The facts are based on documents in F.O. 371/2147.
5. Most of the facts in the rest of the chapter are culled from F.O. 371/2486.
6. *Orientations* (London, 1937) 167; cf. 216, 230, 252 *et passim.*
7. The full text is in F.O. 371/2147.
8. The report was printed for the Committee of Imperial Defence as secret CAB/42/3/1.
9. *Memories of a Turkish Statesman 1913–1919*, 205–6.
10. *Orientations*, 177. Authoritative British sources completely refute Storrs. Thus, for example, Lord Hardinge wrote in a comment on a dispatch from Wingate dated 10 April 1917 that the Arab revolt was 'very cheap at the price' (F.O. 371/3040).

CHAPTER 9

1. *Memories of a Turkish Statesman, 1913–1919*, 168, 169.
2. A. P. Wavell, *The Palestine Campaigns* (London, 3rd ed. 1940) 56.
3. F.O. 371/2781. See dispatch No. 282 dated 25 October 1916 from McMahon to Grey.
4. F.O. 371/3044. See private note dated 11 February 1917 from Wingate to Balfour (sent with a special messenger).
5. F.O. 371/2781.

6. *The Times* (11 December 1917) p. 7, col. 6.
7. Full text in Allenby's telegram dispatched from Jerusalem at 5.15 p.m. on 11 December to Chief of the Imperial General Staff – F.O. 371/3061, later printed in *Military Operation – Egypt and Palestine*, pt i, by C. Falls (H.M.S.O., 1930) 260–6.
8. *Seven Pillars of Wisdom* (London, 1955) 462, 464.
9. *The Diaries of Theodor Herzl*, 352–4.
10. *Al-Manār*, xvii (1332/1914) 707–8.
11. N. Barbour, *Nisi Dominus, a Survey of Palestine Controversy* (London, 1946) 53.
12. See one of them and a reference to another in Cmd. 3530 (*Shaw Report*, 1930) 126–7.
13. F.O. 371/2767.
14. F.O. 371/2492.
15. Cmd. 5964 – Miscellaneous No. 4 (1939) 3–5.
16. F.O. 371/3380. Dispatch No. 33 dated 19 February 1918 from Wingate to Balfour.
17. Text in Cmd. 5964 (1939) 5–6.
18. ʿAbdullah Ibn al-Ḥusain, *Mudhakkirāti* (Jerusalem, 1945) 143.
19. F.O. 371/3384: Allenby's telegram of 17 October 1918 to the War Office (with copy to the Foreign Office).
20. Secret report by General Edward Spears (Paris) dated 2 November 1918 to the War Office. See F.O. 371/3414.
21. Telegram of 18 January 1919. F.O. 371/4144.

CHAPTER 10

1. *Seven Pillars of Wisdom*, 24.
2. F.O. 371/4162.
3. F.O. 371/4182 paper 125609.
4. *My Diary of the Conference of Paris with Documents*. In volume i (New York, 1924) p. 67, Miller describes the document laconically but erroneously as 'an agreement between the King of the Hijaz and the Zionists'. In vol iii, pp.188–9, he publishes the agreement under No. 141.
5. See my article ('by an Arab student') in *The Palestine Post*, Jerusalem, 19 July 1936, challenging Weizmann's story, later expanded and submitted over my signature to the Palestine Royal Commission in January 1937.
6. As reported in Cheetham's telegram on 1 February 1919. F.O. 371/4173.
7. Cf. texts of Faisal's speeches on the eve of the commission's arrival in Sātiʿ al-Ḥuṣri, *Yaum Maisalūn* (Beirut, 1948) 201–17.
8. F.O. 371/4183.
9. Full Arabic text in Ḥāfiẓ Wahbah, *Jazīrat al-ʿArab*, 389–94.
10. F.O. 371/3395.

11. Telegram No. 200 sent by the Foreign Office to Allenby on 8 March at 9.15 p.m.
12. Cf. Cmd. 3530 (1930) p. 127.
13. Al-Ḥuṣri, *Yaum Maisalūn*, 125–7.
14. Samuel's report for March 1921, in F.O. 371/6375.

CHAPTER 11

1. F.O. 371/6453. Telegram dated 25 January 1921.
2. Cited in W. E. Hocking, *The Spirit of World Politics* (New York, 1932) 287.
3. *Minutes of the Permanent Mandates Commission* (8th session) 191.
4. *Minutes of the Permanent Mandates Commission* (18th session) 121, 122, 123.
5. For a judicious summary of the steps that led to this result see A. J. Toynbee, *Survey of International Affairs, 1938*, i (London, 1941) 479–92.
6. G. T. Havard, *Report on Economic and Commercial Conditions in Syria and the Lebanon, 1936–38* (London, H.M.S.O., 1938) 4. (The author was British consul-general in Beirut at the time.)
7. Ṣāti' al-Ḥuṣri, *Ḥauliyyah*, i (Cairo, 1949) 76 f.
8. Ministère des Affaires étrangères, *Rapport à la Société des Nations sur la situation de la Syrie et du Liban* (*Année 1938*), (Paris, 1939) p. 46.
9. *The Times*, 30 May 1941.
10. On French suspicions of British designs see S. H. Longrigg, *Syria and Lebanon under French Mandate* (London, 1958) 319 f. *et passim.*
11. From a longer version quoted by G. E. Kirk, *The Middle East in the War* (London, 1952) 282–3.
12. Ḥuṣri, *Ḥauliyyah*, i, 99.

CHAPTER 12

1. In *My Memoirs Completed*, trans. H. W. Glidden (Washington, 1954) 29, 'Abdullah expresses regret that the end of the French mandate did not lead to Syrian unity and that he could not achieve it by force.
2. *First Statement* and *Second Statement* are available in an English version issued by the Directorate General of Information (Damascus, 1952).
3. For the names of the members of the Syrian Cabinets from 28 December 1946 to 6 March 1958 see G. H. Torrey, *Syrian Politics and the Military, 1945–1958* (Ohio State University Press, 1963) 405–15.
4. The mission's report was published as *The Economic Development of Syria* (Johns Hopkins Press, Baltimore, 1955).

5. D. Warriner, *Land Reform and Development in the Middle East* (London, 1957) 71, 73.
6. P. Seale, *The Struggle for Syria* (London, 1965) 262.
7. For a concise exposition see G. Barraclough, *Survey of International Affairs, 1956–58* (London, 1962) 163 f.
8. E. Y. Asfour, *Syria: Development and Monetary Policy* (Harvard, 1959) 81.
9. *Chronology of Arab Politics* (issued quarterly since January 1963 by the American University of Beirut) vol. i, no. 1, 58–60.
10. *Maḥāḍir Mubāḥathāt al-Waḥdah*, 1963. For an English summary translation see *Arab Political Documents* (issued annually since 1963 by the American University of Beirut) i, 75–217.
11. Text in *Arab Political Documents, 1963*, 227–46.
12. *The Times*, 18 January 1964.
13. M. Kerr, *The Arab Cold War 1958–1964* (London, 1965) 139.
14. Syrian Arab Republic, Ministry of Planning, *Implementation Report on the First Five Years Development Plan* (Damascus, mimeograph, 1963) 75–9.
15. *Implementation Report* (1964) 7–8, 34 f., 119 f.
16. *Chronology of Arab Politics* vol. ii, no. 2, 179 f.
17. Text in *Arab Political Documents, 1964*, 136–41.
18. *The Economist*, 4 March 1967.

Bibliography

THE list below includes only the principal sources used or quoted in the text or cited in the notes, classified in groups to facilitate reference. I have deliberately refrained from foisting upon the reader the long bibliographical lists so fashionable these days. Having read practically all the literature pertaining to the subject of this book, I doubt the utility of listing together numerous modern works, the good, the indifferent and the downright bad. The specialist needs little or no guidance, but the uninitiated may be deceived. Selective lists also have similar pitfalls. With very few exceptions I have therefore listed no modern works here, not even those actually cited in the notes.

I would, however, mention two books containing between them fairly long lists of references. The first, *La Syrie: précis historique* by the Jesuit Henri Lammens, covers the story down to 1920, but the non-specialist reader must be on his guard against this author's anti-Islamic and anti-Arab bias. The second book, more judicious and not unsympathetic to the Arab and French point of view, is *Syria and Lebanon under the French Mandate*, by Stephen H. Longrigg. There is no authoritative and comprehensive work on the last two decades, but the recent venture by the department of political science at the American University of Beirut in publishing a quarterly digest of the Arabic and foreign press reports and an annual collection of documents deserves special notice.

An asterisk against a source denotes its special importance.

MANUSCRIPT SOURCES

*London, Public Record Office:

(*a*) Consular reports from 1841 and diplomatic correspondence from 1878.

(*b*) Cabinet and Foreign Office papers from 1914 to 1921.

Paris, Archives du Ministère des Affaires étrangères: Consular reports for the 1820s and the 1880s.
Washington, National Archives: Occasional consular reports from 1851.

PRINTED ORIGINAL SOURCES

Rabbath, A., *Documents inédits pour servir à l'histoire du christianisme en orient* (Paris, 1910) vol. ii.
*Rustum, A. J., *A Calendar of the State Papers from the Royal Archives of Egypt Relating to the Affairs of Syria*. 4 vols (Beirut, 1940–3).
— *Material for a Corpus of Arabic Documents Relating to the History of Syria under Mehemet Ali*. 5 vols (Beirut, 1930–4).

OFFICIAL REPORTS AND MINUTES

*French Ministry for Foreign Affairs: *Rapport(s) à la Société des Nations sur la situation de la Syrie et du Liban* (annual up to 1938).
*League of Nations: *Minutes of the Permanent Mandates Commission* (from 1925).
Great Britain, Board of Trade: Report(s) on the Trade [Industry and Finance] of Syria by consuls Satow and Havard (from 1920 to 1936).
*The Syrian Republic: *First Statement* (Damascus, 1952).
Second Statement (Damascus, 1952).
Implementation Report on the First Five Years Plan (Damascus, 1963).
Implementation Report (Damascus, 1964).
*United Arab Republic: *Maḥāḍir Mubāḥathāt al-Waḥdah* (Cairo, 1963).
American Board of Commissioners for Foreign Missions (Boston), *Annual Reports* (from 1868).
*American University of Beirut: *Arab Political Documents* (annual from 1963).
Church Missionary Society (London), *Proceedings* (from 1887).
International Bank of Reconstruction and Development: *Economic Development of Syria* (Johns Hopkins Press, Baltimore, 1955).

WORKS BY EYE-WITNESSES

*'Abdur-Raḥmān al-Jabarti, *'Ajā'ib al-Athār fi at-Tarājim wa al-Akhbār* (Cairo, A.H. 1297) vol. ii.
*Burckhardt, J. L., *Travels in Syria and the Holy Land* (London, 1822).
*Sāṭi' al-Ḥuṣri, *Yaum Maisalūn* (Beirut, 1948).

*Volney, C.-F., *Travels through Syria and Egypt in the years 1783, 1784 and 1785* (London, 1787).

MEMOIRS OF EYE-WITNESSES

'Abdullah Ibn al-Ḥusain, *Mudhakkirāti* (Jerusalem, 1945).
[Ahmad] Jamal Pasha, *Memories of a Turkish Statesman* (London, 1922).
Lawrence, T. E., *Seven Pillars of Wisdom* (London, 1955 ed.).
Storrs, R., *Orientations* (London, 1937).

PRINCIPAL NEWSPAPERS AND JOURNALS QUOTED

**Ḥadīqat al-Akhbār* (Beirut, 1858, 1866).
Journal de Constantinople, Écho de l'Orient (1855).
**Al-Manār* (Cairo), 1909, 1910, 1913, 1914.
Al-Mashriq (Beirut) 1931.
The Missionary Herald (Boston) 1855, 1860.
Al-Muqtaṭaf (Cairo) 1882–3.
**Revue de l'académie arabe* (Damascus) 1929.
**The Times* (London) 1878, 1898, 1917, 1919, 1941, 1964.

COMPLEMENTARY WORKS ON THE CULTURAL HISTORY OF SYRIA

Tibawi, A. L., *American Interests in Syria 1800–1901* (Oxford, 1966).
— *British Interests in Palestine 1800–1901* (Oxford, 1961).
— *Russian Cultural Penetration of Syria and Palestine in the Nineteenth Century* (London, 1966).

Index

THE substance of the book is classified below principally under subjects and persons. However, persons who played a relatively insignificant part in the events are excluded because whatever part they did play is included in the subject entries. For the same reason most place-names do not appear in this index. As in the text of the book, care has been taken not to baffle the general reader with ghosts. The Arabic definitive article *al*, when it occurs at the beginning of a name or a word, has been disregarded in listing entries.